Advances in Social & Organizational Psychology

A Tribute to Ralph Rosnow

Advances
in Social
& Organizational
Psychology
A Tribute to Ralph Rosnow

Edited by

Donald A. Hantula
Temple University

LAWRENCE ERLBAUM ASSOCIATES, PUBLISHERS

2006   Mahwah, New Jersey   London

Lawrence Erlbaum Associates, Inc., Publishers
10 Industrial Avenue
Mahwah, New Jersey 07430
www.erlbaum.com

Cover design by Tomai Maridou

Library of Congress Cataloging-in-Publication Data

Advances in social & organizational psychology : a tribute to Ralph
   Rosnow / edited by Donald A. Hantula
      p. cm.
   Includes bibliographical references and index.
ISBN 0-8058-5590-4 (cloth : alk. paper)
   1. Social psychology. 2. Organizational behavior. 3. Psychology—
   Research. 4. Rosnow, Ralph L.   I. Rownow, Ralph.   II. Hantula,
   Donald A.

HM1033.A39 2006   2005050732
                                                        CIP

Printed in the United States of America
10   9   8   7   6   5   4   3   2   1

Contents

III Social and Organizational Psychology

IV Theory and Epistemology

Preface

This volume started as an idea on a cool early spring night during a dinner in Ralph Rosnow's honor. Ralph announced his retirement as the Thaddeus Bolton Professor of Psychology and his longtime friend and co-author, Bob Rosenthal, had come to Philadelphia to deliver the Uriel Foa Memorial Lecture at Temple University and to celebrate Ralph's retirement. After the lecture, we presented Ralph with a folio of letters written by students, colleagues, and friends remembering Ralph's wisdom, sage advice, and counsel, and his impact on their lives. Ralph's good works as a colleague, mentor, and teacher were expressed eloquently in those letters by those privileged to know him personally, but his profound influence on Psychology and the practice of social research extends far beyond this circle of friends. Capturing an effect of that size required something more formal, such as this volume.

Phone calls, emails, and letters went to colleagues, friends, and former students asking for chapters as a tribute to the intellectual legacy of Ralph Rosnow's career. Those who responded were asked to contribute an original work of scholarship that showcased how Ralph's work had informed their own research and writing. The breadth of both the contributors and topics demonstrates how much of a difference Ralph's work has made across both social and organizational psychology. Three generations of scholarship are represented herein; chapters from Ralph's dissertation adviser, colleagues and coauthors throughout his career, and his students. The topics range from new thinking about data analysis and interpretation, to substantive theoretical issues in social and organizational psychology, to more philosophical treatments of the future direction of psychological research and theory.

While this volume was being assembled some contributors changed their topics and chapters, new contributors were added, and some had to drop out of the project for various reasons. For those who had to withdraw, your published works throughout your careers stand as powerful testimony to Ralph's influence, and your desire to be part of this volume is appreciated. In one particularly sad instance, Ralph's longtime colleague Phil Bersh passed away before his chapter was completed. Professor Bersh's intended topic was a review and critique of classical conditioning paradigms within social psychology. Phil Bersh studied basic Pavlovian processes during his long and illustrious career and was fond of pointing out that Ralph's first publications were in verbal conditioning, and that although each started at nearly the same place and had taken seemingly divergent paths, by the end their metatheoretical bases were not altogether that different.

The chapters illustrate the wide rage of Ralph's influence. Some summarize robust research programs and point toward future directions, whereas others are careful reconsiderations and point to the tentativeness of our knowledge. All chapters acknowledge Ralph's considerable theoretical and methodological acumen and strive to emulate his subtle but powerful command of the language.

As a tribute to both Ralph's contextualist perspective and his appreciation of history, the first chapter reviews Thaddeus Bolton's legacy. Bolton was a pioneer of American psychology and Ralph held the Bolton chair at Temple University. As Peter Crabb points out, both Thaddeus Bolton and Ralph Rosnow had an abiding interest in measurement issues and application of psychological knowledge.

The first major section of the volume focuses on what is perhaps Ralph's greatest contribution to psychology, advancing our knowledge of the methods and ethics of research. Chapters by longtime collaborators Bob Rosenthal and Don Rubin and by Howard Wainer and MaryLu Rosenthal introduce refinements in research methodology. The chapters by David Strohmetz, Allan Kimmel, and Peter Blanck, and colleagues raise ongoing ethical issues in the conduct of psychological research. Those by Strohmetz and Kimmel revisit the thorny problems of artifact in behavioral research that Ralph identified and pursued some 3 decades ago and still challenge researchers today.

Although perhaps best known for his methodological acumen, Ralph also studied substantive areas within both social and organizational psychology. He encouraged his students and colleagues to pursue their own particular interests in social and organizational psychology. The variety of topics that Ralph did not necessarily study, but instead inspired others to tackle, is well represented in this section. Four of the chapters cover topics in organizational psychology (consumer behavior, rumor, decision making, and leadership) and three are in the domain of social psychology (science and social issues, smiling, and values). It is noteworthy that only one chapter, by former students Nick DiFonzo and Prashant Bordia on rumor in organizational contexts, summarizes advances in a research program identified with Ralph Rosnow.

The fourth and final section includes sage contributions from eminent psychologists who bring the perspectives of their long careers to bear on issues of theory and epistemology that Ralph wrestled with throughout his career. Each author offers a humble optimism about what we can know within the epistemological limits of psychology. Bob Perloff's chapter shows how the strains of Ralph Rosnow's work will be heard in generations to come and William McGuire uses a perspectivist position to raise 20 questions on epistemology for future generations to solve. The volume ends as Ralph's career began, with Bob Lana's re-examination of the experiment and its interpretation in social psychology. Bob was Ralph's dissertation adviser (and also long-time colleague as well as precedent in the Bolton chair). Ralph learned the craft of experimental research and importance of epistemology from Bob—their later collaborations led to a re-evaluation of the experiment in social psychology and a paradigm shift in the interpretation and evaluation of knowledge gleaned from experiments.

The following chapters place Ralph's career and work in the context of 20th century Psychology and show how his influence will guide the field into the 21st century. The authors built on a solid foundation to showcase the new vistas that could be seen when standing on the shoulders of a giant. I thank the authors for their contributions, Bob Rosenthal for his encouragement, LEA for their patience, and especially Ralph Rosnow for serving as the stimulus for this project. On behalf of the contributors, thank you for your wisdom, your guidance, and your kindness.

—Donald A. Hantula

I
Context

1

The Bolton Legacy[1]

Peter B. Crabb
Pennsylvania State University–Abington

Ralph Rosnow held the Thaddeus L. Bolton Professorship in Psychology at Temple University from 1981 to 2001, making his tenure in that post the longest since the honor was established in 1955. During that period, in 1984, I began my graduate training in social psychology with Professor Rosnow. I could hardly have predicted that I would soon be "doing history," but during my second year I found myself immersed in his work on contextualism and the Pepperian notion that the proper unit of analysis in social psychology should be the transitory historic event in its context (Pepper, 1942/1970). My task was to explore the obscure strand of events running through the history of American psychology that led to the Thaddeus L. Bolton Professorship of Psychology at Temple.

I had no clue where to begin. I found a mention of Bolton in Boring's *A History of Experimental Psychology* (1950), but little else at first. Slowly, however, as one source led to another, a picture of this pioneering American psychologist emerged. His story, I think, provides a sense of what American psychology must have been like during its early years, and an idea of how the discipline's beginnings continue to reverberate to this day.

[1]The following individuals and institutions graciously provided information and access to documents: Miriam I. Crawford, Conwellana-Templana Collection, Temple University Libraries; Catherine T. Sizer, Arthur W. Mellon Library, American Psychological Association; Stuart W. Campbell, University Archivist, Clark University; D. Johnson, K. Ross Toole Archives, University of Montana; Joseph G. Svoboda, University Archives, University of Nebraska, Lincoln; Nan E. Young, Assistant Librarian, University of Washington Archives; Dr. Terry Sheldahl, Columbia College–Fort Stewart; the late Hughbert C. Hamilton, Department of Psychology, Temple University; and the staff of the Free Library of Philadelphia. I thank Ralph Rosnow for helpful comments. Ilene Karp assisted with preparation of the typescript.

EDUCATION

Thaddeus Lincoln Bolton was born on July 27, 1865, in the farming community of Sonora, Illinois. His parents, William and Amelia Dortt Bolton, sent him to Mt. Morris Academy, where his teachers were graduates of the University of Michigan (Marquis, 1939). Bolton must have been greatly influenced by his teachers because, at age 21, he entered the classics program at the University of Michigan. He worked his way through college as a carpenter's helper ("Dr. Bolton, Psychology Professor, Plays," 1930), and received his A.B. degree in 1889 (Clark University, 1891).

Following his graduation, he spent a year as an administrator in the public school system in Vulcan, Michigan. School administration did not appeal to him, apparently, because in 1890 he entered the psychology program at the newly established Clark University in Worcester, Massachusetts (Clark University,1891; H. C. Hamilton, personal communication, February 27, 1985). Twenty-five years old and unmarried, Bolton arrived in Worcester in the autumn of Clark's second year.

Clark University's president was G. Stanley Hall, an educator, seminarian, evolutionist, philosopher, literarian, and a psychologist who actively recruited faculty and students from throughout North America and Europe (Ross, 1972). Under the sponsorship of businessman Jonus Clark, Hall established a university that closely resembled the German *Instituten* he had visited as a student. In Hall's words:

> The university ... should represent the state of science *per se*. It should be strong in the fields where science is highly developed, and should pay less attention to other departments of knowledge which have not reached the scientific stage.... It should be a laboratory of the highest possible human development in those lines where educational values are the criterion of what is taught or not taught and the increase of knowledge and its diffusion among the few fit should be its ideal (quoted in Ross, 1972, p. 200)

With an emphasis on research and graduate training, Hall intended Clark to be elitist and distinct from traditional American universities. He considered psychology to be a science on a par with the four other scientific divisions of the University: biology, chemistry, physics, and mathematics (Ross, 1972). The humanities were excluded altogether from the original curriculum at Clark.

It was in this stimulating and highly competitive environment that Bolton began his work as a scholar in psychology (Clark University, 1891). Figure 1.1 shows Bolton (first row, far left) and the Clark psychological department at the end of Bolton's second year. Although Hall took a special interest in overseeing students in the psychology depart-

FIG. 1.1.   Psychological department, Clark University, June 4, 1892. Front row, from left: T. L. Bolton, F. Boas, H. H. Donaldson, G. S. Hall, E. C. Sanford, W. H. Burnham, E. W. Scripture. Back row, from left: J. S. Lemon, G. M. West, W. O. Krohn, F. B. Dresslar, J. E. Rossignol, W. L. Bryan, A. Fraser, J. A. Bergstrom. (Courtesy of Clark University Archives.)

ment, Bolton's primary mentor was Edmund C. Sanford. Sanford had been a student of Hall's at Johns Hopkins and was the head of Clark's new psychology laboratory, which was in competition with William James' laboratory at Harvard (Ross, 1972). Sanford had a passion for devising instrumentation and is credited with the first laboratory manual for the new science (Sanford, 1891-1896), predating even Edward B. Titchener's famous manual (Boring, 1950).

The zeitgeist for Sanford's "psycho-physical" laboratory was derived from Wilhelm Wundt's laboratory at the University of Leipzig (Boring, 1950). Parallelism—the idea that thought and consciousness operated in parallel with neurophysiological processes—was the guiding theory. Boring describes this psychology as:

> *introspective* because consciousness was its subject-matter.... It was *sensationalistic* because sensation shows what the nature of consciousness is.... It was *elementalistic,* because the whole conception at the start was of a mental chemistry, and it seemed as if sensations, images and feelings might well be the elements which make up those compounds that are the stuff of psychology. And it was *associationistic* because association is the very principle of compounding, and be-

cause the British school had shown how you can get perception and meaning out of the association of parts. (Boring, 1950, p. 385)

During his first year Bolton completed a study that was an extension of work started by the anthropologist Franz Boas. Boas had just been appointed docent of anthropology at Clark (Ross, 1972) and was associated with the psychology department until 1892 (White, 1963). Boas had gathered a variety of physical, perceptual, and intellectual measurements on several thousand Worcester-area schoolchildren. Using Boas' data and procedure, Bolton filled out the sample with additional data so that all school grades were represented. The part of the study that concerned memory, with a sample of more than 1,500 children, yielded Bolton's first published paper in the *American Journal of Psychology* (Bolton, 1891–1892). Teachers in the schools read series of numbers and then asked the students to remember the numbers in the order in which they were presented. Bolton concluded that the limit of memory in his subjects was six digits, that memory span increased with age but not with intellectual capacity, that girls were superior to boys in memory tasks, and that the capacity to remember could be increased with practice.

This first study clearly owed a debt to the work of Ebbinghaus (1885/1964), but there is no acknowledgment of him. Bolton cited only research by Boas, Sanford, Hall, and Joseph Jastrow. The practice of ignoring the European roots of theory and research appears to have been endemic in G. Stanley Hall's sphere of influence (Ross, 1972) and was no doubt an attempt to legitimize the emerging purely American psychology.

Bolton also worked with Henry Donaldson in his physiology laboratory (Donaldson & Bolton, 1891–1892). Donaldson and Bolton studied the cranial nerves of 11 fresh cadavers, including the blind and deaf-mute woman Laura Bridgman who, when she had been alive, was the subject of a study by Hall (1879). The purpose was to determine whether Bridgman's pathology could be detected in the size of her cranial nerves. Slices of nerves were mounted on glass microscope slides, and a shadow of each section, enlarged 25 times, was projected onto paper. A pencil tracing was made of the shadow, the tracing was placed over a sheet of tin foil, and a disk the size of the projection was then cut out with a scalpel. Four foil disks were obtained for each section; the disks were weighed together and the mean weight was taken as the measure to be used for comparison with other individuals. Donaldson and Bolton estimated the error of this procedure to be less than 1%. The authors concluded that Bridgman's optic nerves and olfactory bulb were markedly smaller than were those of the rest of the sample.

Bolton then expanded on earlier work by Hall and Jastrow (1886) that examined thresholds for the perception of elements of tones (Bolton, 1893). The assumption was that tones are composed of many clicklike subsounds that humans are able to perceive only as a unity. Three subjects were exposed to two groups of clicks per trial, using a battery- and pendulum-driven "time-marker" device that generated very rapid clicking sounds (10 per .11 second). Intervals between the clicks could be varied from 0.11 to .0075 second. Subjects were told that a group of 4 to 10 clicks would be presented first, and that a group of clicks of the same number plus or minus 1 would follow. The task was to determine the number of clicks in the second group. Bolton found that, contrary to what was expected, subjects made more errors when larger groups of clicks (i.e., the standard plus 1) were presented, suggesting that they did not perceive the unity of larger numbers of clicks. Bolton expressed surprise at the results when he presented his findings at the American Psychological Association meeting in Philadelphia in 1892 (Bolton, 1893). On hearing this, Joseph Jastrow, who was then the director of a new laboratory at the University of Wisconsin, instigated a scene familiar to many novice psychologists when he publicly admonished Bolton for not knowing that he and Hall had found similar results in their study conducted at Johns Hopkins 6 years earlier. Sanford rose and countered this attack on his student by observing that in fact no such finding had been reported by Hall and Jastrow in "the very condensed account of their experiments" (Sanford, 1893, p. 301).

After only 3 years at Clark, Bolton completed his doctoral dissertation. Entitled *Rhythm*, this research extended his study of the perception of clicks. The dissertation examined the idea that experience and activity are organized into recurring periods, a hot topic at the time. Bolton's thesis was that the mind's activity occurs in rhythmic waves. When incoming sensory data are not organized with rhythmic cues for intervals, the mind, capable of finite spans of attention, organizes the data according to the mind's characteristics. In this way, the mind is both shaped by experience and constitutes it. Bolton succinctly expressed the psychophysicalism of his time when he argued that "this rhythm in the attention, and hence in conscious activity, finds its counterpart in the activity of the nerve cell, which we have seen reason for believing was a series of explosions—an alternation of periods of activity and periods of repose" (1894, p. 221).

Bolton anticipated "crisis" research in social psychology that occurred almost 80 years later (e.g., Rosenthal & Rosnow, 1975) when he discussed the influence of subject characteristics on his experimental results. He distinguished between three types of subjects: "those persons who yield immediately to any suggestion that is offered"; "those who take a moderately critical attitude"; and "those persons who are excessively critical" (Bolton, 1894, pp. 208–209). Accounting for subject characteristics is important, according to Bolton, because "in a study like this, which is purely introspective, the experimenter must rely upon the integrity of his subjects" (Bolton, 1894, p. 208) and "It is a fact which every psychologist must understand that certain classes of persons are incapable of introspection" (Bolton, 1894, p. 209). Bolton indicated that of the three types only the "moderately critical" subject was acceptable for introspection research.

The question examined in the first study of 30 subjects was whether uniformly spaced clicks could be perceived as one group, two groups, three groups, and so on. The apparatus used was a modification of a chronograph developed by Wundt (1893), which consisted of a battery-powered motor that turned a drive shaft. Attached to the shaft were two-pronged wooden arms that, when turned, struck two keys each along a brass keyboard. When depressed by one of the turning arms, the keys closed circuits for a specific time interval (e.g., .323 second). The circuits were connected to a telephone receiver, which generated audible clicks. The arms on the shaft could be arranged to generate a variety of groups of clicks that were uniform or accented.

To interpret between-subjects differences in perceptions of groups of clicks, Bolton emphasized subjects' reports of childhood experiences: "Several of the subjects testify to have known of their tendency to group the puffs of the locomotive, even in early childhood, and they have taken great delight in it" (Bolton, 1894, pp. 204–205). Thus, he concluded that perception of groups of clicks was a product of experiences with natural, mechanical, and literary rhythms, in addition to neurophysiological constraints.

In a second study, Bolton used an instrument designed by Sanford that consisted of a tuning fork whose tone could be mechanically interrupted by motor-driven notched disks. Nine disks were used to produce nine different sequences of tones. The tones could be uniform in duration, length, and number of intervals, or they could be varied in any rhythmic sequence. The object of the study "was to determine where the rhythmical groups began, with the long or short sounds" (Bolton, 1894, p. 232). Eleven of the subjects in the first study participated in the second study.

Bolton found that accented sounds tended to signal the start of a group of tones, a principle that he felt had implications for artistic expression. For example, Edgar Allan Poe's principle of poetry holds that "the regular foot must continue long enough in the line, and be sufficiently prominent in the verse to thoroughly establish itself" (Bolton, 1894, p. 238). In music, variation in the rhythm of measures produces what is perceived to be melody: "The melody is a new and higher unifying agency, which corresponds in a way to the use of rhymes in poetry. The temporal sequence of the accents is always preserved" (Bolton, 1894, p. 238). Bolton concluded that the perception and production of these expressive forms flow from a single organizing mechanism in the brain.

Bolton's dissertation was his last work devoted specifically to the topic of rhythm. He finished his course work during the 1893–1894 academic year and received his doctorate that spring.

EARLY CAREER

Bolton's first teaching post was at the State Normal School in Worcester ("Dr. T. L. Bolton," 1948). He stayed only a year, but retained an affiliation with the school until 1898 (Bolton & Haskell, 1898). In 1895, he moved to San Jose State College in California, where again he stayed only one year. Such brief affiliations were characteristic of Bolton's early career, at least in part because of some disagreeable personality traits. He was de-scribed by colleagues as having "a certain rawness that he has never been able to overcome" (Miller, 1912a) and as being plagued by "some peculiar-ities" (Hill, 1912) and "limitations" (Miller, 1912b). He was a "straightfor-ward, honest, and plainspoken fellow, whom some people might perhaps regards as tactless now and then" (Anonymous, 1912). His personality ap-pears to have precipitated scraps and controversies that led to his resigna-tion or dismissal from a number of posts (H. C. Hamilton, personal communication, February 27, 1985).

After San Jose, Bolton moved up the coast to Seattle, where he took a professorship in philosophy and education at the University of Washington. His teaching load was three courses per term, three terms per year. One of his courses was psychology, which was "devoted mainly to the physiology and psychology of sense perception and to brain physiology, as a basis for the study of instinct, habit, impulse, memory, imagination, and attention" (Uni-versity of Washington, 1896–1897, p. 58). The text for the course was Wil-liam James' *Text-book of Psychology: Briefer Course* (1892). Another course, problems in psychology, was "devoted to a study of animal psychology, hyp-notism, crime, suicide, insanity, etc." (University of Washington, 1896–1897, p. 58). Compared with 21st-century academic specialization, it was incredible that Bolton also taught history of ancient and mediæval phi-losophy and education, conference upon the study of children, history of modern philosophy, history of modern education, recent educational thought, and seminary in English philosophy.

After a year at Washington, Bolton left the United States to continue his education in Germany (Murchison, 1932). Retracing G. Stanley Hall's steps 20 years earlier, Bolton toured the Universities of Leipzig, Berlin, and Hei-delberg during 1898 and 1899 (Ross, 1972). Wundt, Hering, and Ludwig were at Leipzig, Stumpf was at Berlin, and Kraepelin, although a psychia-trist, dominated psychology at Heidelberg (Boring, 1950).

Perhaps out of loyalty to Hall and his disillusionment with Wundt's more speculative ideas and questionable laboratory techniques (Ross, 1972), Bolton appears to have been most drawn to Emil Kraepelin's work on fatigue at Heidelberg. He published a series of papers on fatigue in Kraepelin's jour-nal *Psychologische Arbeiten* (Bolton, 1902) and in American journals (Bolton, 1903b; Bolton & Miller, 1904; Bolton & Withey, 1907). These studies focused on physiological problems of work capacity and efficiency, and served as the cornerstone of his career.

When he returned to the United States in 1899, Bolton found a position as instructor of philosophy at the University of Nebraska in Lincoln (J. G. Svoboda, personal communication, March 11, 1985). He was elected professor of psychology in 1904, and his subsequent years at Nebraska were among his most productive. He published nine papers and served on the editorial committee of the *University of Nebraska Studies* from 1904 to 1907.

During this period he pursued his interest in fatigue, which he defined as "a decreased capacity for work which finds its cause either in a reduced supply of energy producing substance in the nerve and muscle cells or in the toxic effects of waste products in the blood" (Bolton, 1903b, p. 110). Following Kraepelin, Bolton drew a distinction between fatigue and weariness. Fatigue (Ermüdung) "is an organic condition which, while it lasts, reduces in proportion to its amount the capacity for work" (Bolton, 1903b, p. 121). Weariness, (Müdigokeit) "shall express the intellectual state of being tired" (Bolton, 1903b, p. 121).

Bolton contended that research could provide teachers with tools for diagnosing fatigue among children in their classes. His list of symptoms of fatigue included "restlessness, sleeplessness, fidget, muscular twitching and jerkings—incipient chorea—stumbling, trembling, unsteadiness, stammering and some other disorders of speech, irritability, heedlessness, distraction, lack of interest, loss of memory, feeble attitudes, drooping hands and head, slowness, inaccuracy, headaches, etc." (Bolton, 1903b, p. 121). Several instruments that could be used to measure fatigue had been devised, including Francis Galton's dynamometer, which measured strength of hand grip, and the ergograph, which measured the work capacity of muscles and had been developed by Mosso at the University of Turin (Bolton, 1903b; Bolton & Miller, 1904). Bolton had seen the ergograph used in laboratories at Heidelberg and Leipzig, and he decided to assess its validity for measuring work capacity of fingers (Bolton & Miller, 1904).

Bolton and his graduate assistant Eleanora Miller served as the subjects, or "reagents" as they called them. Bolton and the ergograph used in these studies are shown in Fig. 1.2. The ergograph sat on a table and the subject's first and third fingers of either hand were immobilized in "stalls" while the wrist was secured in a plaster cast. The middle finger was harnessed to two cables that passed through pulleys. Weights were attached to the end of one cable (6.84 kg. for Bolton and 3.58 kg. for Miller), while the other cable activated a pen on a motor-driven drum. The height and frequency of the middle finger's movements were recorded on the drum.

The trials on the ergograph were conducted over 3½ months. Contractions were paced to the beat of a metronome: "No great gain [in contraction capacity] seems to have been possible until the movement could be done

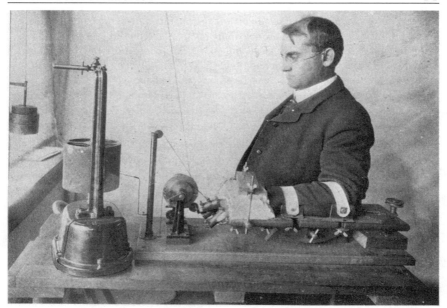

FIG. 1.2.   Bolton demonstrates the ergograph. (From Bolton & Miller, 1904).

rhythmically" (Bolton & Miller, 1904, p 101). The results indicated that an increased capacity for middle finger movements was made possible by practice. "Inurement" was detected as steep increases in capacity followed by plateaus of unchanging performance. These plateaus were identified as periods of fatigue, and Bolton concluded that they were necessary for practice gain. There appeared to be no ceiling on practice gain, and because work capacity increased for both Bolton and Miller over the trials, Bolton concluded that the validity of the ergograph as a tool for diagnosing fatigue was poor.

Bolton then approached the issue of motor strength and control from a different angle (Bolton, 1903a). Schoolchildren from the Lincoln-area public schools were administered several tests of motor power and coordination. The children were assigned to two groups, based on what would today be called socioeconomic status: "those from the best wards in the city … and others from the lower wards" (1903a, p. 353). Three tests of motor strength and control found that affluent children scored higher than did poorer children on all tasks. Affluent children also showed greater gains in performance between ages eight and nine than did poorer children. Bolton concluded that environment plays a considerable role in the growth of motor power and skill. He invoked Fechner's psychophysical psychology when he wrote that:

every new movement acquired adds a new piece of furniture to the mental house-
hold. Movement may not be the sole source of mental representation, but representations of movements do enter into our mental constitutions, so that the
higher our motor development has progressed, the more will our consciousnesses
be built up from this source.... Accordingly, mind and movement must develop
together; for without movement there is no mind. (Bolton, 1903a, p. 366)

Bolton's work at Nebraska turned as well to questions about personality
and social behavior. He proposed that four principles govern how people exercise power over one another (Bolton, 1907). His premise was that "The
process by which one becomes a person among other persons is slow and
gradual and personality is attained only after much struggle and conflict and
its course of development is devious and winding" (Bolton, 1907, p. 30).
The strategies used in these struggles were homologous to instinctive dominance and subordination behaviors among nonhuman animals.

The first principle was "self-exaltation"—a tendency to display oneself,
to feel important, and to gain approval from others. Bolton reported some
naturalistic observations to support his view that for adults, as well as children, opportunities for successfully manipulating some aspect of the environment can promote positive self-regard:

on a certain street near the sidewalk stands a stone post with a flat top. In this is a
ring held fast by a staple. The writer observed himself turning this ring from one
side to the other as he passed and wishing to test other people in this respect, he
concealed himself on the opposite side of the street to observe how other people
behaved toward the ring. More than a dozen persons were observed to turn the
ring in a short time. It made no difference which way the ring was turned; the pass-
erby turned it to the opposite side. It appears to be one of the best ways to attain a
self feeling by working our wills upon something. (Bolton, 1907, p. 35)

Other principles were the "law of depreciation," a tendency to inflict in-
jury on others for one's own gain; the "law of self protection and self recov-
ery," which includes defensive rejoinders ("sticks and stones ..."), polite lies,
and rumormongering; and the "law of self surrender," the paradoxical notion that humility can be a powerful social tool. Bolton concluded that "every appearance of a personality distinguishing itself among other
personalities arouses some antagonism—depreciates others' selves and so
such an appearance must give room for other personalities to triumph in
some other way" (1907, p. 56).

One may wonder how much of this "dog-eat-dog" view of personality
and social behavior was shaped by Bolton's own experiences with campus
politics. By 1907, he had become embroiled in a conflict with the administration at Nebraska, perhaps due to his unfulfilled expectation that he
should be appointed department head (H. C. Hamilton, personal commu-

nication, February 27, 1985). He resigned from the University of Nebraska at the close of the spring semester in 1908 (J. G. Svoboda, personal communication, March 11, 1985). Despite this unfortunate end to his career there, he mentored several students who went on to become well-known psychologists in their own right, including Edwin R. Guthrie, later at the University of Washington (Guthrie, 1959), and Harry Hollingworth and Leta Stetter, later at Columbia University (H. C. Hamilton, personal communication, February 27, 1985).

Bolton applied for a number of positions that spring, including a professorship in the department of experimental psychology at the University of Texas, and dean of the school of education at the State University of Kentucky (J. G. Svoboda, personal communication, March 11, 1985). He wound up at the Tempe Normal School (now Arizona State University) and taught there until 1912, spending summers at the University of Kansas (Marquis, 1939). While at Tempe, Bolton founded and edited the *Arizona Journal of Education* (Marquis, 1939).

In 1912 , Bolton was wooed by Edwin B. Craighead, president of the University of Montana. Following a bout of appendicitis (Bolton, 1912a), Bolton arrived in Missoula and assumed the position of chair of psychology (Bolton, 1912b; Craighead, 1912a) at an annual salary of $2,000 (Craighead, 1913). In a letter to a colleague at Columbia University, Craighead explained why he had chosen Bolton over a number of other candidates:

> I appointed Dr. T. L. Bolton instead of the two splendid men recommended by you, because: (1) Bolton seems to be a more current psychologist. He is a starred man of Cattell's science and while I do not consider this a great importance, the common rabble does. Cattell has all sorts of wooden men in his list and he has left out some men who will be remembered forever; (2) Bolton is an author of distinction and unquestionably a scholar. (Craighead, 1912b)

In the next paragraph, Craighead admitted to misgivings about Bolton's personality: "I am not sure, however, that I have made a wise decision. I judge that Kirby is a saner, perhaps a better poised man" (Craighead, 1912b).

In the winter of 1913, Bolton was asked by the governor of Montana to look into reports of strange occurrences at the home of the MacDonald family in a remote area outside Missoula ("Dr. Bolton Cites," 1922; "Mary Ellen Ghost," 1922). Bolton spent an evening at the family's house, where he witnessed an animated family séance. Mr. and Mrs. MacDonald claimed that they were in touch with a number of spirits of deceased people whom they had known. The appearance of the spirits was always accompanied by knocking sounds emanating from the bedroom of their adopted daughter, who allegedly was asleep at the time. In a written report to the MacDonalds, Bolton pronounced the occurrences to be an unwitting hoax. The family had undoubtedly fallen victim to "their own self-illusion" ("Dr. Bolton Cites," 1922, p. 2), and he suggested that the daughter was making the knocking sounds while in a somnambulistic state brought on by the parents' talk about ghostly visitations. Unhappy with Bolton's report, Mrs. MacDonald complained to the governor, who then summoned Bolton to his office. Bolton stuck to his analysis of the events, and the governor was placed in the awkward position of wanting to appease his constituents in the face of contradictory evidence presented by his own expert.

The MacDonald case must have stood as a point of contention between the governor and Bolton. In June 1915, Bolton was dismissed along with several of his colleagues and the university's president, Craighead. Although he denied it in a letter (Bolton, 1915a), it is possible that Bolton was vying for Craighead's position, and was involved with the others in squabbles intended to oust the president. The governor and the state board of education "cleaned house" of everyone involved in the disruption (Anonymous, 1916). Although Bolton and a few of his colleagues were later reinstated, he was forced to take a year's leave of absence and never returned to the University of Montana (Bolton, 1915a, 1915b).

YEARS AT TEMPLE UNIVERSITY

Bolton moved east in the summer of 1915 to Springfield, Massachusetts, not far from his alma mater in Worcester (Bolton, 1915b). From the temporary haven of a post as a school psychologist (Sheldahl, in preparation), he submitted applications to Boston University's department of education (Anonymous, 1916; Wilde, 1916) and Temple University in Philadelphia. Bolton accepted an offer from Temple, and appears to have started there during the 1917–1918 academic year (Marquis, 1939).

At that time, there was no department of psychology at Temple, and there were only two psychologists, George F. Miller and Lorle I. Stecher (Temple University, 1917–1918). Bolton no doubt played an active role in lobbying for an autonomous department, and may have used what was for him the atypical interpersonal strategy of ingratiating himself with Laura Carnell, who was actually operating the university for founder and president Russell Conwell (H. C. Hamilton, personal communication, February 27, 1985). Bolton's experience with setting up laboratories and single-handedly running departments proved to be an asset that he could successfully exchange for stability and security he probably had never known. In 1924, the department of psychology was established, additional faculty were hired, and a full curriculum of psychology courses was offered. Bolton, shown in Fig. 1.3, was appointed the department's first chairman (Temple University, 1924–1925).

Psychology journals were then buzzing with the New Psychology— John B. Watson's behaviorism. (Watson studied with Bolton's old physi-

FIG. 1.3. Thaddeus Lincoln Bolton, chair, department of psychology, Temple University. (Courtesy of the Conwellana-Templana Collection, Temple University Libraries. Photo: Bachrach.)

ology professor, H. H. Donaldson, at the University of Chicago; Boring, 1950.) The zeitgeist created by G. Stanley Hall, William James, Wilhelm Wundt, Edward Titchener, and other founders of modern psychology was slipping away. Bolton himself had become an anachronism, clinging to old ideas and themes. Perhaps because of this, he came to rely on a number of alternative outlets for his research and commentary. These included education journals (Bolton, 1921), vanity books (Bolton, 1923, 1927b), a pamphlet (1924), a business training manual (1926), and popular press interviews and articles. It was at this time, too, that he married Martha Louise Busse (Marquis, 1939).

One old theme that resurfaced in Bolton's work was intellectual ability. In a 1921 article, he argued that despite the rapidly changing demands of modern society, the study of classical Greek and Latin could be justified by the "useful habits of study," "transferable increased mental power," and "transferable technique and information" that students could acquire (Bolton, 1921, p. 206). Bolton likened the intellect to a muscle: The more it is used in a focused, directed manner, the greater its capacity. He argued that the use of the Army Alpha and Army Beta tests during the First World War, under the supervision of Robert M. Yerkes, illustrated this point. Men who were successful in the highly technical field of engineering also scored higher on the intelligence scales than did recruits with no engineering aptitude or experience. Bolton cautioned that "intelligence level is a matter of heredity and can not be much affected by any form of training. Let us suggest that the amount of the effect which study may work towards raising the intelligence level does not exceed ten per cent" (Bolton, 1921, pp. 207–208).

Also echoing his earlier studies of children, Bolton pursued questions concerning psychomotor development. He gave a lecture to the Baby Welfare Association of Philadelphia that was, in effect, a demonstration and endorsement of a device called the "Health Bowl" (Bolton, 1924). This was a large steel saucer with a seat mounted on top. Bolton strapped a boy who was a "clinical type of the Mongolian" into the Health Bowl to illustrate his ideas about the sense of equilibrium. Bolton argued that "there are what I call critical periods in the development of the child. In the post-birth life of the child the most critical period is just this period of assisting at the right time and the tendency to sit and stand" (Bolton, 1924, p. 23). The Health Bowl purportedly would help maximize motor skills and growth and would overcome any tendency to retardation. Bolton claimed that the Health Bowl aided development by forcing children to hold their heads up, sit up straight, and kick with the feet in order to turn around and see and hear as much of their surroundings as possible. He explained that movement that tilts the semicircular canals off their optimal planes causes a pleasurable dizziness. Bolton purported that the repeated motor activity that produced self-induced dizziness, along with having to right oneself with opposing motor activity, strengthened the muscles and nerves of the neck and shoulders. Other alleged benefits of the Health Bowl were improved sitting and standing postures, walking, heart function, bowel function, and even vocabulary acquisition and speech comprehension. Sounding a bit like a snake-oil salesperson, Bolton added that, "I don't doubt at all that we will be able to see how this instrument ... aids the growth of the teeth" (Bolton, 1924, p. 23).

Bolton also returned to his work on fatigue with a study of diet and fatigue that was reported in *Scientific American* ("Diet Causes Fatigue," 1930; "Dr. Bolton Experiments," 1930). Bolton and Clarence H. Smeltzer administered tests of physical dexterity, coordination, endurance, and mental alertness to 20 female office workers. The tests were given at varying times of the normal workday in order to plot fatigue curves. Bolton and Smeltzer found that performance was poor at the start of the day, then peaked at about 2:30 P.M., and dropped off steadily until quitting time. Subjects were then assigned to three treatment groups and a control group. Each treatment group received a different diet during the day, varying by the time of a meal or snack and type and quantity of food. The subjects were given performance tests periodically during the day. After some 500,000 calculations, Bolton concluded that the group that received a high-calorie diet in the afternoon was more productive, and that to maximize performance during the busiest time of day, office workers "would do well to keep in the drawer of the desk a box of good candy or candied fruit. When energy flags in mid-afternoon, these quick-action foods will act as an emergency ration and supply the calories needed for the rest of the day's work" ("Diet Causes Fatigue," 1930, p. 223). Bolton added that "special emphasis should be laid upon the support these findings give to the opinions of those who have held that reducing diets are responsible for impairing the efficiency of the modern business girl" ("Diet Causes Fatigue," 1930, p. 223).

Bolton lent his expertise to other issues that were of interest to the general public, notably in the press (H. C. Hamilton, personal communication, February 27, 1985). His views of sports fans were quoted on the front page of *The New York Times*:

> A man who would stand in line for hours for a seat in the bleachers and then shout himself hoarse rooting for his favorite baseball team is not well balanced mentally, in the opinion of Dr. Thaddeus L. Bolton, Professor of Psychology at Temple University. He may not be abnormal, but he is not gifted with good mental poise, Dr. Bolton said today.
>
> "The well-balanced man," said Dr. Bolton, "will not become fanatical in his love for one particular sport to the exclusion of all others. If he does, he is suffering from a mental hypertrophy."
>
> "A hypertrophy," explained Dr. Bolton, "is a growth. There are mental and physical hypertrophies. Physically they manifest themselves in the form of corns, bunions, boils, &c.; mentally, in the case of the baseball fan, by a tendency toward over-ardent, hysterical devotion to the one particular sport" ("Ball Fan," 1927, p. 1).

Also appearing in *The New York Times* was an article entitled "Anatomy of Laughter: Its Origins and Uses," in which Bolton contended that laughter evolved in humans as a response to the successful hunt or battle. Laughter thus serves as a "socializing agent": "We laugh to hold ourselves together as a social group" (Bolton, 1927a, p. 18). Echoing his "Laws of Personal Growth," Bolton observed in another *New York Times* article that people often laugh at the failure or misfortune of others, in order to gain dominance: "A man walks down the street, steps on a banana peel and we laugh ... we triumph in the fact that we did not slip and fall" ("Many Animals Laugh," 1927, p. 19).

Other popular press coverage of Bolton's ideas included work on handedness ("Tests Right-Handedness," 1930) and the origin and function of slogans ("Dr. Bolton Traces," 1932). During this period he also pursued his hobbies of furniture making and woodcarving, from which a number of departments at Temple benefited:

> This same recreation of Dr. Bolton's supplies the psychology department with much of its wooden apparatus. One may find a tube rack here, a little wooden cabinet there, a table somewhere else, all of them—if one only knew—breathing the spirit of play.... The biology department, the Dental School, and the psychology department are all indebted to him for the designing of the tables which they use in their work ("Dr. Bolton Plays," 1930, p. 4).

THE BOLTON PROFESSORSHIP

Bolton retired as professor and chairman of Temple's department of psychology at the end of the 1936–1937 academic year ("Bolton, Wallace," 1937), at the age of 71. His legacy extended well beyond homemade furniture. In February 1947, Bolton established a trust fund of $61,000 (Temple University Development Office, n.d.; "Trust Fund," 1947) for the Thaddeus L. Bolton Professorship of Psychology. Temple faculty members who held the Professorship include Clarence H. Smeltzer (1955–1968), Hughbert C. Hamilton (1968–1970), Robert E. Lana (1974–1981), and Ralph Rosnow (1981–2001; see Fig. 1.4). It was traditional for standing

FIG. 1.4. Ralph L. Rosnow, Thaddeus L. Bolton Professor of Psychology, 1981 to 2001. (Photo: Zohrab Kazanjian.)

Bolton Professors to nominate their successors. The Bolton endowment has supported psychological research by these scholars and their graduate students, including the research that made this chapter possible.

Bolton was 82 years old when he died at Temple University Hospital on January 3, 1948. Although obituaries were published in the *American Psychologist* (American Psychological Association, 1948), *The New York Times* ("Dr. Bolton Dies," 1948), and *The Philadelphia Inquirer* ("Dr. T. L. Bolton," 1948), it is curious that a scholar whose career touched so many of the great figures in American and European intellectual history could have dropped so utterly into obscurity. I have been unable to find even one mention of him in recent histories of psychology. Yet, Bolton was an exemplary figure in early American psychology, and the breadth of his interests anticipated many of the most vital areas of contemporary psychology. It is true that he was something of a dilettante, but it is only fair to say that, like most early psychologists, Bolton was an enthusiastic and capable generalist. He was a prodigious traveler and an "academic gypsy," having taught in some of the finest psychology departments in the United States. He published in the top journals of his day. It is to his credit that Bolton's unlikely legacy continues today through the Bolton Professorship and the rich tradition of research and training it has supported.

Ralph Rosnow distinguished the Bolton legacy by continuing Bolton's commitment to innovative research methodology and his emphasis on applied psychological research. Like Bolton, Professor Rosnow is an intrepid methodologist, having published numerous articles and several popular textbooks that continue to appear in new editions. Also like Bolton, his work on areas such as rumor and gossip and interpersonal acumen demonstrates his commitment to applying knowledge to real-world problems. Not least of all, Ralph Rosnow, like Thaddeus Bolton, ably served as a dedicated teacher, colleague, and friend to several generations of psychologists.

REFERENCES

American Psychological Association. (1948). Thaddeus L. Bolton. *American Psychologist, 3*, 115.

Anonymous. (1912, September 29). Letter to E. B. Craighead.

Anonymous. (1916, July 31). Letter to A. H. Wilde.

Ball fan lacks mental poise, says Philadelphia savant. (1927, July 27). *The New York Times*, p. 1.

Bolton, T. L. (1891–1892). The growth of memory in school children. *American Journal of Psychology, 4*, 362–380.

Bolton, T. L. (1893). On the discrimination of groups of rapid clicks. *American Journal of Psychology, 5*, 294–301.

Bolton, T. L. (1894). Rhythm. *American Journal of Psychology, 6*, 145–238.

Bolton, T. L. (1902). Uber die Beziehungen zwischen Ermüdung, Raumsinn der Haut und Muskelleistung. *Psychologische Arbeiten, 5*, 175–234.

Bolton, T. L. (1903a). The relation of motor power to intelligence. *American Journal of Psychology, 14*, 351–367.

Bolton, T. L. (1903b). The fatigue problem. *Journal of Pedagogy, 16*, 97–123.

Bolton, T. L. (1907). Some social laws of personal growth. *Journal of Pedagogy, 20*, 29–56.

Bolton, T. L. (1912a, September 28). Letter to E. B. Craighead.

Bolton, T. L (1912b, October 1). Telegram to E. B Craighead.

Bolton, T. L. (1915a, October 27). Letter to Professor Scheuch.

Bolton, T. L. (1915b, November 28). Letter to Professor Scheuch.

Bolton, T. L. (1921). What is the disciplinary value of the classics? *School and Society, 14*, 205–210.

Bolton, T. L. (1923). *The family record of Peter Bolton, the son of Peter of Plockington, England*. Philadelphia: Author.

Bolton, T. L. (1924). *Lecture on the health bowl*. Philadelphia: Henry Karr.

Bolton, T. L. (1926). *Application of tests and measurements to shorthand and typing*. New York: Gregg.

Bolton, T. L. (1927a, October 9). Anatomy of laughter: Its origins and uses. *The New York Times*, p.18.

Bolton, T. L. (1927b). *Geneaology of the Dart, Darte, Dartt, Dort family*. Philadelphia: Cooper.

Bolton, T. L., & Haskell, E. M. (1898). Knowledge from the standpoint of association. *Educational Review, 15*, 474–499.

Bolton, T. L., & Miller, E. T. (1904). Validity of the ergograph as a measurer of work capacity. *University of Nebraska Studies, 4*, 79–128.

Bolton, T. L., & Withey, D. L. (1907). On the relation of muscle sense to pressure sense. *University of Nebraska Studies, 7*, 175–195.

Bolton, Wallace, Heller retire. (1937, September 29). *Temple University News*, p. 3.

Boring, E. G. (1950). *A history of experimental psychology* (2nd ed.). New York: Appleton-Century-Crofts.

Clark University. (1891). Second annual report of the president. Worcester, MA: Author.

Craighead. E. B. (1912a, October 1). Letter to T. L. Bolton.

Craighead, E. B. (1912b, October 3). Letter to C. J. Keyser.

Craighead, E. B. (1913, July 31). Letter to T. L. Bolton.

Diet causes fatigue. (1930, March). *Scientific American*, p. 223.

Donaldson, H. H., & Bolton, T. L. (1891–1892). The size of cranial nerves in man as indicated by the areas of their cross-sections. *American Journal of Psychology, 4*, 224–229.

Dr. Bolton cites his ghost investigations. (1922, March 20). *Temple University News*, pp. 1–2.

Dr. Bolton experiments. (1930, April 4). *Temple University News*, p. 1.

Dr. T. L. Bolton, psychologist, dies. (1948, January 4). *The Philadelphia Inquirer*.

Dr. Bolton dies; psychologist, was 82. (1948, January 4). *The New York Times*, p. 52.

Dr. Bolton, psychology professor, "plays" at wood carving and design. (1930, March 21). *Temple University Weekly*, p. 4.

Dr. Bolton traces origin of slogans. (1932, April 1). *Temple University News*, p. 4.

Ebbinghaus, H. (1885/1964). *Memory*. New York: Dover.

Guthrie, E. R. (1959). Association by contiguity. In S. Koch (Ed.), *Psychology: A study of a science* (pp. 158–197). New York: McGraw-Hill.

Hall, G. S. (1879). Laura Bridgman. *Mind, 4*, 149–172.

Hall, G. S., & Jastrow, J. (1886). Studies of rhythm. *Mind*, *11*, 55–62.

Hill, A. R. (1912, September 21). Telegram to E. B. Craighead.

James, W. (1892). *Text-book of psychology: Briefer course*. New York: Henry Holt.

Many animals laugh, scientist contends. (1927, September 2). *The New York Times*, p. 19.

Marquis, A. N. (Ed.). (1939). *Who's who in Pennsylvania* (Vol. 1). Chicago: Author.

Mary Ellen ghost heard in Montana. (1922, March 18). *The New York Times*, p. 13.

Miller, W. (1912a, September 21). Telegram to E. B. Craighead.

Miller, W. (1912b, September 30). Telegram to E. B. Craighead.

Murchison, C. (Ed.). (1932). *The psychological register* (Vol. 3). Worcester, MA: Clark University Press.

Pepper, S. C. (1942/1970). *World hypotheses*. Berkeley, CA: University of California Press.

Rosenthal, R., and Rosnow, R. L. (Eds.) (1975). *The volunteer subject*. New York: Wiley.

Ross, D. (1972). *G. Stanley Hall: The psychologist as prophet*. Chicago: University of Illinois Press.

Sanford, E. C. (1891–1896). Course in experimental psychology, Part I: Sensation and perception. *American Journal of Psychology*, *4–7*.

Sanford, E. C. (1893). Introduction. Minor studies form the Psychological Laboratory of Clark University. *American Journal of Psychology*, *5*, 294, 301.

Sheldahl, T. (in preparation). *Thaddeus Lincoln Bolton: 1865–1948: Psychologist, educationist, and academic survivor*.

Temple University. (1917–1918). *Catalogue*. Philadelphia: Author.

Temple University. (1924–1925). *Catalogue*. Philadelphia: Author.

Temple University Development Office. (n.d.). *The Thaddeus Lincoln Bolton professorship of psychology*. Philadelphia: Temple University.

Tests right-handedness. (1930, July 20). *The New York Times*, p. 6.

Trust fund used to start foundation. (1947, February 21). *Temple University News*, p. 6.

University of Washington (1896–1897). *Catalog*. Seattle: Author.

White, L. A. (1963). *The ethnography and ethnology of Franz Boas*. Austin: Texas Memorial Museum.

Wilde, A. H. (1916, July 27). Letter to University of Montana.

Wundt, W. (1893). *Grundzüge der Physiologischen Psychologie* (Vol. II, 4th ed.). Leipzig: Verlag von Wilhelm Engelmann.

II

Methods and Ethics
of Research

2

Praising Pearson Properly: Correlations, Contrasts, and Construct Validity

Robert Rosenthal
University of California, Riverside

Even prior to praising Pearson properly I want to praise our dedicatee, Ralph Rosnow. I cannot praise him properly because that would leave no space for Pearson, so I will be brief: Ralph is my oldest friend—colleague—collaborator—teacher—coach—and mentor. He has been ruining my character and spoiling me for over 35 years, beginning back when we both started the Boston phases of our careers in the early 1960s. He spoiled me when he invited me to collaborate with him in his ongoing research program. He educated me in matters historical, philosophical, and theoretical. And then, whenever I needed cheering up, he wrote a book—and put my name on it. (That does wonders for your morale!) I must have needed a lot of cheering up because Ralph did that a lot of times, and he's still doing it, I'm happy (but embarrassed) to report. Thank you, Ralph!

Not in this century, the 21st, nor in the last, the 20th, but in the 19th century, Karl Pearson published the equation for the product moment correlation that now bears his name (Pearson, 1896; Stigler, 1986). Old as this correlational metric is, I want to suggest that it remains as perhaps the most nearly universally applicable index of effect size. It is difficult to imagine a situation in which a Pearson r, or its equivalent, could not appropriately be used to index the magnitude of an effect. And because all Pearson rs, and their equivalents, are based on focused comparisons, or contrasts, rather than on diffuse or omnibus comparisons (e.g., F tests with more than one df in the numerator, or χ^2 tests with $df > 1$), there is far greater conceptual clarity in the employment of r than in the employment of effect size estimates based on $df > 1$.

By the use of simple displays, Pearson rs can be made readily understandable to policy experts who are unfamiliar with more complex statistical ideas such as standard deviation units. The interpretation of Pearson rs that do not differ significantly from the null value (usually zero) can be clarified by the use of simple devices like the counternull value of the obtained r (Rosenthal & Rubin, 1982, 1994; Rosnow & Rosenthal, 1996).

In some areas of behavioral and biomedical research, effect size indices such as odds ratios and relative risks are commonly employed. It is often the case that these indices operate in ways that can be quite misleading. In such situations we can use Pearson rs to standardize these indices and make them more consistently useful and interpretable (Rosenthal, 2000; Rosenthal, Rosnow, & Rubin, 2000). In the domain of reliability of measurement, we run considerable risks when we try to get by with such noncorrelational indices as percent agreement or with indices based on more than a single df.

When three or more conditions are being compared in experimental or observational research, different subtypes of Pearson rs have been found useful. Two of these subtypes of r—$r_{\text{alerting-CV}}$ and $r_{\text{contrast-CV}}$—have recently been applied to the problem of construct validation, permitting a useful quantification of this most complex of the types of validity of our measures.

To praise Pearson properly (i.e., thoroughly, fully) would take much more space than we have here. Accordingly, the remainder of this chapter focuses on just two topics, both of them relevant to psychometric issues: risks we run in not using Pearson's r-based indices of reliability, and benefits that can flow from using Pearson's r to quantify construct validity. Before beginning those topics, it is worth noting that long ago Pearson (1904) found a new and exciting application of his r. He used it in what must surely have been one of the earliest of meta-analyses.

Pearson was interested in the effects of vaccination for smallpox on survival, and he collected the results of six experiments examining this relationship. Table 2.1 shows these six rs rounded to two decimal places. Pearson summarized these six correlations as an r of .6. Table 2.1 shows a few more details about his results than Pearson reported, including the mean, median, standard deviation, 95% confidence interval, one sample t, p, and r_{contrast} all based on a random effects approach (i.e., treating studies, rather than patients, as sampling units; Rosenthal & DiMatteo, 2002).

TABLE 2.1
Karl Pearson's (1904) Meta-Analysis: Correlations
Between Smallpox Vaccination and Survival

Study	Pearson r
1	.60
2	.66
3	.77
4	.58
5	.58
6	.63
Mean	.64
Median	.61
S	.072
Standard error $(S / \sqrt{6})$	.029
95% Confidence interval	From .56
	To .72
One sample $t_{(5)}$	21.68
p	.000002
r	.99

Note. Calculations were carried out on untransformed rs because Fisher's Z_r transformation had not yet been invented (and because of the homogeneity of the obtained rs).

SOME ALTERNATIVES TO USING PEARSON'S r-BASED INDICES OF RELIABILITY AND WHY WE SHOULD NOT USE THEM

Percent Agreement

It has long been common practice for some researchers to index the reliability of judges' categorizations using percent agreement defined as

$$\left(\frac{A}{A + D}\right)100 \tag{1}$$

where A represents the number of agreements and D represents the number of disagreements (Rosenthal & Rosnow, 1991). Table 2.2 shows how percent agreement can be a very misleading indicator of interjudge reliability. In Part A of Table 2.2, we find that two researchers, Smith and Jones, each had two judges evaluate a series of 100 film clips of children for the presence or absence of frowning behavior. Both Smith and Jones found their judges to show 98% agreement, but Smith's 98% agreement was a hollow victory indeed. The correlation between Judges A and B was actually slightly negative,

$$r = -.01, \left(\chi^2_{(1)} = 0.01 \right).$$

Jones's 98% agreement, on the other hand, was associated with an r of $+.96, \left(\chi^2_{(1)} = 92.16 \right)$.

Part B of Table 2.2 shows two additional cases of percent agreement obtained by researchers Brown and Green. This time, the two investigators both obtained an apparently chance level of agreement (i.e., 50%). Both results, however, are very far from reflecting chance agreement, both with $p = .0009$. Most surprising, perhaps, is that Brown obtained a substantial negative reliability ($r = -.33$), whereas Green obtained a substantial posi-

TABLE 2.2
Examples of Percent Agreement

A. *Two Cases of 98% Agreement*

	Smith's Results			Jones's Results	
	Judge A			Judge C	
Judge B	Frown	No Frown	Judge D	Frown	No Frown
Frown	98	1	Frown	49	1
No frown	1	0	No frown	1	49

Agreement = 98%, but $r_{AB} = -.01$;   Agreement = 98%, but $r_{CD} = +.96$;
$\chi^2 (1) = 0.01$ $\chi^2 (1) = 92.16$

B. *Two Cases of 50% Agreement*

	Brown's Results			Green's Results	
	Judge E			Judge G	
Judge F	Frown	No Frown	Judge H	Frown	No Frown
Frown	50	25	Frown	25	50
No frown	25	0	No frown	0	25

Agreement = 50%, but $r_{EF} = -.33$;   Agreement = 50%, but $r_{GH} = +.33$;
$\chi^2 = 11.11$ $\chi^2 = 11.11$

tive reliability ($r = +.33$)—another illustration that percent agreement is not a very informative index of reliability.

Multi-*df* Interjudge Reliability

Among the first psychologists to appreciate the problems of percent agreement as an index of reliability was Jacob Cohen (1960). He developed an index, kappa, that solved the problem of the percent agreement index by adjusting for any agreement based simply on lack of variability (e.g., the lack of variability shown in Table 2.2A, where both of Smith's judges found 99% of the film clips to show frowning behavior).

Table 2.3 gives an example of the type of situation in which *kappa* is often employed. Two clinical diagnosticians have examined 100 people and assigned them to one of four classifications: schizophrenic, neurotic, normal, and brain damaged. Only three quantities are required to compute *kappa*:

O = observed number on which the two judges have agreed, i.e., the number on the diagonal of agreement; in this example:
$$13 + 12 + 12 + 13 = 50.$$

E = expected number under the hypothesis of only chance agreement for the cells on the diagonal of agreement. For each cell, the expected number is the product of the row total and the column total divided by the

TABLE 2.3
**Results of Two Diagnosticians' Classification of 100 Persons
Into One of Four Categories**

	Judge 1				
	A	*B*	*C*	*D*	
Judge 2	*Schizophrenic*	*Neurotic*	*Normal*	*Brain Damaged*	*Σ*
A Schizophrenic	13	0	0	12	25
B Neurotic	0	12	13	0	25
C Normal	0	13	12	0	25
D Brain damaged	12	0	0	13	25
Σ	25	25	25	25	100

$$kappa(df = 9) = \frac{O - E}{N - E} = \frac{50 - 25}{100 - 25} = .333$$

total number of cases. In this example, the expected number is:
$(25 \times 25)/100 + (25 \times 25)/100 + (25 \times 25)/100 + (25 \times 25)/100 = 6.25 + 6.25 + 6.25 + 6.25 = 25.$

N = total number of cases classified; in this example, $N = 100$.

In the present example, *kappa* is computed from

$$kappa = \frac{O - E}{N - E} = \frac{50 - 25}{100 - 25} = .333 \tag{2}$$

Although *kappa* is clearly an improvement over percent agreement as an index of reliability, it does raise some serious questions. When *kappa* is based on tables larger than a 2 × 2—for example, a 3 × 3, a 4 × 4 (as in Table 2.3), or larger—as it often is, *kappa* suffers from the same problem as does any statistic on $df > 1$. This problem, the problem of diffuse or omnibus procedures, is that for most values of *kappa* we cannot tell which focused or specific judgments are made reliably and which are made unreliably. Only when *kappa* approaches unity is the actual interpretation of a value of *kappa* straightforward (i.e., essentially all judgments are made reliably; Rosenthal, 1991). We illustrate the difficulty in interpreting *kappa* by returning to Table 2.3.

The 4 × 4 table we see, based on 9 *df*, can be decomposed into a series of six pairwise 2 × 2 tables, each based on a single *df* and addressing a very specific, conceptually clear question of the reliability of dichotomous judgments: A versus B, A versus C, A versus D, B versus C, B versus D, and C versus D. Table 2.4 shows the results of computing *kappa* separately for each of these six 2 × 2 tables.

Of the six focused or specific reliabilities computed, four are *kappas* of 1.00, and two are *kappas* near zero (.04 and −.04). The mean of the six 1 *df kappas* is .667, and the median and the mode are 1.00; none of these values being predictable from the omnibus 9 *df kappa* value of .33. To show even more clearly how little relation there is between the omnibus values of *kappa* and the associated 1 *df kappas* (i.e., the focused reliability *kappas*), Tables 2.5 and 2.6 have been prepared. Table 2.5 shows an omnibus 9 *df kappa* value of .33, exactly the same value as that shown in Table 2.3.

Table 2.6 shows the six focused reliabilities of $df = 1$ associated with the omnibus value of *kappa* (.33) of Table 2.5. We see that of these six focused *kappas*, four are *kappas* of .00, one is a *kappa* of +1.00, and one is a *kappa* of −1.00. The mean, the median, and the modal focused *kappa* all show a value of .00. We can summarize the two omnibus *kappas* of Tables 2.3 and 2.5 and their associated focused *kappas* as follows:

	Example 1	Example 2
Omnibus kappa	.33	.33
Mean focused kappa	.67	.00
Median focused kappa	1.00	.00
Modal focused kappa	1.00	.00

TABLE 2.4

Breakdown of the Nine *df* Omnibus Table of Counts of Table 2.3 into Six Specific (Focused) Reliabilities of *df* = 1 Each

	A Schizophrenic	B Neurotic	Σ		A Schizophrenic	C Normal	Σ
A Schizophrenic	13	0	13	A Schizophrenic	13	0	13
B Neurotic	0	12	12	C Normal	0	12	12
Σ	13	12	25	Σ	13	12	25
	kappa = 1.00				*kappa* = 1.00		

	A Schizophrenic	D Brain Damaged	Σ		B Neurotic	C Normal	Σ
A Schizophrenic	13	12	25	B Neurotic	12	13	25
D Brain damaged	12	13	25	C Normal	13	12	25
Σ	25	25	50	Σ	25	25	50
	kappa = .04				*kappa* = −.04		

	B Neurotic	D Brain Damaged	Σ		C Normal	D Brain Damaged	Σ
B Neurotic	12	0	12	C Normal	12	0	12
D Brain damaged	0	13	13	D Brain damaged	0	13	13
Σ	12	13	25	Σ	12	13	25
	kappa = 1.00				*kappa* = 1.00		

TABLE 2.5
**Alternative Results of Two Diagnosticians' Classification
of 100 Persons Into One of Four Categories**

Judge 2	Judge 1				
	A	B	C	D	Σ
A	25	0	0	0	25
B	0	0	25	0	25
C	0	25	0	0	25
D	0	0	0	25	25
Σ	25	25	25	25	100

$$kappa(df = 9) = \frac{O-E}{N-E} = \frac{50-25}{100-25} = .333$$

TABLE 2.6
**Breakdown of the 9 *df* Omnibus Table of Counts of Table 2.5
Into Six Specific (Focused) Reliabilities of *df* = 1 Each**

	A	B	Σ
A	25	0	25
B	0	0	0
Σ	25	0	25

kappa = .00

	A	C	Σ
A	25	0	25
C	0	0	0
Σ	25	0	25

kappa = .00

	A	D	Σ
A	25	0	25
D	0	25	25
Σ	25	25	50

kappa = 1.00

	B	C	Σ
B	0	25	25
C	25	0	25
Σ	25	25	50

kappa = −1.00

	B	D	Σ
B	0	0	0
D	0	25	25
Σ	0	25	25

kappa = .00

	C	D	Σ
C	0	0	0
D	0	25	25
Σ	0	25	25

kappa = .00

Thus we have two identical *kappas:* one made up primarily of perfect reliabilities, the other made up primarily of zero reliabilities.

We might think that these examples are extreme and perhaps due in part to the values of *kappa* being quite modest (i.e., .33). That is not the case, however. Consider the following table of counts, where once again two diagnosticians have classified patients into one of four categories: A, B, C, or D.

	A	B	C	D	Σ
A	300	0	0	0	300
B	0	0	10	0	10
C	0	10	0	0	10
D	0	0	0	300	300
Σ	300	10	10	300	620

The preceding table yields a *kappa* of .94, but the six pairwise *kappas* (or *r*s) are .00, .00, .00, .00, +1.00, and −1.00, for a mean, median, and modal *kappa* (or *r*) of .00. This is not a very reassuring result; diagnosticians *can* distinguish A from D, but they *can't* distinguish A from B or C, or B from C or D, or C from D, despite the *kappa* value of .94!

Single-*df* Interjudge Reliability

Although the greatest limitations on *kappa* occur when *kappa* is based on *df* > 1, there are some problems with *kappa* even when it is based on a 2 × 2 table of counts where *df* = 1. The basic problem under these conditions is that very often *kappa* is not equivalent to the product moment correlation computed from exactly the same 2 × 2 table of counts. This is certainly not a criticism of *kappa*, because it never pretended to be a product moment correlation. The limitation, however, is that we cannot apply various interpretive procedures or displays to *kappa* that we can apply to product moment correlations. Examples include the use of the *coefficient of determination* (i.e., r^2) and the *binomial effect size display* (Rosenthal & Rubin, 1979, 1982; Rosnow, Rosenthal, & Rubin, 2000).

Here we need only indicate the conditions under which a 1 *df kappa* is or is not equivalent to a product moment correlation (referred to as a Pearson *r* in the general case, and sometimes referred to as *phi*—or ϕ—in the case of a 2 × 2 table of counts). *Kappa* and *r* are equivalent when the row totals for Levels A and B are identical to the column totals for Levels A and B, respectively. Consider the following example:

	Judge 1		
Judge 2	A	B	Σ
A	70	10	80
B	10	10	20
Σ	80	20	100

For these data, where the marginal totals for Level A are identical for Judges 1 and 2 (i.e., 80),

$$kappa(df = 1) = \frac{O - E}{N - E} = \frac{80 - 68}{100 - 68} = .375,$$

and r (or equivalently, phi) yields the identical value of .375. Therefore, we could meaningfully compute a coefficient of determination or a *binomial effect size display* for this particular *kappa* because it is equivalent to a Pearson r or *phi* (ϕ).

Now consider the following example, in which we have the same four cell entries and the same marginal totals as in the preceding example. The only thing that has changed is the location of the cell with the largest count (70), so that the marginal totals for Level A differ for Judges 1 and 2 (20 vs. 80).

	Judge 1		
Judge 2	A	B	Σ
A	10	70	80
B	10	10	20
Σ	20	80	100

In this example,

$$kappa(df = 1) = \frac{O - E}{N - E} = \frac{20 - 32}{100 - 32} = -.176,$$

but r (or ϕ) yields a markedly different value of $-.375$. We can, therefore, compute a meaningful coefficient of determination and *binomial effect size display* for r, but we cannot do so for *kappa*.

USING PEARSON'S r
TO QUANTIFY CONSTRUCT VALIDITY

Construct validity is one of the most important concepts in all of psychology. Yet, despite the importance of this concept, no simple metric can be employed to quantify the extent to which a measure can be described as construct valid. Researchers typically establish construct validity by presenting correlations between a measure of a construct and a number of other measures that should, theoretically, be associated with it (convergent validity) or vary independently of it (discriminant validity).

The aim of construct validation is to embed a purported measure of a construct in a nomological network; that is, to establish its relation to other variables with which it should, theoretically, be associated positively, negatively, or practically not at all (Cronbach & Meehl, 1955). A procedure designed to help quantify construct validity should provide a summary index not only of *whether* the measure correlates positively, negatively, or not at all with a series of other measures, but also the relative magnitude of those correlations. Or, put another way, it should be an index of the extent to which the researcher has accurately predicted the pattern of findings in the convergent-discriminant validity array. Such a metric should also provide a test of the statistical significance of the match between observed and expected correlations, and provide confidence intervals for that match, taking into account the likelihood that some of the validating variables may not be independent of one another.

Drew Westen and I have presented two effect size estimates (both Pearson rs) for quantifying construct validity (Westen & Rosenthal, 2003). These two rs are variants on two of four rs described elsewhere in considerable detail (Rosenthal et al., 2000; Rosnow et al., 2000). The two variants were designed to summarize the pattern of findings represented in a convergent-discriminant validity matrix for a given measure. These metrics provide simple estimates of validity that can be compared across studies, constructs, and measures. Both metrics provide a quantified index of the degree of convergence between the observed pattern of correlations and the theoretically predicted pattern of correlations— that is, of the degree of agreement of the data with the theory underlying the construct and the measure.

Contrasts and Construct Validity

In their classic paper on construct validation, Cronbach and Meehl (1955) considered the possibility of developing an overall coefficient for indexing construct validity, but noted the difficulty of providing anything more than a broad indication of the upper and lower bounds of validity. However, developments since that time, particularly in the concept of the multi-trait multi-method matrix (MTMM; Campbell & Fiske, 1959; Shrout & Fiske, 1995), have led to continued efforts to derive more quantitative, less impressionistic ways to index the extent to which a measure is doing its job. Thus, a number of researchers have developed techniques to try to separate

out true variance on a measure of a trait from method variance, often based
on the principle that method effects and trait effects (and their interactions) should be distinguishable using analysis of variance, confirmatory
factor analysis (because trait and method variance should load on different
factors), structural equation modeling, and related statistical procedures
(Cudeck, 1988; Hammond, Hamm, & Grassia, 1986; Kenny, 1995;
Reichardt & Coleman, 1995; Wothke, 1995). Our procedures are in many
respects related, but are simple, readily applied, and designed to address the
most common case in which a researcher wants to validate a single measure
by correlating it with multiple other measures.

The approach we proposed, based on contrast analysis, asks a highly specific, focused question with one degree of freedom. The question it addresses is whether the researcher has accurately predicted the magnitude of
correlations between a single predictor variable and multiple criterion variables. Rosenthal et al. (2000) have outlined the advantages of focused questions of this sort, but the major advantage is that these procedures, based on
one degree of freedom, provide a single answer to a single question; in this
case, how well does this measure predict an array of correlations with other
measures in a way predicted by theory?

The procedures that Drew Westen and I proposed derive primarily from
developments in contrast analysis (Meng, Rosenthal, & Rubin, 1992;
Rosenthal & Rosnow, 1985; Rosenthal et al., 2000; Rosnow et al., 2000)—
a set of techniques usually employed in the analysis of variance to test specific hypotheses about the relative magnitude of a series of means. Although researchers have most commonly applied this method to analysis
of variance in experimental designs, contrast analysis is equally applicable
to correlational data. Just as researchers can construct contrasts to test the
relative ordering of means, they can equally construct contrasts to assess
the relative ordering of correlation coefficients, even when those correlation coefficients are correlated with one another (Meng et al., 1992;
Rosenthal et al., 2000).

Two Pearson rs for Construct Validity: $r_{alerting\text{-}CV}$ and $r_{contrast\text{-}CV}$

Two Pearson rs provide convenient and informative indices of construct
validity, each in its own way. The first of these correlations, $r_{alerting\text{-}CV}$, is the
simple correlation between (a) the pattern of correlations *predicted* between the measure being validated and the k variables correlated with
that measure, and (b) the pattern of correlations actually *obtained*. It is
called an "alerting" correlation because it is a rough, readily interpretable
index that can alert the researcher to possible trends of interest
(Rosenthal et al., 2000; Rosnow et al., 2000).

For example, suppose we were developing a new measure of interpersonal skill. We have administered our new measure to a sample of participants to whom we have also administered four other measures. Our construct of interpersonal skill is such that we predict it will correlate with the four other measures as follows: verbal IQ, r predicted roughly as .5; nonverbal decoding skill, r predicted roughly as .5; agreeableness, r predicted roughly also as .5; and conscientiousness, r predicted as .1. To compute $r_{alerting\text{-}CV}$ we simply correlate these predicted values (arranged as a column of data) with the obtained values (arranged as a second column of data). More accurate results are obtained when the correlations (rs) are first transformed into their Fisher Z_r equivalents in order to improve normality (Meng et al., 1992; Steiger, 1980).

Thus, suppose the obtained values, Z_r transformed, were .74, .59, .60, and –.03. The correlation between this column of data and our predicted values (.5, .5, .5, .1) yields an $r_{alerting\text{-}CV}$ of .98. The magnitude of this correlation suggests that our predicted pattern of values provided a very accurate portrayal of the pattern or profile of correlations actually obtained.

The effect size correlation $r_{alerting\text{-}CV}$ becomes increasingly useful as we include more and more variables in our convergent-discriminant validity matrix. If only two variables are to be correlated with our new measure, $r_{alerting\text{-}CV}$ can take on values of only $+1.00$ or -1.00. As more variables are added, $r_{alerting\text{-}CV}$ becomes more informative. To put it another way, $r_{alerting\text{-}CV}$ provides an unstable index when the number of criterion variables is small, but becomes progressively more useful as the researcher makes bolder hypotheses about the relation between the target measure and a range of criterion variables—that is, as the nomological net gets wider. We typically do not compute p levels for $r_{alerting\text{-}CV}$, but it can be used to help in the computation of significance levels for our other effect size correlation, $r_{contrast\text{-}CV}$.

Our second correlation, $r_{contrast\text{-}CV}$, shares with $r_{alerting\text{-}CV}$ the characteristic that it will be larger as the match between expected and obtained correlations is higher. In addition, however, $r_{contrast\text{-}CV}$ uses information about (a) the median intercorrelation among the variables to be correlated with the measure being validated, and (b) the absolute values of the correlations between the measure being validated and the variables with which it is being correlated. A desirable feature of $r_{contrast\text{-}CV}$ is that its interpretation is not limited in the same way as is $r_{alerting\text{-}CV}$ when there are only a few variables in the convergent-discriminant validity matrix. Computational details for $r_{contrast\text{-}CV}$ were provided in appendix A of Westen and Rosenthal (2003) and, in a less directly applicable form, in Meng et al. (1992).

Table 2.7 shows the intercorrelations among our five variables, including the new measure we are in the process of validating, and the four variables for which we have predicted the correlations with the new measure that

TABLE 2.7

Correlations Between a New Measure of Interpersonal Skill
and Four Other Measures (N = 15)

Other Measures	New Measure (Y)	Verbal IQ (A)	Nonverbal Decoding (B)	Agreeableness (C)
A Verbal IQ	.63	—		
B Nonverbal Decoding	.53	.38	—	
C Agreeableness	.54	.36	.38	—
D Conscientiousness	−.03	−.19	.12	.60

Note.   Contrast weights for Measures A, B, C, D are +1, +1, +1, −3, respectively, based on predicted correlations with the new measure of +.50, +.50, +.50, +.10.

would contribute to its construct validation. We have already reported $r_{alerting\text{-}CV}$ as .98; we now report $r_{contrast\text{-}CV}$ to be .60. The equations given in Westen and Rosenthal (2003) and in Meng et al. (1992) also yielded a χ^2 (on $k - 1$ df) testing the heterogeneity of the set of correlations of the validating variables with the common dependent variable (i.e., the new measure). For the data of Table 2.7, this $\chi^2 (3) = 5.71$. Interestingly, the Z test of significance of $r_{contrast\text{-}CV}$ can be obtained by multiplying $r_{alerting\text{-}CV}$ by the square root of the χ^2 test for heterogeneity; in this example,

$$Z = r_{alerting-CV} \sqrt{\chi^2 (k - 1)} = (.98)\sqrt{5.71} = 2.34, p = .0096. \qquad (3)$$

We can also get $r_{contrast\text{-}CV}$ from Equation (4)

$$r_{contrast-CV} = \frac{Z}{\sqrt{N}} \qquad (4)$$

which in this example yields

$$r_{contrast-CV} = \frac{2.34}{\sqrt{15}} = .604.$$

In addition, we can get $r_{contrast\text{-}CV}$ from Equation (5) employing t instead of Z.

$$r_{contrast-CV} = \sqrt{\frac{t^2_{contrast}}{t^2_{contrast} + df}} \tag{5}$$

We get t from the p associated with Z (.0096 in this case) and therefore find $t_{(13)}$ to be 2.67. Then from Equation 5 we find

$$r_{contrast-CV} = \sqrt{\frac{(2.67)^2}{(2.67)^2 + 13}} = .595$$

a value slightly lower than the .604 obtained from Equation 4. With large samples, Equations 4 and 5 tend to give the same values; with smaller sample sizes, Equation 5 employing t tends to be more accurate.

To come now to a close, let me repeat that in this chapter I have been able to only scratch the surface of all the contributions to our field that have flowed from Pearson and his r. We owe Pearson a great deal, and we, and especially I, owe Ralph Rosnow a great deal as well for all his contributions both substantive and methodological. Thank you, Karl, and thank you, Ralph!

REFERENCES

Campbell, D. T., & Fiske, D. (1959). Convergent and discriminant validation by the multitrait-multimethod matrix. *Psychological Bulletin, 56,* 81–105.

Cohen, J. (1960). A coefficient of agreement for nominal scales. *Educational and Psychological Measurement, 20,* 37–46.

Cronbach, L., & Meehl, P. (1955). Construct validity in psychological tests. *Psychological Bulletin, 52,* 281–302.

Cudeck, R. (1988). Multiplicative models and MTMM matrices. *Journal of Educational Statistics, 13,* 131–147.

Hammond, K. R., Hamm, R. M., & Grassia, J. (1986). Generalizing over conditions by combining the multitrait-multimethod matrix and the representative design of experiments. *Psychological Bulletin, 100,* 257–269.

Kenny, D. A. (1995). The multitrait-multimethod matrix: Design, analysis, and conceptual issues. In P. Shrout & S. Fiske (Eds.), *Personality research, methods, and theory: A festschrift honoring Donald W. Fiske* (pp. 111–124). Mahwah, NJ: Lawrence Erlbaum Associates.

Meng, X. L., Rosenthal, R., & Rubin, D. B. (1992). Comparing correlated correlation coefficients. *Psychological Bulletin, 111,* 172–175.

Pearson, K. (1896). Mathematical contributions to the theory of evolution—III. Regression, heredity and panmixia. *Philosophical Transactions of the Royal Society of London (series A), 187,* 253–318.

Pearson, K. (1904, November 5). Report on certain enteric fever inoculation statistics. *British Medical Journal,* pp. 1243–1246.

Reichardt, C., & Coleman, S.C. (1995). The criteria for convergent and discriminant validity in a multitrait-multimethod matrix. *Multivariate Behavioral Research, 30,* 513–538.

Rosenthal, R. (1991). Some indices of the reliability of peer review. *Behavioral and Brain Sciences, 14,* 160–161.

Rosenthal, R. (2000). Effect sizes in behavioral and biomedical research: Estimation and interpretation. In L. Bickman (Ed.), *Validity and social experimentation: Donald Campbell's legacy* (Vol. 1, pp. 121–139). Thousand Oaks, CA: Sage.

Rosenthal, R., & DiMatteo, M. R. (2002). Meta-analysis. In J. Wixted (Ed.), *Stevens' handbook of experimental psychology* (3rd ed., Vol. IV, pp. 391–428). New York: Wiley.

Rosenthal, R., & Rosnow, R. L. (1985). *Contrast analysis: Focused comparisons in the analysis of variance.* New York: Cambridge University Press.

Rosenthal, R., & Rosnow, R. L. (1991). *Essentials of behavioral research* (2nd ed.). New York: McGraw-Hill.

Rosenthal, R., Rosnow, R. L., & Rubin, D. B. (2000). *Contrasts and effect sizes in behavioral research: A correlational approach.* New York: Cambridge University Press.

Rosenthal, R., & Rubin, D. B. (1979). A note on percent variance explained as a measure of the importance of effects. *Journal of Applied Social Psychology, 9,* 395–396.

Rosenthal, R., & Rubin, D. B. (1982). A simple, general purpose display of magnitude of experimental effect. *Journal of Educational Psychology, 74,* 166–169.

Rosenthal, R., & Rubin, D. B. (1994). The counternull value of an effect size: A new statistic. *Psychological Science, 5,* 329–334.

Rosnow, R. L., & Rosenthal, R. (1996). Computing contrasts, effect sizes, and counternulls on other people's published data: General procedures for research consumers. *Psychological Methods, 1,* 331–340.

Rosnow, R. L., Rosenthal, R., & Rubin, D. B. (2000). Contrasts and correlations in effect-size estimation. *Psychological Science, 11,* 446–453.

Shrout, P., & Fiske, S. (Eds.). (1995). *Personality research, methods, and theory: A festschrift honoring Donald W. Fiske.* Hillsdale, NJ: Lawrence Erlbaum Associates.

Steiger, J. H. (1980). Tests for comparing elements of a correlation matrix. *Psychological Bulletin, 87,* 245–251.

Stigler, S. M. (1986). *The history of statistics: The measurement of uncertainty before 1900.* Cambridge, MA: Harvard University Press.

Westen, D., & Rosenthal, R. (2003). Quantifying construct validity: Two simple measures. *Journal of Personality and Social Psychology, 84,* 608–618.

Wothke, W. (1995). Covariance components analysis of the multitrait-multimethod matrix. In P. Shrout & S. Fiske (Eds.), *Personality research, methods, and theory: A festschrift honoring Donald W. Fiske* (pp. 125–144). Mahwah, NJ: Lawrence Erlbaum Associates.

3

Estimating Treatment Effects From Nonrandomized Studies Using Subclassification on Propensity Scores[1]

Donald B. Rubin
Harvard University

The aim of many analyses of social science and medical data sets is to draw causal inferences about the relative effects of treatments, such as different methods of treating psychologically disturbed patients or cancer patients. The data available to compare many such treatments are not based on the results of carefully conducted randomized clinical trials, but rather are collected while observing systems as they operate in "normal" practice, without any interventions implemented by randomized assignment rules. Such data are relatively inexpensive to obtain, however, and often do represent the spectrum of actual practice better than do the settings of randomized experiments. Consequently, it is sensible to try to estimate the effects of treatments from such datasets, even if only to help design a new randomized experiment or shed light on the generalizability of results from existing randomized experiments. Standard methods of analysis using routine statistical software (e.g., linear or logistic regressions), however, can be quite decep-

---

[1]This chapter is an expansion of Rubin (1997) and was written in January 2003; consequently, the analogous article written today would differ to reflect more current literature.

tive for these objectives because they provide no warnings about their propriety. Propensity score methods, introduced by Rosenbaum and Rubin (1983a), are more reliable tools for addressing such objectives because the assumptions needed to make their answers appropriate are more assessable and transparent to the investigator. Subclassification on propensity scores is a particularly straightforward technique and is the topic of this chapter. Because these techniques are so straightforward, they seem especially appropriate to review in this Festschrift for Ralph Rosnow, who has made such substantial contributions to the teaching and dissemination of straightforward statistical methods in psychological research. It has been a true pleasure to work with Ralph as a friend and collaborator (e.g., Rosenthal, Rosnow, & Rubin, 2002).

SUBCLASSIFICATION
ON ONE CONFOUNDING VARIABLE

Before describing how subclassification on propensity scores can be used in the statistical analysis of an observational study with many confounding background characteristics, we begin with an example showing how subclassification can be used to adjust for a single confounding covariate, such as age, in a study of smoking and mortality. We then show how propensity scores methods can be used to generalize subclassification on a single confounding covariate to the case with many confounding covariates, such as age, region of the country, and gender.

The potential for an observational database (i.e., not from a randomized experiment) to suggest causal effects of treatments is indicated by Table 3.1, adapted from Cochran (1968), which concerns mortality rates per thousand in three large databases from the United States, the United Kingdom, and Canada for nonsmokers, cigarette smokers, and cigar and pipe smokers. The treatment factor here involves the three levels of smoking. It appears from the death rates in Part A of Table 3.1 that cigarette smoking is good for health, especially relative to cigar and pipe smoking, clearly a result contrary to current wisdom. A problem with the naive conclusion from Part A is exposed in Part B of Table 3.1, which gives the average ages of the subpopulations: Age is correlated with both death rates and smoking behavior. Age in this example is a "confounding" covariate, and conclusions regarding the effects of smoking should be adjusted for differences in age distributions across subpopulations.

TABLE 3.1
Comparing Death Rates for Three Smoking Groups in Each of Three Databases (from Cochran, 1968)

	Canadian Study			UK Study			US Study		
	No Smoke	Cigarette	Cigar & Pipe	No Smoke	Cigarette	Cigar & Pipe	No Smoke	Cigarette	Cigar & Pipe
A: Death rates per 1,000 person years									
	20.2	20.5	35.5	11.3	14.1	20.7	13.5	13.5	17.4
B: Average age in years									
	54.9	50.5	65.9	49.1	49.8	55.7	57.0	53.2	59.7
C: Adjusted death rates using K subclasses									
K = 2	20.2	26.4	24.0	11.3	12.7	13.6	13.5	16.4	14.9
K = 3	20.2	28.3	21.2	11.3	12.8	12.0	13.5	17.7	14.2
K = 9–11	20.2	29.5	19.8	11.3	14.8	11.0	13.5	21.2	13.7

A straightforward way of adjusting for age is to: (a) divide the population into age categories of approximately equal size (e.g., two categories = younger, older; or three categories = young, middle aged, old; or four categories, etc.); (b) compare death rates within an age category (e.g., within the younger population, compare death rates for the three treatment groups and similarly for the older population); and (c) average over the age-group-specific comparisons to obtain overall estimates of the age-adjusted death rates per 1,000 for each of the three treatment groups. Part C of Table 3.1 shows the results for different numbers of categories of age, where the subclass age boundaries were defined to have equal numbers of nonsmokers in each subclass. These results, especially with 9–11 subclasses, align better with our current understanding of the effects of smoking than does Part A. Incidentally, having approximately equal numbers of nonsmokers within each subclass is not necessary, but if the nonsmokers are considered the baseline group, it is a convenient and efficient choice because then the overall estimated effect is the simple unweighted average of the subclass specific results. That is, the mortality rates in all three groups are being "standardized" (Finch, 1988) to the age distribution of nonsmokers as defined by their subclass counts.

Cochran (1968) called this method "subclassification" and offered theoretical results showing that as long as the treatment groups overlap in their age distributions (i.e., as long as there are reasonable numbers of subjects from each treatment condition in each subclass), comparisons using five or six subclasses will typically remove 90% or more of the bias present in the raw comparisons in Part A. More than five subclasses were used in the final rows of Part C in Table 3.1 because the large sizes of the datasets made it possible to do so.

A particular statistical model such as a linear regression (or a logistic regression, or in other settings a hazard model) could have been used to adjust for age, but subclassification has two distinct advantages over such models, at least for offering initial trustworthy comparisons that are easy to communicate. First, if the treatment groups do not adequately overlap on the confounding covariate age, the investigator will see it immediately and be warned. Thus, if members of one treatment group have ages outside the range of another group's ages, it will be obvious, because one or more age-specific subclasses will consist solely of members exposed to one treatment (or nearly so). In contrast, there is nothing in the standard output of any regression modeling software that will display this critical fact. The reason for this apparent omission is that such models predict an outcome (e.g., mortality) from regressors (e.g., age and treatment indicators), and standard regression diagnostics do not include the careful analysis of the joint distribution of the regressors (e.g., a comparison of the distributions of age across treatment groups). When the overlap on age distributions across treatment groups is too limited, the database, no matter how large, cannot support causal conclusions about the differential effects of the treatments. For an extreme example, if the database consists of 70-year-old smokers and 40-year-old nonsmokers, the comparison of 5-year survival rates among 70-year-old smokers and 40-year-old nonsmokers provides essentially no information about the effect of smoking versus nonsmoking for either 70-year-olds or 40-year-olds, or any other age group.

The second reason for preferring subclassification to model-based adjustment concerns more promising situations like that in Table 3.1, where the treatment groups overlap enough on the confounding covariate so that a comparison is possible. When estimating the treatment effect, subclassification does not rely on any particular functional form (e.g., linearity) for the relationship between the outcome (mortality) and covariate (age) within each treatment group, whereas models do rely on such assumptions. If the treatment groups have similar distributions of the covariate, common assumptions like linearity are usually harmless, but when the treatment groups have rather different covariate distributions, model-based methods of adjustment are dependent on the specific form of the model (e.g., linearity, log-linearity), and their answers are influenced by untrustworthy extrapolations. Simulations documenting the fragility of linear regression methods appeared in Rubin (1973) for the basic case of one covariate.

If standard models can be so dangerous, why are they so commonly used for such adjustments when examining databases for estimates of causal effects? One reason is the ease of automatic data analysis using existing, pervasive software on plentiful, speedy hardware. Nevertheless, although standard modeling software can automatically "handle" many regressor variables and produce results, these results can be remarkably misleading. In fact, when there are many confounding covariates, the issues of lack of adequate overlap and reliance on untrustworthy model-based extrapolations are even more serious than with only one confounding covariate, as documented by simulations in Rubin (1979, Table 2) and Rubin and Thomas (2000, Table 4). One reason for the increased problem is that small differences on many covariates can accumulate into a substantial overall difference. For example, if one treatment group is a little older, has a little higher cholesterol, has a little more familial history of cancer, and so on, that group may be substantially less healthy. Another reason for the increased problem with many covariates rather than one covariate is that diagnosing nonlinear relationships between outcomes and many covariates is more complicated. Moreover, standard comparisons of means between the groups (like those in Table 3.1B) or even comparisons of histograms for each confounding covariate between the treatment groups, although adequate with one covariate, are inadequate with more than one. The groups may differ in a multivariate direction to an extent that cannot be discerned from separate analyses of each covariate. This multivariate direction is closely related to the statistical concept of the "best linear discriminant" and intuitively is the single combination of the covariates on which the treatment groups are farthest apart.

A second reason for the dominance of modeling over subclassification is the seeming difficulty of using subclassification when there are many confounding covariates in need of adjustment, which is the common case. Fortunately, subclassification techniques can be applied with many covariates with nearly the same reliability as with only one covariate. The key idea is to use "propensity score" techniques introduced by Rosenbaum and Rubin (1983a); these can be viewed as important extensions of discriminant matching techniques, which calculate the best linear discriminant between the treatment groups and match on it (Rubin, 1980). Since their introduction two decades ago, propensity score methods have been used in a variety of applied problems in medical and other research disciplines, and they are becoming very popular. The appendix to this chapter lists references primarily in the medical area. Nevertheless, propensity score methods have not been used nearly as frequently as they should have been relative to model-based methods.

PROPENSITY SCORE METHODS

Propensity score methods generally have to be applied to treatment groups two at a time. Therefore, in an example with three treatment conditions, there are generally three distinct propensity scores, one for each two-group treatment comparison (e.g., for the example of Table 3.1, nonsmokers versus cigarette smokers, nonsmokers versus cigar and pipe smokers, and cigarette smokers versus cigar and pipe smokers). To describe the way propensity scores work, we therefore assume two treatment conditions. Situations with more than two treatment groups are considered later.

The basic idea of propensity score methods is to replace the collection of confounding covariates in the observational study with one function of these covariates, called the propensity score (i.e., the propensity to receive Treatment 1 rather than Treatment 2), and then to use this score just as if it were the only confounding covariate. Thus, the collection of predictors is collapsed into a single composite predictor.

The propensity score is found by predicting treatment group membership (i.e., the indicator variable for being in Treatment 1 vs. Treatment 2) from the confounding covariates; for example, by a logistic regression or a discriminant analysis (e.g., least squares regression). In this prediction of treatment group membership, it is critically important that the outcome variable (e.g., mortality) plays no role; the prediction of treatment group only involves the covariates. Each subject in the database then has an esti-mated propensity score, which is the estimated probability, as determined by that subject's covariate values, of being exposed to Treatment 1 versus Treatment 2. This propensity score is then the single summarized confounding covariate to be used for subclassification.

Subclassification into five or more groups on the propensity score then has the rather remarkable property of adjusting for all of the covariates that went into its estimation, no matter how many! This is a "large-sample" claim that relies on certain conditions addressed in technical statistical pub-lications (Rosenbaum & Rubin, 1983a; Rubin & Thomas, 1992a, 1992b), but nevertheless it is an extremely useful guide for practice (Rubin & Thomas, 1996). The intuition behind the claim's validity is fairly straight-forward and proceeds as follows.

Suppose that two subjects, one exposed to Treatment 1 and the other exposed to Treatment 2, were presented to us with the same value of the propensity score. These two subjects would then have the same predicted probability of being assigned to Treatment 1 versus Treatment 2, and thus, as far as we can tell from their values of the confounding covariates, a coin was tossed to decide which one received Treatment 1 and which one re-ceived Treatment 2. Now suppose that we have a collection of Treatment 1 subjects and a collection of Treatment 2 subjects, such that the distribu-tions of the propensity scores are the same in both groups, as is approxi-mately true within each propensity subclass. Then, in Subclass 1, the subjects who received Treatment 1 were essentially randomly chosen from the pool of all subjects in Subclass 1, and analogously for each subclass. As a result, within each subclass, the multivariate distribution of the covariates used to estimate the propensity score differs only randomly be-tween the two treatment groups. The formal proof of this result with true propensity scores appeared in Rosenbaum and Rubin (1983a). Research on how well this theoretical result is satisfied when using estimated rather than true propensity scores is the topic of technical statistical publications (Drake, 1993; Rubin, 1984; Rubin & Thomas, 1992a, 1992b, 1996). Generally, the conclusion is that using estimated propensity scores in place of true propensity scores works very well.

EXAMPLE: PROPENSITY SUBCLASSIFICATION

In the 1990s, the U.S. Government Accounting Office (GAO, 1994) summarized results from randomized experiments comparing mastectomy (removal of breast, but not the pectoral muscle, plus nodal dissection but no radiation) and breast-conservation therapy (lumpectomy, nodal dissection, and radiation) for the treatment of breast cancer for node-negative patients. Table 3.2 is adopted from their Table 2, and the results provide no evidence of any differential treatment effect, at least for the type of women who participated in these informed-consent clinical trials and received the kind of care dispensed at the centers participating in these trials. The question remained, however, how broadly

TABLE 3.2

Estimated 5-year Survival Rates for Node-Negative Patients
in Six Randomized Experiments (U.S. General Accounting Office, 1994)

Study	Treatment	n	Estimate
US-NCI*	Breast conservation	74	93.9%
	Mastectomy	67	94.7%
Milan*	Breast conservation	257	93.5%
	Mastectomy	263	93.0%
French*	Breast conservation	59	94.9%
	Mastectomy	62	95.2%
Danish**	Breast conservation	289	87.4%
	Mastectomy	288	85.9%
EORTC**	Breast conservation	238	89.0%
	Mastectomy	237	90.0%
US-NSABP**	Breast conservation	330	89.0%
	Mastectomy	309	88.0%

*Single center.
**Multicenter.

these results could be generalized (i.e., to other node-negative women and other medical facilities). The General Accounting Office (GAO) used the National Cancer Institute's SEER (Surveillance, Epidemiology and End Results) observational database to address this question. Restrictions (e.g., node-negative diagnosis, age 70 or younger, tumor 4 cm. or smaller, etc., as detailed in GAO, 1994, in its Tables 4 and I.3) were applied to correspond to criteria for the randomized experiments, and these reduced the database to 1,106 women receiving breast-conservation therapy and 4,220 receiving mastectomy.

The GAO used propensity score methods on the SEER database to compare the two treatments for breast cancer. First, approximately 30 potential confounding covariates and interactions were identified: year of diagnosis (1983–1985), age category (four levels), tumor size, geographical registry (nine levels), race (four levels), marital status (four levels), and interactions of year and registry. A logistic regression was then used to predict treatment (mastectomy vs. conservation therapy) from these confounding covariates based on the data from the 5,326 (1,106 + 4220) women. Each woman was then assigned an estimated propensity score—her estimated probability, based on her covariate values, of receiving breast conservation therapy rather than mastectomy. The group of 5,326 was then divided into five approximately equal-size subclasses based on their individual propensity scores, just as if these propensity scores comprised the only covariate: 1,064 were in the most mastectomy-oriented subclass, 1,070 in the next subclass, 1,059 in the middle subclass, 1,067 in the next subclass, and 1,066 were in the most breast-conservation-oriented subclass.

Before examining any outcomes (i.e., any 5-year survival results)—and the "before" is critical—the subclasses were checked for balance on the covariates. Recall that propensity score theory claims that if the propensity scores are relatively constant within each subclass, then the distribution of all covariates should be approximately the same in both treatment groups within each subclass. This balance was found to be satisfactory. If important within-subclass differences between treatment groups had been found on some covariates, then either the propensity score prediction model would need to be reformulated, or it would have been concluded that the covariate distributions did not overlap sufficiently to allow subclassification to adjust for these covariates. This process of cycling between checking for balance on the covariates and reformulating the propensity score model was described in Rosenbaum and Rubin (1984) in the context of a study investigating coronary bypass surgery, and also in Rubin (2002) in the context of investigating the health effects of smoking. For example, if the variances of an important covariate were found to differ importantly between treatment and control groups, then the square of that covariate would have been included in the revised propensity score model. For another example, if the correlations between two important covariates differed between the groups, then the product of the covariates would have been added to the propensity score model.

If "checking for balance" had been allowed to include the examination of estimated causal effects, then the selection of a particular propensity score model could have been used to bias the estimate of the causal effect in a "preferred" direction. This point is critical: The unbiased design of an observational study requires us to check for balance in covariates without allowing the influence of the associated estimates of causal effects. Rubin (2002) developed this theme more extensively.

For the GAO study, the estimates of 5-year survival rates based on the resulting propensity score subclassification are given in Table 3.3, taken from Tables 5 and 7 in the GAO study (1994). Several features of this table are particularly striking, especially when compared to the randomized experiments; results in Table 3.2. First, the general conclusion of similar performance of both treatments is maintained. Second, although overall survival is quite similar across treatment groups, there is an indication that survival

TABLE 3.3

Estimated 5-year Survival Rates for Node-Negative Patients
in SEER Database Within Each of Five Propensity Score Subclasses
(U.S. General Accounting Office, 1994)

Propensity Score Subclass	Treatment	n	Estimate
1	Breast conservation	56	85.6%
	Mastectomy	1,008	86.7%
2	Breast conservation	106	82.8%
	Mastectomy	964	83.4%
3	Breast conservation	193	85.2%
	Mastectomy	866	88.8%
4	Breast conservation	289	88.7%
	Mastectomy	778	87.3%
5	Breast conservation	462	89.0%
	Mastectomy	604	88.5%

in general practice may be slightly lower than suggested from the population of women and type of clinic participating in the randomized clinical trials, especially in the single clinic studies.

Third, there is a slight indication that, in general practice, women and their doctors may be making efficacious choices. More precisely, women in Propensity Subclasses 1–3, which are composed of patients whose characteristics (including age, size of tumor, and region of country) make them relatively more likely to receive mastectomy than breast conservation therapy, seem to show better 5-year survival under mastectomy than under breast conservation surgery. In contrast, for Propensity Subclasses 4–5, composed of patients whose characteristics make them relatively more likely to receive breast conservation therapy than mastectomy, there appears to be no advantage to mastectomy, and possibly a slight advantage to breast conservation therapy. Of course, this third interpretation is subject to two caveats. First, we have only adjusted for the covariates that were used to estimate the propensity score and, hence, other hidden covariates might alter this interpretation; in a randomized experiment, the effects of these "hidden" covariates are reflected in the standard errors of the estimates, but in an observational study these effects create bias not reflected in standard errors. Second, the sampling variability (i.e., standard errors) of the results do not permit firm conclusions about this point, even if the collection of confounding covariates used to estimate the propensity score were sufficient to remove all bias in this observational study.

The basic conclusion of the GAO analyses is, however, clear: Even though there is no randomized assignment in the SEER database, the propensity score analyses do appear to provide useful suggestive results, especially when coupled with the results of the randomized experiments, with which they are scientifically consistent.

MORE THAN TWO TREATMENT CONDITIONS

With more than two treatment conditions, there is generally a different propensity score for each pair of treatment groups being compared (i.e., with three treatment groups labeled A, B, and C, there are three propensity scores: A vs. B, A vs. C, and B vs. C). At first, this may seem to be a limitation of propensity score technology relative to a model-based analysis, but in fact it is not a limitation but an important strength and points to further weaknesses in a model-based approach. We see this by exploring a range of hypothetical modifications to Cochran's (1968) smoking example.

First, consider what we could have learned if the nonsmokers and cigarette smokers had adequately overlapping age distributions, but the cigar/pipe smokers were substantially older than either of the other groups, with essentially no overlap with either the cigarette smokers or the nonsmokers. When there are more than two groups, one particular two-group comparison (nonsmokers vs. cigarette smokers in this example) may have adequate overlap, whereas the other comparisons (those involving cigar/pipe smokers in this example) may have inadequate overlap. A typical model-based analysis would use all the data to provide estimates for all three two-group comparisons, even using cigar/pipe smokers' data to influence the nonsmokers versus cigarette smokers comparison, with no warning of either (a) the extreme extrapolations involved in two of the three two-group comparisons or (b) the use of the cigar/pipe smokers data to help compare the nonsmokers and cigarette smokers, even though the cigar/pipe smokers are substantially older than are both the nonsmokers and the cigarette smokers.

Let us again modify the Cochran smoking example, but now include an additional covariate, some index of socioeconomic status (SES). Also suppose that nonsmokers and cigarette smokers have adequate overlap in their age distributions but not much overlap in their SES distributions, with nonsmokers typically having higher SES values. In contrast, suppose that nonsmokers and cigar/pipe smokers have substantial overlap in their SES distributions, but have essentially no overlap in their age distributions. This scenario illustrates that with more than two groups and more than one covariate, the comparison of one pair of groups can be compromised by one covariate and the comparison of another pair of groups can be compromised by a different covariate. As earlier, typical model-based analyses provide no warning that comparisons may be based on extreme extrapolations, nor that the extrapolations are using data from groups not in the pair of groups being compared.

Now suppose that the nonsmokers and cigarette smokers have the same age distributions and adequately overlapping SES distributions. For this comparison, age needs no adjustment but SES does. The propensity score for the comparison would essentially equal SES because it, and not age, would predict being a cigarette smoker versus being a nonsmoker; thus, for this comparison, adjusting for the propensity score would be the same as adjusting for SES. Also suppose that the nonsmokers and cigar/pipe smokers have the same SES distributions, so SES needs no adjustment, and adequately overlapping age distributions that do need adjustment. The propensity score for this comparison would equal age, and hence adjusting for it would be the same as adjusting for age. Thus, the propensity score for a comparison of one pair of groups generally needs to be different than for a comparison of a different pair of groups. To complete the current scenario, suppose cigarette and cigar/pipe smokers had adequate overlap in both age and SES, and both needed adjustment. The propensity score for this comparison would involve both age and SES, because both help to predict cigarette group versus cigar/pipe group membership, and adjusting for this propensity score would adjust for both age and SES. Clearly, in general, different propensity score models are needed to adjust appropriately for different comparisons. Estimating all effects using one model in this case with three groups and adequate overlap on all covariates can be even more deceptive than estimation in the two-group setting, because the model being used to compare one pair of groups (e.g., nonsmokers vs. cigarette smokers) is affected by the third group's data (e.g., cigar/pipe smokers), which possibly have covariate values rather different from either of the two groups being compared.

In some cases with more than two groups, the different propensity scores can be similar enough to be combined into a common one, as when there is one historical control group, one randomized control group, and a randomized treated group. Or, in other cases, one propensity score estimated as the probability of receiving the treatment a patient did receive (Imbens, 2000) can be used to calculate weighted estimates of average effects. These are important directions for further work.

LIMITATIONS OF PROPENSITY SCORES

Despite the broad utility of propensity score methods, it is important when addressing causal questions from nonrandomized studies to keep in mind that even propensity score methods can only adjust for observed confounding covariates and not unobserved ones. This is always a limitation of nonrandomized studies relative to randomized studies, where the randomization tends to balance the distribution of all covariates, observed and unobserved.

In observational studies, confidence in causal conclusions must be built by seeing how consistent the obtained answers are with other evidence (e.g., from related experiments) and how sensitive the conclusions are to reasonable deviations from assumptions, as illustrated in Connors et al. (1996) using techniques from Rosenbaum and Rubin (1983b). Such sensitivity analyses suppose that a relevant but unobserved covariate has been left out of the propensity score model. By explicating how this hypothetical unmeasurable covariate is related to treatment assignment and to outcome, we can obtain an estimate of the treatment effect that adjusts for it as well as measured covariates, and thereby investigate how answers might change if such a covariate were available for adjustment. Of course, medical knowledge is needed when accessing whether the posited relationships involving the hypothetical unmeasured covariate are realistic or extreme. Of particular relevance to Connors et al. (1996), clarifications of nomenclature and extended sensitivity analysis reported in Lin, Psaty, and Kronmal (1997) moderated the initial conclusions in Connors et al. (1996).

Another limitation of propensity score methods is that they work better in larger samples for the same reason that randomized experiments work better in larger samples. The distributional balance of observed covariates created by subclassifying on the propensity score is an *expected* balance, just as the balance of all covariates in a randomized experiment is an *expected* balance. In a small randomized experiment, random imbalances of some covariates can be substantial despite the randomization; analogously, in a small observational study, substantial imbalances of some covariates may be unavoidable despite subclassification using a sensibly estimated propensity score. The larger the study, the more minor are such random imbalances. One way to create better balance in randomized experiments is to randomize within blocks of patients who are similar on prognostically important covariates. Just as blocking on such covariates can be beneficial in a randomized experiment, blocking or matching on them in special ways can be used with propensity score methods (Rubin & Thomas, 2000). Additional model-based adjustments can also be helpful following propensity score adjustment (Rubin & Thomas, 2000), just as in a randomized experiment.

Another possible limitation of propensity score methods is its handling of prognostically weak covariates included in the propensity score estimation. A covariate related to treatment assignment but not to outcomes is treated the same as a covariate with the same relationship with treatment assignment but strongly related to outcomes. This feature can be a limitation of propensity scores in that the inclusion of irrelevant covariates reduces the efficiency of the control on the relevant covariates. More recent work, however, suggests that, at least in modest or large studies, the biasing effects of leaving out even a weakly predictive covariate dominate the efficiency gains from not using such a covariate (Rubin & Thomas, 1996, 2000). Thus, in practice, this limitation may not be substantial if investigators use some judgment.

Finally, a current limitation in the application of propensity score methods concerns how to handle missing data in the covariates. In such a situation, the general objective is to achieve balance on the observed values of covariates and the observed patterns of missing data. The computational software required to achieve this objective is far more complex than for the case without missing data. Fortunately, the method described in D'Agostino and Rubin (2000) seems to be quite successful in practice, and software for it and propensity score methods is being developed.

CONCLUSION

Observational databases can address, although not necessarily settle, important social and medical science questions concerning causal effects of treatments. Addressing these causal questions using standard statistical (or econometric or psychometric, or neural net, etc.) models can be fraught with pitfalls because of their possible reliance on unwarranted assumptions and extrapolations without any warning. Subclassification on propensity scores is more reliable; it generalizes the straightforward technique of subclassification with one confounding covariate to allow simultaneous adjustment for many covariates. One critical advantage of propensity score methods is that they can warn the investigator that, because of inadequately overlapping covariate distributions, a particular database cannot address the causal question at hand without either relying on untrustworthy model-dependent extrapolations or restricting attention to the type of subject adequately represented in both treatment groups. Because of this advantage, any causal questions put to a database should be first attacked using propensity score methods while blinded to outcome data to see if the question can be legitimately addressed. If so, then subclassification on a well-estimated propensity score can be used to provide reliable results, which are adjusted for the covariates used to estimate the propensity score and which can be displayed in a transparent manner. After that, modeling can play a useful role. For example, standard statistical models, such as least squares regression, can be safely applied within propensity score subclasses to adjust for minor within-subclass differences in covariate distributions between treatment groups. This, in fact, was done in the U.S. GAO (1994) example. Of course, it always must be remembered that propensity scores only adjust for the observed covariates that went into their estimation.

REFERENCES

Cochran, W. G. (1968). The effectiveness of adjustment by subclassification in removing bias in observational studies. *Biometrics, 24,* 295–313.

Connors, A. F., et al. (1996). The effectiveness of right heart catheterization in the initial care of critically ill patients. *Journal of the American Medical Association, 276,* 889–897.

D'Agostino, R., Jr., & Rubin, D. B. (2000). Estimation and use of propensity scores with incomplete data. *Journal of the American Statistical Association, 95,* 749–759.

Drake, C. (1993). Effects of misspecification of the propensity score on estimators of treatment effect. *Biometrics, 49,* 1231–1236.

Finch, P. E. (1988). Standardization. In S. Kotz & N. L. Johnson (Eds.), *Encyclopedia of statistical sciences* (Vol. 8, pp. 629–632). New York: Wiley.

Imbens, G. W. (2000). The role of the propensity score in estimating dose-response functions. *Biometrika, 87*, 706–710.

Lin, D. Y., Psaty, B. M., & Kronmal, R. A. (1997). Assessing the sensitivity of regression results to unmeasured confounders in observational studies (Tech. Rep. No. 144). Seattle: University of Washington School of Public Health, Department of Biostatistics.

Rosenbaum, P., & Rubin, D. B. (1983a). The central role of the propensity score in observational studies for causal effects. *Biometrika, 70*, 41–55.

Rosenbaum, P. R. & Rubin, D. B. (1983b). Assessing sensitivity to an unobserved binary covariate in an observational study with binary outcome. *The Journal of the Royal Statistical Society, Series B, 45*, 212–218.

Rosenbaum, P. R., & Rubin, D. B. (1984). Reducing bias in observational studies using sub-classification on the propensity score. *Journal of the American Statistical Association, 79*, 516–524.

Rosenthal, R., Rosnow, R., & Rubin, D. B. (2002). *Contrasts and effect sizes in behavioral research: A correlational approach.* Cambridge, UK: Cambridge University Press.

Rubin, D. B. (1973). The use of matched sampling and regression adjustment to remove bias in observational studies. *Biometrics, 29*, 184–203.

Rubin, D. B. (1979). Using multivariate matched sampling and regression adjustment to control bias in observational studies. *The Journal of the American Statistical Association, 74*, 318–328.

Rubin, D. B. (1980). Bias reduction using Mahalanobis' metric matching. *Biometrics, 36*, 295–298.

Rubin, D. B. (1984). Assessing the fit of logistic regressions using the implied discriminant analysis. Discussion of "Graphical methods for assessing logistic regression models" by Landwehr, Pregibone, & Smith. *Journal of the American Statistical Association, 79*, 79–80.

Rubin, D. B. (1997). Estimating causal effects from large data sets using propensity scores. *Annals of Internal Medicine, 127*, 757–763

Rubin, D. B. (2002). Using propensity scores to help design observational studies: Application to the tobacco litigation. *Health Services & Outcomes Research Methodology, 2*, 169–188.

Rubin, D. B., & Thomas, N. (1992a). Affinely invariant matching methods with ellipsoidal distributions. *The Annals of Statistics, 20*, 1079–1093.

Rubin, D. B., & Thomas, N. (1992b). Characterizing the effect of matching using linear propensity score methods with normal covariates. *Biometrika, 79*, 797–809.

Rubin, D. B., & Thomas, N. (1996). Matching using estimated propensity scores: relating theory to practice. Biometrics, 52, 249-264.

Rubin, D.B., & Thomas, N. (2000). Combining propensity score matching with additional adjustments for prognostic covariates. *Journal of the American Statistical Association, Applications, 95*, 573–585.

U.S. General Accounting Office. (1994). Breast conservation versus mastectomy: Patient survival in day-to-day medical practice and randomized studies (Report No. GAO-PEMD-95-9). Washington DC: Author.

Appendix
Some Publications on or Utilizing Propensity Scores

Aiken, L., Smith, H., & Lake, E. (1994). Lower Medicare mortality among a set of hospitals known for good nursing care. *Medical Care, 32,* 771–787.

Ayanian, J. Z., Landrum, M. B., Guadagnoli, E., & Gaccione, P. (2002). Specialty of ambulatory care physicians and mortality among elderly patients after myocardial infarction. *The New England Journal of Medicine, 347,* 1678–1686.

Baxter, J., Beilman, G., & Abrams, J. (1997). Effectiveness of right heart catheterization: Time for a randomized trial [Letter to the editor]. *Journal of the American Medical Association, 277,* 108.

Braitman L. E., & Rosenbaum P. R. (2002). Rare outcomes, common treatments: Analytic strategies using propensity scores. *Annals of Internal Medicine, 137,* 693–695.

Cook, E. F., & Goldman, L. (1988). Asymmetric stratification: An outline for an efficient method for controlling confounding in cohort studies. *American Journal of Epidemiology, 127,* 626–639.

Cook, E. F., & Goldman, L. (1989). Performance of tests of significance based on stratification by a multivariate confounder score or by a propensity score. *Journal of Clinical Epidemiology, 42,* 317–324.

D'Agostino, R. B., Jr. (1998). Propensity score methods for bias reduction in the comparison of a treatment to a non-randomized control group. *Statistics in Medicine, 17,* 2265–2281.

Drake, C., & Fisher, L. (1995). Prognostic models and the propensity score. *International Journal of Epidemiology, 24,* 185–187.

Eastwood, E. A., & Fisher, G. A. (1988). Skills acquisition among matched samples of institutionalized and community-based persons with mental retardation. *American Journal on Mental Retardation, 93,* 75–83.

Ferguson, T. B., Jr., Coombs, L. P., & Peterson. E. D. (2002). Preoperative beta-blocker use and mortality and morbidity following CABG surgery in North America. *Journal of the American Medical Association, 287,* 2221–2227. [Erratum appears in *Journal of the American Medical Association, 287,* 3212.]

Fiebach, N. H., et al. (1990). Outcomes in patients with myocardial-infarction who are initially admitted to stepdown units—data from the multicenter chest pain study. *American Journal of Medicine, 89,* 15–20.

Gu, X. S., & Rosenbaum, P. R. (1993). Comparison of multivariate matching methods: Structures, distances, and algorithms. *Journal of Computational and Graphical Statistics, 2,* 405–520.

Gum, P. A. et al. (2001). Aspirin use and all-cause mortality among patients being evaluated for known or suspected coronary artery disease: A propensity analysis. *Journal of the American Medical Association, 286,* 1187–1194.

Harrell, F. E. et al. (1990). Statistical methods in SUPPORT. *Journal of Clinical Epidemiology, 43,* S89–S98.

Henderson, R. C., et al. (2002). Bone density and metabolism in children and adolescents with moderate to severe cerebral palsy. *Pediatrics, 110,* e5.

Joffe, M. M., & Rosenbaum, P.R. (1999). Propensity scores. *American Journal of Epidemiology, 150,* 327–333.

Kane, R., et al. (1991). Improving primary care in nursing homes. *Journal of the American Geriatric Society, 39,* 359–367.

Kramer, A., et al. (1997). Outcomes and costs after hip fracture and stroke: A comparison of rehabilitation settings. *Journal of the American Medical Association, 277,* 396–404.

Lavori, P. W., & Keller, M. B. (1988). Improving the aggregate performance of psychiatric diagnostic methods when not all subjects receive the standard test. *Statistics in Medicine, 7,* 723–737.

Lavori, P. W., Keller, M. B., & Endicott, J. (1988). Improving the validity of Rh-Rdc diagnosis of major affective disorder in uninterviewed relatives in family studies—a model based approach. *Journal of Psychiatric Research, 22,* 249–259.

Malloy, M., et al. (1990). Exposure to a chloride-deficient formula during infancy: Outcome at ages 9 and 10 years. *Pediatrics, 86,* 601–610.

Mehta, R. L., et al. (2002). Diuretics, mortality, and nonrecovery of renal function in acute renal failure. *Journal of the American Medical Association, 288,* 2547–2553.

Mehta, R. L., et al. (2002). Nephrology consultation in acute renal failure: Does timing matter? *American Journal of Medicine, 113,* 456–461.

Myers, W. O., et al. (1987). Medical versus early surgical therapy in patients with triple-vessel disease and mild angina pectoris: A CASS registry of survival. *Annals of Thoracic Surgery, 44,* 471–486.

Phillips, C. S., et al. (1997). Effects of residence in Alzheimer disease special care units on functional outcomes. *Journal of the American Medical Association, 278,* 1340–1344.

Raby, K., et al. (1989). Correlation between preoperative ischemia and major cardiac events after peripheral vascular surgery. *The New England Journal of Medicine, 321,* 1296–1300.

Reinisch, J., Sanders, S., Mortensen, E., & Rubin, D. B. (1995). In utero exposure to phenobarbital and intelligence deficits in adult men. *Journal of the American Medical Association, 274,* 1518–1525.

Rosenbaum, P. R., & Rubin, D. B. (1985a). Constructing a control group using multivariate matched sampling methods that incorporate the propensity score. *The American Statistician, 39,* 33–38.

Rosenbaum, P. R., & Rubin, D. B. (1985b). The bias due to incomplete matching. *Biometrics, 41,* 103–116.

Salmon, D. P., et al. (2002). Alzheimer's disease can be accurately diagnosed in very mildly impaired individuals. *Neurology, 59,* 1022–1028.

Soumerai, S., et al. (1997). Adverse outcomes of underuse of beta-blockers in elderly survivors of acute myocardial infarction. *Journal of the American Medical Association, 277,* 115–121.

Stamou, S. C., et al. (2002). Stroke after conventional versus minimally invasive coronary artery bypass. *Annals of Thoracic Surgery, 74,* 394–399.

Stone, R. A., et al. (1995). Propensity score adjustment for pretreatment differences between hospitalized and ambulatory patients with community-acquired pneumonia.
Medical Care, 33, 56–66.

Teufelsbauer, H., et al. (2002). Endovascular stent grafting versus open surgical operation in patients with infrarenal aortic aneurysms: A propensity score-adjusted analysis. *Circulation, 106,* 782–787.

Van Den Eeden, S., et al. (1998). Quality of life, health care utilization, and costs among
women undergoing hysterectomy in a managed-care setting. *American Journal of Ob-
stetric Gynecology, 178,* 91–100.

Willoughby, A., et al. (1990). Population-based study of the development outcome of
children exposed to chloride-deficient infant formula. *Pediatrics, 85,* 485–490.

4

On Model-Based Inferences: A Fitting Tribute to a Giant

Howard Wainer[1]
National Board of Medical Examiners

I first met Ralph Rosnow in October 1968. I was a new assistant professor, and Ralph spotted me right away. He had 18 or 20 irons in the fire and needed some statistical help on one or two of them.[2] After we met, he gave me some data and asked that I analyze them. To aid in this task he provided the epigrammatic advice "Think Fisher, not Pearson." This became his parting mantra each time we met over the next several months. He never told me exactly what he meant by it, so I was forced to guess.

My first guess was that he felt that I should do an analysis of variance and not a regression analysis of his data. This puzzled me, because it was well known, even then, that they were just two sides of the same coin. My next guess was that he was interested in effect sizes, but that too can be done within the context of a regression analysis. However, once I understood the great subtlety of Ralph's mind, I realized that he surely was trying to lead me away from the problems associated with trying to draw inferences from a model that is certain to be less than perfect. Of course, such temptations exist for all empirically based models, but they are especially alluring within the context of complex regression models. One has only to peruse the factor analysis literature to see how many otherwise sensible people are led down the dark path to

---

[1]This work was supported by the research budget of the National Board, and the author is delighted to be able to acknowledge this help.

[2]At least two of those irons resulted in papers we published together; see Rosnow, Wainer, & Arms, 1969, 1970.

flights of contentless fancy from regression coefficients that are so unstable that even their signs are not accurately established. Indeed, the current hot area of data mining (e.g., http://icdm04.cs.uni-dortmund.de/) exhibits this same difficulty that Ralph so presciently foresaw more than 3 decades ago. Because of these difficulties, data mining has, alas, more in common with the ganzwelt[3] of Wundt's 19th-century laboratory in Leipzig than it does to 21st-century statistical analysis.

It took me some time to appreciate what Ralph was trying to teach me, and even longer to learn what to do about it. This chapter is my attempt to elucidate what Ralph was able to summarize in his four memorable words. I'm sorry it has taken me so long to do it.

Some sort of formal quantitative model underlies most of modern scientific inference. The paradigm usually followed is to fit a model to data, note the quality of the fit, and, if it is deemed acceptable, draw inferences from the model as if it were true. A common measure of fit is some function of the sum of the squares of the deviations of the description of the data by the model from the actual data. The squared correlation between the data and the model is one usual measure. When the goal of the investigation is simply to accurately summarize the data, a high correlation between data and model justifies such an approach. But if the goal is deeper and tries to provide insights into the underlying processes that gave rise to the data, or to extrapolate beyond the data, we must be much more cautious.

To illustrate this, let us consider the growth record of a normal male. If we wish to provide a parsimonious model for his growth so that we can offer sensible interpolations between measurements, we can fit a linear function to his growth record. Such a model is shown in Figure 4.1. The model represents his height (in centimeters) as a linear function of his age (in years):

$$\text{Height} = 81.6 + 5.8 \text{ (age)} \qquad (1)$$

The squared correlation between this model and his actual height is 0.97. By most contemporary scientific standards for model fit, this would be deemed more than adequate. However, such a model has severe restrictions for use. It works well enough for interpolating, but as soon as we stray from the domain of the data we run into serious problems. For example, extrapolating downward to see how large he was at birth yields a hefty 32 inches—not a size to endear him to his mother. Indeed, extrapolating back to conception, we would be forced to conclude that either he was the product of a 2½-foot-long egg and sperm or that his gestation period lasted more than 14 years. Extrapolating upward, we would be forced to conclude that if

---

[3] A *ganzwelt*, for those who have forgotten, was an absolutely uniform visual field, like something you would experience if half a ping-pong ball were glued over each of your eyes. What Wundt and his associates found was that after you stared at nothing for awhile, you would start to see things. So it is with data mining.

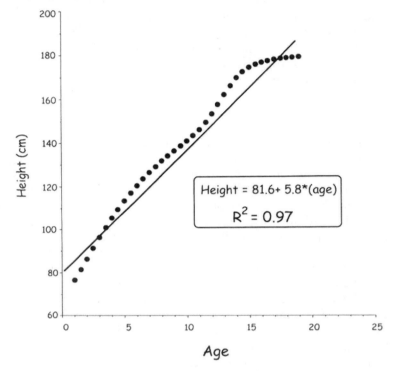

FIG. 4.1. The growth pattern of a normal male (from Bock et al., 1973) showing that a good linear fit does not mean an accurate representation of the underlying biological phenomenon.

he lived to the biblically prescribed three score and ten years, he would have folded his tent from the impressive altitude of 16 feet. Clearly, there are sharp limits to model-based inference, even for models whose fit is as impressive as this one.

A BETTER MODEL

A linear model is an often-used first choice for many phenomena, principally because of its ease of application. Also, because all functions can be well approximated by a linear function over short distances, this is not an unintelligent first approximation.[4] Indeed, the spectacular fit merely reflects that children start out small and end up big, and any model with that characteristic will provide a reasonable approximation. However, we know

---

[4]All differentiable functions can be approximated to any specified degree of accuracy with a Taylor polynomial expansion. The first two terms of the Taylor expansion are, of course, linear.

that human growth is self-limiting, and a model that does not reflect some sort of upper asymptote is bound to have severe limitations. We can also see trends in the residuals in Figure 4.1 that suggest a systematic lack of fit.

Many forms of growth with a constraint can be thought of as the solution to the differential equation

$$dy/dt = a(f - y),\tag{2}$$

which postulates that the speed of growth (dy/dt) is proportional to the amount of room/resources left to grow in ($f - y$, where f is the upper asymptote). Solving Equation 2 yields a logistic function, which is often used to represent such things as growth of bacteria within a closed container. A logistic function has the attractive property of manifesting what is essentially exponential growth initially, and then slowing down after passing the half-way point in its journey toward its eventual upper limit.

Such a model was proposed by Burt (1937) to fit human growth from a presumed zero point at conception. He suggested using the sum of several logistic functions, in which each one was polynomial in time. The set of functions he used was enormously flexible and fit the data very well indeed, but it required a minimum of 10 parameters per subject.[5] Such parameters were not only difficult to interpret, but were so poorly conditioned that accurate estimation was practically impossible.

A simplified and more workable version of this model was proposed by Bock et al. (1973), who offered the two-component logistic mixture

$$y = \frac{a_1}{1 + e^{-b_1(t-c_1)}} + \frac{f - a_1}{1 + e^{-b_2(t-c_2)}}\tag{3}$$

in which the first term on the right describes the prepubertal growth of the subject and the second term describes the contribution of the adolescent growth spurt. The parameters are interpreted as follows:

a_1 is the upper asymptote of the prepubertal component.

b_1 is the slope of the prepubertal component at its midpoint, and is used in the calculation of the peak height velocity ($v_1 = a_1 b_1/4$)) due to prepubertal growth.

c_1 is the age at which the peak velocity of this component is reached.

f is final stature.

---

[5]"With four parameters I can fit an elephant, and with five I can make it wag its tail" (Henri Poincaré, 1896).

The two parameters of the adolescent component of growth (b_2 and c_2) are interpreted in a parallel fashion.

The five parameters—$a_1, b_1, c_1, b_2,$ and c_2—were fit using maximum likelihood under the assumption of normally distributed measurement error (Wainer & Petersen, 1972), but f is assumed known. This innocent-appearing assumption was made in order to force the function through the observed final point and avoid the intuitively uncomfortable position of having to interpret an individual curve that did not terminate at mature stature. Bock et al. (1973) also made the prescient assertion that fixing f is "essential to prevent the estimation procedure from reversing the roles of the two components" (p. 65).

Over the years since its first publication, this model has been applied successfully in many different situations, providing summary descriptions as well as allowing scientific inferences. Among the areas of application were comparing the different longitudinal growth studies (Thissen, Bock, Wainer, & Roche, 1976), comparing growth patterns of normal children and children with Down Syndrome (Rarick, Wainer, Thissen, & Seefeldt, 1975), examining the growth of children with renal insufficiency (Potter et al., 1978), and studying the hereditary and environmental determinants of growth in height in a longitudinal sample of children and youth of Guatemalan and European ancestry (Johnson, Wainer, Thissen, & MacVean, 1976).

FITTING THE MODEL TO A GIANT

This unblemished record of successful application within widely varying circumstances led me to try the model out on Robert Pershing Wadlow. Wadlow—at 8 feet, 11 inches in height—is listed in the *Guinness Book of World Records* (Young, 1998) as the tallest human ever measured. He was born in Alton, Illinois, on February 22, 1918, and died on July 15, 1940. He is thought to have been a "pituitary giant"—someone who grows enormously due to an overactive pituitary gland. He was of normal size at birth, but was 6 feet tall when he was 8 and almost 7 feet tall when he was 12. His growth record is shown in Table 4.1. After all, I said to myself, if the model worked on Down syndrome children, Guatemalan children, and children with renal insufficiency, why wouldn't it work on the growth pattern manifested by an acknowledged giant with a pituitary problem?

Proceeding cautiously, I repeated what I did for the male of normal stature that was shown in Figure 4.1, and fit a linear function to Wadlow's growth record. The result of this parallel analysis is shown in Figure 4.2, and the fitted straight-line model that represents his height as a linear function of his age is:

$$\text{Height} = 126.5 + 6.9 \times (\text{age}) \tag{4}$$

TABLE 4.1
Remarkable Growth Record of Robert P. Wadlow

Age	HT (in.)	HT (ft.)	HT (cm.)
5	60.0	5.00	152
6			
7			
8	72.0	6.00	183
9	74.5	6.21	189
10	77.0	6.42	196
11	79.0	6.58	201
12	82.5	6.88	210
13	86.0	7.17	218
14	89.5	7.46	227
15	92.0	7.67	234
16	94.5	7.88	240
17	96.5	8.04	245
18	99.5	8.29	253
19	101.5	8.46	258
20	103.5	8.63	263
21	104.5	8.71	265
22	107.0	8.92	272

And the squared correlation between this model and his actual height is a remarkable 0.99.

It is interesting to compare this result with the more normal result in Equation 1. The intercept terms are quite different, but the slopes suggest that Robert Wadlow only grew 1 centimeter a year faster than would a male of normal stature. Extrapolations from Wadlow's model are no more useful than they were for the anonymous male in Figure 4.1. Indeed, had Mr. Wadlow not expired prematurely, this model would predict his stature at death to exceed 20 feet!

I had fond hopes of being able to make more reasonable inferences from the double logistic growth model described in Equation 3. However, to be able to use the double logistic I had to observe Wadlow's final stature. Although a compelling argument could be made that his height at death was his final stature, an examination of Figure 4.2 suggests that Wadlow's growth pattern does not exhibit the asymptotic pattern seen in Figure 4.1.

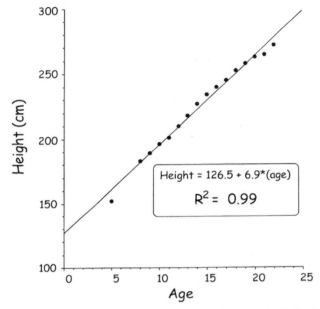

FIG. 4.2.   The growth pattern of Robert Pershing Wadlow (1918–1940), the world's tallest man (from Young, 1998).

Thus, I was forced to guess his final length. My preliminary guess was that his final stature would be about 278 centimeters (9 feet, 1.5 inches), which I then inserted into the model. The result of the fitting (shown in Figure 4.3) was remarkable. It, too, had a R^2 of 0.99, but it seemed to follow the pattern of growth much more faithfully, thus providing evidence that this growth model, which had been so valuable in other applications, would once again prove its mettle.

Once I found that the model fit like a glove, I felt that I could safely interpret the parameters of the model. The most startling aspect of Wadlow's growth was that most of his unusual stature was contained in his adolescent growth spurt. A typical male growth spurt contributes about 29 centimeters to final stature, whereas for Wadlow it was more than three times that. His prepubertal growth, although certainly impressive, was only about 20% greater than normal.[6] Thus, one might infer that whatever caused Wadlow's unusual stature was due largely to adolescent growth and hence was likely to be steroidal in origin.

[6]A normal male has prepubertal growth of about 150 centimeters and adolescent growth of about 30 centimeters. According to this parameterization of the model, Wadlow's prepubertal growth is about 5 standard deviations higher than normal, whereas his adolescent component is more than 10 standard deviations greater than normal.

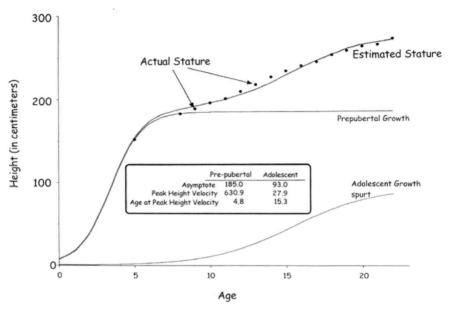

FIG. 4.3. The result of fitting the double-logistic function to Robert Wadlow's growth data, when the final stature was estimated to be 278 centimeters, yielded a very big adolescent growth spurt.

I checked the fit again, this time by plotting the fitted values against his actual stature (Figure 4.4), and confirmed my earlier conclusion, although I did see systematic trends in the residuals. To try to get rid of those trends, I decided to manipulate the final asymptote a little. Reducing it below 278 made matters worse, and so, noticing that Wadlow had grown 7 centimeters in his 22nd year, I tried to increase it. I drew some smooth curves through the growth data and convinced myself that 284 centimeters was actually a more believable final estimate. The result was revealing (see Figure 4.5). First, the fit clearly deteriorated, although with an R^2 of 0.95 it was still impressive. Second, the asymptote of the adolescent component was estimated to be 34 centimeters, well within normal bounds. The prepubertal component was now estimated to be 250 centimeters.

Thus, a relatively small change in the asymptote yielded a profound change in the gross interpretation of the model's parameters. Which interpretation is the right one? How can we tell? All three of the models that I fit yielded R^2 values that most researchers dream about; hence, they provided no guidance.

This sensitivity of outcome to something that is unknown was somewhat presaged by Darrell Bock's (Bock et al., 1973) warning that was quoted ear-

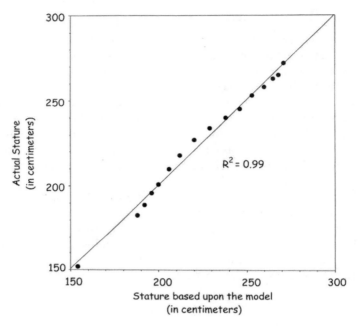

FIG. 4.4. A plot of the fitted values from the double-logistic model shown in Figure 4.3 against the Wadlow's actual height shows small consistent variation in the residuals.

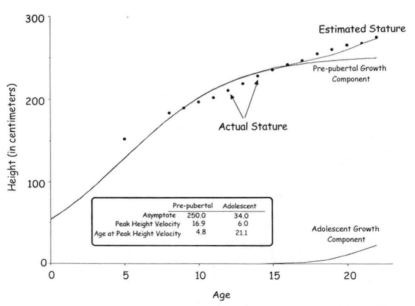

	Pre-pubertal	Adolescent
Asymptote	250.0	34.0
Peak Height Velocity	16.9	6.0
Age at Peak Height Velocity	4.8	21.1

FIG. 4.5. The result of fitting the double-logistic function to Robert Wadlow's growth data, when the final stature was estimated to be 284 centimeters, yielded a small adolescent growth spurt.

lier. Yet, the two components did not simply reverse their location. Instead, they held their locations in time but in some sense reversed their contributions to the abnormal portions of Wadlow's stature. Moreover, because we could see that Robert Wadlow was more than 7 feet tall when he was 13, this fit corresponded more closely with what we might expect from a medical point of view. Thus, because it seemed plausible to ascribe unusual growth to the prepubertal component, the outcome shown in Figure 4.5 seems more acceptable. However, the fit is far from perfect. Indeed, when the fitted values are plotted against Wadlow's actual stature (see Figure 4.6), the systematic shortcomings of the fit are clear.

The variability of our inferences about the contribution of the Robert Wadlow's adolescent growth spurt to his final stature was certainly due, at least in part, to the fact that the double-logistic growth model did not fit perfectly. I thought that perhaps a better-fitting model would ameliorate this difficulty. An improved growth model was proposed and implemented by Bock and Thissen (1983); it uses three logistic components that represent

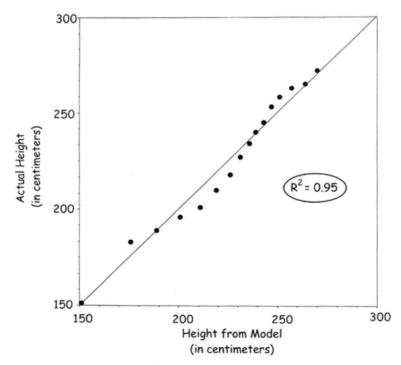

FIG. 4.6.   A plot of the fitted values from the double-logistic model shown in Figure 4.5 against Wadlow's actual height also shows small, consistent variation in the residuals.

infantile growth, midchildhood growth, and adolescent growth. As we might expect, a model with three more parameters fits better (see Figure 4.7, and remember Poincaré's observation that was quoted earlier), but not perfectly.[7] The triple logistic indicates adolescent growth that is a little below the population mean (19.9 centimeters for Wadlow vs. 21.8 centimeters for the male population mean). Can we believe that Wadlow's adolescent growth spurt was of normal size? How much would this change with modest adjustments in the assumed final asymptote? A very small change in the fitting procedure (omitting the last data point) alters the estimate of the adolescent asymptote to 21.6 centimeters, suggesting that there is nothing in the data, once that point is removed, to cause the fitting algorithm to move the estimate from the prior.

So where does this leave us? What value is a model if our interpretations are critically dependent on something that we cannot know? Is the only conclusion that we can reach from this investigation that the remaining un-

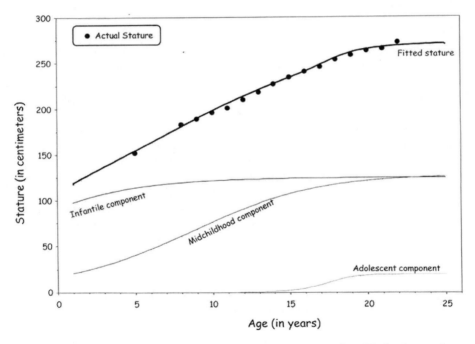

FIG. 4.7. The result of fitting the triple-logistic function to Robert Wadlow's growth data, when the final stature was estimated to be 272 centimeters.

[7] I am grateful to Darrell Bock for providing this fit, and to David Thissen for aiding in the interpretation of the output.

certainty of interpretation makes model-based reasoning impossible? Surely, just because these models are demonstrably false (as are all models) does not mean that they are worthless. Newtonian mechanics has similar limits yet remains a useful approximation a century after Einstein provided a more accurate alternative.

Statistics is often called the science of uncertainty. Uncertainty does not mean simple ignorance—instead, it is that state of knowledge in which a range of possibilities and some idea of their relative chances of occurrence are available. Thus my point is not simply the old platitude that "the more you learn, the more you realize that you do not know"—that may be true, but it comes dangerously close to suggesting that learning can be futile, which is quite the antithesis of my message. Rather, it is my intention to argue that the real gains in science need not come through reducing uncertainty, but they will always entail a better understanding of uncertainty.

A natural, if unanticipated, consequence of 3 centuries of scientific exploration that has followed Newton's *Principia* has been an increase in uncertainty, or at least an increase in our awareness of uncertainty. There's an aphorism I like, because it says much in few words: "A man with one watch knows what time it is; a man with two watches is never sure." Newton gave the scientific world its first watch, and for a while we knew what time it was. But even in astronomy that certainty was short lived, as questions were asked that went beyond the bounds of developed theory, and improved instruments revealed discrepancies even within that theory. Slowly, astronomers acquired a second watch, and a consequent loss of certainty.

The second asymptote I used when fitting the double-logistic growth model provided the second watch. It helped us understand the limits of inference possible with the model. And this is the message that I would like to leave—that models are always wrong, but they can be useful. However, the limits on their usefulness must be ascertained and included in any description of them. An important tool in such investigations is a sensitivity study, one in which the accuracy of the underlying assumptions of the model are varied and the consequent variation in conclusions is noted.

REFERENCES

Bock, R. D., & Thissen, D. (1980). Statistical problems of fitting curves for individual growth in stature. In E. F. Johnson, A. F. Roche, & C. Susanne (Eds.), *Human physical growth and development: Methodologies & factors* (pp. 265–290). New York: Plenum.

Bock, R. D., & Thissen, D. (1983). *TRIFIT: A program for fitting and displaying triple logistic growth curves*. Mooresville, IN: Scientific Software.

Bock, R. D., Wainer, H., Petersen, A., Thissen, D., Murray, J., & Roche, A. (1973). A parameterization for individual human growth curves. *Human Biology, 45,* 63–80.

Burt, C. (1937). *The backward child.* New York: Appleton-Century.

Johnson, E. F., Wainer, H., Thissen, D., & MacVean, R. (1976). Hereditary and environmental determinants of growth in height in a longitudinal sample of children and youth of Guatemalan and European ancestry. *American Journal of Physical Anthropology, 44,* 469–475.

Poincaré, H. (1896). *Calcul des probabilité. Leçons professées pendant le deuxième semester 1893–1894.* Paris: Gauthier-Villars.

Potter, D. E., Broyer, M., Chantler, C., Gruskin, A., Holliday, M. A., Roche, A. F., Sharer, S., & Thissen, D. (1978). Measurement of growth in children with renal insufficiency. *Kidney International, 14,* 378–382.

Rarick, G. L., Wainer, H., Thissen, D., & Seefeldt, V. (1975). A double logistic comparison of growth patterns of normal children and children with Down's syndrome. *Annals of Human Biology, 2,* 339–346.

Rosnow, R., Wainer, H., & Arms, R. (1969). Anderson's personality-trait words rated by men and women as a function of sex of stimulus. *Psychological Reports, 24,* 787–790.

Rosnow, R., Wainer, H, & Arms, R. (1970). Personality and group impressions formation as a function of the amount of overlap in evaluative meaning of the stimulus elements. *Sociometry, 33,* 472–484.

Thissen, D., Bock, R. D., Wainer, H., & Roche, A. F. (1976). Individual growth in stature: A comparison of four growth studies in the U.S.A. *Annals of Human Biology, 3,* 529–542.

Wainer, H., & Petersen, A. (1972). *GROFIT: A FORTRAN program for the estimation of parameters of a human growth curve* (Res. Mem. No. 17). Chicago: Department of Education Statistical Laboratory, University of Chicago.

Young, M. (1998). *Guinness book of world records 1998.* New York: Bantam.

5

Retrieving Literature for Meta-Analysis: Can We Really Find It All?

MaryLu C. Rosenthal
OCS America

In earlier times, researchers planning to conduct a meta-analysis systematically leafed through printed volumes of abstracts (e.g., *Psychological Abstracts* and/or *Sociological Abstracts*) to find citations and abstracts for journal articles and dissertations. They collected references from published and unpublished papers, and read relevant conference proceedings. They sought out studies by making personal contact with colleagues (either friends, acquaintances, or strangers) who were doing relevant research or knew other people who were doing relevant research. They contacted those colleagues and requested copies of their "file drawer" articles—those written but not submitted for publication, or submitted but rejected for publication.

Those methods of collecting studies are still used, and during the last 20 or so years a few new ones have been added to the list. The truly scholarly scientist uses them all. Ralph Rosnow, whose methodological contributions underlie research procedures widely adopted by behavioral scientists, uses the most sophisticated modern technology *and* the older traditional retrieval practices to find information about behavioral and biomedical research relevant to his domains of scholarly work.

Harris Cooper (1998) provided detailed descriptions of essentially all the methods for locating research studies. He divided both the old and the new retrieval methods into three groups:

1. *Informal channels* (in which there is no restriction, e.g., peer review, on the quality of the studies available): personal contact and personal solic-itation (often called the "invisible college"), electronic colleges (scientists sending—via the Internet—information to known and unknown col-leagues through mailing lists and newsgroups), and the World Wide Web.

2. *Formal channels* (in which there are restrictions on the kind and quality of the studies): conference papers, traditional journals, electronic journals, and reference lists found in research reports.

3. *Secondary channels* (in which an organization or company provides information about completed and in-progress research): research bibliog-raphies, research registers, and citation and reference databases [the last being the information source described by Cooper, 1998, as "likely to prove most fruitful to research synthesists (meta-analysts) ..." (p. 60)].

Our focus is on those reference databases—tools that have made the process of finding references and abstracts of studies easier and faster for the meta-analyst in the social, behavioral, and medical sciences. This chapter does not describe for the meta-analyst the selection of databases or the keywords to use for searching, nor the "click-on, then click-on" se-quences when using the computer to search these databases; excellent de-scriptions and helpful hints for selecting and using electronic bibliographic databases are found elsewhere (Cooper, 1998; Lipsey & Wilson, 2001; Rosnow & Rosnow, 2003). Instead, this chapter reviews some of the his-tory of reference databases, defines some relevant vocabulary, and pres-ents some examples of the differences among these rich sources of bibliographic information.

HISTORICAL BACKGROUND

Developed during the 1970s, many bibliographic reference databases cor-responded to a printed version of the same information. Although a num-ber of the database developers did include the records contained in the earlier printed versions, many simply started their online products with-out attempting to add what had originally been in the print form, so the printed abstracts and indexes remained useful and valuable tools (Rosenthal, 1985).

During the 1970s and early 1980s, computer-readable databases were available only through intermediaries: (a) Librarians in college, university, or corporate research libraries would perform literature searches for their patrons; and (b) private information/research brokers would provide searches and document delivery services for a fee (Reed & Baxter, 1994; Rosenthal, 1985). When these databases were in their early years, special training was needed to conduct searches. Each database had its own "language"; this language included not only the fields to be used in the searching procedure, but also particular commands and the insertions of commas, semicolons, and slashes in unlikely places (this was especially true for databases produced by the federal government). Librarians or information specialists kept the instruction manuals open beside the computer; memorizing these "languages" was not a simple task.

A few government-produced databases were sold on magnetic tape and updated periodically, but most searches had to be done online. At the beginning, providers and vendors of these databases charged for each minute spent online. The librarian (or other information professional) was always aware of the mounting costs with each of these minutes, which made leisurely searching difficult. Later, database vendors began to charge flat user fees to corporations and universities.

During the late 1980s and early 1990s, the database providers wanted to expand their markets by developing user-friendly search software (Reed & Baxter, 1994). It became simpler to search, and not as much training was needed. Putting bibliographic databases on CD-ROMs further improved searching in several important ways: They were user-friendly; they were accessible on either a single-user workstation or a local area network; they allowed unlimited, inexpensive search activity (online per-minute costs were no longer a concern); and they allowed the user to download citations into word processing or database programs for future use (Reed & Baxter, 1994).

By 2002, much of the pre-1970s printed bibliographic information had been added to the computer-readable databases, so the searcher needed to use fewer print sources to find published materials. (A recent search of the American Psychological Association's PsycINFO, using the keywords *paradoxical psychotherapy*, turned up records of publications as early as 1948.) Today's scientists tracking down empirical studies online (or using databases via a local area network or on CD-ROMs) would *expect* that 30 years of improved technology would have made the hunt a simple one. They would need to look in fewer sources for studies, and everything written on a given research hypothesis (whether published, unpublished, or in progress) would be found in one big comprehensive source. In fact, the searching process is still rather complicated and relies almost as much on serendipity as it did 30 years ago.

Databases, Records, and Fields

The word *database* did not show up in the 1970 edition of the *American Heritage Dictionary of the English Language* (Morris, 1970)—although *data pro-*

cessing did—so perhaps in 1970 *database* was considered a technical term used only by computer scientists. *The Dictionary of Computer Terms* (Covington & Downing, 1992) defined the word *database* as "a collection of data stored on a computer storage medium, that can be used for more than one purpose" (pp. 92–93).

Perhaps without recognizing it, people have long been using various kinds of noncomputerized versions of a database (a **base,** or filing system, for storing **data,** or information). Library card catalogs, office files, or any other system for organizing and reorganizing a collection of pieces of information by hand are databases. The data (or information) stored in card catalog drawers or filing cabinets can be used and arranged in various ways and used for more than one purpose (just as in *The Dictionary of Computer Terms'* definition of the word *database*). One may think of the *whole* card catalog, or the *whole* filing cabinet, as a **database.**

Library catalog cards can be arranged in alphabetical order by the authors' names, book titles, or book subjects. Office file folders may be arranged by customers' names or customers' zip codes. One may think of each catalog card (which holds all the information about a single book), or each file folder (which holds all the information about a single customer) as a database **record.**

Think of the pieces of information about a book we see on a library catalog card, or the pieces of information we write on an application for a driver's license. Each of these pieces of information (the title of the book, the author's name, the subject the book is about; or in the case of the application, your name, your address, your telephone number) fall into categories: a "title" category, an "author's name" category, a "your address" category, and so on. In a computer-readable database, these categories are called **fields.** These fields are used for searching; using a database, we can search on the author category **(field)** to find articles and books by a particular author, just as we would search the section of the card catalog drawer for cards **(records)** labeled "Hemingway" to find books by that author, or search a section of the file cabinet under the zip code category **(field)** "02150" to find the files **(records)** of the customers in Chelsea, Massachusetts.

Fields in the Computer-Readable Database.   Modern computer-readable databases allow searching on many different fields. For example, using the PsycINFO database, the scientists may do Subject or Keyword searches; those search the Title, the Thesaurus (controlled subject terms), Abstract, Key Phrase, Descriptors, Identifiers and, for books, Tables of Contents. Other types of searches are for words in a Title, or on an author's name, Author's Affiliation, Language in which the document was published, ISBN, Year of Publication, Publisher, Publication Type (there are 49 Publication Types in PsycINFO), Journal Title, Classification Code for the 22 different areas of psychology, and a number of additional fields.

Table 5.1 shows a sample **record** from the **database** PsycINFO (from the vendor Cambridge Scientific Abstracts). The **fields** listed in the first column (with their abbreviations and full names given) are but a few of the fields available through PsycINFO. Individual vendors decide what fields of information they will provide. This **record** was among eight retrieved from a search on the Author **field** = Rosnow, and Keyword (Descriptors) **field** = ethics.

DATABASE SEARCHING IN THE 21ST CENTURY

It would be every meta-analyst's dream to have all published and unpublished empirical studies listed in one huge database, and to have that huge database available through the Internet. No more having to be networked to your university or college library computer, no more reading the conference programs cover to cover, and no more correspondence inquiring about the possibility of unpublished studies. Just go online and retrieve all the information needed!

The Internet search engines that we all know and love (e.g., Google) are enormously productive at finding information on events, products, companies, and people; in seconds they produce for us a list of thousands of newspaper articles, magazine articles, and books. The search engines even put the results in a convenient order of relevance. A 2002 search for the term *paradoxical intervention* using the search engine Google yielded 22,700 results in 0.17 seconds. The results of the search yielded mostly Web sites, ranging from advertisements (from publishers and personal authors, and from organizations selling both therapy instruction to professionals and the therapy itself) to anything that included the words *paradoxical* and *intervention* somewhere in their texts. There were also descriptions of some scholarly and interesting television and radio programs included in our retrievals, and practical do-it-yourself instructions for applying the techniques in everyday life. Serious meta-analytic researchers would find only a few empirical studies in these World Wide Web results. And, unless scientists have listed their unpublished papers on their Web pages, unpublished materials remain fugitive.

An Abundance of Materials

During the 1980s, several large printed volumes conveniently provided complete descriptions of all online and CD-ROM databases, listing the disciplines they served and giving contact information about the organizations that produced them and the vendors that sold them (Bowker Co., 1983; Cuadra Associates, 1979; Gale Research Co., 1983/1986; Hall & Brown, 1983; Williams, 1979/1982). Now, the Gale Research Company offers its "Electronic Reference Shelf," the *Gale Directory of Online, Portable, and*

TABLE 5.1
Names of Fields, and the Information Contained in Each, in a Sample Record (of Eight Retrieved) From a Search of AU (Author) = Rosnow and KW (Keyword) = Ethics Using the Cambridge Scientific Abstracts Version of PsycINFO

Field	Record
TI (Title)	Hedgehogs, foxes, and the evolving social contract in psychological science: Ethical challenges and methodological opportunities
AU (Author)	Rosnow, Ralph L.
AF (Author's Affiliation)	Temple U., Dept of Psychology, Philadelphia, PA, US [Rosnow]
SO (Source)	Psychological Methods. Vol 2 (4), Dec., 1997, pp. 345–356
IP (Information Provider)	http://www.apa.org/journals/met/html
IS (ISSN)	1082-989X (Print)
PB (Publisher)	American Psychological Assn, US, http://www.apa.org
AB (Abstract)	This article is addressed primarily to new researchers who feel burdened by an expanding body of ethical rules and regulations. Moral dilemmas proliferate as researchers try to strike a balance between ethical accountability and the technical demands of scientific practices. The challenge is to expand existing knowledge and abide by an evolving social contract that is responsive to current ethical sensitivities.. This article illustrates dilemmas faced by researchers, examines some of the events leading up to the present situation and shows how researchers might exploit this situation, so that science and society can both benefit. (PsycINFO Database Record (c) 2002 APA, all rights reserved) (journal abstract)
LA (Language)	English
PY (Publication Year)	1997
PT (Publication Type)	Print (Paper) ; Journal Article
FE (Features)	References; Peer Reviewed
DE (Descriptors)	Experimental Ethics; Experimentation; Methodology; Professional Ethics
ID (Identifier)	ethical challenges & methodological opportunities in psychology research
CL (Classification)	3450 Professional Ethics & Standards & Liability

*The same record may appear differently depending on which vendor's version is being used. APA provides many fields in the PsycINFO database; some vendors use some of those fields, and some vendors use others.

Note. This table is based on a Cambridge Scientific Abstracts version of an American Psychological Association (2002c) PsycInfo record.

Internet Databases (Thomson Dialog, 2002), containing information on 11,000 database products, 3600 database producers, and 2000 database vendors! This compilation of information that once was in print form is now contained in several separate computer-readable databases, and can be purchased through an online vendor or on CD-ROM, diskette, or magnetic tape (Thomson Dialog, 2002). People once joked about librarians "reading books about books"; now librarians read databases about databases!

Six Searches for Meta-Analyses

If there has been such an explosion in the sources for bibliographic information, it could be that there is now much more scholarly work being done and many more publications being produced. To examine this possibility, I did a search of the PsycINFO database, using several combinations of fields, to look for a possible increase in the number of one kind of study—meta-analyses—since 1970.

The two particular sources of PsycINFO available for this search were the PsycINFO database leased by the University of California Digital Library (CDL) from the American Psychological Association (APA), and the version of PsycINFO sold by the vendor Cambridge Scientific Abstracts (CSA). The searches used the CDL's Power Search option and the CSA's Advanced Search, and the same six search strategies for each. Between the two versions of PsycINFO, the number of citations found were never the same for any of the six search strategies employed. For the combined three time periods searched (1970–1979, 1980–1989, 1990–1999), the numbers totaled to similar numbers of citations, but, for any given time period, there are some large differences in the numbers of citations (in one case more than 200) between the two versions of the PsycINFO database. Table 5.2 shows the increase over time in the number of articles about the subject of "meta-analysis" and an increase in the number of meta-analyses reported.

Search 1 used *Meta Analysis* (the space between the two parts of the term is used instead of a hyphen in the PsycINFO database, and both parts are capitalized) as a Keyword (KW) in all Publication Types (PT). The results simply indicate that with each group of years there was a growing number of articles about meta-analysis, and interest in that type of research. In Search 2, when *Meta Analysis* was used as a Title Word (TI) in all Publication Types (PT), there were fewer publications cited, but the number of articles *did* become substantially larger in each 10-year period of the 30 years searched.

With the idea of finding "true" meta-analyses (i.e., studies that are themselves meta-analyses), Search 3 used *Meta Analysis* as a Keyword and *Meta Analysis* as a Publication Type; this search yielded fewer citations, but there was still an increase through the years from 1970 to 1999. However, using *Meta Analysis* as a Publication Type did not give reliable results. For the

TABLE 5.2
Results of PsycINFO Searches: Six Searches for Each of Two Versions of PsycINFO

Publication Type	Dates	CDL1 Keyword: Meta-Analysis — Citations		CSA2 Keyword: Meta-Analysis — Citations		CDL1 Title Words: Meta-Analysis — Citations		CSA2 Title Words: Meta-Analysis — Citations	
		Number	Percentage	Number	Percentage	Number	Percentage	Number	Percentage
		Search 1		*Search 3*		*Search 2*		*Search 2*	
All publication types	1970–1979	27*	1%	16*	0%	8*	1%	8*	1%
	1980–1989	980	27%	919	28%	462	30%	458	30%
	1990–1999	2585	72%	2371	72%	1089	70%	1081	70%
Σ		3592		3306		1559		1547	
		Search 3				*Search 4*		*Search 4*	
Meta-analysis	1970–1979	7**	0%	7**	0%	1	0%	1**	0%
	1980–1989	629	24%	628	24%	323	25%	321	24%
	1990–1999	1954	75%	1942	75%	993	75%	989	75%
Σ		2590		2577		1317		1311	
		Search 5				*Search 6*		*Search 6*	
Empirical study	1970–1979	0	0%	0	0%	0	0%	0	0%
	1980–1989	184	26%	175	29%	86	35%	84	35%
	1990–1999	512	74%	427	71%	159	65%	155	65%
Σ		696		602		245		239	

[1]This version of PsycINFO is leased by the American Psychological Association to the provider, University of California Digital Library (CDL).

[2]The vendor of this version of PsycINFO is Cambridge Scientific Abstracts (CSA). The results of these searches are from November 2, 2002. In August, 2002, these same searches on the CSA version of PsycINFO produced different numbers of records for the year span 1980-1989. In every case, at least 10% fewer records were retrieved in the later (November) searches (16% fewer records on average).

*The Smith and Glass (1977) article is found here where no "publication type" is specified.

**Some of these articles were commentaries on the meta-analysis presented in Smith and Glass (1977). The article itself was not assigned a publication type and would not be found specifying *meta analysis* as the publication type

1970–1979 time span, both versions of PsycINFO (the California Digital Library and Cambridge Scientific Abstracts) found seven articles. The articles were all commentaries, and responses to commentaries, about a well-known 1977 meta-analysis (Smith & Glass, 1977), but there was no citation to that article itself! The complete records of the citations showed that the commentaries had been assigned Publication Type designations of "Journal Article; Comment; Meta Analysis," whereas the Smith and Glass article was assigned only the Publication Type "Journal Article."

Search 4, using *Meta Analysis* as a Title word and *Meta Analysis* as a Publication Type yielded one citation from both PsycINFO versions for the time period 1970–1979. There was no Smith and Glass (1977) article there, of course, because by limiting our search by entering a Publication Type, we once again excluded that article.

Searches 5 and 6 looked (as a meta-analyst might) for empirical studies only. These searches used *Empirical Studies* as the Publication Type, with *Meta Analysis* as either the Keyword or as the Title Word. We know that there were meta-analytic empirical studies during that time period, and we know that the Publication Type designation was used as early as 1976, yet there were no citations for meta-analyses as empirical studies for the years 1970–1979.

The searches listed in Table 5.2 would seem to indicate that using a *broad* search strategy (without specifying a Publication Type) might be the wiser course to follow. For the purposes of the meta-analyst seeking many studies, a search using the "subject," "keyword," or "descriptor," or "identifiers" fields yields more records because it is less specific. Although scientists then have to read more citations and abstracts than are actually relevant, they can be more confident that they are not missing some important studies.

FREE TEXT
ND CONTROLLED VOCABULARY SEARCHING

"Free-text searching" allows searching on almost any word in the text of a document's title or abstract; the only words that are not used for searching are called "stop words"; for example, articles (*a, an, the*), pronouns, and conjunctions. **"Controlled vocabulary"** refers to the terms or "descriptors" that make up the "thesaurus"—a hierarchy of terms appropriate for a particular database. Online versions of thesauri are set up so that searchers may browse through them while working with the database, making it possible to find related or alternative terms to search.

Each thesaurus is different from all others (even when they are used for databases representing similar disciplines), the terms scientists use may or may not be included in a given thesaurus, and consulting many thesauri is time consuming and not always productive. For these reasons, many scientists and librarians, when searching multiple databases, simply enter terms as "keywords" or "key phrases," using free-text rather than controlled vocabulary searching. Fidel (1991) found that the more databases involved in a search, the less likely scientists are to take the time required to consult thesauri. She suggested that the standardization of thesauri would increase the use of searches using the controlled vocabulary (descriptors) method, thereby leading to more exacting retrieval. She observed, however, that the competition among database providers might prohibit the kind of cooperation necessary for this kind of standardization (Fidel, 1991). To illustrate the differences in thesauri, I consulted three, looking for the term *meta-analysis*.

APA's *Thesaurus of Psychological Index Terms* (2002) is structured so that searchers may see how the subject they wish to search is related to Broader Terms, Related Terms, and Narrower Terms. For example, the term *meta-analysis* falls under two Broader Terms: *Methodology* and *Statistical Analysis,* and is related to *Literature Review.*

PubMed's thesaurus uses MeSH (medical subject headings), the National Library of Medicine's controlled vocabulary. There is a MeSH Browser with a hierarchy called a "MeSH tree." For example, the term *meta-analysis* appears on four branches of the MeSH tree: Analytical, Diagnostic and Therapeutic Techniques and Equipment; Biological Sciences; Physical Sciences; and Health Care.

The Biosis database uses the Taxonomic Guide as its thesaurus. The term *meta-analysis* does not appear in the guide's hierarchical structure under any of the four main headings of "Animals," "Bacteria," "Plants," and "Viruses," so that the ability to do a free-text search was essential when using the Biosis database.

System-Generated Thesauri versus Human-Generated Thesauri

System-generated or "automatic" thesauri are more comprehensive than are those generated by human beings. An example of the development of an "automatic" thesaurus could be when indexing documents' titles and abstracts, a computer program is written to filter out "stop words" and "stop-verbs" (verbs that serve only as verbs; e.g., *write* and *generate*); the program then indexes only nouns or noun phrases (containing adjectives and nouns) found in titles and abstracts (Chen, Martinez, Kirchhoff, Ng, & Schatz, 1998).

Human-generated indexes and thesauri tend to be more precise and rich in semantics, and they offer scientists alternative terms to use in their searches. The term *indexing uncertainty* is used for the problem that arises when human indexers try to select the correct terms to assign to a document. People tend to use different terms for the same information, and Chen et al. (1998, p. 207) stated that "studies have revealed that, on average, the probability of any two people using the same term to describe an object is less than 20%". For example, a colleague reported a PsycINFO Keyword search for *Health Care* among *Latinos;* his search retrieved many records that did not contain the word *Latinos* in the title or abstract (M. Yonezawa, personal communication, September 27, 2002). Apparently, the indexers at PsycINFO realize that many people use the terms *Latinos* and *Hispanics* interchangeably (even though they are technically different), and thus the indexers assigned both terms as "descriptors" for documents about either Latinos or Hispanics. That kind of indexing makes it possible to retrieve an article such as "Modern Racism on Campus: A Survey of Attitudes and Perceptions" (Sydell & Nelson, 2000) through a Keyword search using either the word *Hispanics* or the word *Latinos,* even though the word *Latinos* does not appear in the title or the abstract of the article.

Human-generated thesauri, however, require constant maintenance because of the development and changes in the social, behavioral, and medical sciences and technology. If thesauri changes are *not* done consistently and continuously to keep pace with the multitude of terms and the changing vocabulary, it is called the "knowledge acquisition bottleneck" (Chen et al., 1998, p. 207).

An example of what may be the optimal solution for combining the best features of system-generated (automatic) thesauri with the best features of human-generated thesauri is a project underway at the National Library of Medicine. The project incorporates human-generated thesauri into an automated system called the National Library of Medicine's Unified Medical Language System (UMLS). The UMLS objective is "an intelligent automated system that understands biomedical terms and their interrelationships" (Chen et al., 1998, p. 207), one that combines the best attributes of human-generated thesauri (precision and semantic richness) with automatic thesauri (comprehensiveness).

SAMPLE SEARCHES ON SEVERAL DATABASES

Search Plan

Subject.   In planning an illustrative search of the literature, it seemed appropriate to select a topic that might be studied by a range of social, medical, and behavioral scientists. I selected the subject of *paradoxical psychotherapy* or *paradoxical intervention* (also called *paradoxical intention*) because of its use and study in a variety of possible settings: biological, medical, psychiatric, psychological, and sociological. According to an article in *The Corsini Encyclopedia of Psychology and Behavioral Science,* "Paradoxical psychotherapy ... is an intervention in which therapists create a paradox by reinforcing the behavior to be changed, ... and telling the patient to change by remaining unchanged" (Shoham, 2001, p. 1129).

The PsycINFO *Thesaurus of Psychological Index Terms* (American Psychological Association, 2002b) included the term *Paradoxical Techniques*, but does not list *paradoxical psychotherapy* or *paradoxical intervention*. However, it is possible to search on them as Keywords (words in either the Abstract or the Title, or on the lists of Descriptors or Identifiers). The *Thesaurus* listed *Paradoxical Techniques*, defined as: "Techniques designed to disrupt dysfunctional behavior patterns through systematically encouraging them, thus allaying anticipatory anxiety, creating resistance to the symptomatic behavior, or enabling clients to achieve voluntary control over this behavior" (American Psychological Association, 2002b). All three terms—*paradoxical techniques, paradoxical psychotherapy,* and *paradoxical intervention*—were used for the searches.

Strategy.   Because of the differences in controlled vocabularies (described earlier), I did not use Descriptors listed in thesauri. The search option available in all databases was the Keyword or Subject search, and so, to maintain consistency among the searches, I used this free-text searching method. For the three databases that retrieved the most records (the two versions of PsycINFO plus PubMed), I searched twice, limiting the search to a Publication Type on the second searches.

Years and databases searched.   I limited my searches to literature for the years 1980–2002 (in some databases the date ranges available for searching were different; those are noted in Table 5.3). I selected the following bibliographic databases, which support the disciplines for the social, medical, and behavioral sciences:

ABI/Inform (via the California Digital Library, or CDL).

Anthropological Literature (via CDL).

Biosis Previews (two versions via two providers: CDL and the vendor Ovid).

Current Contents (via CDL).

Digital Dissertations–Dissertations Abstracts International (via the vendor UMI Proquest).

ERIC (via the vendor Cambridge Scientific Abstracts, or CSA).

FirstSearch (via FirstSearch/OCLC).

Medline/PubMed (via the National Center for Biotechnology Information, National Library of Medicine).

PsycINFO (two versions via two providers: CDL and the vendor CSA).

Sociological Abstracts (via CSA).

TABLE 5.3
Comparison of Numbers of Citations Found in Searches
on Three Keywords or Search Terms for the Years 1980–2002

| | Keywords/Phrase | | |
| | Paradoxical Techniques | Paradoxical Psychotherapy | Paradoxical Intervention |
Database	Number of Records Retrieved	Number of Records Retrieved	Number of Records Retrieved
PsycINFO (CDL version)	625	241	185
+ publication type: empirical study	283	65	92
PsycINFO (CSA version)	452	157	152
+ publication type: empirical study	241	2	51
Medline/PubMed (no specified field)	765	189	125
+ publication type: randomized control trial	20	11	7
Biosis (CDL) 1985–2002	143	21	66
Biosis (Ovid) 1990–2002	2	3	6
ABI/Inform	0	4	0
Anthropological Literature	0	1	0
Dissertation Abstracts International	9	2	18
Current Contents*	2	4	10
ERIC	25	0	1
OCLC FirstSearch	3	8	4

*This version of Current Contents provides a Title Words search, but not a Keyword search.

Results of the Searches

Table 5.3 compares the number of citations retrieved from various databases that seem relevant to our topic. The results show different yields
from identical searches of identical databases from two different database vendors. These results strongly indicated that, not only should scientists (looking for materials) search several different databases for their
subject, but they should also include in their search databases from as
many vendors as possible.

   PsycINFO.   Using the term *paradoxical techniques*, the search retrieved
625 citations from the CDL version of PsycINFO, whereas the CSA version
of PsycINFO yielded only 452 citations. With the term *paradoxical psychotherapy*, the CDL PsycINFO produced 241 citations compared to the CSA's

PsycINFO's 157. For the search on the term *paradoxical intervention,* the score was 185 to 152, with the CDL PsycINFO winning again!

The differences between the two versions of PsycINFO (in the number of citations retrieved) was so dramatic that I contacted Michael Yonezawa, Reference/Electronic Resources Librarian at the University of California, Riverside, to ask why these differences occurred. He and Lorna Lueck, PsycINFO Resource Liaison at the University of California, Santa Barbara, provided me with a detailed and technical explanation about the way each database searches its records (L. Lueck, personal communication, September 27, 2002. M. Yonezawa, personal communication, September 27, 2002). For our purposes, here, I simplify that explanation:

1. A Keyword search using the CDL version of PsycINFO is an "automatic" search, and it searches on the following fields: Abstract, Key Phrase, Thesaurus Terms, Title, and (in books) Table of Contents. It automatically includes the results from any match of terms (also called "Subject Headings") in PsycINFO's thesaurus; and the term *paradoxical techniques* is in the thesaurus (L. Lueck, personal communication, September 27, 2002.)

The CDL version searches on the two words—for example, *paradoxical* and *techniques*—and it is not necessary for the two words to be displayed together as long as they are in the indexed fields that are being searched (California Digital Library Services, personal communication, September 27, 2002). Say, for example, a scientist wants to search on the term *paradoxical techniques.* An abstract might state that "in this study the psychotherapeutic methods can be described as 'paradoxical,'" an example in which the keyword *paradoxical* appears without the word *techniques,* but nevertheless is a description of a document that certainly seems to be relevant to the search.

2. A Keyword search using the CSA version of PsycINFO searches on the Abstract, Descriptors, Identifiers, and Title fields. The search engine is not looking for the two words; instead, it is looking for the whole term *paradoxical techniques* (L. Lueck, personal communication, September 27, 2002). In a Keyword it is necessary for the two words to be displayed together in the indexed fields being searched (California Digital Library Services, personal communication, September 27, 2002). Thus, in order to retrieve the article "The Paradox: A Crucial Element in Psychotherapy" (Jenkins, 1991) we had to search on the Keywords *paradoxical* and *psychotherapy* because nowhere in the title or abstract do these words appear together.

We should note here that the differences in the searching methods in these two versions of the database do not always produce different numbers of citations. For example, in a search using the author *Rosnow* and the keyword *ethics*, both database versions retrieved eight publications, including Rosnow's 1997 "Hedgehogs, Foxes, and the Evolving Contract in Psychological Science: Ethical Challenges and Methodological Opportunities" (Rosnow, 1997). The CDL PsycINFO retrieved this record using the word *ethics* as part of *experimental ethics* and *professional ethics* in the Thesaurus Terms field. The CAS PsycINFO used the same terms (*experimental ethics* and *professional ethics*) but found them in the Descriptors field.

According to an advertisement issued by the American Psychological Association (APA), PsycINFO is available from the following vendors: APA, Aries Systems, Cambridge Scientific Abstracts, DataStar (Switzerland), Dialog, DIMDI (Germany), EBSCO, Elsevier Science ScienceDirect, Hogrefe & Huber (Switzerland), NISC, OCLC, Ovid Technologies, Proquest, and SilverPlatter Information. (A comprehensive comparison of these various versions of PsycINFO would be an interesting undertaking).

Biosis. Table 5.3 also shows a sizable difference in number of records found between two versions of Biosis—the CDL (California Digital Library) version, and Biosis as sold by the vendor Ovid Technologies.

PubMed. The Medline/PubMed search on *paradoxical intervention* yielded 125 records, but many of the titles suggest that the content is probably about medical interventions, and perhaps only about 35 are really relevant to the search. When the searcher enters a phrase, PubMed first tries to match the phrase to MeSH. If it does not find the phrase as a match to MeSH, it then searches each word of the phrase as text words, and the words *paradoxical* and *intervention* did not appear together in many of the records. A careful reading of the abstract of each citation would be necessary to assess each one's value as part of a collection of articles about paradoxical psychotherapy.

The Medline/PubMed citation yield for the term *paradoxical psychotherapy* was 189, and a reading of the titles suggests that these publications are more relevant than are those that were found under the subject search *paradoxical intervention*. Only 24 of the 189 found were also found in PsycINFO, but some other than those 24 articles appeared to be quite relevant to the topic. For example, an abstract for an article titled "The Ethical Use of Paradoxical Interventions in Psychotherapy" (Foreman, 1990) was found in both the PubMed and Current Contents searches. It clearly met our search criteria, but it was not found in either PsycINFO database because it was published in the *Journal of Medical Ethics*, a journal that is not among the 1,800 journals that PsycINFO *does* index (American Psychological Association, 2002a).

Overlap Among Databases

Searches on the term *paradoxical techniques* yielded large numbers of records, but because the term as used in Biosis and PubMed often refers to medical and biological techniques not related to psychotherapy, I did not compare the yields of the searches using that term. I did, however, compare the overlap in the searches using the terms *paradoxical psychotherapy* and *paradoxical intervention*. Using all the records found under those terms, I compared all other databases (listed in Table 5.3) against the CDL version of PsycINFO. Table 5. 4 shows the number of records *not* found in that version of PschINFO but found in eight other databases. These results seem to reinforce the notion that using a variety of databases for searching is useful.

CONCLUSION

The searches reported here are simply examples that point up some reference databases' differences and idiosyncrasies. Vendors of reference databases are uneven in their coverage, and not every database can index every publication relevant to a particular scientist's interest. The meta-analyst may make use of the following suggestions:

1. Select a variety of terms to search. Do not limit the search the first time it is done; use free-text rather than thesauri (keeping in mind that not

TABLE 5.4

Number of Citations Found in Databases Other Than PsycINFO in Searches on Two Keywords or Search Terms for the Years 1980–2002

Database	*Number of Records Not Found in CDL Version of PsycINFO*	
	Paradoxical Psychotherapy	*Paradoxical Intervention*
ABI/Inform	0	3
Anthropological Literature	1	0
Biosis (CDL) 1985–2002	16	5
Current Contents	3	8
Dissertation Abstracts International	2	4
Medline/PubMed	164	19
PsycINFO (CSA)	2	4
OCLC FirstSearch	4	2
Σ	192	45

all records are thoroughly indexed and assigned appropriate Descriptors). A broad search yields more records than are relevant, but it is much easier to limit the search after looking at what the broad search has yielded.

2. Search a number of databases (even some that might seem less relevant to the search) and, if possible, search the same database from two different vendors. There is never complete overlap between two databases, and often there is not complete overlap even between two different versions of the same database.

3. If searching many databases (as is advised), devise a structured method for keeping records: names of databases searched, the search strategy used in the searches, and information about the relevant records retrieved. It is useful to build a database for these data, with authors in one field, dates in another, and so on, so that it can be searched in different ways (Lipsey & Wilson, 2001; Rosenthal, 1994).

Computer-readable reference databases are but one method for collecting studies. They have somewhat simplified the process and certainly decreased the amount of time once needed for using abstracts, but the searching process is still rather complicated for the scientist attempting to collect all the empirical studies on a given research question. Perhaps in the future, as providers and vendors compete for business, they will develop and standardize search procedures to make them more user friendly.

REFERENCES

American Psychological Association. (2002a). *PsycINFO journal coverage list.* Washington, DC: Author.

American Psychological Association. (2002b). *Thesaurus of psychological index terms.* Retrieved July 23, 2002, from the PsycINFO Database. http://www/csa2.com/hybin/ids52/thescli...esults.html

American Psychological Association. (2002c). Record retrieved October 2, 2002, from the PsycInfo Database: http://www.csa2/htbin/ids60/proccskel.cgi?fn= adresults_list.html&ctx=/wais/idstmp/ctx

Bowker Co. (1983). *Information industry marketplace: An international directory of information products and services.* New York: Author.

Chen, H., Martinez, J., Kirchhoff, A., Ng, T. D., & Schatz, B. R. (1998). Alleviating search uncertainty through concept associations: automatic indexing, co-occurrence analysis, and parallel computing. *Journal of the American Society for Information Science, 49,* 206–216.

Cooper, H. M. (1998). *Integrating research: A guide for literature reviews* (3rd ed.). Thousand Oaks, CA: Sage.

Covington, M. A., & Downing, D. (1992). *Dictionary of computer terms* (3rd ed.). Hauppauge, NY: Barron's.

Cuadra Associates. (1979). *Directory of online databases.* Santa Monica, CA: Author.

Fidel, R. (1991). Searchers' selection of search keys II: Controlled vocabulary or free-text searching. *Journal of the American Society for Information Science, 42,* 501–514.

Foreman, D. M. (1990). The ethical use of paradoxical techniques in psychotherapy. *Journal of Medical Ethics, 16,* 200–205. Abstract retrieved October 2, 2002, from http://www.ncbi.nlm.nih.gov/entrez/query.fcgi?cmd=Retrieve&db= PubMed& list_uids=2287C

Gale Research Co. (1983, 1986). *Abstracting and indexing services directory.* Detroit: Author.

Hall, J. L., & Brown, M. J. (1983). Online bibliographic databases: An international directory. London: ASLIB.

Jenkins, H. (1991). The paradox: A crucial element in psychotherapy. *Magyar Pszichologiai, 47,* 361–380. Abstract retrieved October 2, 2002, from http//www.dbs. cdlib.org/mw/mwcgi?sesid=2658121237&ZS9.1/CM&CScs=9&Cdisplay

Lipsey, M. W., & Wilson, D. B. (2001). *Practical meta analysis.* Thousand Oaks, CA: Sage.

Morris, W. (Ed.). (1970). *American heritage dictionary of the English language.* New York: American Heritage Publishing Co.

Reed, J. G., & Baxter, P. M. (1994). Using reference databases. In H. Cooper & L. V. Hedges (Eds.), *Handbook of research synthesis* (pp. 85–94). New York: Russell Sage Foundation.

Rosenthal, M. C. (1985). Bibliographic retrieval for the social and behavioral scientist. *Research in Higher Education, 22*(4), 315–333.

Rosenthal, M. C. (1994). The fugitive literature. In H. Cooper & L. V. Hedges (Eds.), *Handbook of research synthesis* (pp. 85–94). New York: Russell Sage Foundation.

Rosnow, R. L. (1997) Hedgehogs, foxes, and the evolving contract in psychological science: Ethical challenges and methodological opportunities. *Psychological Methods, 2,* 345–356. Abstract retrieved October 2, 2002, from http//www.csa2.com/htbin/ids60/procskel.egi ?fn=advresults_list.html

Rosnow, R L., & Rosnow, M. (2003). *Writing papers in psychology: A student guide* (6th ed.). Belmont, CA.: Wadsworth.

Shoham, V. (2001). Paradoxical intervention. In W. E. Craighead & C. B. Nemeroff (Eds.), The Corsini encyclopedia of psychology and behavioral science (3rd ed., Vol. 3, pp. 1129–1131). New York: Wiley.

Smith, M. L., & Glass, G. V. (1977). Meta analysis of psychotherapy outcome studies. *American Psychologist, 32*(9) 752–760. Abstract retrieved September 7, 2002, from http//www.csa2.com/htbin/ids52/procskel.cgi

Sydell, E. J., & Nelson, E. S. (2000). Modern racism on campus: A survey of attitudes and perceptions. *Social Science Journal, 37,* 627–635. Abstract retrieved October 11, 2002, from http//www.dbs.cdlib.org/mw/mwcgi?sesid=2429728710&ZS4.2/ CM&CScs=4&Cdisplay

Thomson Dialog. (2002). *Gale directory of online, portable, and internet databases.* Retrieved September 2, 2002, from http://library.dialog.com.bluesheets/html/bl0230.html

Williams, M. E. (1979/1982). *Computer-readable databases: A directory and data sourcebook.* White Plains: NY: Knowledge Industry Publications.

6

Rebuilding the Ship at Sea: Coping With Artifacts in Behavioral Research

David B. Strohmetz
Monmouth University

We are as sailors who are forced to rebuild their ship on the open sea, without ever being able to start fresh from the bottom up.

—Otto Neurath (1921)

Ralph Rosnow and Bob Rosenthal began their book *People Studying People* (1997) with this epigraph to characterize the nature of science. They wanted to convey the notion that, in order to advance, science must have its flaws and weaknesses continually identified and improved on by scientists who never have the benefit of simply "starting over" in the pursuit of knowledge. Therefore, it becomes incumbent on current researchers to pass on what they have learned about these flaws and limitations to future generations. In this light, the career of Ralph Rosnow has exemplified one of being the consummate researcher—a scientist who not only advanced our understanding of psychological phenomena, as other chapters in this book attest, but also one who has sought to improve behavioral research as a scientific endeavor (e.g., see Kimmel, chap. 7, this volume). This chapter focuses on Ralph's contributions to our understanding of what has become commonly known as the "social psychology of the experiment" (Rosnow, Strohmetz, & Aditya, 2000).

It is not surprising that among Ralph's many interests was the nature of the psychological experiment itself. An underlying theme in Ralph's work has been his interest in how people give meaning to their social situations. Ralph recognized, as Rosenzweig did back in 1933, that this is true even within the context of the psychological experiment. Contrary to the implicit view of early psychologists who hoped to simply apply the methodology used in the natural sciences to the study of psychological phenomenon, humans are not merely reagents reacting to experimental stimuli of interest to the researcher (Rosnow, 1983, 1993). Rather, they are sentient and thinking organisms who are often aware that they are filling the role of "research subject." In this role, they are not merely reacting to the experimental stimuli, but are also seeking to understand the purpose of the experiment and how they should be behave accordingly (Strohmetz & Rosnow, 1994). As such, the conclusions that research participants draw concerning the experiment can sometimes influence their behavior as much as the independent variable of interest, threatening the validity of otherwise carefully controlled studies. *Research artifact* is the term commonly used to refer to those factors that can lead to these systematic, uncontrolled biases in an experiment (Rosenthal & Rosnow, 1991).

Similar to the sailors in Neurath's metaphor, Ralph's career illustrates both his dissatisfaction with simply pointing out the "weak planks" in behavior research stemming from the artifact problem and his desire to improve the ship of science. This chapter focuses on a theoretical model first proposed by Ralph (Rosnow & Aiken, 1973; Rosnow & Davis 1977) and later refined by Strohmetz and Rosnow (1994) that conceptualizes how artifacts may be introduced into a research study. This model provides a "blueprint" for identifying and replacing scientific planks weakened by the problem of research artifacts by suggesting ways in which this problem may be controlled or minimized.

BACKGROUND OF THE PROBLEM

Although recognition of the problem of artifacts in behavioral research is now commonly accepted, this has not always been the case, despite early indications to the contrary. As early as 1885, Hermann Ebbinghaus acknowledged the problem of artifacts in human subject research (as cited in Rosenthal & Rosnow, 1991). There were other early indications that the methodology used to investigate phenomena in the natural sciences may be problematic for behavioral science research. For example, a turn-of-the-century horse, named "Clever Hans," showed how artifacts can simply result from an observer's expectations or hypotheses (Pfungst, 1911/1965). Clever Hans was credited with extraordinary intellectual abilities such as mathematical reasoning. Through a systematic investigation, a German psychologist, Oskar Pfungst, revealed that the "cleverness" of Clever Hans was due not to his intellectual abilities but rather to his abilities to respond to the subtle, unintentional cues of his questioners. Although Pfungst's investigation dramatically demonstrated the impact that expectations can have on even animal behavior, the broader implications may not have been fully recognized by early behavioral scientists.

A series of field experiments conducted at the Western Electric Company's Hawthorne Works in Illinois between 1924 and 1932 provided another indication that the straightforward application of the methodology used in the natural sciences may be problematic for the behavioral sciences (Roethlisberger & Dickson, 1939). Roethlisberger and Dickson were interested in the effect of workplace conditions on worker productivity and job satisfaction. Although what actually occurred during these experiments have been the subject of much controversy and misinterpretations (see Adair, 1984; Gillespie, 1988; Olson, Verley, Santos, & Salas, 2004; Parsons, 1974, 1992), the findings indicated that humans are reactive, not passive participants in the research process. This idea has become known as the *Hawthorne effect*—a term first coined by French (1953) to represent the idea that the simple act of observing can influence the behavior of those being observed. Over the years, the term *Hawthorne effect* has also become viewed as a *placebo effect* in psychological research because of its connotations about the power of suggestion in behavioral research (Sommer, 1968).

The challenging nature of conducting research involving humans did not go completely unheeded by early psychologists. In what is now considered a landmark paper, Rosenzweig (1933) argued that psychologists must recognize that research participants do not react to experimental stimuli in a naïve manner. Rather, they are implicit psychologists themselves who are interested not only in the purpose of the experiment but also what it reveals about them. Rosenzweig suggested that this interest can influence the participants' experimental behaviors.

Despite signs early in the history of psychology that the methodology utilized in the natural sciences could not simply be applied to the study of humans, little acknowledgment was given to the potential problem that unidentified artifacts create when evaluating the validity of behavioral research outcomes and their implications. However, it was obvious that there must have been some underlying feeling that psychological observations were not immune from unconscious biases, as evident from the frequent use of deception in behavioral research (Rosnow, 1983). McGuire (1969) characterized psychology as being in the "ignorance" stage of interest in this problem, when researchers were seemingly unaware of the problem and, if made aware, simply denied its existence.

Nevertheless, evidence concerning the artifact problem kept mounting until it could no longer be denied or ignored. According to McGuire (1969), researchers now entered the second stage—the "coping phase"— in which the focus became on identifying potential research artifacts and developing procedures that would reduce their threat to the validity of a study. Finally, McGuire suggested that the natural progression of interest in the research artifact finally led to the third stage—the exploitation stage. It is at this point that the variables that were once viewed as a threat to one's research that must be minimized or controlled now became variables of interest in their own right. As is evident in the discussion of his theoretical model, Ralph's research into artifacts, particularly into the nature of the volunteer subject, characterizes McGuire's last stage in the life of an artifact—the exploitation stage.

Ralph's goal was not to simply develop a list of potential research artifacts, but rather to develop an overall theory of how artifacts may be introduced into an otherwise well-designed study, thereby jeopardizing the validity of the conclusions that can be drawn from that study. In the spirit of Kurt Lewin, who once wrote, "There is nothing as practical as a good theory" (Lewin, 1951), the benefit of developing a theory of how artifacts can jeopardize one's study is that it implies strategies that one can implement to prevent or minimize potential research artifacts. In this sense, Ralph is like one of Neurath's sailors as he passes his wisdom on to future sailors who will assume the responsibility of rebuilding and maintaining the ship of science.

THE MODEL

By the 1970s, the problem of artifacts in behavioral research became so evident that researchers could no longer claim ignorance and had to develop coping strategies for dealing with this issue (Rosnow, 1981). Ralph recognized that what was lacking in the attempt to cope with the artifact problem was a conceptual framework by which one could identify (and subsequently control or eliminate) potential artifacts that can emerge during the course of an experiment (Rosnow & Rosenthal, 1997). Such a framework (see Fig. 6.1) was first proposed by Rosnow and Aiken (1973) and later refined by Rosnow and Davis (1977) as well as by Strohmetz and Rosnow (1994). The premise behind this model is that the typical experimental situation is, in essence, a social interaction. However, what makes this social interaction different from other social interactions is that when the research participant agrees to enter into this interaction, he or she is making an explicit agreement to fulfill a specific role, namely the role of the "research participant" (Orne, 1962). As part of this agreement, the participant assumes a subservient role, agreeing to fulfill the experimenter's requests, often without question. Orne (1962) illustrated this idea in a field experiment. When individuals who agreed only to do a favor for the experimenter were asked to perform five pushups, they typically responded, "Why?" However, when they were asked to do five pushups after agreeing to participate in a brief experiment, their question became, "Where?"

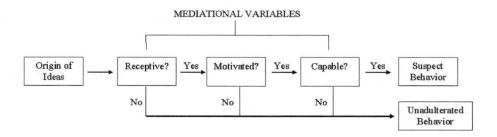

FIG. 6.1.   A mediational model of research artifacts.

Despite assuming a subservient role to the experimenter's requests, the participant is often unaware of what behavioral expectations will be made of him or her in the experimental situation. As such, the participant will look to situational cues for guidance as to how he or she should behave in these novel situations. The implication is that the behavior of the research participant may not only be due to the influence of the independent variable but also due to other, more subtle situational cues that are not obvious to the experimenter.

Ralph suggested that if one views the experiment as a social interaction influenced by role expectations and behavioral norms, then one might develop a model describing the process by which artifacts can be introduced into an experimental situation. Ralph proposed a five-step mediatory model to characterize this process. Key to this model is the role of three mediatory variables. These variables are central in determining the likelihood that a research participant's behavior is due to the "unadulterated effects" of the experimental variables of interest rather than to one or more research artifacts.

The first mediatory variable is receptivity. In order for a participant's behavior to be influenced by an artifact, the participant must first be receptive to the presence of an artifact. Next, the participant must be motivated to act on the knowledge of this task-orienting cue. Finally, even if the participant is aware of and motivated to act on an artifact, he or she must have the capability to actually change his or her behavior in response to the artifact. Strohmetz and Rosnow (1994) characterized this process as a Markov process (see Fig. 6.1). They suggested that when there is a high likelihood that the participants are not only receptive to potential task-oriented cues but are also motivated and capable of acting on these cues, researchers should be especially concerned with the probability that the participants' behaviors are due to artifacts rather than to the variables of interest. One of the advantages of this model is that it suggests not only possible avenues of research in the investigation of artifacts in their own right (McGuire, 1969), but also ways that researchers can minimize the possibility that the effects of their variables of interest on behavior have been compromised by the presence of research artifacts.

Origin of Ideas

Although in an ideal world a research participant would enter the experimental situation naïve to not only the purpose of the study but also what behaviors he or she would be expected to engage in, this may not necessarily be the case in actual studies. The participant may already have formed conclusions about the experiment as well as his or her role, which can influence the person's behavior as much if not more so than can the variables of interest. What may serve as the basis for these conclusions? Because in American psychology many experiments rely heavily on college students as their participants (Higbee & Wells, 1972; Jung, 1969; Schultz, 1969; Smart, 1966), one potential source may stem simply from the use of this population. Campus scuttlebutt or rumors may provide the participant with a wealth of information as to the "true" purpose of the experiment (Orne, 1962; for more discussion on the nature of rumors, see Rosnow, 1991).

Another source may simply be what information participants have been exposed to during the course of their education. For example, information presented during class lectures that students attend can influence their behaviors in subsequent experimental studies. Orne (1970) showed how the behavior that one exhibits while hypnotized can reflect prior beliefs about hypnosis. During a classroom lecture on hypnosis, Orne announced that one characteristic behavior induced by hypnosis was "catalepsy of the dominant hand." Although seemingly plausible, this was a novel behavioral characteristic of hypnosis that Orne concocted to test whether or not one's behavior during a hypnosis experiment resulted from the hypnotic state itself or one's prior beliefs of how a hypnotized person should act. In another class, Orne gave the same lecture, but omitted the mention of this characteristic as a typical hypnotic behavior. Approximately 1 month later, Orne recruited volunteer students from both classes for a hypnosis experiment. After hypnotizing the participants, Orne did observe individuals displaying catalepsy of the dominant hand. However, all of these individuals were from the class that had learned that this behavior was supposedly exhibited by people when they were hypnotized. The implication is that if prior to entering the experimental situation research participants have developed ideas about what behaviors are expected of them, questions must be raised as to whether the participants' behaviors are due to the variables of interest or to participants' a priori beliefs about how they are supposed to behave in the experiment.

Receptivity

Even if a participant enters an experimental situation with a priori beliefs concerning the purpose of the experiment, the participant may still be apprehensive and uncertain as to the exact behaviors that will be expected of him or her (Hendrick, 1977). Orne (1962) argued that in order to reduce this uncertainty, research participants will engage in a type of problem-solving behavior, trying to discern the "true" purpose of the study. Orne referred to the cues that participants use to formulate these personal hypotheses about the study as the "demand characteristics" of the experimental situation. Although every experimental situation will have demand characteristics present to some degree (Brenner & Bungard, 1981), the extent to which they are salient to the participant will have an impact on whether these cues have introduced a potential artifact into the experimental situation (Orne, 1962).

Based on this assumption, the second step in the proposed model is the mediatory step of receptivity. Participants must be aware of the presence of the demand characteristics if they are to alter their behavior accordingly. If participants are unaware of the presence of these behavior-orienting cues, then there is increased confidence that their experimental behaviors are unadulterated by these demand characteristics. However, if the demand characteristics are salient, the question must be raised concerning whether the participants are responding to the independent variables of interest, the demand characteristics, or a combination of both.

There are at least two sources of demand characteristics in every experimental situation. The first source is the experiment itself. Sometimes, participants glean what the purpose of the experiment is as well as what is expected of them from the experimental procedure. Pretest-posttest research designs commonly used in attitude change and learning studies provide an example of this possibility, because the pretest may sensitize participants that some change in attitude or behavior is expected of them (Lana, 1969).

A second, rich source of demand characteristics is the experimenter himself or herself (Rosenthal, 1969, 1976). Personal characteristics of the experimenter—such as physical attractiveness, gender, or attire—can influence the behavior of research participants (Barnes & Rosenthal, 1985; Rosenthal, 1967). The experimenter, who has a vested interest in the outcome of the experiment, may even unintentionally influence the behavior of the participants in the study. In an experimental variation of the self-fulfilling prophecy (Merton, 1948), the experimenter may unconsciously convey his or her expectations as to how the participant should behave in response to the experimental treatment. For example, Rosenthal and Fode (1963b) conducted a study in which student-experimenters had participants evaluate how successful or unsuccessful they thought people were simply based on the people's facial photographs. Although all of the student-experimenters were given identical instructions on how to conduct the study, they were given differing expectations as to the purpose of the study. Half of the student-experimenters were informed that the study was to replicate a well-established finding that participants will give the photographs high successful ratings, whereas the remaining student-experimenters were told that they would be replicating the finding that people will give the photographs high failure ratings. The results revealed that student-experimenters who were expecting high success ratings did indeed obtained higher success photo ratings than did those who expected high failure ratings.

Interestingly, Rosenthal and his colleagues found that this interpersonal expectancy effect (Rosenthal, 1985, 1994) was not limited to research involving humans. Rosenthal and Fode (1963a) gave 12 student-experimenters five rats each to train to run a maze with visual cues. Half of the student-experimenters were led to believe that their rats had been specifically bred to easily learn this task, whereas the other student-experimenters were informed that their rats had been bred for "maze dullness." Although there were no initial differences between the two groups of rats, rats trained by student-experimenters who held high expectations for them learned to run the maze significantly quicker than did their fellow "maze dull" rats. The implication of this and other similar studies (Rosenthal, 1994; Rosenthal & Rubin, 1978) is that an experimenter's unintentional behaviors can convey messages as to the purpose of the experiment as well as to the expected role of the participant in the experiment.

The second step in this artifact model suggests that if participants are receptive to or aware of the presence of demand characteristics, then questions must be raised as to whether or not the resulting behavior is a reflection of the experimental treatment or a reflection of a research artifact. If participants are either unaware of, or not receptive to, the presence of task-orienting cues, then there can be increased confidence that their behavior has not been influenced by such cues.

Motivation

The next step in the model, motivation, reflects the recognition that it is not only necessary for participants to be receptive to the presence of demand characteristics in the experimental situation, but they must also be motivated to alter their experimental behavior in response to this awareness. Even if a participant is cognizant of potential task-orienting cues, if the person is not motivated to act on this knowledge, then the researcher can have increased confidence that the participant's behavior was not due to these potential research artifacts. However, if the participant is not only aware of the demand characteristics, but also motivated to act on them, then there is increased concern that the experimental outcome may be the result of a research artifact.

What type of motivations may guide a participant's behavior during the experiment? Orne (1962) argued that individuals frequently enter experimental situations because they wish to help the cause of science. As such, they are willing to engage in a wide range of behaviors with remarkable diligence simply because they are participating in a study.

This desire to engage in any behavior that will seemingly help the cause of the science became evident to Orne (1962) as he attempted to develop a meaningless task that most individuals would either refuse to do outright or quit doing after a short period of time. Orne told participants that their task was to sum adjacent numbers in rows of random numbers that filled an entire sheet of paper. To do this task, the participant would need to do 224 separate calculations. The experimenter then gave the participants approximately 2,000 sheets of numbers and told them to continue to work until the experimenter returned. Orne reasoned that the participants would quickly learn that this was an impossible task (they would have to do some 448,000 calculations!) and therefore would stop working on the task. However, after 5½ hours, it was the experimenter, not the participants, who gave up! Trying to make the task appear even more meaningless, Orne had another set of participants engage in the same task with the added instruction that they were to tear each completed worksheet up into a minimum of 32 separate pieces before starting the next page of calculation. Again, the participants engaged in this task with extraordinary diligence.

Based on these and similar findings, Orne reasoned that one powerful motivation underlying participants' experimental behavior is the belief that regardless of what they will be asked to do, it will somehow contribute to the cause of science and ultimately to humankind in general. Because of this belief, Orne posited that participants will want to do whatever is necessary to ensure that they have made a useful contribution and that the experiment is considered a success. Orne referred to these research participants as being "good subjects" because they want to help the experimenter achieve his or her experimental aims (see also Rosnow, 1970). This motivation to be a "good subject" may explain an interesting finding by Resnick and Schwartz (1973). To assess the impact that full adoption of the then-proposed ethical standards for collecting data, Resnick and Schwartz conducted a study in which one group was given full disclosure of the purpose of the study while the other group was treated under the prevailing procedures of the day. Resnick and Schwartz had extreme difficulty recruiting participants for the study once they had fully disclosed the true purpose and hypotheses of the study. Resnick and Schwartz speculated that because so much was being disclosed, the potential participants did not take the research study very seriously. In other words, the participants were not motivated to help the researcher and the cause of science because they may have believed the fully disclosed study to be a joke and therefore a waste of their time.

If the motivation to help the cause of science by being a good subject is an important determinant in one's responsiveness to demand characteristics, then one must consider which participants are most likely to have this motivation. Rosenthal and Rosnow (1975) speculated that individuals who volunteer to participate in research are more likely to be motivated by this cause and therefore willing to play the role of the "good subject." In a series of studies, Rosnow and his colleagues (e.g., Goldstein, Rosnow, Goodstadt, & Suls, 1972; Rosnow, Rosenthal, McConochie, & Arms, 1969; Rosnow & Suls, 1970) showed that one's volunteer status was an important factor in determining how accommodating participants were to salient demand characteristics. For example, Rosnow and Suls (1970) found that volunteers were more sensitized by pretesting and subsequently more accommodating to one-sided attitude manipulations than were nonvolunteers. Similarly, Goldstein et al. (1972) found that volunteers for a verbal operant conditioning study were more responsive to the verbal reinforcement than were nonvolunteers for the study.

In an early application of meta-analysis, Rosenthal and Rosnow (1975) examined the literature comparing characteristics of volunteers and nonvolunteers for research, and found systematic differences that have the potential of threatening the internal, external, and construct validity of a study. In general, Rosenthal and Rosnow discerned that, compared to nonvolunteers, volunteers tend to be better educated, higher in social class, more intelligent, higher in need for social approval, and more sociable. Rosenthal and Rosnow argued that the volunteer status of the research participants might be a determinant of the outcome of a study (Rosenthal & Rosnow, 1975; Rosnow & Rosenthal, 1976). For example, in addition to the experimental studies previously discussed (Goldstein et al., 1972; Rosnow & Suls, 1970), Strohmetz, Alterman, and Walter (1990) determined that volunteer differences can raise validity concerns in randomized clinical research studies.

Whereas Orne (1962) argued that research participants are motivated by the desire to help the cause of science, Rosenberg (1965, 1969) suggested that participants are motivated by a desire to "look good." Rosenberg argued that when one enters an experimental situation, one is very aware that his or her behavior will be evaluated in some way by the experimenter. This awareness will induce some anxiety in the participant, as evidenced by questions frequently heard during experimental debriefings, such as, "How did I do—were my responses (answers) normal?" "What were you really trying to find out, whether I'm some kind of neurotic?" "Did I react the same as most people do?" (Rosenberg, 1969, p. 282). Because of this anxiety, Rosenberg suggested that participants are motivated to form hypotheses as to the best way to obtain a favorable evaluation from the experimenter. If the perceived demand characteristics provide the participant with an opportunity to obtain such an evaluation, then the person will be motivated to alter his or her behavior in response to these cues. In situations where acquiescing to the demand characteristics may lead to an unfavorable evaluation, research participants will be more motivated to earn a positive evaluation rather than help the cause of science. For example, Rosnow, Goodstadt, Suls, and Gitter (1973) noted that when participants were put in a situation that created a conflict between "looking good" and "being a good subject," participants tended to respond in a manner that favored a positive evaluation (see also Sigall, Aronson, & Van Hoose, 1970).

Obedience to authority may be a third motivation for participants to act on their awareness of demand characteristics operating in the experimental situation. Participants may perceive task-orienting cues as indications of how the experimenter expects the participants to behave. Consequently, the participants will behave in this manner simply because the experimenter is viewed as an authority figure whose desires are to be fulfilled (Hendrick, 1977; Rosnow & Rosenthal, 1997). Rosnow and Rosenthal (1997) described this motivation as the desire to be "faithful subjects."

The recognition of demand characteristics presented in an experimental situation does not immediately imply that the experimental results have been influenced by these task-orienting cues. Participants must also be motivated to alter their experimental behavior as a result of this awareness. If the participant is motivated by a desire to be a "good subject," then he or she would be especially likely to acquiesce to demand characteristics that provide indications of the experimenter's hypotheses and expectations. If the participant's experimental behavior is motivated by a desire to "look good," then he or she would likely be influenced by task-orienting cues that can help the participant to alleviate his or her evaluation apprehension. Finally, if the participant has a strong desire to be a "faithful subject," then he or she will comply with the demand characteristics simply because the experimenter is viewed as an authority figure.

Capability

The third and final mediational variable in this model concerns whether or not the participants have the capability of altering their behavior even if they are receptive to the presence of demand characteristics and motivated to act on this awareness. For example, participants may not be biologically capable of altering their behavior in response to task-orienting cues. Likewise, to respond to these cues may require behaviors that are outside the bounds of the participant's normal capabilities. In these situations, it is unlikely that the participant's response to the independent variable has been adulterated by the presence of demand characteristics.

Rosnow and Rosenthal (1997; Rosnow & Aiken, 1973; Rosnow & Davis, 1977; Strohmetz & Rosnow, 1994) have suggested this step may be least important in raising concern over whether or not participants' behavior may have been due to artifacts rather than the independent variable. Experimenters are very unlikely to design a study in which participants are incapable of responding in ways consistent with the experimenters' own expectations for the reason that such a design would most likely also preclude the participants from being able to perform the behaviors of interest.

Outcome Behavior

The final step in this theoretical model is the decision of whether or not the participant's behavior should be considered an adulterated response to the independent variable under investigation. If a research participant is not only receptive to the presence of possible demand characteristics in the experimental situation but also motivated and capable of responding to those cues, then suspicions must be raised about the participant's behavior. The experimenter will not be able to clearly discern whether or not the participant's behavior is the result of the effect of the independent variable or the result of some other uncontrolled factors operating in the experimental situation. If any of these mediational steps are missing, then the chain leading to suspect behavior is broken and the experimenter can be more confident that the participant's behavior is due to the independent variable of interest rather than to research artifacts (Strohmetz & Rosnow, 1994).

MINIMIZING RESEARCH ARTIFACTS

One of the benefits of this model is that it provides, using Neurath's metaphor, a blueprint for future sailors as to how to strengthen the ship of science with respect to experimental design. The model suggests that an experimenter can have more confidence that the behavior under investigation is the result of the independent variable of interest rather than other uncontrolled factors if measures are taken at each step that will break the chain. For example, if demand characteristics are made less salient, then participants will be less receptive to their presence. If care is taken to reduce the participants' motivations to alter their behaviors in response to task-orienting cues, then the experimenter can be more confident that the resulting behaviors were due to research artifacts.

Receptivity

One way to diminish the potential that the research participants' behaviors are due to artifacts is to decrease or eliminate the likelihood that participants are aware of the presence of possible demand characteristics. For example, if the participant is unaware that he or she is participating in a study, as in the case of field studies using unobtrusive observational measures, than the participant will not be receptive to the presence of possible task-orienting cues. Although such studies might provide reassurance to the experimenter as to the unadulterated nature of the participants' reactions to the independent variable under investigation, they are limiting in that study of some behavioral phenomena necessitate the use of experimental designs in laboratory settings. Also, such studies can raise ethical concerns such as the issue of informed consent (Rosnow, 1997; Rosnow & Rosenthal, 1997).

The relationship between the experimental treatment and the measurement procedures can enhance the participants' receptivity to task-orienting cues, such as in the case of pretest-posttest designs. One option is to eliminate the use of pretesting in favor of posttest-only designs. However, this is not always possible given the researcher's question of interest. Another solution is to directly evaluate the effects that the use of pretesting may have had on behavioral responses by employing the use of the Solomon four-group design (Solomon, 1949; Solomon & Lessac, 1968; see also Rosenthal & Rosnow, 1991; Rosnow & Rosenthal, 2002). For example, Rosnow and Suls (1970) utilized the Solomon design in an attitude-change study to investigate the divergent effects that attitude manipulations can have on volunteer and nonvolunteer research participants.

Because task-orienting cues can result from the temporal proximity of the participant's exposure to treatment and measurement procedures, researchers may reduce receptivity to these cues by separating the experimental treatment and measurement procedures in both time and place. For example, one person may be responsible for implementing the experimental treatment whereas another individual, ideally at a later time, administers the outcome measures. This separation of treatment and measurement procedures may help make the connection between these two procedures more ambiguous, thus reducing the probability that participants will perceive this relationship as a potential source of task-orienting cues.

In an effort to reduce participants' receptivity to potential demand characteristics, special attention must be given to the experimenter's own behavior as a source of research artifacts. Although certainly standardization and restriction of communication between the experimenter and the research participant may reduce receptivity, one must also be aware that the experimenter's unconscious behavior can lead to an experimenter expectancy effect. One way of minimizing this potential bias is to incorporate the use of computers in the presentation of experimental instructions and possibly even treatment manipulations (Rosenthal, 1976, 1977). Another way is to employ the use of "blind" experimental procedures. For example, the experimenter who interacts with the participant is kept unaware of whether the participant is in the experimental or control condition. Likewise, this experimenter who interacts with the participant is unaware of, or has limited knowledge of, the experimental hypotheses, so that these expectations cannot be inadvertently communicated to the participant.

One strategy for examining the potential for an experimenter bias is to include experimenter expectancy in the experimental design as an independent variable in its own right (Rosenthal, 1966). For example, Burnham (1966; reported in Rosenthal, 1966, 1976) employed an expectancy control design into a study on the effects of brain lesions on discrimination learning in rats. Experimenters were given rats that had received either lesioning surgery to remove parts of their brain or superficial (i.e., sham) surgery that gave the appearance of brain lesioning but involved no destruction of the brain. To manipulate experimenter expectancy, Burnham informed half of the experimenters that their rats had received the lesioning surgery while the other half were told that their rats had received the sham surgery. Burnham found that although the actual lesioning of the rat's brain had effect on the rat's discrimination learning, so too did the experimenter's expectancy. Regardless of whether they had been lesioned or not, rats in the sham surgery expectancy group performed significantly better than did rats in the lesion surgery expectancy group. The benefit of employing the expectancy control designs in studies such as Burnham's is that it allows one to estimate the degree to which experimenter bias may have impacted the experimental results.

One additional method of reducing one's receptivity to the presence of demand characteristics is to make irrelevant task-orienting cues more salient than are the true experimental cues. For example, the experimenter might incorporate the use of deception into the experimental design. However, such strategies can give rise to other issues, such as ethical considerations (Kimmel, 1981, 1988; Rosnow & Rosenthal, 1997).

Motivation

Another avenue for avoiding the introduction of research artifacts into one's study is to reduce the motivation of participants to alter their behaviors in response to the presence of task-orienting cues. However, manipulating participants' motivations may be more difficult than minimizing their receptivity. Therefore, the following suggestions may be more tenuous in controlling or eliminating research artifacts.

To lessen possible feelings of evaluation apprehension, the experimental setting as well as procedure should be made as innocuous and nonthreatening as possible. For example, when appropriate, experimenters may wish to emphasize to participants the anonymity or confidentiality of their responses. Esposito, Agard, and Rosnow (1984) discerned that written assurances of confidentiality significantly reduced response distortion due to socially desirable responding on a personality measure. However, attempts to make a study innocuous or nonthreatening also have the potential for reducing the experimental and mundane realism of the study (cf. Aronson & Carlsmith, 1968).

As Rosenthal and Rosnow (1975) noted, the volunteer status of a participant is related to one's motivation to acquiesce to demand characteristics present in a situation. Consequently, attempts should be made to minimize the potential for a volunteer bias. For example, experimenters should be sensitive to the sampling methods they employ when recruiting research participants. When asking individuals to volunteer for a research study, special efforts should be made to portray the study to be as interesting and nonthreatening as possible (see Rosenthal & Rosnow, 1975; Rosenthal & Rosnow, 1976, for ways of reducing volunteer bias). The goal should be to alleviate the fears of unfavorable evaluation that may dissuade an individual from volunteering to participate in the study. However, while trying to minimize the potential for a volunteer bias, the experimenter must also be wary of the tactical and ethical concerns that may arise as a result of these efforts (see Blanck, Bellack, Rosnow, Rotheram-Borus, & Schooler, 1992).

Finally, an experimenter may be able to minimize participants' motivations to respond to demand characteristics rather than only to the independent variable by explicitly informing them that the experimental purpose cannot be disclosed and that the participants should not try to ascertain the experimenter's motives and expectations. This would create a new set of role demands that are in direct conflict with any perceived demand characteristics. Participants desiring to fulfill their role as a research participant would feel compelled not to respond to any salient task-orienting cues present in the experimental situation. However, if a participant is already suspicious or distrustful of the experimenter, this manipulation of the participant's motivation may do more harm than good in reducing the likelihood that the participant will respond to perceived demand characteristics (Strohmetz & Rosnow, 1994).

IDENTIFYING THE PRESENCE
OF RESEARCH ARTIFACTS

Despite well-meaning intentions and careful experimental design, a researcher may still be concerned that his or her study has been compromised by research artifacts. Orne (1962, 1969; see also Rosnow & Rosenthal, 1997) suggested several strategies for identifying research artifacts that may be operating in an experimental situation. One such strategy is a carefully conducted postexperimental inquiry during which the participant is given the opportunity to reflect on his or her research experience and subsequent behavior. However, Orne (1969) cautioned that the demand characteristics that were operating during the experiment may still be present during this inquiry, leading to a "pact of ignorance" between the experimenter and the participant.

Another strategy for identifying potential research artifacts involves the use of "quasi-control subjects" (Orne, 1962, 1969). These are individuals who are asked to step out of their traditional role as research participants in order to become "coinvestigators" or aides to the experimenter. In this new role, these individuals are asked to reflect on their experiences and identify ways in which their experimental behavior may have been compromised or influenced by factors other than the independent variable. For example, these quasi-control subjects might be asked not to actually participate in the study but rather to imagine that they are participating in the study as the experimental procedure is described to them. These quasi-control subjects would then be asked to describe how they might have behaved if they had actually participated in the study. Similarities between the predicted responses of the quasi-control subjects and the responses of the actual participants might indicate the degree to which the observed experimental behaviors were due to the real participants' guesses as to how they should act rather than to the independent variable under investigation.

Orne (1962, 1969) suggested that an experimenter may also wish to use "sacrifice groups" of quasi-control subjects. In this case, the research participation of the quasi-control subjects is terminated at various stages during the experiment. These individuals are then questioned concerning their perceptions and beliefs about the experiment up to the point at which their involvement was ended. The use of sacrifice groups allows for the identification of not only potential research artifacts but also the point at which these artifacts may have compromised the participants' responses.

Finally, Rosnow and Aiken (1973) posited that potential research artifacts might be identified by observing the dependent variable in different contexts in which the demand characteristics may not also be operating. Orne, Sheehan, and Evans (1968) employed this strategy to test the effectiveness of a posthypnotic suggestion. A hypnotized group of participants and a control group of participants who were simulating being hypnotized were given the hypnotic suggestion that they should touch their forehead whenever they heard the word *experiment* during the subsequent 2 days. Although both groups responded to this hypnotic suggestion within the original experimental setting, none of the control group participants responded once they were outside of that situation. Five out the 17 hypnotized participants, however, still responded to the hypnotic suggestion even the next day. This led Orne et al. to conclude that posthypnotic behavior is not limited to the experimental setting.

CONCLUSION

During the early part of Ralph Rosnow's career, the field of social psychology was under such criticism that some concluded the discipline was experiencing a "crisis" (Rosnow, 1981). Rather than becoming disillusioned by the critiques being leveled at the field with respect to its methodological deficiencies, Ralph saw this as an opportunity for scientific inquiry. Through his work on research artifacts, particularly with respect to the volunteer subject problem, Ralph has given future scientists a blueprint as to which timbers need shoring up in this ship of exploration that we call "science." To this end, his work has made a valuable contribution to our understanding of how we can best investigate matters involving behavioral phenomena.

REFERENCES

Adair, J. G. (1984). The Hawthorne effect: A reconsideration of the methodological artifact. *Journal of Applied Psychology, 69,* 334–345.

Aronson, E., & Carlsmith, J. M. (1968). Experimentation in social psychology. In G. Lindzey & E. Aronson (Eds.), *The handbook of social psychology* (2nd ed., Vol. 2, pp. 1–79). Reading, MA: Addison-Wesley.

Barnes, M. L., & Rosenthal, R. (1985). Interpersonal effects of experimenter attractiveness, attire, and gender. *Journal of Personality and Social Psychology, 48,* 435–446.

Blanck, P. D., Bellack, A. S., Rosnow, R. L., Rotheram-Borus, M. J., & Schooler, N. R. (1992). Scientific rewards and conflicts of ethical choices in human subjects research. *American Psychology, 47,* 959–965.

Brenner, M., & Bungard, W. (1981). What to do with social reactivity in psychological experimentation? In M. Brenner (Ed.), *Social method and social life* (pp. 89–114). London: Academic Press.

Esposito, J. L., Agard, E., & Rosnow, R. L. (1984). Can confidentiality of data pay off? *Personality and Individual Differences, 5,* 477–480.

French, J. R. P. (1953). Experiments in field settings. In L. Festinger & D. Katz (Eds.), *Research methods in the behavioral sciences* (pp. 98–135). New York: Holt.

Gillespie, R. (1988). The Hawthorne experiments and the politics of experimentation. In J. Morawski (Ed.), *The rise of experimentation in American psychology* (pp. 114–137). New Haven, CT: Yale University Press.

Goldstein, J. H., Rosnow, R. L., Goodstadt, B., & Suls, J. M. (1972). The "good subject" in verbal operant conditioning research. *Journal of Experimental Research in Personality, 6,* 29–33.

Hendrick, C. (1977). Role-taking, role-playing, and the laboratory experiment. *Personality and Social Psychology Bulletin, 3,* 467–478.

Higbee, K. L., & Wells, M. G. (1972). Some research trends in social psychology during the 1960s. *American Psychologist, 27,* 963–966.

Jung, J. (1969). Current practices and problems in the use of college students for psychological research. *Canadian Psychologist, 10,* 280–290.

Kimmel, A. J. (Ed.). (1981). *Ethics in human subject research.* San Francisco: Jossey-Bass.

Kimmel, A. J. (1988). *Ethics and values in applied social research.* Beverly Hills, CA: Sage.

Lana, R. E. (1969). Pretest sensitization. In R. Rosenthal & R. L. Rosnow (Eds.), *Artifact in behavior research* (pp. 119–141). New York: Academic Press.

Lewin, K. (1951). Problems of research in social psychology. In D. Cartwright (Ed.), *Field theory in social science* (pp. 155–169). New York: Harper & Row.

McGuire, W. J. (1969). Suspiciousness of experimenter's intent. In R. Rosenthal & R. L. Rosnow (Eds.), *Artifact in behavioral research* (pp. 13–57). New York: Academic Press.

Merton, R. K. (1948). The self-fulfilling prophecy. *Antioch Review, 8,* 193–210.

Neurath, O. (1921). *Antispengler* (T. Parzen, Trans.). Munich: Callwey.

Olson, R., Verley, J., Santos, L., & Salas, C. (2004). What we teach students about the Hawthorne studies: A review of content within a sample of introductory I-O and OB textbooks. *The Industrial-Organizational Psychologist, 41* (3), 23–39.

Orne, M. T. (1962). On the social psychology of the psychological experiment: With particular reference to demand characteristics and their implications. *American Psychologist, 17,* 776–783.

Orne, M. T. (1969). Demand characteristics and the concept of quasi-controls. In R. Rosenthal & R. L. Rosnow (Eds.), *Artifact in behavioral research* (pp. 143–179). New York: Academic Press.

Orne, M. T. (1970). Hypnosis, motivation, and ecological validity of the psychological experiment. In W. J. Arnold & M. M. Page (Eds.), *Nebraska symposium on motivation* (Vol. 18, pp. 187–265). Lincoln: University of Nebraska Press.

Orne, M. T., Sheehan, P. W., & Evans, F. J. (1968). Occurrence of posthypnotic behavior outside the experimental setting. *Journal of Personality and Social Psychology, 9,* 189–196.

Parsons, H. M. (1974). What happened at Hawthorne? *Science, 183,* 922–932.

Parsons, H. M. (1992). Hawthorne: An early OBM experiment. *Journal of Organizational Behavior Management, 12,* 27–43.

Pfungst, O. (1965). *Clever Hans (The horse of Mr. Von Osten).* New York: Holt, Rinehart & Winston. (Original work published 1911)

Resnick, J. H., & Schwartz, T. (1973). Ethical standards as an independent variable in psychological research. *American Psychologist, 28,* 134–139.

Roethlisberger, F. J., & Dickson, W. J. (1939). *Management and the worker.* Cambridge, MA: Harvard University Press.

Rosenberg, M. J. (1965). When dissonance fails: On eliminating evaluation apprehension from attitude measurement. *Journal of Personality and Social Psychology, 1,* 28–42.

Rosenberg, M. J. (1969). The conditions and consequences of evaluation apprehension. In R. Rosenthal & R. L. Rosnow (Eds.), *Artifact in behavioral research* (pp. 279–349). New York: Academic Press.

Rosenthal, R. (1966). *Experimenter effects in behavioral research.* New York: Appleton-Century-Crofts.

Rosenthal, R. (1967). Covert communication in the psychological experiment. *Psychological Bulletin, 67,* 356–367.

Rosenthal, R. (1969). Interpersonal expectations. In R. Rosenthal & R. L. Rosnow (Eds.), *Artifact in behavioral research* (pp. 181–277). Academic Press: New York.

Rosenthal, R. (1976). *Experimenter effects in behavioral research* (Rev. ed.). New York: Appleton-Century-Crofts.

Rosenthal, R. (1977). Biasing effects of experimenters. *ETC: A Review of General Semantics, 34,* 253–264.

Rosenthal, R. (1985). From unconscious experimenter bias to teacher expectancy effects. In J. G. Dusek, V. C. Hall, & W. J. Meyer (Eds.), *Teacher expectancies* (pp. 37–65). Hillsdale, NJ: Lawrence Erlbaum Associates.

Rosenthal, R. (1994). Interpersonal expectancy effects: A 30-year perspective. *Current Directions in Psychological Science, 3,* 176–179.

Rosenthal, R., & Fode, K. L. (1963a). The effect of experimenter bias on the performance of the albino rat. *Behavioral Science, 8,* 183–189.

Rosenthal, R., & Fode, K. L. (1963b). Three experiments in experimenter bias. *Psychological Reports, 12,* 491–511.

Rosenthal, R., & Rosnow, R. L. (1975). *The volunteer subject.* New York: Wiley.

Rosenthal, R., & Rosnow, R. L. (1991). *Essentials of behavioral research: Methods and data analysis* (2nd ed.). New York: McGraw-Hill.

Rosenthal, R., & Rubin, D. B. (1978). Interpersonal expectancy effects: The first 345 studies. *Behavioral and Brain Sciences, 3,* 377–415.

Rosenzweig, S. (1933). The experimental situation as a psychological problem. *Psychological Review, 40,* 337–354.

Rosnow, R. L. (1970, June). When he lends a helping hand, bite it. *Psychology Today,* pp. 26–30.

Rosnow, R. L. (1981). *Paradigms in transition: The methodology of social inquiry.* New York: Oxford University Press.

Rosnow, R. L. (1983). Von Osten's horse, Hamlet's question, and the mechanistic view of causality: Implications for a post-crisis social psychology. *Journal of Mind and Behavior, 4,* 319–338.

Rosnow, R. L. (1991). Inside rumor: A personal journey. *American Psychologist, 46,* 484–496.

Rosnow, R. L. (1993). Toward methodological pluralism and theoretical ecumenism: A response to Leaf. *New Ideas in Psychology, 11,* 35–37.

Rosnow, R. L. (1997). Hedgehogs, foxes, and the evolving social contract in psychological science: Ethical challenges and methodological opportunities. *Psychological Methods, 2,* 345–356.

Rosnow, R. L., & Aiken, L. S. (1973). Mediation of artifacts in behavioral research. *Journal of Experimental Social Psychology, 9,* 181–201.

Rosnow, R. L., & Davis, D. J. (1977). Demand characteristics and the psychological experiment. *ETC: A Review of General Semantics, 34,* 301–313.

Rosnow, R. L., Goodstadt, B. E., Suls, J. M., & Gitter, A. G. (1973). More on the social psychology of the experiment: When compliance turns to self-defense. *Journal of Personality and Social Psychology, 27,* 337–343.

Rosnow, R. L., & Rosenthal, R. (1976). The volunteer subject revisited. *Australian Journal of Psychology, 28,* 97–108.

Rosnow, R. L., & Rosenthal, R. (1997). *People studying people: Artifacts and ethics in behavioral research.* New York: Freeman.

Rosnow, R. L., & Rosenthal, R. (2002). *Beginning behavioral research: A conceptual primer* (4th ed.). Upper Saddle River, NJ: Prentice-Hall.

Rosnow, R. L., Rosenthal, R., McConochie, R., & Arms, R. L. (1969). Volunteer effects on experimental outcomes. *Educational and Psychological Measurement, 29,* 825–846.

Rosnow, R. L., Strohmetz, D., & Aditya, R. (2000). Artifact in research. In A. E. Kazdin (Ed.), *Encyclopedia of psychology* (Vol. 1, pp. 242–245). New York: Oxford University Press & American Psychological Association.

Rosnow, R. L., & Suls, J. M. (1970). Reactive effects of pretesting in attitude research. *Journal of Personality and Social Psychology, 15,* 338–343.

Schultz, D. P. (1969). The human subject in psychological research. *Psychological Bulletin, 72,* 214–228.

Sigall, H., Aronson, E., & Van Hoose, T. (1970). The cooperative subject: Myth or reality? *Journal of Experimental Social Psychology, 6,* 1–10.

Smart, R. G. (1966). Subject selection bias in psychological research. *Canadian Psychologist, 7a,* 115–121.

Solomon, R. L. (1949). An extension of control group design. *Psychological Bulletin, 46,* 137–150.

Solomon, R. L., & Lessac, M. S. (1968). A control group design for experimental studies of developmental processes. *Psychological Bulletin, 70,* 145–150.

Sommer, R. (1968). Hawthorne dogma. *Psychological Bulletin, 70,* 592–595.

Strohmetz, D. B., Alterman, A. I., & Walter, D. (1990). Subject selection bias in alcoholics volunteering for a treatment study. *Alcoholism: Clinical and Experimental Research, 14,* 736–738.

Strohmetz, D. B., & Rosnow, R. L. (1994). A mediational model of research artifacts. In J. Brzeziński (Ed.), *Probability in theory-building: Experimental and non-experimental approaches to scientific research in psychology* (pp. 177–196). Amsterdam: Editions Rodopi.

7

From Artifacts to Ethics: The Delicate Balance Between Methodological and Moral Concerns in Behavioral Research

Allan J. Kimmel
ESCP-EAP, European School of Management

Even experienced researchers often find themselves caught between the Scylla of methodological and theoretical requirements and the Charybdis of ethical dictates and moral sensitivities.

—Rosnow (1997, p. 345)

In little more than a quarter century, a mere heartbeat in the history of modern science, the ethical pendulum has swung from one extreme to the other for behavioral science researchers. Where once ethical considerations played a minor role, if at all, in the research process, today they have a formidable influence on most of the decisions relative to the planning and conduct of a research investigation, from the recruitment of research participants to the subsequent application of the research findings. This shift to ethics in the research environment should be abundantly clear to senior experimenters who—in light of increasingly stricter ethical codes, federal regulations, and institutional review boards—no doubt are finding it more and more difficult to carry out their investigations using the traditional arsenal of manipulations and controls of their science. Indeed, it is interesting to ponder how different the face of social psychology, for example, might be today if Solomon Asch, Leon Festinger, Stanley Schachter, and other pioneers of the discipline had to run their (now classic) deception studies past the ethical review boards now in place at the universities where once they were employed.

Despite the growing protections now offered to participants in the research process, recent developments in ethical regulation have complicated the conduct of research for many behavioral scientists. Confronted by an increasingly daunting array of ethical guidelines, governmental regulations, and institutional review, investigators often are compelled to weigh methodological and ethical requirements in order to choose whether and how to pursue particular research questions. The practical difficulties imposed by attempts to cope with these two sets of demands often are linked to the recognition that the most methodologically sound study is not necessarily the most ethical one, and vice versa.

It is this delicate balance between methodological and moral concerns that provides the central theme of this chapter and brings us face to face with some of the issues developed in one of Ralph Rosnow's most enlightening books, *Paradigms in Transition: The Methodology of Social Inquiry.* That 1981 book articulated how the experimental research paradigm adopted within the discipline of social psychology was not ideally suited to the field because of the very nature of the focus of study—the social nature of human behavior.

Unlike researchers in the physical sciences (the Heisenberg uncertainty principle notwithstanding), psychologists and investigators in related disciplines are forced to grapple with a range of problems linked to their attempts to study conscious, problem-solving participants whose reactions are apt to be influenced or distorted by the very acts of observation and measurement. In Rosnow's view, this mismatch between research paradigm and subject to a large extent explains the crisis of confidence that emerged within social psychology during the 1970s. Specifically, Rosnow traced the crisis back to three specific "assaults" against the discipline's basic positivistic approach to the study of human social behavior: artifacts, ethics, and relevance. In the discussion that follows, the focus is placed squarely on some of the problems associated with the first two of these assaults through an emphasis on the intimate connections between ethical and methodological issues.

ETHICAL REGULATION
AND THE BEHAVIORAL RESEARCH PROCESS

Prior to the 1960s, the idea had not yet taken hold that systematic attention to researchers' moral obligations to study participants and to society as a whole represented an integral element of the research process (Kelman, 1996). This is not meant to imply that behavioral scientists were immoral or lacking in ethical sensitivities; rather, times were different then and the scientific climate was such that considerations related to research ethics were not regarded as representing a critical aspect of decision making in the selection of research design and methods. In fact, several of the now well-known investigations in psychology and related disciplines that eventually became the focal point of ethical debate—such as Stanley Milgram's (1963) ingenious obedience experiments, the Stanford prison simulation (Haney, Banks, & Zimbardo, 1973), and the Tuskegee syphilis study (cf. Jones, 1993)—initially were lauded as innovative examples of research with potentially major benefits to science and society. Perhaps reflecting unresolved attitudes regarding research ethics at the time, Milgram encountered academic tenure difficulties at Harvard University because of some early ethical concerns generated by his obedience studies, but was awarded the American Association for the Advancement of Science's (AAAS) prize for research in 1964 (Blass, 2004).

There are several possible reasons why the moral dimension was underplayed for so long by behavioral scientists. When placed in historical context, the apparent failure to recognize the ethical implications of such research methodologies as deception, disguised participant observation, and the employment of potentially harmful psychological manipulations may be linked to some of the same forces that led psychologists to ignore the experimenter–participant artifact problem for so long, despite earlier warnings about the methodological problems inherent in the study of conscious human beings (e.g., Rosenzweig, 1933). For example, Suls and Rosnow (1988) surmised that systematic biases linked to the human interactions within the research situation might have been seen as impeding the progress and growing influence of behavioral research as a firmly established scientific enterprise within the United States. Better to ignore these potentially biasing factors than to acknowledge inherent weaknesses in the application of the positivistic approach to the study of human behavior.

Part and parcel of the widespread optimism regarding the potential of psychological research for understanding and application, which was given impetus as a result of psychologists' successful contributions during WWII, academic researchers proceeded full steam ahead with their empirical research programs. Explicitly acknowledged or not, the prevailing presumption was that this research enterprise was oriented to the betterment of humankind, whether the ultimate goal was to increase levels of satisfaction in the workplace, improve group relations, or contribute to personal development. With such a prevailing zeitgeist it is not difficult to understand why so few behavioral scientists paused to consider the moral soundness of their research activities. If, as Suls and Rosnow also surmised, the classical mechanistic approach adopted by experimental psychologists contributed to the illusion that human research was being carried out in an impartial and passive manner, it stands to reason that sensitivities regarding any possible harms that could come to research participants would have been anything but salient.

Another possible explanation for the oversight regarding the ethical dimension of research is the long-standing view held by many basic researchers that their work is morally neutral, particularly when the predominant goal is the disinterested and impersonal pursuit of scientific knowledge for its own sake. This position of scientific impartiality suggests that although research findings can be used for good or bad ends, the creation of knowledge is ethically neutral and morality has little to do with the conduct of science (at least a positivistic one). Alternatively, researchers may have been uncomfortable with moral reflection altogether, particularly when it failed to yield definitive answers; after all, few mechanisms for guidance were available for helping to resolve ethical dilemmas prior to the 1970s. It may have been easier for researchers simply to overlook vague moral questions than to struggle with any complex ethical dilemmas imposed by their research methodologies, an oversight that was more than consistent with the tradition of the field.

A variety of developments can be identified as ultimately having brought greater attention to the moral underpinnings of behavioral research. In retrospect, much of the impetus for ethical progress in psychology was sparked by a significant increase in the employment of deception and other ethically questionable research practices. Often cited along these lines are studies from the 1960s, like Project Camelot in political science (Horowitz, 1967), the "tearoom trade" research in sociology (Humphreys, 1970), and the obedience research in psychology (Milgram, 1963), each of which aroused considerable controversy among researchers and the general public.

By the mid-1970s, the practice of deceiving research participants in psychological research had become commonplace, and awareness regarding deceptive methods had grown among the public. According to various estimates, the percentage of studies using deception in social psychology alone rose from around 20% in 1960 to nearly 70% in 1975 (e.g., Adair, Dushenko, & Lindsay, 1985; McNamara & Woods, 1977). Although deception arguably proved to be the most pervasive ethical issue in psychological research, other practices also aroused concern, including the invasion of participants' right to privacy, failure to protect the anonymity of respondents or the confidentiality of data, unobtrusive observations of unsuspecting participants, and the use of risky experimental manipulations. The extensive debate surrounding the appropriateness of these practices, aroused by public concerns about some of the more flagrant research cases, sparked a significant movement toward the development of federal and professional research guidelines and the evolution of the institutional review process (Kimmel, 2003).

Ethical developments have continued unabated through the present era, prompting some critics to question whether we have entered a period of overregulation in the research context. The expanded influence of external review has brought with it a growing concern that review boards either do not effectively protect participants from harm or else overstep their intended role in an effort to force behavioral and social research into a biomedical mold, thereby making it increasingly difficult for many researchers to proceed with their studies as intended. Mueller and Furedy (2001) pointed out some of the difficulties inherent in attempts to assess review board performance, including the misconception that "a problem found" with a research proposal equates with "an incident avoided."

In order to ensure the protection and welfare of participants, review boards typically attempt to ascertain that the anticipated benefits of an investigation are greater than any risks posed, and that informed consent procedures are adequate. Where once this formal review process emphasized the protection of participants from "extraordinary risks," the identification of even everyday risk now is obligatory for all proposals. Along these lines, Mueller (2003) argued that the regulatory approach commonly followed by many IRBs is to eliminate all risk (including everyday risks; e.g., simple embarrassment) rather than to exercise the best judgment in evaluating research proposals. As a consequence, in the view of some observers, over time participation in research has become much safer than many of the everyday activities in which people engage (Diener, 2001). Rosnow (1997) expressed this sentiment somewhat differently when he noted that contemporary researchers are subjected to a higher level of professional ethical accountability than is the case for other professionals who supposedly serve as society's guardians of human rights—such as lawyers, politicians, and journalists—who routinely engage in various forms of deception.

THE LINK BETWEEN ETHICS AND ARTIFACTS

The recognition that decisions about particular research questions and associated methodological issues are inextricably bound to ethical considerations is no more apparent than when one considers the inseparable relationship between artifacts and ethics. As described earlier, ethical developments in psychology were promulgated as a function of the dramatic rise in the use of deceptive methodologies, a trend that was best exemplified by research carried out within the discipline of social psychology. However, it was not by chance that psychologists turned to deception as a primary research tool. Deception largely emerged as a practical remedy to the experimenter–participant artifact problem—the recognition that participants come to the research setting not as passive automatons who respond mechanistically to the manipulations to which they are subjected (hence, the ethically pejorative term *research subject*), but rather as conscious, active problem solvers who attempt to guess the investigator's hypotheses in order to do the right (or good) thing. Assistance in this problem-solving activity comes from the multiple sources of demand characteristics available to participants both before (e.g., campus scuttlebutt about ongoing research studies) and during (e.g., research instructions) the actual study (Rosnow, 2002).

Ethical Standards for Psychologists: The APA Code

Largely in response to the changing nature of research in psychology and the ensuing public debates generated by controversial deception studies, the American Psychological Association (APA) has taken steps to codify (and periodically modify) ethical standards intended to guide human participant researchers. The APA code of ethics has served as a model for other professional associations around the world (Kimmel, 1996; Leach & Harbin, 1997), and is unique in that its principles have been derived largely through an empirical approach based on a survey of critical incidents pertaining to ethical dilemmas experienced by the association's members. The current version of the code (APA, 2002) is the result of a 50-year history of development and revision, and is presumed to reflect the values of APA members as well as the moral growth of the psychology discipline (Jones, 2001).

The code emphasizes voluntary participation and informed consent as fundamental prerequisites for research with human participants. The standard pertaining to deception in the current version of the code (APA, 2002) significantly restricts its use for research purposes by dictating that (a) deception should be used only if a study's results are likely to be sufficiently important (because of "the study's significant prospective scientific, educational, or applied value," p. 1070), (b) an alternative nondeceptive procedure is not feasible, (c) the research is not likely to cause physical pain or severe emotional distress, and (d) the deception is to be explained to participants as early as possible as part of a debriefing.

Although deception is permitted under the code and is commonly used in psychology and other fields of human research (e.g., Kimmel, 2001), the practice has been questioned by critics who argue that any use of deception is wrong and may result in a variety of negative consequences. Adair et al. (1985) succinctly summarized some of the key concerns about its frequent use in psychology by suggesting that deception:

violates the individual's right to voluntarily choose to participate, abuses the basic interpersonal relationship between experimenter and subject, contributes to deception as a societal value and practice, is a questionable base for development of the discipline, is contrary to our professional roles as teachers or scientists, and will ultimately lead to a loss of trust in the profession and science of psychology. (p. 61)

Although some critics are opposed to any use of deception (e.g., Ortmann & Hertwig, 1997), others favor a more restricted use and express concern that the ethical standards for deception are to be applied within a cost-benefit framework that permits the researcher to consider whether the benefits of the research outweigh possible harm to participants. Indeed, this criterion has fueled extensive debate regarding interpretation of existing professional standards and their implementation. However, the code acknowledges that most psychologists will have to obtain institutional approval prior to conducting research and this constraint partially addresses the cost-benefit problem.

The Ethics/Artifact Dilemma

In light of the various methodological problems imposed by research artifacts, current guidelines for the conduct of research necessitate that researchers walk a fine line in responding to scientific and ethical demands. Investigations into widely researched social psychology topics such as attitudes, aggression, prejudice, intimate relationships, group dynamics, impression formation, and social identity represent sensitive areas that typically cannot be studied in traditional ways (e.g., experimental laboratory investigations) with the full awareness of research participants. Dating back to Rosenthal and Rosnow's (1969) seminal book *Artifact in Behavioral Research*, it has long been assumed that if researchers had to provide participants with full information about their experimental plans and procedures, the resulting psychology of human behavior might very well be based on the kinds of behavior for which participants believe experimenters are looking.

It now is rather evident that a completely informed consent obtained during investigations into social psychological phenomena such as altruism and prejudice could cause participants to behave differently in order to present a more socially acceptable (as opposed to a natural or typical) image to the researcher. It has been empirically demonstrated that informing participants of the true purpose and procedures of a study can serve to distort participant responses and severely jeopardize the tenability of inferred causal relationships (e.g., Resnick & Schwartz, 1973). This effect is not limited to social psychological research; for example, Broder (1998) cited certain studies of memory, incidental learning, and cognitive illusions that could not have been carried out without deception. In this light, informed consent essentially operates as an independent variable—studies conducted with or without it may come up with vastly different results. By opting for deception as a means to reduce demand clarity (e.g., by generating alternative and irrelevant demands), researchers can proceed with greater confidence that participants are responding to the experimental variables under study and not to uncontrolled factors linked to the social nature of the researcher–participant interaction (Rosnow, Strohmetz, & Aditya, 2000; Strohmetz & Rosnow, 1994).

In short, the primary justification for using deception in laboratory settings is a purely methodological one—that if researchers conformed to the letter of the law regarding informed consent and did not deceive participants at all, then many investigations would be either impossible to conduct or would result in biased findings. It should be noted that, in addition to deception, other strategies have been utilized for circumventing the potential validity problems linked to experimenter–participant artifacts, such as the employment of unobtrusive observations in naturalistic settings. Such research approaches also have given rise to ethical concerns, including the fear that they impinge on individual rights to privacy, confidentiality, and voluntary participation in research. As Table 7.1 summarizes, various alternatives to deception have been suggested; however, for a majority of researchers, recourse to some form of deception has long served as the preferred artifact coping mechanism. This has included the widespread use of both active deceptions (e.g., the employment of research "confederates" who act out predetermined roles, untrue statements about the researcher's identity, incorrect information about research procedures and instructions, and false feedback) and passive deceptions (e.g., failure to disclose aspects of the study procedure or instruments, concealed observation, and the use of psychometric tests not described as such).

ASSESSING THE EVIDENCE: HOW EFFECTIVE IS DECEPTION AS AN ARTIFACT COPING MECHANISM?

Whereas the consequences of research deception have been given relatively scant attention by psychologists from either an ethical (at least through a normative analysis) or disciplinary perspective, its methodological implications have been extensively examined. Table 7.2 reveals that various attempts have been made to ascertain the extent to which deception lives up to its supporters' claims that it serves as an effective mechanism for coping with the artifact problem. Researchers have focused their attention specifically on issues directed to the very core of the methodological bases on which the use of deception procedures depend, including (a) that the level of naiveté among research participants is high and

TABLE 7.1
Research Alternatives to Deception

Research Alternative	Methodology
Quasi-controls (e.g., Rosenthal & Rosnow, 1991)	Participants are asked to reflect on what is happening during a study and to describe how they think they might be affected by the procedure. If no demand characteristics are detected, the researcher would develop a less deceptive manipulation and have the quasi-controls once again reflect on the study. If they remain unaware of the demands of the study, the researcher could then use this lower level of deception to carry out the intended investigation. (Key strength: Deception can be minimized without risking a corresponding increase in demand cues. Key drawbacks: Quasi-controls are time consuming and often more costly to carry out.)
Simulations (e.g., Geller, 1982)	Conditions are created that mimic the natural environment and participants are asked to pretend or act as if the mock situation were real. Variations include field simulations (simulations in highly realistic staged settings), role-playing simulations (see the next item in the table), and game simulations (participants take on roles in staged situations lasting until a desired outcome has been attained or a specified length of time has passed). (Key strength: This approach preserves the key elements thought to underlie the dynamics of real-world phenomenon under study. Key drawbacks: Simulations are sometimes characterized by intrinsic deceptions; mundane realism is sometimes suspect.)
Forewarning (e.g., Allen, 1983)	Prospective research participants are informed before a study begins that deception may be used and are then given the opportunity to agree to place themselves in a situation in which they may be misled or else decline further participation. (*Key strength*: Forewarning reduces the ethical problems associated with deception by having subjects agree to the possibility that they may be misled. *Key drawback*: Forewarning may arouse subjects' search for demand characteristics and efforts to discover procedures involving mistruths.)
Role playing (e.g., Greenberg, 1967)	Research participants are enlisted as active collaborators in the investigation. Each participant is told what the study is about and is then asked to play a role as if he or she were actually participating in the actual study. (Key strengths: In contrast to deception studies, participants in role-playing studies are fully informed; the strategy allows for a wide latitude of response, is capable of exploring complex behavior, and is a more humanistic alternative to deception research. Key drawback: Role-playing results may not replicate the results that would have been obtained in traditional research, especially counterintuitive ones.)

TABLE 7.2
Summary of Methodological, Ethical,
and Disciplinary Consequences of Deception

Issues Linked to Deception	Degree of Effects[1]	Research Evidence
A. Methodological		
Participant suspiciousness (use of deception leads to an increase in suspiciousness among subject pools)	Medium to high (> 25%) levels of S suspicions.	Gallo et al. (1973); Glinski et al. (1970); Stricker et al. (1967); Willis & Willis (1970);
	Low (0%–25%) levels	Adair et al. (1985); Kimmel (2001); Stricker (1967)
Leakage (participants divulge crucial information into the subject pool)	Extensive	Diener et al. (1972); Glinski et al. (1970); Lichtenstein (1970); Lipton & Garza (1978);
	Low	Aronson (1966); Walsh & Stillman (1974)
Effects of subject suspicions (suspicions linked to the use of deception influence current or future research performance)	Significant effects (between naive and aware participants)	Allen (1966); Cook & Perrin (1971); Golding & Lichtenstein (1970); Levy (1967); Newberry (1973); Silverman et al. (1970)
	No effects	Brock & Becker (1966); Cook & Perrin (1971); Fillenbaum (1966)
Forewarning (participants' preknowledge of deception alters experimental performance)	Little effect on performance	Allen (1983); Gallo et al. (1973); Wiener & Erker (1986)
	Significant effects (between forewarned Ss and uninformed controls)	Finney (1987); Golding & Lichentenstein (1970); Levy (1967); Turner & Simons (1974)
Effectiveness of debriefing on the mitigation of negative deception effects (false beliefs, negative affect, inflicted insight)	Effective (conventional debrief) Ineffective (conventional debrief)	Holmes (1973); Holmes & Bennett (1974) Aronson (1966); Ross et al. (1975); Valins (1974); Walster et al. (1967); Wegner et al. (1985)
	Effective (explicit debrief)	Misra (1992); Ring et al. (1970); Toy et al. (1989)

B. Ethical		
Effects of deception on participants (deception has immediate or delayed harmful effects on participants)	No effects	Milgram (1964); Ring et al. (1970)
Participant reactions to deception (participants have adverse reactions to having been deceived; e.g., believe their rights have been violated)	Positive reactions only	Christiansen (1988); Clark & Word (1974); Finney (1987); Pihl et al. (1981); Smith (1981); Smith & Richardson (1983)
	Negative reactions	Allen (1983); Cook et al. (1970)
Participant reactions to debriefing (participants appreciate and value the procedure)	High	Toy et al. (1989)
	Low	Sharpe et al. (1992)
C. Disciplinary		
Effects of deception on perceptions of the discipline (deception reflects poorly on the discipline and the image of researchers)	Mixed effects	Sharpe et al. (1992)
	Positive effects	Clark & Word (1974); Gerdes (1979)
General population reactions to deception (objections to the use of deception for research purposes among the general public)	No objections	Collins et al. (1979); Epstein et al. (1973); Farr & Seaver (1975); Rugg (1975); Sullivan & Deiker (1973)
	Objections	Singer (1984)

*This column represents the extent to which the anticipated adverse consequences of deception noted in the first column were apparent. For the issues linked to debriefing, this column reflects the extent of debriefing in reducing adverse deception effects or leading to favorable evaluations of the debriefing procedure.

that the procedure does not produce cues that suggest to participants that deception is taking place, (b) that participant suspiciousness of deception or prior experience in deception studies does not alter the experimental effect, and (c) that any negative effects resulting from the use of deception (e.g., false beliefs, negative affect, and inflicted insight) can be mitigated by a careful debriefing process or else offset by forewarning and limited informed consent procedures.

Section A in Table 7.2 provides an overview of studies that have examined these three key methodological assumptions and, in general, the results are anything but clear-cut. Overall, the body of research suggests that under some circumstances deception actually may exacerbate the artifact problem. Other evidence points to the efficacy of deception in offsetting some of the undesirable methodological consequences associated with experimenter–participant artifacts. The current state of knowledge with regard to each methodological assumption is summarized in the sections that follow.

Assumption 1: Participant Naiveté Levels Are High

Critics have long argued that a continuing rise in the use of research deception ultimately would reduce the pool of naive participants. That is, it was reasoned that as investigators relied more and more on deceptive methodologies, this approach would become common knowledge and a growing number of participants would arrive at the research laboratory with the expectation that they would be deceived. Regardless of the source of this expectation—whether conveyed by mass-mediated accounts of deception studies, informal conversations with previously deceived participants, descriptions of deception in psychology textbooks, or the like—it was feared that suspicious participants would be more likely to see through a study's deceptions (Strohmetz & Rosnow, 1994). Of course, if this were the case, not only would it obviate the utility of deception in the first place, but it would also lead to the possibility that participants would be skeptical of informed consent procedures and expect to be deceived even when no deception was used.

Consistent with these fears, the findings pertaining to naiveté levels among current or prospective participants show that, within certain research circumstances, the continued employment of deception does in fact have the capacity to reduce the pool of naive research participants. This is apparent from evidence that research participants who have been debriefed may communicate the true purpose and other details of studies to future participants, even when instructed not to do so; this tendency is referred to as *leakage* (Diener, Matthews, & Smith, 1972; Lipton & Garza, 1978).

Despite the findings showing that deception can undermine participant naiveté levels, there is little evidence suggesting that this is a common outcome. Overall estimates of suspiciousness regarding deceptions, research hypotheses, and the nature of experimental manipulations and assessment techniques have revealed extremely low levels of suspicion among research participants. With the exception of a handful of early experiments on conformity to group pressure revealing rather extensive suspicions (e.g., Glinski, Glinski, & Slatin, 1970; Stricker, Messick, & Jackson, 1967), more recent estimates of the overall percentage of participants identified as suspicious have ranged from only 1.8% to 3% (Adair, Dushenko, & Lindsay, 1985; Kimmel, 2001, 2004). For example, I investigated the prevalence of research practices in psychology and marketing research over a 40-year period by content analyzing empirical articles published in the *Journal of Personality and Social Psychology* (JPSP), the *Journal of Marketing Research* (JMR), and the *Journal of Consumer Research* (JCR). Across 66 investigations reporting suspiciousness checks, only 230 out of 10,028 participants (2.3%) were identified as harboring skepticism about the true experimental purpose or manipulations (Kimmel, 2004).

Over the years, there has been surprisingly little research on the extent of suspiciousness or leakage in the research setting, and investigators do not routinely probe levels of participant suspiciousness (Adair et al., 1985; Kimmel, 2001, 2004; Stricker, 1967). Based on the results to date, there does not appear to be any indication of a rise in participant sophistication corresponding to the ongoing use of deception in behavioral studies. Nevertheless, this conclusion must be somewhat tempered by the recognition that participants cannot always be counted on to be totally forthcoming in revealing their suspicions or knowledge about research procedures and hypotheses.

Similarly, the quality of suspiciousness checks by researchers may be called into question, particularly if such efforts represent only cursory attempts to demonstrate the soundness of experimental manipulations. In some early investigations, researchers found that when they assessed suspiciousness by asking their participants up to three postexperimental questions, only about 5% of the participants were classified as suspicious; this percentage increased to about 40% when more extended questioning was utilized (Page, 1973; Spielberger, 1962). More research clearly is needed on the levels and sources of participant suspiciousness, extent of leakage, the impact of prior experience in deception studies on perceptions of researchers' honesty, and so on. In addition, investigators need to more carefully evaluate the procedures they use to assess perceptions of the study and levels of participant suspiciousness (Taylor & Shepperd, 1996).

It is interesting to conjecture about how recent ethical developments may be linked indirectly to low rates of participant suspiciousness. Concerns about the suspiciousness problem have always been predicated on the likelihood that an increase in the employment of deception (or at least steadily high rates of use) would gradually erode the pool of naive research participants. For example, in his review of the social conformity literature covering the period 1954–1973, Stang (1976) reported an increase in the percentage of suspicious participants over time, corresponding to a period in social psychology when deception rates rose to such high levels that deception had essentially become the methodological standard. However, in more recent years, the rates in psychology have declined to the extent that less than 40% of human participant studies involve some form of active or passive deception (Kimmel, 2001, 2004; Nicks, Korn, & Mainieri, 1997; Vitelli, 1988). Concurrently, researchers have become more inclined to utilize alternative procedures that circumvent some of the ethical issues, such as nondeceptive field and survey research. The apparent shifts from active to passive deception and from experimental laboratory research to nonexperimental field investigations may be a sign of the growing impact of stricter ethical guidelines and review mechanisms on the research approach selected by empirical psychologists.

In short, despite the fact that many psychologists are still apt to deceive their participants, the prevalence and apparent intensity of deception have declined during recent decades, which would seem to undermine to some extent the argument that subject pools will inevitably become less naive. It has been more than 30 years since critics of deception first warned about deception leading to the inevitable loss of naive research participants, yet to date there seems to be little evidence suggesting that subject pools are any more contaminated than in the past.

Assumption 2: Suspiciousness of Deception Does Not Alter the Experimental Effect

The issue of whether or not deception leads to greater levels of suspiciousness bears little import if, in fact, skepticism regarding research procedures or purpose does not have an impact on experimental performance and it turns out that naive and suspicious individuals behave similarly under the same experimental conditions. Apart from the moral considerations engendered by artifact coping strategies, the potential for suspiciousness to influence research performance probably has aroused the greatest concern among researchers. Mistrust of the experimental procedure could alter participants' reactions enough to cause misleading results or invalidation of an investigation altogether.

Research on the effects of distrust on experimental performance has focused on various manifestations of the issue, including the general effects of self-reported suspiciousness (e.g., Stang, 1976; Stricker, 1967), the effects of experimentally induced suspicions through the use of some variation of forewarning (or prebriefing; e.g., Allen, 1983; Finney, 1987), and the influence of prior experience in deception experiments on subsequent research performance (e.g., Cook & Perrin, 1971; Fillenbaum, 1966). Overall, the extant empirical evidence regarding the effects of subject distrust is mixed, with some studies showing that the results produced by suspicious or preinformed participants (who are made aware that deception is to be utilized in the investigation) can differ substantially from those of naive participants. For example, Newberry (1973) carried out two experiments in which individuals who had received prior information from a confederate consistently used it, whether intentionally or not, to improve their performance on various problem-solving tasks. Similarly, Stang (1976) reviewed nine conformity studies that systematically compared suspicious and naive participants (identified via postexperimental interviews) and concluded that suspicious individuals tended to show less conformity than did those classified as nonsuspicious.

Other investigations have revealed that previous experience in deception research can affect performance in subsequent experiments, with prior deception resulting in an increased tendency for favorable self-presentation (e.g., Silverman, Shulman, & Wiesenthal, 1970). However, some researchers have been unable to obtain performance effects from persons with foreknowledge about a deceptive investigation (e.g., Allen, 1983; Wiener & Erker, 1986). Such disparities in the findings likely are linked to a variety of methodological considerations, including the specific procedure utilized for making the relevant comparisons between suspicious and nonsuspicious participants, the degree of specificity of the suspicions, the types of persons studied, and the nature and degree of deceptions involved in the research. With respect to forewarning, there is evidence that experimental performance is more likely to be altered to the extent that participants receive explicit details about the deceptive nature of the investigation (e.g., after receiving a detailed tipoff of the true experimental purpose from a confederate) than when they are merely informed that the study *might* involve deception. Additionally, if a prior deception is seen as mild and legitimate, participants simply may accept it and behave naturally, adhering to the instructions in current or later studies despite their suspicions.

The degree of intensity of the deceptions in a study is an important consideration, not only with respect to the methodological implications of participant suspiciousness, but also to general ethical concerns. Deception severity can be defined in terms of the potential adverse costs or likelihood of risks posed for the various parties involved in the research process. Studies such as Milgram's obedience experiments inevitably aroused strong critical reactions in large part because of the perceived intensity of the deceptions employed. As an example of a field study employing a severe deception, a Columbia Business School professor sent letters on university letterhead stationery to 240 New York City restaurants, falsely claiming he had suffered food poisoning after dining at the restaurant in celebration of his wedding anniversary (Kifner, 2001). The intention was to investigate vendor response to consumer complaints. Although some suspicions were aroused (e.g., unlike genuine food poisoning cases, the letter did not specify what had been eaten), the overall emotional impact on the restaurant owners who received the letter was dramatic. Reflecting the adverse consequences induced by the study, an editorial in *The New York Times* ("Spoiling the Broth," 2001) claimed that the resulting review of hygiene procedures "caused a reign of terror in the city's top restaurants" (p. 3). Reactions to the study resulted in a formal apology from the school's dean and the researcher, and prompted the introduction of new procedures governing research at Columbia.

An example of a study involving mild deception would be one in which participants are not informed that they will be asked later to rate their degree of liking for different nonsense syllables on a list they have been asked to memorize. It is unlikely that such a deception would arouse much suspicion for a participant and, even if it did, it is difficult to imagine that it would appear meaningful enough to significantly influence performance on the experimental task. In fact, much research in psychology tends to involve these sorts of mundane procedures, which arouse little interest for the typical undergraduate likely to end up in the subject pool. In such studies, the primary motive may simply be to get it over with in order to receive the promised incentive, without any concern for altering one's natural performance on the research task.

Another way of viewing the mild versus severe deception distinction has largely been confined to discussions within the area of marketing research. Toy, Olson, and Wright (1989) defined "severe deceptions" as those that create false beliefs about central, important issues related to participants' self-concept or personal behavior, as when an experimental manipulation leads participants to believe that they lack self-confidence. "Mild deceptions" are those that create false beliefs about relatively unimportant issues that are peripheral to participants' self-concept, such as misleading them about the research sponsor or study purpose. Severe deceptions can be expected to create negative affect both during and after participation in the research (e.g., upset or anxiety linked to a reduced self-image), whereas mild deceptions are unlikely to create negative beliefs and affect until the debriefing session at the end of the study (e.g., disappointment that the study was not really supported by an environmental protection group).

Given this distinction, we might anticipate different kinds of performance effects depending on whether a mild or severe deception is used. Assuming they have any impact at all on participants, mild deceptions would be unlikely to affect performance in the investigation during which they are employed, but could influence performance in subsequent experiments. For severe deceptions, performance could be affected in the ongoing study as well as subsequent ones. The fact that social psychologists are more likely to employ severe deceptions that are relevant to the fundamental beliefs and values of research participants than are investigators in related fields, such as consumer research, to some extent explains why deception has been such a central issue in social psychology.

Another important consideration related to performance effects concerns the empirical issue of whether more (or less) statistical conclusion bias will be created by the decision either to use or not use deception (cf. Shadish, Cook, & Campbell, 2001). That is, even when a researcher chooses not to deceive, this decision will not offset the tendency for participants to conjecture about the true purpose of the study, with each person theoretically generating his or her own hypothesis. These multiple hypotheses could be seen as operating as a form of error variance to the extent that they influence dependent measure values. In this regard, it might be argued that by opting for deception, a reduction in error variance would result as a function of the deception having led to greater homogeneity among participants (T. A. Shimp, personal communication, October 29, 2002).

The issue of suspicion adds a further complication to these considerations given the possibility that suspiciousness can operate differentially across the conditions of a study (Diener & Crandall, 1978). Because different treatments are likely to cause dissimilar levels of suspicion, apparent treatment effects in some studies could be attributed to varying suspiciousness rates. If the rate of suspicion is not distributed randomly across treatment conditions, omitting the data obtained from suspicious participants can serve to increase the apparent treatment effects. Furthermore, the decision to eliminate suspicious persons from the study could lead to the loss of truly random assignment to conditions. As a result, it would be difficult for the researcher to rule out the possibility that treatment effects were caused by selection biases or, for that matter, undetected suspicion that exists differentially across conditions (Diener & Crandall, 1978). Although there are no easy solutions to these problems, researchers should at least attempt to assess the effectiveness of each deception used in an investigation and the extent to which participants idiosyncratically perceived the experiment and its rationale (Adair et al., 1985).

Assumption 3: Debriefing Can Offset the Negative Effects of Deception

Ethical guidelines typically necessitate that all deceived participants be fully debriefed within a reasonable period following their involvement in a study. This requirement is often cited as an important safeguard against some of the potential risks inherent in the use of deception. The debriefing session can function as a means of assessing whether participants were adversely affected by the research procedures. It also provides an opportunity to probe for suspicions and to eliminate lasting false impressions about the study. However, the effectiveness of debriefing for achieving these objectives is not entirely evident, particularly in cases in which the debriefing procedure involves only a perfunctory attempt by the researcher to inform participants that they were deceived. In order to be effective, the debriefing may require both "dehoaxing" (i.e., convincing deceived participants that the information they had been given was in fact fraudulent, and relieving any anxiety resulting from that information) and "desensitizing" (i.e., helping deceived participants to deal with new information about themselves that was acquired as a consequence of their behavior during the study).

It is possible that the realization that one has been deceived could result in a loss of self-esteem and embarrassment, in addition to creating a negative attitude toward the researcher or science (Baumrind, 1985). Accordingly, it is important to recognize that the debriefing process, although designed to resolve ethical problems and provide a methodological check on research methods, can have unintended adverse effects on participants (Toy, Wright, & Olson, 2001). In some cases, it may be appropriate to withhold certain information during the debriefing (e.g., about individual differences) when it is judged that awareness could cause more harm than good to participants.

Unless it is carried out with care and heightened vigilance, there is the possibility that persons already deceived once may question the validity of the information provided during the debriefing (Holmes, 1976). The so-called "perseverance process," whereby perceptions and beliefs created during a study continue after they have been discredited, also may cast doubt on the effectiveness of debriefings to undo the effects of deceptive manipulations. It has been shown that self-relevant and non-self-relevant perceptions (e.g., created by deceptive feedback following experimental tasks) may become cognitively detached from the evidence that created them; as a result, even after the basis for the perceptions are disconfirmed (via a debriefing), individuals may tend to cling to the original beliefs (Ross, Lepper, & Hubbard, 1975). It is for these reasons that some researchers have recommended a process approach to debriefing, focusing on the psychological processes that underlie the effects of deception and debriefing and structuring postexperimental procedures accordingly (see Aronson & Carlsmith, 1968; Mills, 1976; Toy et al., 2001, for specific suggestions for designing thorough process-oriented debriefings). On the whole, it appears that unlike conventional debriefings, which involve only a cursory explanation of the deception, explicit debriefings (i.e., those that describe the perseverance effect or clearly provide participants with justification for their experimental behavior) can substantially reduce false beliefs or negative feelings linked to the use of deception (e.g., Misra, 1992).

With a consideration of the potential effectiveness of the debriefing process in mind, certain severe deceptions could be seen as preferable to others according to how readily their effects are likely to be reduced or eliminated. Consider, for example, a self-esteem manipulation that is carried out by having participants write a paragraph about a time when they were proud or not proud of themselves. On the surface, this procedure would seem to be ethically preferable to the more standard one whereby participants are given false feedback about their performance on a test. The paragraph method involves less deception (i.e., although participants are not told that their self-esteem is being manipulated, they are not lied to about their performance abilities) and might appear to have lower potential for harming participants. Nonetheless, in the view of some researchers who have used both procedures, the test manipulation—even though it involves more deception—is preferable to the paragraph approach because it is easier to undo (J. G. Klein, personal communication, October 29, 2002).

For the test manipulation, it is relatively easy to convincingly debrief participants about the bogus nature of the test and the feedback they received (e.g., that the test was impossible to successfully complete, that everyone does very poorly, that the feedback was false). By contrast, there is no such straightforward approach for eliminating any residual effects participants might experience from the paragraph manipulation. Although some researchers have their participants write a positive paragraph at the end of the study, the effectiveness of this approach for eliminating negative thoughts and feelings induced during the experiment remains uncertain. Even given these points, studies involving more severe deceptions likely will be harder to justify when current ethical principles are applied, and are more likely to encounter problems when subjected to committee review.

Summary: Deception in Perspective

A review of the literature on the effects of deception leaves more questions unanswered than answered. Many of the empirical investigations in psychology on whether deception results in the contamination of subject pools, the influence of participant suspicions on experimental effects, and the like, now are quite dated. The fact that recent surveys suggest that the use of deception has declined in recent years in psychology as progressively more psychologists utilize nonlaboratory and nonexperimental research approaches additionally means that those earlier surveys (conducted when deception was used as a matter of course) are even less relevant today. However, it is clear that, for many research situations, deception does not have the negative methodological effects its critics have long contended. The position that all deception is bad and to be avoided is more a moral issue than a methodological one. Certain mundane deceptions that do not have any potential for causing harm or arousing suspicions are acceptable under current ethical codes, and represent acceptable recourses for counteracting threats stemming from experimenter–participant artifacts.

The factors that have emerged as particularly relevant to questions related to the impact of deception concern the nature and intensity of the deceptions employed and the quality of the debriefing following a deceptive investigation. Whereas some researchers have chosen to define deception solely in terms of sins of commission, the impact of passive deception is as important to consider as that of active deception. Findings suggest that active and passive deceptions may differentially influence research results and participant reactions to having been deceived, adding credence to Hey's (1998) comment that "there is a world of difference between not telling subjects things and telling them the wrong things" (p. 397). As more psychologists move to nonlaboratory settings where participants often are unaware of their involvement in a scientific study, issues related to passive deception no doubt will grow in importance in both a methodological and an ethical sense (Sieber, Iannuzzo, & Rodriguez, 1995). From an ethical point of view, sins of omission are generally easier to justify than are instances of intentional lying (e.g., Baumrind, 1985; McDaniel & Starmer, 1998).

Debriefing is a required element for all research employing deception that has the potential to adversely affect participants, yet there still is much to be learned about how to most effectively carry out a postexperimental interview, and how debriefing functions to reduce undesirable methodological and ethical outcomes. Because not all debriefings are alike, the nature of the debriefing protocol can be expected to serve as an important mediating factor in explaining some of the varying effects of deception on participant suspiciousness, attitude toward the investigation and science in general, and performance effects in subsequent research studies.

Clearly, the time is due for an updated empirical evaluation of these issues, either via strong inference studies or systematic meta-analyses that consider a wide range of mediating factors (severity of deceptions used, active vs. passive deceptions, volunteer vs. nonvolunteer samples, etc.). If, as some research has shown, participants not only evaluate deception research more favorably than do researchers (e.g., Aguinis & Henle, 2001), but also find (nonharmful) deception studies to be more interesting and intellectually stimulating than nondeception studies (Finney, 1987; Smith & Richardson, 1983), this would suggest that deception has the potential to increase the value of the research experience from an ethical perspective (assuming that the deception does not also exacerbate the methodological problems associated with having participants try to figure out the deceptions). Only by conducting the appropriate comparative analyses will a clearer picture emerge as to how deception operates and the specific conditions under which its effects are likely to be beneficial for behavioral researchers and other parties involved in the research process.

THE ARTIFACT–ETHICS DILEMMA:
A LOOK TO THE FUTURE

Since the publication of *Paradigms in Transition*, in which Ralph Rosnow explicated the problems imposed by the clash between artifacts and values, no simple solutions have emerged by which investigators can circumvent or cope with the inevitable dilemmas without having to resort to some sort of compromise between scientific rigor and moral strictures. The emergence of various alternatives to research deception such as role playing and quasi-controls notwithstanding, psychologists have yet to reach a consensus—and there is no reason to expect that they ever could—as to how to most effectively balance ethical and methodological demands.

It is informative to look at how other related fields have dealt with similar challenges associated with human research. Although sociologists and anthropologists have essentially followed psychology's lead in responding to ethical considerations related to research practices (Kimmel, 1988, 1996; Smith, Klein, & Kimmel, 2002), researchers in economics have taken a more aggressive tact. For nearly 20 years, experimental economists have essentially adopted a de facto prohibition against the use of deception in research, largely based on concerns that deception contaminates subject pools and may not guarantee that participants will really believe what they have been told about the research environment (Bonetti, 1998; McDaniel & Starmer, 1998). That a similar such approach could eventually emerge for all behavioral and social science research is a possibility that has been dreaded by researchers who view increasingly restrictive professional and governmental regulatory mechanisms as significant threats to the research process.

Despite considerable debate about the decision to forbid deception in experimental economics research, it generally is argued by supporters of the policy that almost all economics research can be conducted without the use of deception, through the development of alternative procedures (e.g., Bardsley, 2000), guarantees of participant anonymity, and substantial monetary rewards based on outcomes (the latter of which ensures that participants are strongly motivated). Whether forbidding deception would meet with similar success in psychology is another question entirely, where the range of research questions is broader and more likely to arouse self-relevant concerns and participant role playing.

Alternatively, a brighter future for behavioral researchers could come from the adoption of a new model governing the researcher–participant relationship. One possibility is suggested by a modified version of social contract theory (Kimmel & Smith, 2001; Smith et al., 2002), as originally developed in various forms by Jourard (1967), Schuler (1982), and Lawson (1995). According to this contractarian approach, individual researchers and their research participants develop an agreement governing their interaction and the research procedures and methods to be used. Such an approach, when appropriately applied, can provide a more ethical and methodologically rigorous procedure for obtaining informed consent than can current practices.

The imposition of ever-more rigorous policies for protecting the rights and welfare of research participants, although arguably morally justifiable, has come to represent a significant threat to researchers' freedom to pursue significant scientific questions (Azar, 2002). Unnecessarily restrictive ethical requirements can undermine the methodology of a study, thereby making the research costlier and less beneficial for all those involved. Nonetheless, recent ethical developments have successfully achieved certain desirable objectives for psychology. It is impressive to recognize the relative rapidity by which the moral imperatives of research practices have entered into the collective psyche of investigators. Less than 50 years ago, research ethics rarely, if ever, represented a formal component of the training and practice of psychologists. The fact that today these matters are considered as a matter of course suggests that psychologists have taken great strides in terms of acknowledging and responding to their ethical and moral responsibilities.

One noteworthy outcome has been to move researchers away from the long-standing positivistic tradition of the laboratory experiment, which was so readily embraced by psychologists for so many years, and to challenge them to seek out alternative and more innovative research approaches (including qualitative, cross-cultural, and contextually oriented ones)—just the sort of outcome that Ralph Rosnow so passionately argued for in *Paradigms in Transition* (1981). In this sense, psychology has come full circle, while further evolving as a legitimate science. The ethical conflicts encountered as a result of efforts to cope with the problems linked to the cognitive problem-solving capabilities of psychology's basic object of inquiry have led to the emergence of stricter research controls, which in turn have had an influence on the way psychologists conduct their scientific investigations.

Further investigations are necessary for clarifying the impact of ethical guidelines and institutional review on research practice and participant behavior, including whether psychologists have begun to eschew the pursuit of certain research questions for fear that their research proposals never would be approved by an institutional review board. Additionally, review board members need to be sufficiently trained and sensitized about the complex methodological issues inherent in the conduct of rigorous research, and also about the hazards of imposing unreasonable restrictions on researchers (Colombo, 1995). Much has changed within the research context since Ralph Rosnow began his long and productive career in social psychology. Gone are the days when the use of deceptive manipulations had become like a game for many researchers, as Herbert Kelman (1967) once lamented, "often played with great skill and virtuosity" (p. 2) and sometimes involving a series of severe deceptions in which one falsehood is built on another. Even so, we still have a long way to go before the artifacts–ethics dilemma can be sufficiently put to rest.

REFERENCES

Adair, J. G., Dushenko, T. W., & Lindsay, R. C. L. (1985). Ethical regulations and their impact on research practice. *American Psychologist, 40,* 59–72.

Aguinis, H., & Henle, C. A. (2001). Empirical assessment of the ethics of the bogus pipeline. *Journal of Applied Social Psychology, 31,* 352–375.

Allen, D. F. (1983). Follow-up analysis of use of forewarning and deception in psychology experiments. *Psychological Reports, 52,* 899–906.

Allen, V. (1966). Effect of knowledge of deception on conformity. *Journal of Social Psychology, 69,* 101–106.

American Psychological Association. (2002). Ethical principles of psychologists and code of conduct. *American Psychologist, 57,* 1060–1073.

Aronson, E. (1966). Avoidance of inter-subject communication. *Psychological Reports, 19,* 238.

Aronson, E., & Carlsmith, J. (1968). Experimentation in social psychology. In G. Lindsay & E. Aronson (Eds.), *The handbook of social psychology* (Vol. 2, pp. 1–79). Cambridge, MA: Addison-Wesley.

Azar, B. (2002). Ethics at the cost of research? *Monitor on Psychology, 33,* 38–40.

Bardsley, N. (2000). *Control without deception* (Tinbergen Institute Discussion Paper). Rotterdam: University of Amsterdam.

Baumrind, D. (1985). Research using intentional deception: Ethical issues revisited. *American Psychologist, 40,* 165–174.

Blass, T. (2004). *The man who shocked the world: The life and legacy of Stanley Milgram.* New York, NY: Basic Books.

Bonetti, S. (1998). Experimental economics and deception. *Journal of Economic Psychology, 19,* 377–395.

Brock, T. C., & Becker, L. A. (1966). Debriefing and susceptibility to subsequent experimental manipulations. *Journal of Experimental Social Psychology, 2,* 314–323.

Broder, A. (1998). Deception can be acceptable. *American Psychologist, 53,* 85–86.

Christensen, L. (1988). Deception in psychological research: When is its use justified? *Personality and Social Psychology Bulletin, 14,* 664–675.

Clark, R. D., & Word, L. E. (1974). Where is the apathetic bystander? Situational characteristics of the emergency. *Journal of Personality and Social Psychology, 29,* 279–287.

Collins, F. L., Jr., Kuhn, I. F., Jr., & King, G. D. (1979). Variables affecting subjects' ethical ratings of proposed experiments. *Psychological Reports, 44,* 155–164.

Colombo, J. (1995). Cost, utility, and judgments of institutional review boards. *Psychological Science, 6,* 318–319.

Cook, T. D., Bean, J. R., Calder, B. J., Frey, R., Krovetz, M. L., & Reisman, S. R. (1970). Demand characteristics and three conceptions of the frequently deceived subject. *Journal of Personality and Social Psychology, 14*, 185–194.

Cook, T. D., & Perrin, B. F. (1971). The effects of suspiciousness of deception and the perceived legitimacy of deception on task performance in an attitude change experiment. *Journal of Personality, 39*, 204–224.

Diener, E. (2001). Over-concern with research ethics. *Dialogue, 16*, 2.

Diener, E., & Crandall, R. (1978). *Ethics in social and behavioral research*. Chicago: The University of Chicago Press.

Diener, E., Matthews, R., & Smith, R. (1972). Leakage of experimental information to potential future subjects by debriefed subjects. *Journal of Experimental Research in Personality, 6*, 264–267.

Epstein, Y. M., Suedfeld, P., & Silverstein, S. J. (1973). The experimental contract: Subjects' expectations of and reactions to some behaviors of experimenters. *American Psychologist, 28*, 212–221.

Farr, J. L., & Seaver, W. B. (1975). Stress and discomfort in psychological research: Subjects' perception of experimental procedures. *American Psychologist, 30*, 770–773.

Fillenbaum, R. S. (1966). Prior deception and subsequent experimental performance: The faithful subject. *Journal of Personality and Social Psychology, 4*, 532–537.

Finney, P. D. (1987). When consent information refers to risk and deception: Implications for social research. *Journal of Social Behavior and Personality, 2*, 37–48.

Gallo, P. S., Smith, S., & Mumford, S. (1973). Effects of deceiving subjects upon experimental results. *Journal of Social Psychology, 89*, 99–107.

Geller, D. M. (1982). Alternatives to deception: Why, what, and how? In J. E. Sieber (Ed.), *The ethics of social research: Surveys and experiments* (pp. 39–55). New York: Springer-Verlag.

Gerdes, E. P. (1979). College students' reactions to social psychological experiments involving deception. *Journal of Social Psychology, 107*, 99–110.

Glinski, R. J., Glinski, B. C., & Slatin, P. T. (1970). Nonnaivety contamination in conformity experiments: Sources, effects, and implications for control. *Journal of Personality and Social Psychology, 16*, 478–485.

Golding, S. L., & Lichtenstein, E. (1970). Confession of awareness and prior knowledge of deceptions as a function of interview set and approval motivation. *Journal of Personality and Social Psychology, 14*, 213–223.

Greenberg, M. (1967). Role playing: An alternative to deception? *Journal of Personality and Social Psychology, 7*, 152–157.

Haney, C., Banks, W. C., & Zimbardo, P. G. (1973). Interpersonal dynamics in a simulated prison. *International Journal of Criminology and Penology, 1*, 69–96.

Hey, J. D. (1998). Experimental economics and deception. *Journal of Economic Psychology, 19*, 397–401.

Holmes, D. (1973). Effectiveness of debriefing after a stress producing deception. *Journal of Research in Personality, 7*, 127–138.

Holmes, D. (1976). Debriefing after psychological experiments. *American Psychologist, 31*, 858–867.

Holmes, D., & Bennett, D. (1974). Experiments to answer questions raised by the use of deception in psychological research. *Journal of Personality and Social Psychology, 29*, 358–367.

Horowitz, I. L. (1967). *The rise and fall of Project Camelot*. Cambridge, MA: MIT Press.

Humphreys, L. (1970). *Tearoom trade*. Chicago: Aldine.

Jones, J. H. (1993). *Bad blood: The Tuskegee syphilis experiment* (Rev. ed.). New York: Free Press.

Jones, S. E. (2001). Ethics code draft published for comment. *Monitor on Psychology, 32,* 76.

Jourard, S. M. (1967). Experimenter–subject dialogue: A paradigm for a humanistic science of psychology. In J. F. T. Bugental (Ed.), *Challenges of humanistic psychology* (pp. 109–116). New York: McGraw-Hill.

Kelman, H. C. (1967). Human use of human subjects: The problem of deception in social psychological experiments. *Psychological Bulletin, 67,* 1–11.

Kelman, H. C. (1996). Foreword. In A. J. Kimmel, *Ethical issues in behavioral research: A survey* (pp. xiii–xv). Cambridge, MA: Blackwell.

Kifner, J. (2001, September 10). A recipe for distress. *The International Herald Tribune,* p. 3.

Kimmel, A. J. (1988). *Ethics and values in applied social research.* Newbury Park, CA: Sage.

Kimmel, A. J. (1996). *Ethical issues in behavioral research: A survey.* Cambridge, MA: Blackwell.

Kimmel, A. J. (2001). Ethical trends in marketing and psychological research. *Ethics & Behavior, 11,* 131–149.

Kimmel, A. J. (2003). Ethical issues in social psychology research. In C. Sansone, C. C. Morf, & A. T. Panter (Eds.), *Handbook of methods in social psychology* (pp. 45–70). Newbury Park, CA: Sage.

Kimmel, A. J. (2004, August). *Ethical trends in psychology and marketing research: An update.* Paper presented at the 112th annual convention of the American Psychological Association, Honolulu, HI.

Kimmel, A. J., & Smith, N. C. (2001). Deception in marketing research: Ethical, methodological, and disciplinary implications. *Psychology & Marketing, 18,* 663–689.

Lawson, C. (1995). Research participation as a contract. *Ethics & Behavior, 5,* 205–215.

Leach, M. M., & Harbin, J. J. (1997). Psychological ethics codes: A comparison of twenty-four countries. *International Journal of Psychology, 32,* 181–192.

Levy, L. H. (1967). Awareness, learning, and the beneficent subject as expert witness. *Journal of Personality and Social Psychology, 6,* 365–370.

Lichtenstein, E. (1970). Please don't talk to anyone about this experiment: Disclosure of deception by debriefed subjects. *Psychological Reports, 26,* 485–486.

Lipton, J. P., & Garza, R. T. (1978). Further evidence for subject pool contamination. *European Journal of Social Psychology, 6,* 363–370.

McDaniel, T., & Starmer, C. (1998). Experimental economics and deception: A comment. *Journal of Economic Psychology, 19,* 403–409.

McNamara, J. R., & Woods, K. M. (1977). Ethical considerations in psychological research: A comparative review. *Behavior Therapy, 8,* 703–708.

Milgram, S. (1963). Behavioral study of obedience. *Journal of Abnormal and Social Psychology, 67,* 371–378.

Milgram, S. (1964). Issues in the study of obedience: A reply to Baumrind. *American Psychologist, 67,* 371–378.

Mills, J. (1976). A procedure for explaining experiments involving deception. *Personality and Social Psychology Bulletin, 2,* 3–13.

Misra, S. (1992). Is conventional debriefing adequate? An ethical issue in consumer research. *Journal of the Academy of Marketing Science, 20,* 269–273.

Mueller, J. (2003). Overkill by IRBs. *APS Observer, 16*(10), 3.

Mueller, J. H., & Furedy, J. J. (2001). Reviewing for risk: What's the evidence that it works? *APS Observer, 14*(7), 1, 26–28.

Newberry, B. H. (1973). Truth-telling in subjects with information about experiments: Who is being deceived? *Journal of Personality and Social Psychology, 25,* 369–374.

Nicks, S. D., Korn, J. H., & Mainieri, T. (1997). The rise and fall of deception in social psychology and personality research, 1921 to 1994. *Ethics & Behavior, 7,* 69–77.

Ortmann, A., & Hertwig, R. (1997). Is deception acceptable? *American Psychologist, 52,* 746–747.

Page, M. M. (1973). On detecting demand awareness by postexperimental questionnaire. *Journal of Social Psychology, 91,* 305–323.

Pihl, R. O., Zacchia, C., & Zeichner, A. (1981). Follow-up analysis of the use of deception and aversive contingencies in psychological experiments. *Psychological Reports, 48,* 927–930.

Resnick, J. H., & Schwartz, T. (1973). Ethical standards as an independent variable in psychological research. *American Psychologist, 28,* 134–139.

Ring, K., Wallston, K., & Corey, M. (1970). Mode of debriefing as a factor affecting subjective reaction to a Milgram-type obedience experiment: An ethical inquiry. *Representative Research in Social Psychology, 1,* 67–88.

Rosenthal, R., & Rosnow, R. L. (1969). *Artifact in behavioral research.* New York: Academic Press.

Rosenthal, R., & Rosnow, R. L. (1991). *Essentials of behavioral research: Methods and data analysis* (2nd ed.). New York: McGraw-Hill.

Rosenzweig, S. (1933). The experimental situation as a psychological problem. *Psychological Review, 40,* 337–354.

Rosnow, R. L. (1981). *Paradigms in transition: The methodology of social inquiry.* New York: Oxford University Press.

Rosnow, R. L. (1997). Hedgehogs, foxes, and the evolving social contract in psychological science: Ethical challenges and methodological opportunities. *Psychological Methods, 2,* 345–356.

Rosnow, R. L. (2002, October 18). The nature and role of demand characteristics in scientific inquiry. Prevention & Treatment, Vol. 5 (Article pre0050037c). Available: http://journals.apa.org/prevention/volume5/pre0050037c.html

Rosnow, R. L., Strohmetz, D. B., & Aditya, R. N. (2000). Artifact in research. In A. E. Kazdin (Ed.), *Encyclopedia of psychology* (Vol. 1, pp. 242–245). New York: Oxford University Press & American Psychological Association.

Ross, L., Lepper, M. R., & Hubbard, M. (1975). Perseverance in self-perception and social perception: Biased attributional processes in the debriefing paradigm. *Journal of Personality and Social Psychology, 32,* 880–892.

Rugg, E. A. (1975). *Ethical judgments of social research involving experimental deception.* Unpublished doctoral dissertation, George Peabody College for Teachers, Nashville, TN.

Schuler, H. (1982). *Ethical problems in psychological research.* New York: Academic Press.

Shadish, W. R., Cook, T. D., & Campbell, D. T. (2001). *Experimental and quasi-experimental designs for generalized causal inference.* Boston: Houghton Mifflin.

Sharpe, D., Adair, J. G., & Roese, N. J. (1992). Twenty years of deception research: A decline in subjects' trust? *Personality and Social Psychology Bulletin, 18,* 585–590.

Sieber, J. E., Iannuzzo, R., & Rodriguez, B. (1995). Deception methods in psychology: Have they changed in 23 years? *Ethics & Behavior, 5,* 67–85.

Silverman, I., Shulman, A. D., & Wiesenthal, D. L. (1970). Effects of deceiving and debriefing psychological subjects on performance in later experiments. *Journal of Personality and Social Psychology, 14,* 203–212.

Singer, E. (1984). Public reactions to some ethical issues of social research: Attitudes and behavior. *Journal of Consumer Research, 11,* 501–509.

Smith, C. P. (1981). How (un)acceptable is research involving deception? *IRB: A Review of Human Subjects Research, 3,* 1–4.

Smith, N. C., Klein, J. G., & Kimmel, A. J. (2002). *The ethics of deception in consumer research.* Unpublished manuscript, London Business School.

Smith, S. S., & Richardson, D. (1983). Amelioration of deception and harm in psychological research: The important role of debriefing. *Journal of Personality and Social Psychology, 44,* 1075–1082.

Spielberger, C. D. (1962). The role of awareness in verbal conditioning. *Journal of Personality, 30,* 73–101.

Spoiling the broth. (2001, September 11). *The New York Times,* p. 3.

Stang, D. J. (1976). Ineffective deception in conformity research: Some causes and consequences. *European Journal of Social Psychology, 6,* 353–367.

Stricker, L. J. (1967). The true deceiver. *Psychological Bulletin, 68,* 13–20.

Stricker, L. J., Messick, S., & Jackson, D. N. (1967). Suspicion of deception: Implications for conformity research. *Journal of Personality and Social Psychology, 5,* 379–389.

Strohmetz, D. G., & Rosnow, R. L. (1994). A mediational model of research artifacts. In J. Brzezinski (Ed.), *Probability in theory building* (pp. 177–196). Amsterdam: Editions Rodopi.

Sullivan, D. S., & Deiker, T. E. (1973). Subject-experimenter perceptions of ethical issues in human research. *American Psychologist, 28,* 587–591.

Suls, J., & Rosnow, R. L. (1988). Concerns about artifacts in psychological experiments. In J. G. Morawski (Ed.), *The rise of experimentation in American psychology* (pp. 163–187). New Haven, CT: Yale University Press.

Taylor, K. M., & Shepperd, J. A. (1996). Probling suspicion among participants in deception research. *American Psychologist, 51,* 886–887.

Toy, D., Olson, J., & Wright, L. (1989). Effects of debriefing in marketing research involving "mild" deceptions. *Psychology and Marketing, 6,* 69–85.

Toy, D., Wright, L., & Olson, J. (2001). A conceptual framework for analyzing deception and debriefing effects in marketing research. *Psychology and Marketing, 18,* 663–689.

Turner, C. W., & Simons, L. S. (1974). Effects of subject sophistication and evaluation apprehension on aggressive responses to weapons. *Journal of Personality and Social Psychology, 30,* 341–348.

Valins, S. (1974). Persistent effects of information about reactions: Ineffectiveness of debriefing. In H. London & R. Nisbett (Eds.), *Thought and feeling* (pp. 116–124). Chicago: Aldine.

Vitelli, R. (1988). The crisis issue assessed: An empirical analysis. *Basic and Applied Social Psychology, 9,* 301–309.

Walsh, W. B., & Stillman, S. M. (1974). Disclosure of deception by debriefed subjects. *Journal of Counseling Psychology, 21,* 315–319.

Walster, E., Berscheid, E., Abrahams, D., & Aronson, V. (1967). Effectiveness of debriefing following deception experiments. *Journal of Personality and Social Psychology, 6,* 371–380.

Wegner, D., Coulton, G., & Wenzlaff, R. (1985). The transparency of denial: Briefing in the debriefing paradigm. *Journal of Personality and Social Psychology, 49,* 338–346.

Wiener, R. L., & Erker, P. V. (1986). The effects of prebriefing misinformed research participants on their attributions of responsibility. *Journal of Psychology, 120,* 397–410.

Willis, R. H., & Willis, Y. A. (1970). Role playing versus deception: An experimental comparison. *Journal of Personality and Social Psychology, 16,* 472–477.

8

Science and Ethics in Conducting, Analyzing, and Reporting Disability Policy Research

Peter Blanck, Helen A. Schartz,
Heather Ritchie, and Robert Rosenthal[1]
*Syracuse University, University of Iowa,
and University of California, Riverside*

With the rise of the disability civil rights movement, a wave of social science research has emerged that focuses on both disability as a natural part of life and the necessity for accommodation of disability in social policies and laws (DeJong, 1979). The new rights paradigm of disability has been examined through the lens of a variety of disciplines—disability studies, psychology, sociology, history, economics, computer science, and law—and from interdisciplinary perspectives (Blanck, 2000; Blanck & Schartz, 2001; Hahn, 1985).

Despite the growing prominence of the disability rights model, the majority of social and policy research conducted to date has not sufficiently in-

[1]The program of research described herein is supported, in part, by grants to the first author from The National Institute on Disability and Rehabilitation Research (NIDRR), U.S. Department of Education grants: (a) "Technology for Independence: A Community-Based Resource Center," #H133A021801; (b) "IT Works," #H133A011803; (c) The Rehabilitation Research and Training Center on Workforce Investment and Employment Policy for People with Disabilities, #H133B980042-99; as well as grants from The University of Iowa College of Law Foundation; The Great Plains ADA and IT Center; and a generous endowment to the LHPDC from Stan and Gail Richards. For information on LHPDC grant funding, see http://disability.law.uiowa.edu

cluded the perspective of persons with disabilities in the research process and as uniquely qualified researchers (Blanck, Ritchie, Schmeling, & Klein, 2003). Nor has prior social science research adequately examined the impact of the rights model of disability on collaboration among disability researchers and researchers from disciplines such as law and the social sciences (Seelman, 2000). Lastly, disability policy research that has been conducted has not been adequately summarized or evaluated using meta-analytic techniques.

This chapter describes a number of scientific and ethical issues relevant to conducting, analyzing, and reporting disability policy research. The chapter bears the imprint of Ralph Rosnow, who has promoted, taught, and conducted social science research in ways consistent with the highest ethical and scientific standards (Rosnow, Rotheram-Borus, Ceci, Blanck, & Koocher, 1993). However, it is not this chapter alone that has profited from Ralph Rosnow's contributions; rather, it is the social sciences more broadly that have been enriched.

The first part of this chapter explores scientific and ethical issues related to the design and conduct of disability policy research. The chapter then discusses how the analysis and reporting of research have implications for the evaluation of disability policy research.

SCIENCE AND ETHICS
IN DISABILITY POLICY RESEARCH

In contrast to the prior medical model that stressed welfare and dependency, the disability civil rights framework proposes that governmental policies foster equality by eliminating the physical, economic, and social barriers that preclude participation of people with disabilities in society (Blanck, Hill, Siegal, & Waterstone, 2003, 2005; Blanck & Millender, 2000; NCD, 1986; Silverstein, 2000). This framework is reflected in laws such as the Americans with Disabilities Act (ADA) of 1990, the reauthorization of the Rehabilitation Act of 1973, the Individuals with Disabilities Education Act (IDEA), the Technology-Related Assistance for Individuals with Disabilities Act, and the Ticket to Work and Work Incentives Improvement Act (TWWIIA) (Blanck, 1998; Blanck & Schartz, 2001). The framework has been applied in research on labor force participation rates, independent living, vocational rehabilitation services, and the provision of health care (Cook & Burke, 2002).

The U.S. Department of Education's National Institute on Disability and Rehabilitation Research (NIDRR) has encouraged the inclusion of social scientists with disabilities in the conduct of disability policy research (NIDRR, 1999). One purpose of Title II of the Rehabilitation Act of 1973, under which NIDRR is authorized, is to increase opportunities for researchers with disabilities (Seelman, 2000; Tewey, 1997). However, the majority of research to date that affects persons with disabilities does not include their unique perspectives as social scientists and participants in the development, design, and conduct of the research. Scotch (2002) asserted that this is because, historically, many people with disabilities have found it difficult to join the ranks of senior social science researchers.

The lack of significant involvement of people with disabilities in the research process as researchers and participants has created a disjuncture between disability policy research and its real-world relevance to persons with disabilities (Blanck, 2004). Recently, disability policy investigators, many with impairments themselves, have been at the forefront of calling for research (and research funding strategies) that incorporates participation from, and the perspective of, the disability community (Barnes, 1992; Gill, 2001; Linton, 1998; Oliver, 1992, 1996; Seelman, 1993, 2000; Stone & Priestley, 1996; Zarb, 1992).

Underlying the critiques of prior disability policy research is the premise that there is a direct relationship between the scientific quality (i.e., usefulness and external validity) and the ethics of the way disability policy research is conducted, analyzed, and reported (cf. Blanck, Bellack, Rotheram-Borus, Rosnow, & Schooler, 1992; Rosenthal & Blanck, 1993). Everything else equal, research of higher scientific quality about persons with disabilities likely is more ethically defensible and relevant to the disability community and policymakers. Similarly, the higher the quality of the research program, the better the investment of participants' time, granting agencies' money, and policymakers' consideration of the findings.

The following sections identify considerations in disability policy research—not all of which are unique to this area of study—related to the methods and procedures employed in the study and recruitment of participants with disabilities. Of course, in evaluating the ethical employment of human participants generally, issues of safety may be distinguished from more subtle issues of research ethics (Blanck et al., 1992). Although research that is unsafe for participants is ethically questionable, perfectly "safe" research, which puts no participant at risk, also may be ethically questionable because of the shortcomings of the design.

Researchers and Issues of Design

Imagine that Congress, for purposes of possible amendment of the ADA, commissions a study on the impact of the law on the employment of persons with disabilities. Congress is aware that critics suggest that the ADA—enacted in part to eliminate discrimination against those with disabilities and thereby enhance their employment opportunities—has failed miserably in its goals.

Anecdotal reports suggest that the employment rates of individuals with disabilities are worsening rather than improving since the ADA went into effect. Those reports lead Congress to question whether the ADA, despite its "good intentions," is a cause of the apparent declines. Some in Congress are quick to conclude that the answer to this question is "yes," if only because the reports of employment rates of individuals with disabilities appear to confirm their general perception that the ADA is an unnecessary, or otherwise "bad," law (Schwochau & Blanck, 2003).

Congress decides to fund a study hypothesizing that the ADA has depressed the employment rates of persons with disabilities (cf. Blanck, Schur, Kruse, Schwochau, & Song, 2003). What many Congressional members may not realize, however, is that how the research question is framed, and particularly how the study defines the term *disability*, can dramatically affect the study's findings and their relevance to ADA policy. For instance, the ADA defines disability as a physical or mental impairment that substantially limits a major life activity, whereas the Social Security Disability Insurance (SSDI) program defines disability as an inability to engage in "substantial gainful activity" and requires a medical assessment of the disabling condition (Schmeling, Schartz, & Blanck, 2005). Thus, at least two research design issues, among others, may be raised: how best to identify the group of individuals with disabilities affected by the ADA, and whether amending the ADA can be expected to improve the employment prospects of those who seek its protections.

The proposed ADA study raises other important, albeit more subtle, ethical issues based on its design. If the purpose of the research is to examine the employment rate of those with disabilities relative to those without disabilities, then it may be sufficient to use a measure that asks individuals whether they are "disabled," or whether they have a disability that prevents or limits their work (Hale, 2001).

However, such an approach, taken without regard to the ADA's language, likely will not yield valid conclusions (Hale 2001; Schwochau & Blanck, 2000). Given the ADA's definition of disability and its requirement that individuals be "qualified," the group of individuals covered by the law is significantly restricted. Neither those whose disability completely prevents them from working nor those whose disability imposes only some functional limitation can expect to be in the ADA-protected population (Blanck, 1997, 1998). Moreover, interpretations of the ADA by courts show that many individuals who consider themselves to have disabilities would not be protected by the ADA, and many who do not consider themselves "disabled" may be covered by the law (Blanck, 2000).

Second, the hypothetical ADA study's central goal is to determine the "causal impact" of the ADA on employment of persons with disabilities. However, the research design does not permit reasonable causal inference because of the absence of randomization or means to evaluate plausible rival hypotheses and potential confounding variables (Cook & Campbell, 1979).

For these reasons alone, the proposed ADA study likely would lead Congress to unwarranted and inaccurate conclusions about the law. Had the research design been improved by including, for instance, a valid articulation of the relevant sample, the ethical issues would have been less acute. The research might have been restricted to a representative random sample of those individuals matched on certain characteristics who would, by several sources, be considered most likely to meet the ADA definition of disability before and after the implementation of the law.

Other design issues are to be considered. As Kruse and Schur (2003) point out, if the ADA is effective in eliminating physical barriers (e.g., promoting accessible transportation) that have historically thwarted the attempts of individuals with disabilities to go to work, over time fewer individuals will consider themselves as having a disability. The study's measure of employment rate pre- and post-ADA is, for these and other reasons, extremely complicated to assess.

Even assuming that the research design issues identified may be addressed adequately, how is Congress to decide whether the ADA should be amended? Whether amendment occurs is, of course, dependent on whether Congress can be persuaded that what has happened, or not happened, since the ADA went into effect deviates from the desired policy goals of the law, and that amendment to the ADA will rectify the situation. It is these public policy questions that are the ultimate queries. In the final part of this chapter, we return to this idea and suggest the importance of meta-analytic techniques to help in their resolution.

Participants and Participatory Action Research (PAR)

Much attention has been devoted to considering ethical issues in the selection and recruitment of human participants in social science research (Grisso, Baldwin, Blanck, & Rotheram-Borus, 1991; Kelman, 1968; Rosenthal & Blanck, 1993). In the classic model of social science research, a researcher, often an academician, gathers data from research participants. The legal and privacy rights of research participants are protected by various informed consent procedures as approved by institutional human subjects committees or review boards (IRBs).

Perhaps as a backlash to the general exclusion of persons with disabilities in the design and conduct of disability policy research, recently there have been initiatives to engage participants with disabilities not as "subjects" of disability policy research, but instead as participants in the research process (Blanck, Ritchie, et al., 2003). The concept of research participant as "collaborator" is not new. What is relatively new, however, is that rather than experiencing research as something that is conducted on the disability community, as historically has been the case, social science researchers are beginning to explore methods that facilitate collaboration between researchers and the disability community in disability policy research. One historical cornerstone of this social science method is participatory action research (PAR; Whyte, 1991).

There are numerous conceptualizations of PAR in a range of disciplinary contexts. In general, PAR promotes the collaboration of researcher and community members in the creation of knowledge that advances community action and change. Most frequently, PAR research is conducted at the local level, drawing on knowledge and expertise of community members (Eriksson, 1999). The PAR team research process is similar to Lewin's (1999) classic spiral of social action represented as interconnected steps of planning, acting, observing, and reflecting, with each cycle influencing the next (McTaggart, 1997; Stringer, 1999). In PAR, the researcher acts more as group facilitator and coinvestigator in problem solving (Greenwood & Levin, 1998; Stringer, 1999).

As Seelman (1993) explained, traditional disability policy research has focused on individuals, and not on "populations and environmental accessibility. The implication is that the problem is located with the individual not with the society." (p. 120). Historically, research that has examined the experience of disability has located study on the individual; thus, at this level, in our hypothetical study Congress might ask, "What is it about individuals with disabilities that do not enable them to benefit from the ADA?"

Little attention has been focused on the interaction between the individual and the environment in which the individual experiences disability. Many disability scholars argue that, in the past, research involving persons with disabilities has created and perpetuated an unequal relationship in which "the interviewer presents as expert and the disabled person as an isolated individual inexperienced in research" (Oliver, 1990, p. 8). Most national surveys have examined disability as functional limitations, and not as a relationship determined by the individual and environmental supports or barriers (Blanck, 2005; Oliver, 1992; Schwochau & Blanck, 2000).

PAR advances a model of research that is embedded in this social context (Oliver, 1992). Whyte (1995) understood that PAR engages community members in the research process—including formulating the questions, designing the research, participating in data collection, interpreting the results, and using the product. By emphasizing participation, PAR promotes collaborative inquiry, empowerment of community partners through mutual decision making, and ownership of ideas (Chataway, 1997; Stone & Priestley, 1996). PAR views individuals as "responsible agents who participate actively in making their own histories and conditions of life"

(McTaggart, 1997, p. 39). In disability policy research, the values of inclu-sion and empowerment advanced by PAR align with the self-determination principles of the disability rights movement.

Prior PAR literature has examined the power dynamics between commu-nity members and researchers (Gaventa, 1993; Mason & Boutilier, 1996; Stone & Priestley, 1996; Zarb, 1992), training persons with disabilities to collect the research data (Morrell-Bellai & Boydell, 1994), methodological concerns (Chataway, 1997; Kondrat & Juliá, 1997; McTaggart, 1997), and conflict resolution during the research process (Simonson & Bushaw, 1993). Other disenfranchised groups in society have used PAR to document experiences of inequity.

PAR has been advanced in feminist research methodology to address women's oppression (Cancian, 1992; Gorelick, 1991; Maguire, 1987, 1993; Mahlstedt, 1999; Reinharz, 1992), in work environments to gain knowledge regarding organizational behavior (Whyte, 1991), in North American com-munity development (Horton, 1993; Jackson, 1993; Puckett & Harkavy, 1999), and in international social development (Anyawu, 1988; Green-wood, 1999; McTaggart, 1997; for a review of the historical use of PAR in North America, see Puckett & Harkavy, 1999).

Bruyère's (1993) Delphi survey of NIDRR Research and Rehabilitation Training Centers found that few disability researchers employed PAR. How-ever, seven years later and with implementation of the ADA, Campbell and Seekins' (2000) analysis of the NIDRR-sponsored research publications found over 500 articles and reports that used one of twelve dimensions of PAR.

Our review of disability research incorporating PAR (Blanck, Ritchie, et al., 2003) indicates its usage in research involving individuals living with mental disability (Mason & Boutilier, 1996; Morrell-Bellai & Boydell, 1994; Ochocka, Janzen, & Nelson, 2002; Rapp, Shera, & Kisthardt, 1993; Townsend, Birch, Langley, & Langille, 2000), individu-als with chronic illness (Low, Shelley, & O'Connor, 2000), members of the deaf and hard-of-hearing community (Taylor, 1999), and individuals with learning difficulties (Rodgers, 1999). Recently, disability policy is-sues have been investigated using PAR, including study of physical ac-cessibility issues (Brydon-Miller, 1993), school-to-work transitioning of youth with disabilities (DePoy, Hartman, & Haslett, 1999), workplace accommodations (Frank, 2003), and collaborations between independ-ent living centers and vocational rehabilitation state and tribal agencies (Temkin & Hanson, 2000).

As with any method of social science study, there are research design and ethical issues associated with PAR in the context of disability policy re-search. One cornerstone of traditional experimental social science research, as articulated by Rosnow and Rosenthal (1997), is consideration of possible biasing effects of the researchers (e.g., observer bias and experimenter expectancy). To assess biasing effects, researchers use randomization techniques and seek to replicate research, the building block of science, to confirm findings with different investigators and participants, and under different conditions.

PAR provides a different, albeit complementary, means for assessing and exploiting bias. In PAR, the research participants themselves are integrated into the research process, so new questions of research validity and generalizability arise; again, "whose truth" is being measured? However, research involves trade-offs, and PAR may give in internal validity what it gains in external or ecological validity. External validity is one measure of the generalizability of the findings to other populations, occasions, and measures (Rosenthal & Rosnow, 1975, 1991; Rosnow & Rosenthal, 2002; Webb, Campbell, Schwartz, & Sechrest, 1966). In PAR, individuals with disabilities enhance external validity by clarifying research design issues that, in turn, may enhance the study's relevance to like communities or policymakers.

If our hypothetical ADA study commissioned by Congress used a PAR approach, participant-researchers might suggest questions about environmental barriers to employment that affect the impact of the ADA, such as participants' access to transportation and health care. They might bring to the study an expertise on improving the response rate from persons with disabilities; for instance, presenting the survey or research instruments in accessible formats to persons with a wide range of disabilities, such as visual, hearing, mobility, and cognitive impairments.

In these and other ways, the participant-researchers enhance the real-world impact of the research. Importantly, PAR can enhance the conduct of subsequent traditional social science study on the topic. In complementary ways, research designs that enhance the generality of research results allow social scientists to view human research participants as yet another "granting agency," which, in reality, they are, because participants must decide whether to grant social scientists their time, attention, and cooperation (Rosenthal, 1994; Rosenthal & Rosnow, 1975).

In disability policy research, a goal related to enhancing the external validity of findings, is to maximize the ways in which disability policy research supports the legitimate goals of the community. Of course, who decides the issue of "legitimacy" is a key question (Melrose, 2001). However, in the absence of meaningful contribution by individuals with disabilities to the research process, findings may have little relevance to daily life. Thus, research validity is enhanced so as to be relevant to the design and outcome of the research; for instance, to address real-world problems relevant to persons with disabilities (Melrose, 2001).

Science and Ethics
in Interpreting Disability Policy Research

Through the scientific process—the conduct and presentation of multiple studies conducted by different researchers—the disability policy community or Congress (as any other research consumer community) evaluates research claims and hyperclaims. Absent systematic information about the participants, research design, and method, stakeholders such as policymakers, the scientific community, granting agencies, and the disability community are limited in their ability to evaluate research claims.

One component of the researcher's ethical obligation is to explain to the participants and to the relevant community of consumers what the research may accomplish (and what it may not). Of course, even when researchers carefully explain their results and the limitations of their findings, consumers of research (even high law courts) may misuse the information.

In passing the ADA, Congress found that some 54,000,000 Americans have disabilities. The U.S. Supreme Court then interpreted this finding to mean that a restricted number of these individuals with disabilities should be afforded the protections of the ADA (Blanck, 2000). Although there is much debate about the origin of the statistics, the National Council on Disability (NCD, 2002) had cautioned Congress that a precise and reliable figure of persons with disabilities is unavailable, "due to differing operational definitions of disability, divergent sources of data, and inconsistent survey methodologies, which together make it impossible to aggregate much of the data that are available" (NCD, 1986, p. 2).

Related to the issue of hyperclaiming is the phenomenon of causism (Rosenthal & Blanck, 1993). *Causism* refers to the tendency to imply a causal relationship where none has been established, and where the research design and data do not support it. Understanding the nature of causism is central to the presentation of research.

Even where experimentally controlled studies are not conducted or desired, as is the case in field-based PAR studies, the characteristics of causism are important to identify. Causism includes the absence of an appropriate real-world basis supporting the causal inference. It includes the inappropriate presence of language directly implying cause-and-effect relationship; for example, phrases such as *the effect of, the impact of, the consequence of,* or *as a result,* where more appropriate language would have been *is related to, is predictable from,* or *may be inferred from.*

As an ethical matter, there may be self-serving benefits (or advocacy goals in the policy community) to the "causist" claim. Thus, the ADA has "impacted" declining employment rates of persons with disabilities and, therefore, the law should be amended. Causism is self-serving because it makes the causist's result appear more important or fundamental than is deserved.

Whereas well-trained social scientists differentiate causist language from inferentially accurate language, research participants, policymakers, the press, and Congress ordinarily cannot. One consequence of knowledge of causism, however, is to invite probing of the design and evaluation of the research. Evaluation of the potential generalizability of a study's results, and of its subsequent usefulness to the relevant community, may include review of participant selection and participation rates.

PAR is one method to foster meaningful understanding of research design and assumptions underlying research methods. In disability policy research, relevant community members help to put findings in context and assess whether they are an appropriate basis for public policy regarding individuals with disabilities

Causism is one example of how social scientists or others can use bad science to misrepresent research results. Poor quality of research design, data analysis, and research reporting lessen the ethical justification and real-world relevance of any research project. This applies not only where deception, discomfort, or embarrassment of the participants is involved but, in many cases, to the most benign research experience for participants.

If, because of the poor quality of the science, no benefit can come of the research study, it is difficult for social scientists to justify the use of participants' time and effort, and the money, space, and resources that have been expended on the research project. When adding the inescapable zero-sum nature of time, attention, effort, money, and other resources to the "no good can come of it" argument, it becomes difficult to justify poor-quality research on any ethical basis.

Rosnow and his colleagues (1993) and Rosenthal (1994) suggested that Institutional Review Boards (IRBs) consider the technical scientific competence of the investigators whose proposals they are asked to evaluate. This will change the work required of IRB to include a focus on methodological expertise. Even then, it is not easy to reach a decision about the scientific competence of the investigator and of the particular proposal. Likewise, it is not easy to come to a decision about the more directly ethical aspects of a proposal.

When social scientists or IRBs are confronted with a questionable research proposal, they ordinarily employ a cost-utility analysis. In such an analysis, the costs of doing a study include the possible negative effects on participants, time, money, effort, and other resources. These are evaluated simultaneously against such utilities as benefits to participants, other people at other times, science, and the investigator. The potential benefits of higher-quality studies and research addressing important topics exceed the potential benefits of lower-quality studies and studies addressing less important topics. Of course, what constitutes an "important" study is open to considerable debate (see Rosnow & Rosenthal, 1984, for a diagram of this type of cost-utility analysis).

The cost-utility model alone is insufficient to answer questions of whether to conduct the study because this calculus fails to consider the costs and utilities of not conducting a particular study. The failure to conduct a study that could be conducted is as much an act to be evaluated on ethical grounds as is the conducting of a study (Kaplan, 1988). The costs of failing to conduct research may accrue to future or present generations, not including the research participants themselves.

Meta-Analysis as an Ethical Imperative in Disability Policy Research

Social scientists often are taught that it is technically improper and probably unethical to analyze and reanalyze their data in many ways. It is not proper to "snoop around" in the data and perform a "fishing expedition."

Social scientists also are taught to test their study's hypotheses with one particular preplanned statistical test, and to take a finding significant at the "p less than .05 level" as the true finding. In evaluating the importance of social science research, policymakers often are led to believe that should a statistical result not be significant at the .05 level—that it is somehow not useful to the issue at hand.

The lack of careful and regular attention by social scientists to research findings that do not yield results significant at the .05 level makes for bad science, bad ethics, and uninformed uses of social science. It makes for bad science because, although snooping does affect statistical significance or p values, it is likely to turn up something new, interesting, and important (Tukey, 1977). It makes for bad ethics, because data collection is expensive in terms of time, effort, money, and other resources, and funders are increasingly willing to attest to this fact. Finally, it makes for uninformed uses of social science research, because the full value of the study and its potential implications are not presented to other researchers and the relevant policy community.

If social science research is worth doing, it is worth analyzing thoroughly. It is worthy of holding up to the light in different ways so that research participants, funding agencies, and policymakers get their full value. Just as important, the fundamental value of data exploitation is knowledge gained. As Tukey (1969) pointed out, social science would be further ahead if data analysts thought of themselves less as clergy blessing data with p less than .05 and more as detectives solving real-world mysteries (Rosenthal & Rosnow, 1991; Rosenthal & Rubin, 1984).

Meta-analysis is a technique to exploit research findings through a set of concepts and procedures employed to quantitatively summarize a domain of research (Rosenthal, 1991a, 1991b). Compared to traditional reviews of the literature, meta-analytic procedures are more accurate, comprehensive, systematic, and statistically more powerful (Cooper & Rosenthal, 1980; Hedges & Olkin, 1985; Mosteller & Bush, 1954), particularly when the meta-analysis includes those studies that were not found to be statistically significant.

Meta-analytic procedures use more of the information in the data, yielding more accurate estimates of the magnitude of the effect or relationship being investigated; more accurate estimates of the overall level of significance of the entire research domain; and more useful information about the variables moderating the magnitude of the effect or relationship being investigated.

Meta-analysis has a unique ability to increase retroactively the benefits and lessen the costs of the studies being summarized. The costs of time, attention, and effort of human participants employed in the individual studies of the meta-analysis are justified when their data enter into a meta-analysis. This is because meta-analysis, or the summarization of studies, increases the utility of all the individual studies (McCartney & Rosenthal, 2000; Rosenthal & DiMatteo, 2001; Rosenthal & Rubin, 1971).

The failure to employ meta-analytic procedures when they could be used has important ethical implications. This is because the opportunity to increase the benefits of past individual studies has been foregone. When resources are employed by scientists to prepare literature reviews, it is fair to ask whether those resources are being used efficiently or ethically.

As in other areas of research, for many types of disability policy issues it also no longer seems acceptable, defensible, or professionally responsible to present to a policymaker the results of individual research studies that claim to contribute to the resolution of controversy (Schmidt, 1992). This is most apparent in instances in which the investigator has not already conducted a meta-analysis to determine whether, in fact, there is a controversy at all. To provide one example: A new study of the effects of psychotherapy may not be worth doing at the present time given prior meta-analytic results (Glass, 1976; Smith, Glass, & Miller, 1980). Prior to the meta-analytic work in this area, the question of the effectiveness of psychotherapy in general was controversial. It is controversial no longer.

Meta-analysis helps to resolve research and policy-based controversies because it eliminates two common errors, or misleading strategies, by social scientists in the evaluation and presentation of research replications. The first error is the belief that when one study obtains a significant effect and a replication does not, there is a failure to replicate the particular effect. This belief is clearly untrue. A failure to replicate is properly measured by the magnitude of difference between the effect sizes of the two studies.

The second error is the belief that if there is a real effect in nature, then each study of that effect will show a significant effect. Even if the effect is substantial in reality, there is a limited chance that all investigators will get results significant at the p less than .05 level.

Meta-analytic procedures increase the utility of individual studies by highlighting implications for how and whether significance testing is performed and reported. Good meta-analytic practice shows little interest in whether the results of an individual study are significant (Rosenthal, Rosnow, & Rubin, 2000). Rather than recording whether a study reached a critical level, say $p = .05$, meta-analysts record the actual level of significance obtained. Getting rid of the all-or-nothing, null-hypothesis decision procedure, and the related state of mind, in the use of social science increases the information value and real-world relevance of the particular study. In turn, this increases the real-world usefulness of the research.

Another way in which meta-analysis increases research real-world relevance and furthers the ethical justification of research studies is by providing accurate estimates of research outcomes, or effect sizes. Effect sizes can be of practical importance even when they are small (Rosenthal, 1991a, 1991b; Rosenthal & Rubin, 1982). Once social scientists and policymakers are aware that effect size—for which r values of .05, .10, and .20, for example, are associated with benefits equivalent to saving 5, 10, or 20 lives per 100 people (or preventing discrimination against individuals with disabilities)—they may more accurately weigh the costs and utilities of undertaking any particular study, as well as the ultimate real-world value of the study.

CONCLUSION

This chapter has highlighted scientific and ethical issues in conducting, analyzing, and reporting disability policy research. An organizing theme has been that the ethical quality of research is not independent of its scientific quality (Rosnow & Rosenthal, 1997). Detailing specifics of this theme serves at least two functions for social scientists, policymakers, and members of the disability community.

First, we hope that this chapter has shown how it is possible simultaneously to improve the quality of science and the quality of ethics in disability policy research. Second, we hope that, in raising more issues than it has answered, this chapter has illustrated to social scientists and policymakers that, in the matter of improving science and ethics, many issues are yet to be resolved.

AUTHORS' NOTE

Correspondence to Peter Blanck, University of Iowa College of Law, 431 Boyd Law Building, Iowa City, IA 52242-1113; e-mail: peter-blanck @uiowa.edu. Blanck is University Professor, Syracuse University, Chairman,

Burton Blatt Institute; and Charles M. & Marion Kierscht Professor of Law, and Professor of Public Health, and of Psychology at the University of Iowa (on leave), and Director of the Law, Health Policy & Disability Center (LHPDC), Ph.D., Harvard University, J.D., Stanford University. Helen A. Schartz is Director of Research, Associate Research Scientist, LHPDC, Ph.D., J.D., University of Iowa. Heather Ritchie was a Research Associate at the LHPDC, M.S.W., University of Iowa. Robert Rosenthal is Distinguished Professor of Psychology, University of California, Riverside, Ph.D., UCLA.

REFERENCES

Anyawu, C. (1988). The technique of PAR in community development. *Community Development Journal, 23,* 11–15.

Barnes, C. (1992). Qualitative research: Valuable or irrelevant? *Disability, Handicap & Society, 7,* 115–123.

Blanck, P. (1997). The economics of the employment provisions of the Americans with Disabilities Act: Part I—Workplace accommodations. *DePaul Law Review, 46,* 877–914.

Blanck, P. (1998). *The Americans with Disabilities Act and the emerging workforce: Employment of people with mental retardation.* Washington, DC: American Association on Mental Retardation.

Blanck, P. (Ed.). (2000). *Employment, disability, and the Americans with Disabilities Act: Issues in law, public policy, and research.* Evanston, IL: Northwestern University Press.

Blanck, P. (2004). Justice for all?: Stories about Americans with disabilities and their civil rights. *Journal of Gender, Race & Justice, 8,* 1–32.

Blanck, P. (Ed.). (2005). *Disability rights.* London: Ashgate.

Blanck, P., Bellack, A., Rotheram-Borus, M. J., Rosnow, R. L., & Schooler, N. (1992). Scientific rewards and conflicts of ethical choices in human subject research. *American Psychologist, 47,* 959–65.

Blanck, P., Hill, E., Siegal, C., & Waterstone, M. (2003). *Disability civil rights law and policy.* St. Paul, MN: Thomson/West

Blanck, P., Hill, E., Siegal, C., & Waterstone, M. (2005). *Disability civil rights law and policy: Cases and materials.* St. Paul, MN: Thomson/West.

Blanck, P., & Millender, M. (2000). Before disability civil rights: Civil War pensions and the politics of disability in America. *Alabama Law Review, 52,* 1–51.

Blanck, P., Morris, M., Schmeling, J., Hsieh, P., Odem, N., & Wagenbach, D. (2003). Americans with Disabilities Act (ADA) Supreme Court cases: Synopsis and implications for the Workforce Development system. *Law, Health Policy, & Disability Center Policy Brief.* Retrieved July 18, 2005, from http://disability.law.uiowa.edu

Blanck, P., Ritchie, H., Schmeling, J. A., & Klein, D. (2003). Technology for independence: A community-based resource center. *Behavioral Sciences & the Law, 21,* 51–62.

Blanck, P., & Schartz, H. (2001). Towards researching a national employment policy for persons with disabilities. In L. R. McConnell (Ed.), *Emerging workforce issues: W.I.A., ticket to work, and partnerships: A report on the 22nd Mary E. Switzer memorial seminar* (pp. 1–10). Alexandria, VA: National Rehabilitation Association.

Blanck, P., Schur, L., Kruse, D., Schwochau, S., & Song. C. (2003). Impact of the ADA's employment provisions. *Stanford Law & Policy Review, 14*(2), 267–90.

Bruyère, S. (1993). Participatory action research: Overview and implications for family member of persons with disabilities. *Journal of Vocational Rehabilitation, 3,* 62–68.

Brydon-Miller, M. (1993). Breaking down barriers: Accessibility self-advocacy in the disabled community. In P. Park, M. Brydon-Miller, B. Hall, & T. Jackson (Eds.), *Voices of change: Participatory research in the United States and Canada* (pp. 125–143). Westport, CT: Bergin & Garvey.

Campbell, M., & Seekins, T. (2000). Whatever happened to PAR? Methodological and administrative challenges of implementing participatory research in applied rehabilitation services. *NIDRR symposium: Best practices in research design and methodology on disability and employment law and policy.* Iowa City: University of Iowa College of Law.

Cancian, F. (1992). Feminist science: Methodologies that challenge inequality. *Gender and Society, 6,* 623–642.

Chataway, C. (1997). An examination of the constraints on mutual inquiry in a participatory action research project. *Journal of Social Issues, 53,* 747–765.

Cook, J. A., & Burke, J. (2002). Public policy and employment of people with disabilities: Exploring new paradigms. *Behavioral Sciences & the Law, 20,* 541–557.

Cook, T. D., & Campbell, D. T. (1979). *Quasi-experimentation: Design and analysis issues for field settings.* Boston, MA: Houghton-Mifflin.

Cooper, H. M., & Rosenthal, R. (1980). Statistical versus traditional procedures for summarizing research findings. *Psychological Bulletin, 87,* 442–449.

DeJong, G. (1979). Independent living: From social movement to analytic paradigm. *Archives of Physical Medicine and Rehabilitation, 60,* 435–446.

DePoy, E., Hartman, A., & Haslett, D. (1999). Critical action research: A model for social work knowing. *Social Work, 44,* 560–568.

Eriksson, K. (1999). Linking social science working life research and work reform: A role for universities. In D. J. Greenwood (Ed.), *Action research: From practice to writing in an international action research development program* (pp. 131–146). Philadelphia: John Benjamins.

Frank, J. J. (2003, February). *The impact of the Americans with Disabilities Act (ADA) on the employment of individuals who are blind or have severe visual impairments: Part I: Elements of the accommodation request process.* NARIC Accession No.: 014680. Project No. H133B010101.

Gaventa, J. (1993). The powerful, the powerless, and the experts: Knowledge struggles in an information age. In P. Park, M. Brydon-Miller, B. Hall, & T. Jackson (Eds.), *Voices of change: Participatory research in the United States and Canada* (pp. 21–40). Westport, CT: Bergin & Garvey.

Gill, C. (2001). The social experience of disability. In G. Albrecht, K. Seelman, & M. Bury (Eds.), *Handbook of disability studies* (pp. 351–372). Thousand Oaks, CA: Sage.

Glass, G. V. (1976). Primary, secondary, and meta-analysis of research. *Educational Researcher, 5,* 3–8.

Gorelick, S. (1991). Contradictions in feminist methodology. *Gender and Society, 5,* 459–477.

Greenwood, D. J. (1999). *Action research: From practice to writing in an international action research development program.* Philadelphia: John Benjamins.

Greenwood, D. J., & Levin, M. (1998). *Introduction to action research: Social research for social change.* Thousand Oaks, CA: Sage.

Grisso, T., Baldwin, E., Blanck, P. D., & Rotheram-Borus, M. J. (1991). Standards in research: APA's mechanism for monitoring the challenges. *American Psychologist, 46,* 758–766.

Hahn, H. (1985). Disability policy and the problem of discrimination. *American Behavioral Scientist, 28,* 293–318.

Hale, T. (2001). The lack of a disability measure in today's current population survey. *Monthly Labor Review, 124,* 38–40.

Hedges, L. V., & Olkin, I. (1985). *Statistical methods for meta-analysis.* Orlando: Academic Press.

Horton, B. (1993). The Appalachian land ownership study: Research and citizen action in Appalachia. In P. Park, M. Brydon-Miller, B. Hall, & T. Jackson (Eds.), *Voices of change: Participatory research in the United States and Canada* (pp. 65–84). Westport, CT: Bergin & Garvey.

Jackson, T. (1993). A way of working: Participatory research and the Aboriginal movement in Canada. In P. Park, M. Brydon-Miller, B. Hall, & T. Jackson (Eds.), *Voices of change: Participatory research in the United States and Canada* (pp. 47–64). Westport, CT: Bergin & Garvey.

Kaplan, J. (1988). The use of animals in research. *Science, 242,* 839–840.

Kelman, H. C. (1968). *A time to speak: On human values and social research.* San Francisco: Jossey-Bass.

Kondrat, M. E., & Juliá, M. (1997). Participation action research: Self-reliant research strategies for human social development. *Social Development Issues, 19,* 32–47.

Kruse, D., & Schur, L. (2003). Employment of people with disabilities following the ADA. *Industrial Relations, 42,* 31–66.

Lewin, K. (1999). Group decision and social change. In T. M. Newcomb & E. L. Hartley (Eds.), *The complete social scientist: A Kurt Lewin reader* (pp. 330–341). Washington, DC: American Psychological Association.

Linton, S. (1998). *Claiming disability: Knowledge and identity.* New York: New York University Press.

Low, J., Shelley, J., & O'Connor, M. (2000). Problematic success: An account of top-down participatory action research with women with multiple sclerosis. *Field Methods, 12,* 29–48.

Maguire, P (1987). *Doing participatory research: A feminist approach.* Amherst: University of Massachusetts Press.

Maguire, P. (1993). Challenges, contradictions, and celebrations: Attempting participatory research as a doctoral student. In P. Park, M. Brydon-Miller, B. Hall, & T. Jackson (Eds.), *Voices of change: Participatory research in the United States and Canada* (pp. 157–176). Westport, CT: Bergin & Garvey.

Mahlstedt, D. (1999). Power, social change, and the process of feminist research. *Psychology of Women Quarterly, 23,* 111–115.

Mason, R., & Boutilier, M. (1996). The challenge of genuine power sharing in participatory research: The gap between theory and practice. *Canadian Journal of Community Mental Health, 15,* 145–152.

McCartney, K., & Rosenthal, R. (2000). Effect size, practical importance, and social policy for children. *Child Development, 71,* 173–180.

McTaggart, R. (1997). Guiding principles for participatory action research. In R. McTaggart (Ed.), *Participatory action research: International contexts and consequences* (pp. 25–43). Albany: State University of New York Press.

Melrose, M. (2001). Maximizing the rigor of action research: Why would you want to? How could you? *Field Methods, 13,* 160–181.

Morrell-Bellai, T., & Boydell, K. (1994). The experience of mental health consumer as researcher. *Canadian Journal of Community Mental Health, 13,* 97–110.

Mosteller, F. M., & Bush, R.R. (1954). Selected quantitative techniques. In G. Lindzey (Ed.), *Handbook of social psychology: Vol. 1 theory and method* (pp. 289–334). Cambridge, MA: Addison-Wesley.

National Council on Disability (NCD). (1986). *An assessment of federal laws and programs affecting persons with disability—with legislative recommendation (February 1986)*. Retrieved from http://ncd.gov/newsroom/publications/1986/pdf/toward.pdf

National Council on Disability (NCD). (2002). *The Americans with Disabilities Act policy brief series: Righting the ADA, no. 3, significance of the ADA finding that some 43 million Americans have disabilities*. Retrieved November 15, 2002, from http://www.ncd.gov/newsroom/publications/pdf/43million.pdf

National Institute on Disability and Rehabilitation Research (NIDRR). (1999). Notice of final long range plan for fiscal years 1999–2004. *Federal Register, 64*(161), 45752–45784.

Ochocka, J., Janzen, R., & Nelson, G. (2002). Sharing power and knowledge: Professional and mental health consumer/survivor researchers working together in a participatory action research project. *Psychiatric Rehabilitation Journal, 25,* 379–387.

Oliver, M. (1990). *The politics of disablement: A sociological approach.* New York: St. Martin's Press.

Oliver, M. (1992). Changing the social relations of research production? *Disability, Handicap & Society, 7,* 101–114.

Oliver, M. (1996). A sociology of disability or a disablist sociology? In L. Barton (Ed.), *Disability & society: Emerging issues and insights* (pp. 18–42). Harlow, UK: Addison Wesley Longman.

Puckett, J., & Harkavy, I. (1999). The action research tradition in the United States: Towards a strategy for revitalizing the social sciences, the University, and the American city. In D. Greenwood (Ed.), *Action research: From practice to writing in an international action research development program* (pp. 147–168). Philadelphia: John Benjamins.

Rapp, C., Shera, W., & Kisthardt, W. (1993). Research strategies for consumer empowerment of people with severe mental illness. *Social Work, 39,* 727–735.

Reinharz, S. (1992). *Feminist methods in social research.* New York: Oxford University Press.

Rodgers, J. (1999). Trying to get it right: Undertaking research involving people with learning difficulties. *Disability & Society, 14,* 421–433.

Rosenthal, R. (1991a). Cumulating psychology: An appreciation of Donald T. Campbell. *Psychological Science, 2,* 213, 217–221.

Rosenthal, R. (1991b). *Meta-analytic procedures for social research* (Rev. ed.). Newbury, CA: Sage.

Rosenthal, R. (1994). Science and ethics in conducting, analyzing, and reporting psychological research. *Psychological Science, 5,* 127–134.

Rosenthal, R., & Blanck, P.D. (1993). Science and ethics in conducting, analyzing, and reporting social science research: Implications for social scientists, judges and lawyers. *Indiana Law Journal, 68,* 1209–1228.

Rosenthal, R., & DiMatteo, M. R. (2001). Meta-analysis: Recent developments in quantitative methods for literature reviews. *Annual Review of Psychology, 52,* 59–82.

Rosenthal, R., & Rosnow, R. L. (1975). *The volunteer subject.* New York: Wiley.

Rosenthal, R., & Rosnow, R. L. (1991). *Essentials of behavioral research: Methods and data Analysis* (2nd ed.). New York: McGraw-Hill.

Rosenthal, R., Rosnow, R. L., & Rubin, D. B. (2000). *Contrasts and effect sizes in behavioral research: A correlational approach.* New York: Cambridge University Press.

Rosenthal, R., & Rubin, D. B. (1971). Pygmalion reaffirmed. In J. D. Elashoff & R. E. Snow (Eds.), *Pygmalion reconsidered; a case study in statistical inference: Reconsideration of the Rosenthal–Jacobson data on teacher expectancy* (pp. 139–155). Worthington, OH: C. A. Jones.

Rosenthal, R., & Rubin, D. B. (1982). A simple, general purpose display of magnitude of experimental effect. *Journal of Educational Psychology, 74,* 166–169.

Rosenthal, R., & Rubin, D. B. (1984). Multiple contrasts and ordered Bonferroni procedures. *Journal of Educational Psychology, 76,* 1028–1034.

Rosnow, R. L., & Rosenthal, R. (1984). *Understanding behavioral science: Research methods for research consumers.* New York: McGraw-Hill.

Rosnow, R. L., & Rosenthal, R. (1997). *People studying people: Artifacts and ethics in behavioral research.* New York: W. H. Freeman.

Rosnow, R. L., & Rosenthal, R. (2002). *Beginning behavioral research: A conceptual primer.* Upper Saddle River, NJ: Prentice-Hall.

Rosnow, R. L., Rotheram-Borus, M. J., Ceci, S. J., Blanck, P. D., & Koocher, G. P. (1993). The Institutional Review Board as a mirror of scientific and ethical standards. *American Psychologist, 48,* 821–826.

Schmeling, J., Schartz, H. A., & Blanck, P. (2005). The new disability law and policy framework: Implications for case managers. In F. Chan, M. J. Leahy, & J. Saunders (Eds.), *Case management for rehabilitation health professionals* (2nd ed., Vol. 1, pp. 88–121). New York: Aspen.

Schmidt, F. L. (1992). What do data really mean? Research findings, meta-analysis, and cumulative knowledge in psychology. *American Psychologist, 47,* 1173–1181.

Schwochau, S., & Blanck, P.D. (2000). The economics of the Americans with Disabilities Act: Part III—does the ADA disable the disabled? *Berkeley Journal of Employment and Labor Law, 21,* 271–313.

Schwochau, S., & Blanck, P. D. (2003). Does the ADA disable the disabled? More comments. *Industrial Relations, 42,* 67–77.

Scotch, R. (2002). Paradigms of American social research on disability: What's new? *Disability Studies Quarterly, 22,* 23–34.

Seelman, K. (1993). Assistive technology policy: A road to independence for individuals with disabilities. *Journal of Social Issues, 49,* 115–136.

Seelman, K. (2000). Science and technology policy: Is disability a missing factor? *Assistive Technology, 12,* 144–153.

Silverstein, R. (2000). Emerging disability policy framework: A guidepost for analyzing public policy. *Iowa Law Review, 85,* 1691–1804.

Simonson, L., & Bushaw, V. A. (1993). Participatory action research: Easier said than done. *American Sociologist, 24*(1), 27–37.

Smith, M. L., Glass, G. V., & Miller, T. J. (1980). *The benefits of psychotherapy.* Baltimore: Johns Hopkins University Press.

Stone, E., & Priestley, M. (1996). Parasites, pawns and partners: Disability research and the role of non-disabled researchers. *British Journal of Sociology, 47,* 699–716.

Stringer, E. T. (1999). *Action research* (2nd ed.). Thousand Oaks, CA: Sage.

Taylor, G. (1999). Empowerment, identity, and participatory research: Using social action research to challenge isolation for deaf and hard of hearing people from minority ethnic communities. *Disability & Society, 14,* 369–384.

Temkin, T., & Hanson, S. (2000). *Participatory action research in a study of exemplary collaborations between independent living centers and publicly-funded vocational rehabilitation agencies.* Oakland, CA: World Institute on Disability.

Tewey, B. P. (1997). *Building participatory action research partnerships in disability and reha-bilitation research.* Washington, DC: U.S. National Institute on Disability and Rehabilitation Research.

Townsend, E., Birch, D. E., Langley, J., & Langille, L. (2000). Participatory research in a mental health clubhouse. *The Occupational Therapy Journal of Research, 20,* 18–44.

Tukey, J. W. (1969). Analyzing data: Sanctification or detective work? *American Psychologist, 24,* 83–91.

Tukey, J. W. (1977). *Exploratory data analysis.* Reading, MA: Addison-Wesley.

Webb, E. J., Campbell, D. T., Schwartz, R. D., & Sechrest, L. (1966). *Unobtrusive measures: Nonreactive research in the social sciences.* Chicago: Rand McNally.

Whyte, W.F. (Ed.). (1991). *Participatory action research.* Newbury Park, CA: Sage.

Whyte, W. F. (1995). Encounters with participatory action research. *Qualitative Sociology, 18,* 289–299.

Zarb, G. (1992). On the road to Damascus: First steps towards changing the relations of disability research production. *Disability, Handicap & Society, 7,* 125–138.

III

Social
and Organizational
Psychology

9

Meta-Analysis, Moral Panic, Congressional Condemnation, and Science: A Personal Journey

Bruce Rind
Temple University

Meta-analysis offers a strong alternative to traditional methods of reviewing research studies (Rosenthal & Rosnow, 1991). Used properly, it can enhance rational assessment of phenomena by removing or substantially reducing subjective bias based on values and emotion. With this in mind, two colleagues and I made use of meta-analysis in the late 1990s to rationally reevaluate claims made about the nature and consequences of child sexual abuse (CSA), a topic particularly vulnerable to value- and emotion-laden thinking (Jenkins, 1998). Our analyses, published in the summer of 1998 in *Psychological Bulletin* (Rind, Tromovitch, & Bauserman, 1998), disputed essential and strongly held assumptions about CSA. Despite the intensity and entrenchment of the assumptions we challenged, widely held in the helping professions, reaction to our publication seemed to be quiet. This appearance of calm was abruptly pierced the next spring, when an avalanche of attacks erupted. By the summer of 1999, exactly 1 year after publication, Congress condemned our study, the first time in the history of the United States that a peer-reviewed scientific study had been so treated. Our attempt to bring rational objectivity to a topic dominated by value- and emotion-based thinking in the end was overwhelmed by this very same thinking.

163

In this sense, our story fits in well with the history of philosophy and science, in which challenges to sacred cows of the day have met similar or worse fates more often than could possibly be summarized in this short chapter.

On July 12, 1999, the House of Representatives voted 355–0 to condemn our study—13 congressmen (all Democrats), however, did abstain. Later that month, the Senate concurred unanimously with a 100–0 vote. Despite this "official" proclamation of our study's invalidity—capping off months of attacks by therapists, child advocates, talk show hosts, journalists, religious organizations, and politicians—the study has, in fact, firmly stood its ground to all serious scrutiny of its scientific merit.

First, the American Association for the Advancement of Science (AAAS), the largest science organization in the United States and the publisher of the prestigious journal *Science,* examined the article. The AAAS concluded, after examining all the materials available to them, that they could find no evidence of improper methodology or other questionable practices. Rather than criticizing us, as various religious, therapeutic, political, and media critics had confidently expected, the AAAS rebuked the critics:

> [W]e found it deeply disturbing that so many of the comments made by those in the political arena and in the media indicate a lack of understanding of the analysis presented by the authors or misrepresented the article's findings. All citizens, especially those in a position of public trust, have a responsibility to be accurate about the evidence that informs their public statements. We see little indication of that from the most vocal on this matter, behavior that the Committee finds very distressing. (quoted in McCarty, 1999, pp. 2–3)

Second, in the fall of 2001, my coauthors and I (Rind, Tromovitch, & Bauserman, 2001) refuted dozens of statistically and methodologically unsound criticisms, as well as inappropriate moral attacks, made by two groups of therapists (Dallam et al., 2001; Ondersma et al., 2001) in *Psychological Bulletin.* One of the groups, Dallam and colleagues, played a key role in facilitating the media and political attacks on our paper by providing these sources with even weaker versions of their unsound criticisms (Dallam, Gleaves, Spiegel, & Kraemer, 1999), which were eventually published in *Psychological Bulletin.*

Third, the March 2002 issue of the *American Psychologist* was devoted to our article and the reaction to it. The individual articles as a whole supported our study and offered no criticism of it, but had much criticism of the critics. Lilienfeld (2002), for example, approaching the issue from a philosophy of science framework, documented a pervasive pattern of illogic in the attacks on our study. Baird (2002), a psychologist and one of the members of the House who abstained in the vote, pointed out the flaws in Congress' judgment of our study, noting that "not more than 10 of the 535 members of the House and Senate had actually read [the article] and that fewer still were qualified to evaluate [it] on scientific merit" (p. 190). He complained that Congress operates on the principle "If a scientific finding does not confirm my policy position, it must not be good science" (p. 190). He called this vote "a low point for the 106th Congress" (p. 190) and added that it was also a low point for the American Psychological Association (APA), which had caved in to political pressures by distancing itself from the study.

The reaction to our study must be viewed as hysterical, particularly when taking into account our study's proven integrity in the face of perhaps the most intense scrutiny ever paid to a psychology article. In retrospect, however, the reaction is hardly surprising at all. As we were publishing our article in 1998, historian Philip Jenkins at Pennsylvania State University was publishing a book on moral panics involving CSA (Jenkins, 1998). His scholarly treatment of this topic made it apparent that the type of reaction we received fit in well with a pattern of related hyperbole spanning from the beginning to the end of the 20th century, with its greatest concentration occurring in the last 2 decades. Before exploring further the reaction to our article, it is important to review the meta-analysis itself—the social events that inspired it, the methodological weaknesses and biases in the field that further suggested it, and the results of the analysis.

THE BACKGROUND INSPIRING THE META-ANALYSIS

In the mid-1980s, several events occurred that played key roles in eventually inspiring the meta-analysis. First was the story of the McMartin preschool case in California, in which seven staff members were accused by hundreds of children of committing bizarre acts of satanic ritual and sexual abuse (Nathan & Snedeker, 1995). Staff members were accused of such things as dressing up as witches and flying through the air; sexually assaulting the children in hot-air balloons, cemeteries, and secret tunnels under the schoolyard; and forcing children to drink the blood of ritually murdered babies. Some advocates for the children's accusations claimed that they were literally true; others claimed that the CSA was true, but that the other alleged events reflected memory distortions caused by the CSA. The liberal 1970s, in which traditional attitudes about sex were relaxed (even in considerations of minors), had been replaced by the Victorian 1890s—Freud's seduction theory that all adult psychological maladjustment stems from early sexual experiences with older persons had been revived. I watched as this renewed view resulted in the spread of McMartin-style cases all around the United States. For example, at the Little Rascals day care center in Edenton, North Carolina, staffers were accused of molesting children in outer space and on ships at sea surrounded by sharks specially trained to prevent the children from escaping ("Innocence Lost," 1991). The

McMartin case turned into the longest and most expensive criminal trial in U.S. history; similar cases in various states across the country (e.g., Little Rascals in North Carolina) became those states' most expensive criminal trials ("Innocence Lost: The Verdict," 1993). It was not difficult to suspect that a social pathology involving sex was upon us, engineered wittingly or unwittingly by certain mental health practitioners and their peculiar theories, by social workers and law-enforcement personnel, and by a sensationalizing media. It seemed clear that a sociological or psychological analysis was in order.

Indication for analysis of basic assumptions about early sex and its consequences was intensified, it seemed to me, by a second wave of panic in the later 1980s. All of a sudden, thousands of adult female children around the country were suing their parents for alleged incest that had supposedly taken place 2, 3, or 4 decades earlier ("Divided Memories," 1995). What had happened was that various therapists around the country, convinced that Freud was right in claiming that all adult neuroses stem from childhood sexual seduction, interpreted all their patients' problems as stemming from incest (Crews, 1998). Patients would come in complaining of problems but recalling nothing about sexual seduction. But under the guidance of their therapists and after many sessions, they often began to recall sketchy events, which after many more sessions crystallized into often rather bizarre memories. Freud's theory had been that sexual seduction is so painful that the mind represses any conscious memory of it in order to cope; however, the memory persists in the unconscious and expresses itself in symptoms, which can only be relieved by bringing the memory back to consciousness.

Freud abandoned the seduction theory in 1897. Women's advocates and various therapists in the 1980s called him a coward for doing this, claiming that he had abandoned the theory so as to help protect certain individuals or the male establishment from the embarrassment of incest. In the meantime, recovered memory therapists performed their "memory work" on countless thousands of patients, leading to a multitude of civil suits ("Divided Memories," 1995). In one not unusual case, presented on *Frontline*'s (1995) "Divided Memories" exposé of the recovered memory movement, a young woman went into therapy simply because she did not know how to relate to her mother. After months of therapy, she developed memories that eventually crystallized into recollections of satanic rituals involving her parents and grandparents. Her therapist diagnosed this patient as having multiple personality disorder with 27 alters (i.e., other personalities). With the therapist's encouragement, she sued her parents for $20 million, claiming that her mother inserted a broomstick into her vagina, as well as spiders, wires, and vegetables, and that her father had sexually assaulted her with tools from a hardware store. At the deposition, when reminded that she had perfect school attendance and pediatric reports at the time these events were purported to have occurred, the young woman was unfazed by the contradiction, dismissively commenting, "Oh, that doesn't matter."

Many people chose to "believe the children," as the saying went (an organization by this name was formed by parents of McMartin children in 1985, because they were enraged that anyone would doubt any details of the McMartin case), and many people chose to believe the adult children as well in the recovered memory cases (Nathan & Snedeker, 1995). To me, it was more like Alice in Wonderland, except it concerned a true nightmare rather than a fairy tale. Child sexual abuse, which had formerly been viewed by mental health professionals as immoral but not particularly psychologically problematic unless accompanied by aggravating circumstances (Jenkins, 1998), had became the highest form of sacrilege and the most devastating imaginable experience.

The bizarre events discussed previously, occasioned by this new thinking, were defended by advocates, it seemed, through practices and theories more akin to shamanism than science, although the advocates assured the public that their arguments were scientific. These events seemed to be the U.S. version of a certain madness that most Americans would readily recognize occurring in other parts of the world, where women are stoned to death in Nigeria for engaging in nonmarital sex, hacked to death in Kashmir for not wearing their veils, and people go on trial for their lives in Pakistan for blasphemy. Regarding the last of these examples, perhaps the following anecdote can serve to convey the sense of skepticism felt by critics of the day-care abuse cases, recovered memory therapy, and related phenomena. In the mid-1990s, two men and a boy of 14 were put on trial in Pakistan for their lives, accused of blasphemy for writing something un-Islamic on a wall (Bagash, 1995). As they were tried, hordes of people gathered outside the courthouse to demand the defendants' executions. Prosecution witnesses were not permitted to report in court what the defendants had allegedly written, because that would itself be blasphemy! The defense attorneys were left with attempting to impeach the credibility of the accusing witnesses by demonstrating that they were self-contradicting in matters such as the times of day when they had allegedly witnessed the crime. The defendants were acquitted. One of the trial judges was subsequently assassinated for rendering this verdict. The American version, although not as deadly, was just as bizarre.

While I watched the day care abuse and recovered memory episodes unfolding, I was also preparing to become a research psychologist, studying social psychology at Temple University. In the spring of 1986, I took a methods course, with a focus on meta-analysis, taught by Ralph Rosnow. For the course, I meta-analyzed studies on conformity behavior of the Asch type, in which participants were pressured by the mere presence of others rather than by explicit commands to agree with statements or ideas that they privately knew were false. This theme, as it turned out, was intimately related to events at the day-care centers, where children were interviewed repeatedly by social workers and others who applied so much pressure for confirmation of crimes that eventually reality and fiction became blurred (Ceci & Bruck, 1993). In this meta-analysis on conformity, I found that effect sizes were heterogeneous across all studies, but were homogeneous when examined within three distinct groups defined by the social psychologist Latané (1981), who argued that conformity was a function of the strength, immediacy, and number of the sources affecting the target. Dr. Rosnow was apparently impressed by this presentation, because immediately afterward I was switched from another faculty member to him as my major professor. For me, this led to increased exposure to the finer points of methodology and statistics, which, in combination with skepticism regarding conventional psychologizing on the issue of CSA, resulted in the methodologically and statistically sophisticated critique of this psychologizing a decade later.

STATISTICAL AND METHODOLOGICAL PROBLEMS SUGGESTING THE NEED FOR META-ANALYSIS

Valid methodology, accurate statistics, and skepticism were three aspects sorely missing from previous literature reviews on CSA. Emphasis of this problem was the focus of the introduction to our 1998 meta-analysis. As we documented, in the nearly two dozen literature reviews of the psychological correlates or effects of CSA done in the 1980s and 1990s (see Rind et al., 1998, for a list), the vast majority subscribed to the "CPIE" view—that is, they concluded that CSA *causes* psychological maladjustment *pervasively* in the population of persons with this history, with *intensely* negative effects that are *equivalent* for males and females. In concluding causation, the reviews generally ignored confounding variables, known to be extremely commonplace in the clinical literature dealing with CSA, or minimized their importance without presenting adequate evidence. The reviews either stated that negative effects are pervasive or implied this by failing to qualify the generalizability of their results, usually based on clinical samples. They indicated that negative effects were intense, not through any sort of measure of effect size, but instead merely by noting that CSA and control groups differed statistically significantly in many of their studies under review. Finally, they argued that the experience was just as traumatic for boys as for girls, most often by examining only female clinical patients and then inferring to all males, clinical patients or not, with a history of CSA.

Regarding the last point, sometimes reviewers examined actual male data to reach their conclusions. To appreciate the argument for the need for skepticism, it is instructive to consider the quality of some of the primary studies and reviews in this area, conducted by child abuse researchers. Bartholow et al. (1994) examined comfort in sexual attractions felt by gay and bisexual men who did or did not have a history of CSA. They found that, on a 5-point scale, where 1 meant *very comfortable* and 5 meant *very uncomfortable*, mean comfort scores were 1.4 for controls and 1.6 for CSA subjects. Due to a large sample size, this very small difference reached statistical significance. The authors used this result to claim a "*lack* of comfort" (italics added) for subjects in the CSA group, even though the mean of this group was well within in the "comfortable" range on the scale.

Mendel (1995), in a literature review, focused on the statistically significant results from Fromuth and Burkhart's (1989) Midwestern sample of male college students to argue that boys are harmed by CSA experiences. However, Mendel paid little attention to Fromuth and Burkhart's Southeastern sample of males, reported in the same article, for whom all CSA-adjustment correlates were nonsignificant with zero effect size. Because the latter sample was 30% larger, Mendel should have given it more weight than the former sample, rather than conveniently ignoring it.

Finkelhor (1984) presented data from his college study on the kind of homosexual behavior experienced as a boy (none, with a peer, or with someone much older) versus recent homosexual activity during the past year. He found higher percentages of recent homosexual behavior when subjects had had sex as a boy with an older partner. In a regression analysis of factors predicting recent homosexual behavior, he presented a table of results of beta weights for age of puberty, proportion of sex education through books and magazines, father's education, and sex with an older partner, which were, respectively, −.14, −.16, −.15, and .16. Finkelhor interpreted these results as showing that sex with an older partner was the "strongest" predictor of recent homosexual activity, and argued that this therefore supported a causal interpretation. In his statistical interpretation, he ignored the fact that −.16 was just as strong as .16 and that −.15 or −.14 were statistically no different than .16. His causal interpretation was without warrant; Finkelhor examined a very limited set of possible confounds and ignored others that were more relevant and self-evident (e.g., already being gay caused greater involvement with men when the subjects were boys and then again when they were adults—an explanation well supported in other research in this area).

The errors in the three examples just discussed not only illustrate the kinds of weaknesses that have often appeared in CSA research, but also suggest an underlying bias to prove that CSA is destructive, irrespective of the data. Finkelhor's comments in this regard are indicative of this bias, in which he tried to have it both ways. On the one hand, he used homosexuality as a symptom, as a negative effect of CSA; on the other, after doing this, he rushed to say that there is nothing wrong with homosexuality, so as to try not to offend gays and their supporters.

Accurate interpretation based on statistical precision was not a strong point in the previous three examples, nor has it been in general in CSA research. Literature reviews in this area have often concluded that CSA causes or is associated with a very long list of symptoms (e.g., depression, anxiety, suicidal ideation; see Rind et al., 1998, for details). The reader is inexorably led by these conclusions to infer that *most* people with a history of CSA will have clinically significant disorders. Keeping in mind that "clinically significant" implies falling two or more standard deviations above the mean, this inference is quite fallacious. In our meta-analyses of national samples (Rind & Tromovitch, 1997) and college samples (Rind et al., 1998), we found that CSA and control groups differed on average by the equivalent of 3 points on an IQ scale. Using IQ research as an analogy, suppose a researcher has found that subjects exposed to some factor have a mean IQ of 97, whereas those not exposed have a mean of 100; suppose further that the researcher concludes that exposure causes or is associated with mental retardation. This conclusion, analogous to concluding that CSA causes or is associated with depression or suicide, is clearly biased. It leads a reader to assume that mental retardation is the *likely* result of exposure. In fact, only 2.39% of exposed subjects will fall in the mental retardation range, which is only slightly higher than the 2.28% among nonexposed persons. Clearly, the assumption that retardation is likely to follow exposure is highly erroneous; in fact, most exposed persons fall in the normal or even superior range. Returning to CSA, we have the same situation: *Most* persons with a history of CSA fall in the normal or superior range of adjustment. Very few will have clinically significant disorders, only slightly more than controls. Moreover, this small increase itself cannot unambiguously be attributed to CSA, because of confounding variables. Previous literature reviews have largely misled readers by stating that CSA causes or is associated with depression or suicide, instead of stating simply that CSA is associated with slightly lower scores on adjustment scales.

Clearly, then, a meta-analytic approach to CSA was in order to force precision and objectivity on a field lacking these qualities. No less important was to conduct a review that was sensitive to the methodological issues of internal and external validity, because almost all previous reviews were not, yet drew conclusions that could only be warranted by taking these two issues into full account.

THE 1998 META-ANALYSIS

In the title of our study, we used the phrase "a meta-analytic examination of assumed properties of child sexual abuse." The key word is *properties* because, as we documented in the introduction, most researchers in this field believe or have come to the conclusion that CSA, typically defined as any sexual experience involving contact or even noncontact sex between someone under 18 and someone 5 or more years older, is by nature invariably psychologically injurious. We critiqued the means by which researchers had come to this view, arguing that the near exclusive focus on clinical samples, scant attention to third variables in correlational research, and qualitative approaches do not warrant such firm conclusions. We maintained that studies based on more representative samples were needed, in which quantitative data were available for both synthesis and examination of confounds. Only then could the "propertied" status of CSA (i.e., the CPIE view) be critically tested. We noted that we had previously conducted a meta-analysis of national probability samples to improve over previous reviews in the areas of precision and external validity (Rind & Tromovitch, 1997). However, we also noted that the national data were weak on third variables for examining internal validity. Thus, the goal of our 1998 study was to replicate and extend the previous meta-analysis by once again focusing on nonclinical and thus more representative samples, but ones in which sufficient data were available regarding confounds for internal validity analysis. We chose college samples, because numerous studies based on college students had been conducted, often including the additional data that we needed.

Our meta-analysis consisted of 59 college samples. We found that the mean magnitude of association between CSA and psychological adjustment was small (effect size $r = .09$). Analyzing by gender, results were $r = .07$ for males and $r = .10$ for females. These effect sizes were smaller than those typically found in clinical studies, which are often in the $r = .30$ range, but they were identical to those in national samples (Rind & Tromovitch, 1997), demonstrating their relevance. The national and college sample results were quite similar in other respects as well. In both cases, a minority of males but a majority of females reported reacting negatively to the CSA experience. Contrasting proportions of male-versus-female negative reactions in the national and college samples resulted in $rs = .31$ in both cases. Self-reported negative effects at any time after the experience occurred for a majority of females but only for a minority of males, in both cases, with contrast differences between the genders of $r = .23$ and $r = .22$ in the national and college samples, respectively. Reports of lasting negative effects were rare for males and constituted a small minority for females in both cases. In the national samples, these figures were 4% for males and 13% for females. In the college data, where more complete information was available on reactions at the time, males reacted positively, neutrally, and negatively 37%, 29%, and 33% of the time, respectively, whereas females' corresponding reactions were 11%, 18%, and 72%.

Some studies based on college samples required that early sexual experiences were unwanted to qualify as CSA. Other studies included as CSA not only unwanted experiences, but also wanted encounters that involved an age discrepancy. For example, if the subject was below age 18 and had a wanted sexual experience with someone 5 years older, then the experience was defined as CSA. Thus, studies could be classed as strictly nonconsenting CSA and as nonconsenting and consenting (i.e., mixed) CSA. In moderator analyses, we took into account these two classes, nonconsent versus mixed, in examining the relation between CSA and psychological adjustment. In the case of males, level of consent moderated outcome, such that the mean effect size ($r = .04$) was statistically non-significant in the mixed category, but statistically significant in the nonconsent category ($r = .10$). These findings indicated that inclusion of willingness eliminated the relationship in the mixed category, implying that willingness itself was not associated with psychological maladjustment in the case of males.

Finally, we examined internal validity by taking into account family environment measures and how they related to CSA and psychological adjustment. Family environment included problems such as physical abuse, emotional abuse or neglect, and parental discord, and positive influences such as emotional support and family cohesion. Across studies that measured family environment, we found via meta-analysis that poor family environment was confounded with CSA, $r = .13$. Furthermore, family environment correlated with psychological adjustment, $r = .29$, substantially more strongly than CSA did, $r = .09$. This three-way relationship among the control variable and the two principle variables suggested that the already small CSA-adjustment relationship would be considerably smaller when taking the control variable into account. We performed this analysis by examining all studies that performed statistical control, factoring out family environment from the CSA-adjustment relation. We found that, before statistical control, CSA-adjustment relations were statistically significant 41% of the time, but after statistical control, they were significant only 17% of the time. This 59% reduction in statistical significance, however, was based on dependent measures (e.g., certain studies contained multiple measures, which were thus dependent). When we examined the reduction in significance rates for independent measures (i.e., one measure per study—percentage reduction), it was 83%.

In short, we used meta-analysis to test the CPIE view that sexual relations defined as CSA cause pervasive psychological harm of an intense nature, regardless of gender, in the population of persons with this history. We found through internal validity analysis that the assumption of causality was weak, the assumption of pervasiveness was unsupported (e.g., a low percentage reported lasting problems), the claim that effects were intense was highly overstated (e.g., most males did not react negatively; the effect sizes were small), and the assumption that boys and girls react the same was false. The finding that the college results mirrored the national results so closely lent huge support to the relevance of the college data in testing the CPIE view. Together, the college and national data strongly suggested that the CPIE view is disconfirmed.

ATTACKS ON OUR STUDY

In July 1998, our meta-analysis was published in *Psychological Bulletin*. All was quiet for many months. However, in December 1998, the National Association for the Research and Treatment of Homosexuality (NARTH) attacked our study on their Web site (www.narth.com). NARTH consists of psychoanalytically oriented therapists who hold traditional religious views on sexuality. In a speech delivered to the organization in 1995, NARTH's president, Charles Socarides, decried the removal of homosexuality from the Diagnostic and Statistical Manul of Mental Disorders (DSM), complaining that this action "has led to a sexual and social dementia." He asserted that homosexuality is "a freedom that cannot be given." NARTH complained that we suggested that not all CSA should be labeled "abuse" and that we used the construct of consent in our analysis. The critique argued that CSA is always abuse and consent is never possible in these relations.

Early in March 1999, a conservative Catholic newsletter, *The Wanderer*, picked up this critique and added commentary to it, characterizing our study as a "pseudo-professional, pseudo-academic analysis." A radio talk-show host in Philadelphia, with this newsletter in hand, contacted one of my co-authors (Tromovitch), who then appeared on his show in mid-March. The host used the interview to launch an attack against Temple University and us. This attack caught the attention of a national talk-show host, Dr. Laura Schlessinger, who then attacked the study for the next 3 months or so beginning later in March. "Dr. Laura" is a religious and social conservative who staunchly espouses "family values" positions. As she noted in one of her newspaper columns, she obtained "three renowned, licensed clinical psychologists and a scientist" to review our study, who unanimously declared it "junk science" (Schlessinger, 1999a, p. E6). Two of the clinicians were from NARTH. One of these, van den Aardweg from Holland, compared us to Nazi doctors. Dr. Laura, on her first radio broadcast attacking our study, called it "garbage research with a dangerous statement at the end," and criticized our use of meta-analysis, stating, "I frankly have never seen this in general science.... This [pooling of studies] is so outrageous" (Schlessinger, 1999b).

Soon Dr. Laura was using sound bites provided to her by psychiatrist Paul J. Fink, president of a group calling itself the Leadership Council for Mental Health, Justice and the Media. This group is an organization of professionals advocating the validity of repressed memories and related therapies. Dr. Laura promoted Fink's sound bite that 60% of the data in our meta-analysis came from one single, outdated study (first broadcast in April 1999). Despite the fact that this claim was completely false—this particular study was *not* included in our meta-analysis—this attack spread all across the media and eventually into the halls of Congress. By April 1999, the Family Research Council, an ultraconservative Christian lobbying group in Washington, DC, joined Dr. Laura, a longtime ally, in the attacks. In May, the Family Research Council organized a press conference, at which Congressman Tom DeLay (R–TX) demanded that the APA denounce our study (Duin, 1999). The APA defended our study initially. During a debate on the MSNBC show *Watch It!* ("Pedophilia Report Controversy," 1999), in response to Congressman Weldon (R–FL), who repeated Fink's sound bites in attacking our study, Raymond Fowler, the CEO of the APA, said, "Well, with all due respect, it isn't a bad study. It's been peer-reviewed by the same principles as any kind of scientific publication. It's been examined by statistical experts. It's a good study."

In fact, Fowler was not merely referring to the original review by experts during the publication phase, but also to recent in-house analysis done after the attacks on the paper had begun. Despite this, Fowler eventually caved in to the enormous pressures coming from Congress. In early June 1999, he e-mailed me that he was "in hand to hand combat with congressmen, talk-show hosts, the Christian Right and the American Psychiatric Association." The very next day, he wrote a letter to Tom DeLay acknowledging "problems" with our study and making unprecedented concessions. He called some of the language in our paper "inflammatory" (i.e., our use of neutral language instead of the term *abuse*), and stated that CSA is never harmless or consensual. He agreed to set up an independent review of our study—the one that was later conducted in the summer by the AAAS. A month later, our study was condemned by the U.S. Congress as "severely flawed," but the APA was formally thanked for seeing it Congress' way.

The controversy quieted down with Congress' proclamation—our critics apparently were satisfied with their victory—but by no means was the situation ended. Psychologist Scott Lilienfeld wrote a critique of our critics' logic, cataloguing a list of fundamental errors. His article was accepted by the APA's flagship journal, the *American Psychologist*. Its editor, Richard McCarty, then secretly had the paper re-reviewed, receiving the hostile rejections that he must have wanted; otherwise, why would he have requested a re-review in secret? When Lilienfeld was informed that his accepted article was now rejected, he pled his case on Internet psychology discussion groups. The response was so intense that the APA and the journal backed down and agreed to publish a special issue of the *American Psychologist*, including Lilienfeld's article, dedicated to our study and the controversy surrounding it. This special issue was published in March 2002.

PSYCHOLOGICAL BULLETIN CRITIQUES AND REBUTTAL

In November 2001, two groups of therapists published critiques of our study in *Psychological Bulletin* (Dallam et al., 2001; Ondersma et al., 2001). Dallam et al. were therapists from the Leadership Council, who had presented an earlier draft of their critique to certain congressmen in 1999 (which was then used as a basis for condemning our study). The draft arguments were weaker and unrefined compared to the *Psychological Bulletin* version. Importantly, this later version was itself quite weak. Nevertheless, Dallam et al.'s group, the Leadership Council, saw it quite differently. Upon publication of the November issue of *Psychological Bulletin*, they issued a press release claiming that the "Controversial Study Defending Child Molesters is Debunked" (www.leadershipcouncil.org). To issue such a comment, the organization must have dismissed or ignored our rebuttal, whose gist is well captured in our abstract (Rind et al., 2001):

> The authors respond to 2 victimological critiques of their 1998 meta-analysis on child sexual abuse (CSA). S. J. Dallam et al. (2001) claimed that B. Rind, P. Tromovitch, and R. Bauserman (1998) committed numerous methodological and statistical errors, and often miscoded and misinterpreted data. The authors show all these claims to be invalid. To the contrary, they demonstrate frequent bias in Dallam et al.'s criticisms. (p. 734)

In our discussion section, we concluded that Dallam et al.'s critique, although more refined and less abrasive, was no better than their 1999 draft provided to Congress. (We previously had characterized the 1999 draft as a "kitchen sink" attack, because it threw every possible criticism our way irrespective of accuracy or relevance, and in the end failed to demonstrate any bias that would necessitate altering any of our basic conclusions; see Rind, Bauserman, & Tromovitch, 2001.)

As we discussed previously (Rind, Tromovitch, & Bauserman, 2000), a good example of a kitchen sink attack was the Family Research Council's critique of Evelyn Hooker's (1957) study on homosexuality (Landass, n.d.). Hooker had examined a nonclinical sample of homosexuals and compared them with a control group on various measures of adjustment; she concluded that the homosexuals were as well adjusted as controls. Her study was a breakthrough in terms of getting research away from clinical samples and contradicting conventional wisdom on a sensitive social issue. Religious conservatives have been upset with this study ever since, and Landass, writing for the Family Research Council (http://www.frc.org), provided a critique. He searched for weaknesses and came up with minor discrepancies between Hooker's text and her tables: She wrote that her subjects' IQs ranged from 90 to 135, but a table showed the lowest IQ to be 91; she reported that the average education for the homosexual subjects was 13.9 years in school, but it was 14.0 years in the table; she reported that the highest educational level of her subjects was the master's level, but in the table it was one year beyond a master's program. In this vein, by citing a volume of trivialities, Landass tried to discredit Hooker's study. He ignored the logic behind it, which was the necessity of examining a nonclinical sample to test the prevailing view that homosexuality is always associated with maladjustment. The parallels between Dallam et al.'s attacks and Landass' attacks are strong. We followed the logic that Hooker did, and Dallam et al. followed the logic of Landass—a kitchen sink attack.

In response to the Leadership Council's press release of November 2001, I developed a spreadsheet (unpublished manuscript) listing the 35 specific criticisms that Dallam et al. (2001) made, along with our rebuttals. Also included were the page numbers in the journal where the criticisms could be found, as well as evaluations of each criticism. I sent this spreadsheet to several listservs for other researchers to read. The following summary appeared at the beginning of the spreadsheet:

> Altogether, Dallam et al. made 35 criticisms. In 11 cases (31%), they misrepresented us. In 8 cases (23%), they made false assertions variously based on false assumptions, misunderstanding methodology, or statistical ignorance. In 18 cases (51%), they exhibited selection bias, for instance, selectively citing only research supporting their view but ignoring equally valid or more valid research contradicting their view. And in 4 cases (11%), their criticisms were patently irrelevant. (p. 1)

Here are some telling examples. To argue that our college data were not generalizable, Dallam et al. asserted that rates of sexual intercourse (a presumed indicator of CSA severity) are much greater in the general population. They based their claim solely on a national study by Finkelhor, Hotaling, Lewis, and Smith (1989), in which rates were two to four times greater. However, in making their claim, they conveniently ignored other national samples with rates equal to or even less than the college samples, although they did reference these same national samples to make other arguments (see Rind et al., 2001, for documentation of this point and those that follow). Moreover, they also ignored Finkelhor et al.'s caution not to rely solely on their data because the measure of intercourse was flawed. In a second attempt to show that our college data were anomalous, Dallam et al. meta-analyzed national samples, coming up with slightly higher mean effect size estimates. But in this analysis, now they omitted the Finkelhor et al. (1989) study, which had low effect sizes, and included instead a few other selected studies based on national samples with higher effect sizes, which they had omitted previously when criticizing us on intercourse rates. In our rebuttal, we showed that meta-analyzing results from all national samples, rather than selected ones, produced mean effect sizes *identical* to the college samples. In these two examples, one can see an approach often used in Dallam et al.'s critique: Cite selectively when the data are supportive, ignore selectively when the data are contradictory, and ignore authors' caveats if they are inconvenient to the point. In a third attempt to show that our college data were anomalous, Dallam et al. listed numerous studies based on junior high and high school samples to argue that (a) effects are more severe in the general population and (b) people with CSA often do not make it to college because of CSA's negative impact, resulting in lower effect sizes in the college population. However, Dallam et al.'s presentation of these younger samples was qualitative. We meta-analyzed results from these same samples and showed that the mean effect sizes were nearly identical to those from the college samples!

Aside from falsely arguing that other research showed our college data were anomalous, Dallam et al. criticized our inclusion criteria for studies. They claimed that we included studies that did not "even purport" to study CSA, listing three examples (Dallam et al., 2001, p. 719). We replied, showing that the authors were unambiguously studying CSA. Moreover, we noted that two of these examples were not included in our meta-analysis, and that the third one had a higher effect size than average among our studies, meaning that including it did not bias the mean result downward, as Dallam et al. implied. This point illustrates another common theme in their attack: Even if their criticism had been correct—which it was not—our final result was unchanged or not biased as implied. In another criticism, they complained that we included studies in which the definition of CSA could include cases in which the CSA occurred after age 17. They cited three examples. We replied, showing that in two of these cases all CSA incidents included in the authors' analysis occurred before the age of 17. We also pointed out that Dallam et al. themselves, in making other points elsewhere in their critique, included studies in which cases of CSA went up to 18 or 19 years of age. Dallam et al. did not look into a mirror when they critiqued us on this point.

Dallam et al. claimed that we erroneously coded a study by Silliman (1993), based on their contacting the author for further information. However, they had to contact Silliman for this because, as we showed in our reply, we coded her results accurately according to how she had presented them. The error was not on our part. Dallam et al. used this point to make their next one, that if we had "properly" coded Silliman, then we would not have excluded several studies from our meta-analysis as outliers. They devoted considerable journal space to this complaint. However, in the end their point was irrelevant, because the estimated mean effect sizes were virtually unchanged. As we noted in rebuttal, we reported two mean effect sizes in our 1998 article: $r = .0948$, based on 54 samples with Silliman uncorrected and including the outliers; and $r = .0921$, based on 51 samples with Silliman uncorrected and without the outliers. But recomputing with Silliman corrected and using all 54 samples, the mean effect size becomes $r = .0969$, which is virtually the same! With this point, Dallam et al. were doing little more than making a mountain out of a molehill. In another attempt to increase the magnitude of the effect sizes to argue that CSA is always devastating, Dallam et al. argued that, because our CSA and control samples were of different size, the effect sizes were underestimated and had to be corrected. They used a formula presented by Becker (1986) to do this, despite the fact that Becker specifically stated in his article that his formula was *not* appropriate for naturally occurring differences in population size, which clearly applied to the college data! Becker added that when a study artificially uses equal sample sizes from two populations with naturally occurring differences in their sizes, then a *reverse* correction of the effect size is in order. This is another case of Dallam et al. ignoring authors' caveats when those warnings got in the way of the point they are trying to make.

Dallam et al. then claimed that we interpreted r^2 as an effect size, despite the fact that methodologists like Rosenthal (1984) had warned not to do so. They presented a partial quote from our 1998 article to make this claim. We replied by presenting the full, not partial, quote, demonstrating unambiguously that it was r, not r^2, that we used as our effect size. Dallam et al. then claimed that we incorrectly concluded that boys with willing participation in CSA were statistically significantly better adjusted than were unwilling boys. They claimed that we "disregarded" the overlapping 95% confidence intervals of the mean effect sizes (rs) for each group, which, they claimed, showed that the two groups were the same. We pointed out in rebuttal that what matters is the 95% confidence interval of the *difference* between independent sample rs, not the 95% confidence intervals of each r. For the former, the confidence interval did not cross zero, indicating statistical significance—that is, our conclusion was correct. In another statistical criticism, Dallam et al. attacked our use of statistical control, claiming that family environment—our control variable—would have to be uncorrelated with CSA to validly hold it constant in examining the relation between CSA and adjustment. This claim is simply false, which Dallam et al. based on an incorrect citation of Pedhazur (1997), as we pointed out in our rebuttal. Continuing this theme, Dallam et al. argued that our use of statistical control was flawed, dubiously claiming that the ANCOVAs and hierarchical regressions we sometimes included were not appropriate. They presented a table of other studies using control whose methods were "more appropriate." In rebuttal, we pointed out that 5 of the 13 "more appropriate" analyses cited by Dallam et al. also used ANCOVAs or hierarchical regressions as their control procedures!

In their 1999 critique presented to various members of Congress, Dallam et al. accusatorily asserted that statements we made based on our data coding of how subjects reacted to their CSA were "ill responsible [sic] and seem to be intent on misleading the reader." They attempted to show the misleading nature of our coding with three examples. We refuted each instance in an earlier rebuttal (Rind et al., 2000). In their 2001 critique, Dallam et al. returned to this theme with three new examples, apparently having given up on the three original ones. In rebuttal, once again we refuted their claims. Let us examine one of them to appreciate the nature of Dallam et al.'s mischief. Fishman (1991) studied boys' reactions to sex with women and with men. Separately for early sexual experiences with women and men, he reported percentages of positive, neutral, and negative reactions. Subjects reported higher percentages of positive reactions to experiences with women and higher percentages of negative reactions to experiences with men. Appropriately, we averaged over all of the experiences to determine overall rates of positive, neutral, and negative reactions with adults, so as to compare results with other studies, which did not differentiate between experiences with men versus women. Dallam et al., however, selectively cited Fishman's values only for the homosexual subsample of contacts—they entirely ignored his data on relations with women. Through this device, they tried to claim that we had misreported the data when we had not, and that boys' reactions are more negative than we were reporting, when they are not.

In addition to these examples, there were many more instances of what can be best characterized as a kitchen sink attack—the attempt to throw everything at our study irrespective of accuracy, relevancy, or importance, so as to create the impression of incompetence and invalidity by volume rather than by substance. Despite using this highly inappropriate approach, and despite the fact that we clearly exposed it in our rebuttal, Dallam et al.'s organization, the Leadership Council, unabashedly announced after publication of the November 2001 *Psychological Bulletin* that our study had been "debunked" (www.leadershipcouncil.org).

The second set of therapists critiquing our study in the November 2001 issue of *Psychological Bulletin,* Ondersma et al. (2001), repeated briefly many of the specious methodological and statistical criticisms used by Dallam et al., which they obtained from Dallam et al.'s 1999 draft given to certain members of Congress. However, Ondersma et al.'s main focus was to argue that our study was another example of the "backlash" against psychotherapists, that our suggestions regarding definitions of CSA were "extra-scientific," that the "moral standard" was the correct way to understand CSA scientifically, and that positive reactions to CSA among many boys is a misattribution. Ondersma et al.'s "backlash," not our definitions, was the bona fide instance of *extra-science*—the term is radical feminist rhetoric used to shoot down dissenting views emotionally rather than argumentatively (Sommers, 1995). To argue that our study was part of this "backlash," Ondersma et al. provided a very selective "sociohistorical" perspective on CSA. Their historical perspective had all the integrity of Marx's historical perspective—a skewed collection of historical events and nonevents, facts and nonfacts, to justify a political agenda. Their chief source for this "perspective" was Olafson, Corwin, and Summit (1993), two of whom served as psychiatrists in the McMartin day-care case, helping to give credibility to this Alice-in-Wonderland mass hysteria. Olafson et al. took Janet and Freud's "discoveries" on memory repression as unquestioned fact—even up to today, more than 100 years later, there has not been a single credible empirical demonstration of repression (Brandon, Boakes, Glaser, & Green, 1998).

Olafson et al.'s article was an advocacy piece justifying the kind of therapeutic practices that produced the day-care abuse hysteria and the recovered memory movement. Far from using scientific argument, their argumentation throughout was patently political, expressed in strident rhetoric, as in the authors' remark that it "remains to be seen whether the current backlash will succeed in resuppressing awareness of sexual abuse, again concealing 'vast aggregates of pain and rage' ... and returning us to the 'shared negative hallucination' that has obscured our vision in the past" (p. 19).

Ondersma et al. continued their critique by characterizing our definitions of CSA as "extra-scientific." We had suggested that researchers use value-neutral terms under certain conditions when discussing CSA, arguing that the language of "abuse" is value-laden and consequently biasing. Ondersma et al. (2001) claimed that value-neutral language was a threat to the moral fabric, because "small but vigorous" minorities would exploit this usage to promote their agendas (p. 712). They argued that what is labeled "abuse" is best determined sociolegally through consensus of a given society. They continued that CSA was never meant to be a scientific term, but rather a social and legal term, and as such should be defined sociolegally. In short, they argued, the moral standard is what is required to define CSA.

Ondersma et al.'s logic was flawed. In criticizing our definition as being "extra-scientific," they were implying that their own approach *was* scientific. However, the use of the moral standard is unambiguously extra-scientific. We rebutted them in our 2001 *Psychological Bulletin* article by noting that our suggestions to use value-neutral terms under certain circumstances was a response to the editor's request to examine the CSA construct more thoughtfully so as to improve its construct validity. The editor made this point because, in our meta-analysis, certain types of CSA were unrelated to harm and did not have the flavor of "abuse" as used in all other scientific contexts. Our original, basic point regarding terminology was that value-laden language does not belong in any kind of scientific discourse, but has permeated the psychiatric and psychological fields in the area of sexual behavior. Value-laden terms have come and gone according to social values—that is, morals standards of the day—rather than because of scientific considerations. Thus, we offered a revised definition for CSA that eschews the "abuse" label when minor participants react positively and perceive their involvement as willing—two circumstances that we showed empirically in our review were not uncommon and were not correlated with negative psychological correlates or consequences, at least in the case of males. To label these experiences in the same way that aggravated assault resulting in trauma is labeled is clearly extra-scientific, because such practice ignores the predictive validity of the term.

In our 2001 rebuttal, we noted that the view among various prominent sexologists is that the "abuse" construct has been abused by abuse researchers. Their argument is that indiscriminate usage of "abuse" terminology exaggerates considerably the impression of harm, even though empirical data show much less harm or even no harm at all, depending on the case and circumstances. Our alignment with their view contradicts Ondersma et al.'s claim that we were extremists. We also noted that as one gets further away from mental health practitioners—to research psychologists, historians, anthropologists, and primatologists—such usage in this context becomes rarer and often nonexistent. Thus, it is in fact those in the mental health field who are extremists with respect to the entire array of scholarly attention to this area. Furthermore, consent is intimately tied to the abuse definition—abuse researchers as well as social and legal institutions define all adult-minor sex as abuse because they assert that minors cannot consent. In our rebuttal, we presented diverse empirical evidence to show that perceived consent moderates outcome in CSA research and is therefore a valid research variable.

Ondersma et al. (2001) were also critical of respondents' reports of positive reactions to their CSA. They argued that positive responders, most of whom were males, were in denial about their victimization. These authors speculated that as boys, and later as men, the positive responders failed to embrace victimhood or perceive trauma because of male socialization or successful indoctrination by the "abuser." Implicit in this argument is that the female experience and perspective comprise the correct standard, and that males who depart from it are aberrant (cf. Sommers, 2001). Former philosophy of logic professor Christina Hoff Sommers (2001) argued in her book *The War Against Boys* that feminists have been attempting to emasculate boys as one means of forcing gender equality. Where boys are clearly different, as they are in sexual behavior and desire, they must be altered to conform to female-typical patterns, because girls in such areas will not easily adopt male-typical patterns. Sommers discussed specifically feminist attempts at emasculating boys' sexuality. In this vein, the characterization by Ondersma et al. (2001) of positive reactions by boys to sexual contacts with older females or males as denial or distortion fits in well with this feminist agenda described by Sommers. It is an argument that ignores for ideological gain the vast array of human and animal data showing the greater and more positive responsiveness of younger males as compared with younger females, especially among adolescents, to sex (Rind et al., 2001). Additionally, Ondersma et al.'s argument is a double standard, because they, as well as victimologists in general, accept uncritically all negative reactions to CSA as genuine. In a culture filled with negative messages about adult–minor sex, and virtually empty of positive ones, negative reactions could easily reflect this cultural influence rather than a primary response of negativity. In such a culture, positive reactions, on the other hand, would seem to be more primary, because they are made in spite of strong influences to react otherwise. Ondersma et al.'s arguments are weakened, if not reversed, by these considerations.

In short, the empirical data supported the construct validity of our approach. Conceptually, our definition reflected concern for historical problems when scientific terminology becomes moralistic. In both cases, our approach was scientific and reflected sensitivity to scientific issues in this area. Our critics were focused on morality, not science. Nevertheless, it was only our approach that they labeled "extra-scientific."

MORAL PANICS, RELIGION, PSYCHIATRY, AND VICTIMISM

We do not claim that our study was definitive. However, we aver that it was soundly conducted and interpreted, and it substantially improved over previous reviews in precision, objectivity, external validity, and internal validity—all important indicators of scientific quality. The exchange we had in *Psychological Bulletin* with Dallam et al. (2001) and Ondersma et al. (2001) is the most direct evidence for our claim. Both groups of therapists failed completely in their statistical and methodological critiques, as we amply demonstrated in our rebuttal (Rind et al., 2001), which was recapped in the previous section. The latter group consistently conflated scientific with moralistic approaches, yet attributed extra-scientific qualities to our treatment. Their conflation repeated the long and sordid history of psychotherapy in the realm of human sexual behavior, where it has consistently medicalized sex based on social and religious values, all the while pretending to be scientific about it (Szasz, 1990). The two critiques are particularly important in the debate between the traditional CPIE view of many therapists (i.e., that CSA is intensely and pervasively destructive to mental health) and those who believe that the issue has been imbued with hyperbole run amok. Their significance lies in the fact that the thinking behind each group had its origins in one of the two panics of the 1980s (day-care abuse and recovered memories), which had much influence on current views that CSA is uniquely destructive. As such, the validity of their critiques can be said to represent the integrity of prevailing views on CSA.

The Ondersma et al. group comes from the American Professional Society of Abuse Counselors (APSAC), for whom they wrote the initial version of their 2001 critique (Ondersma, Chaffin, & Berliner, 1999). APSAC was formed in 1985 as a professional group of therapists concerned that some people were skeptical regarding claims in the McMartin day-care satanic abuse case. At the same meeting at which APSAC was formed for professionals, "Believe the Children" was formed for parents of McMartin children who shared APSAC's point of view (Nathan & Snedeker, 1995). Thus, from the start, APSAC has been an advocate for the reality of satanic and sexual abuse in day care, as well as the CPIE view of CSA, justifying the importance of its members as therapists to deal with the presumed aftermath. The Dallam et al. group (i.e., the Leadership Council) consists of therapists and other professionals supporting the validity of recovered memories and related phenomena such as multiple personality disorder, as well as psychoanalytically oriented techniques to "recover" these memories, thereby "curing" the patients. The organization was formed in part to protect therapists holding these theories and using these techniques from being sued, a practice that began in the mid-1990s. Thus, key representatives of the view that CSA is uniquely destructive not only failed to support their position in their critiques, but offered clear evidence for scientifically minded psychologists and other professionals to be wary of the scientific foundations of their claims, given the weakness or absence of sound science in their attacks.

In closing this chapter, it seems appropriate to examine in context the attacks on our study, an endeavor that requires moving away from the narrow perspective of psychology into more of a sociological and historical perspective—but not the pseudo-sociohistorical perspective presented by Ondersma et al. (2001), used to promote a particular therapeutic and moral agenda. Rather, here we employ a scholarly approach taken by researchers outside the field. Historian Philip Jenkins (1998) provided such a treatment. Briefly, I summarize the gist of his treatise.

Moral Panics

Jenkins (1998) borrowed from British sociological moral panic theory to describe reactions in our society to CSA as a moral panic. This theory holds that moral panics take place regarding some social issue or problem when a wave of irrational public fear exists; when official reaction is out of all proportion to the actual threat; when "experts" perceive the threat in all but identical terms and speak with one voice of rates, diagnoses, prognoses, and solutions; and when media representations universally stress sudden and dramatic increases in the problem that far exceed sober appraisal. Jenkins showed that such a moral panic was occurring in the United States in the mid-1970s, when views of CSA changed in a very short period of time, from viewing CSA as immoral but not especially problematic unless accompanied by aggravating factors, to considering it as something uniquely destructive, requiring far more attention than any other type of problem facing children. The change was so rapid, Jenkins noted, that it could not have reflected definitive empirical data. In fact, as he documented throughout his treatise, the new and evolving view reflected political forces and special interest agendas rather than dispassionate science.

The moral panic that occurred in the mid-1970s was not the first but the third such panic regarding CSA of the 20th century. The first ran from 1890 to about 1920, the second from 1935 to 1957, and the third began about 1976 and has been with us ever since. The first panic died out as moral activism became discredited because of the imposition of Prohibition and the ensuing fiasco, political feminism fragmented, and the media shifted attention to other issues, such as Prohibition gangsterism. The second panic, in which sexual psychopath statutes were passed that permitted indefinite confinement based on psychiatric consultation, died out as criticism grew regarding the "prostitution of medical terminology ... as a basis for social policy" (Jenkins, 1998, p. 91) and the sacrificing of individual rights to "therapeutic fads and jargon" (Jenkins, 1998, p. 92). The current panic, in contrast, has had enormous staying power owing to the institutionalization of the child protection idea and the blame culture of victimization.

In all three panics, the same special interest groups participated and benefited. Initially, they raised concerns of legitimate merit. However, with time they exaggerated the problem for less than charitable reasons. These groups included feminists, therapists, law-enforcement personnel, politicians, religious conservatives, and the media. Jenkins described how each group benefited. Psychiatrists, therapists, and social workers—often allied with law-enforcement interests—gained considerably in numbers, opportunities, and prestige from the sexual threat. Feminists gained in their campaign because this sort of moral panic advanced their more general struggles against perceived victimization and oppression. Politicians benefited by appealing to constituent sentiments of "law and order" and "protecting the weak" from the right and left, respectively. This issue gave moral conservatives a rock-solid front to press for wider morality enforcement. The media enhanced ratings and profitability through their crusading stance.

Jenkins continued, noting that it is worth looking at the current panic in more detail to see how these groups socially constructed the prevailing beliefs about CSA. Feminist campaigns against perceived male oppression and against rape in the late 1960s and early 1970s soon evolved into campaigns against incest. In a pivotal speech delivered at a feminist convention in 1971, feminist Florence Rush characterized incest as a tool used by men to teach females subjugation early on. With this speech, the "incest survivor movement" was begun. Feminists equated incest to rape in its causes and consequences. In 1974, increased interest in physical abuse led to passage of the Child Abuse Prevention and Treatment Act, also known as the Mondale Act. The Mondale Act provided funding for states to set up programs to curb the problems of physical abuse and emotional neglect. The mental health profession expanded and benefited substantially from this legislation. By 1976, feminist campaigns against incest and professionals' concern with child abuse merged, and the focus of the Mondale Act and of state programs shifted very quickly away from physical abuse and emotional neglect to CSA, which has been the chief focus ever since.

Professionals adopted feminist views of incest, derived from the rape model, and then applied this incest model to nonincestuous sex between men and minor females, and eventually to sex between men and boys and between women and boys. The equating of CSA with incest, and thus with rape, produced the view that all CSA was psychologically ruinous. Professionals concerned with child abuse repeatedly expanded definitions of CSA to include noncontact sex as well as sex involving increasingly older minors, which substantially increased the number of "ruined" victims requiring the services of these professionals. Moral conservatives amplified this dogma in their attempt to reverse the general trend in the 1970s of "moral degeneracy." The media enthusiastically sensationalized the issue, creating a sense of national urgency. Legislators responded, taking the risk-free stance for easy political profit that "no policy would be seen as too severe in combating a vast and unqualified evil like child abuse" (Jenkins, 1998, p. 143).

Religion and Psychiatry

Two key sources for the panics, as Jenkins noted, were moral conservatives on the one hand and psychiatrists, therapists, and social workers on the other. Up until the 1800s, clerics were the designated experts in sexual behavior (Szasz, 1990), who derived their authority from the Church and from Christian precepts dating back to St. Paul, Chrysostrum, Origen, and Augustine, in which ascetic philosophy replaced the more positive sexual outlook of the Greeks and Romans. The antisexual views of the Church evolved from anti-body, anti-empirical philosophies of the Pythagoreans, Plato, and the Neo-Platonists, which Augustine fixed into Church doctrine in the 4th century A.D. (Hergenhahn, 1986). In these philosophies, sensual experience was evil, especially if sexual; the goal of life was to live in a world of rationality, and later faith and spirituality, uncorrupted by the body. Ideally, sex was to be reserved for procreation only. In exchange for sensual and sexual sacrifice, people were promised eternal bliss, a small price for many to pay at a time when believers expected their impoverished material world to end in their lifetime (Bullough & Bullough, 1977). It was not until the Medieval Church grew stronger and was then able to extend its control over the peoples of Europe, however, that guilt about sex became a central feature of Western life. The Church grew obsessed with restricting sex, at one point going so far as to make intercourse within marriage illegal on Sundays, Wednesdays, and Fridays, as well as 40 days before Easter, 40 days before Christmas, and from the time of conception to 40 days after parturition (Marmor, 1971). Since this point, one of Christianity's chief occupations has been controlling and restricting sex, labeling virtually all nonprocreative sexual behaviors as sins.

When medicine rose in prestige, influence, and power 2 centuries ago, the clinician began to replace the cleric as the expert on sex, and now was granted authority by the state to diagnose, intervene, and treat. Behaviors that had been labeled sin now were called sickness. Psychiatry classified sexual disease not on the basis of science, but rather on that of morality (Szasz, 1990). Two hundred years ago, psychiatry had deemed female erotic response and desire as a mental disorder, because society disapproved on moral grounds. At that time and up until recently, psychiatry labeled masturbation a sickness, because society saw it as immoral. Up until a generation ago, psychiatry also labeled homosexuality as a mental illness, because society viewed it as morally wrong (Szasz, 1990).

Christianity and psychiatry have worked hand in hand to define sexual normalcy and deviancy in philosophical and moral terms, but certainly not in scientific terms. Christianity may have vested so much energy into controlling sex because it intuitively has known that this practice produces guilt (cf. Marmor, 1971). Given such guilt, the sinner relieves it through expiation granted by the Church. The Church gains in power by inducing guilt, because it alone can relieve the guilt, thus making parishioners dependent on the Church. Psychiatry's interest in rigidly insisting that socially disapproved sexual behavior is pathological is analogous to the Church's interest: Psychiatrists gain money and status by serving as state-designated experts to control behavior (Jenkins, 1998).

In view of this background, it is no surprise that the two groups most vocal in attacking our meta-analysis were religious conservatives and various mental health professionals. Historically, these groups have had vested interest in combating sexual sin and sickness. Their focus on the CSA problem intensified so much after the sexual revolution of the 1970s undoubtedly because most other forms of sexuality lost much of their taboo status, narrowing the range of targets. Both groups played key roles in the panics of the 1980s and 1990s, benefiting substantially in the process as outlined by Jenkins (1998). Our article threatened this privilege, and thus prompted vigorous attack.

Victimism

Although moral conservatives and therapists played an important role in building the moral panic, most important in terms of sparking the panic was the women's movement, radical feminism, and the culture of victimology. The first wave of feminism in the late 1960s was focused on equal rights and opportunities, which Christina Hoff Sommers (1995) labeled "equity feminism." But then a more combative, hostile version branched off, which saw female oppression and victimhood as being ubiquitously at the hands of males and the "patriarchy," and spoke of "backlash" as an assumed, undeclared war by males against females. Sommers labeled this version "gender feminism." In this context, genuine concern about judicial response to the problem of rape and incest became politicized not merely as a means of stemming these problems, but also as powerful weapons in the wider "war" against perceived male oppression.

Gender feminists became "injustice collectors," gathering atrocity stories, irrespective of veridicality, and disseminating them to galvanize the troops—to produce "fighting madness," as one prominent gender feminist leader put it (Sommers, 1995). Gloria Steinum told her readers that 150,000 women and girls died each year from anorexia nervosa caused by the androcentric system; however, the correct value, according to the Center for Disease Control, is about 100 (and not necessarily from the "androcentric system"). Patricia Ireland, the president of NOW in 1994, claimed in a television interview that battery of pregnant women was the number one cause of birth defects in this country. *Time* magazine added some details, reporting that this finding came from a study conducted by the March of Dimes. The claim was without merit; the March of Dimes had conducted no such study. In 1993, another factoid proliferated—that research had shown a 40% rise in battery of women on Superbowl Sunday. This falsehood came to be known as the Superbowl hoax (Sommers, 1995). Gender feminists' most successful hyperbole, however, was in the domain of sexual victimology. "One in four" became their official figure for rapes of woman by men, based on a study conducted for Gloria Steinum's *Ms.* Magazine, in which the researchers inflated the numbers fourfold by including cases in which respondents themselves did not consider the episode to have been rape (e.g., in half of these cases, the women viewed the experience as a miscommunication with their partner rather than as an act of aggression; Sommers, 1995).

In this context of persuasion and propaganda in the so-called gender wars, CSA achieved its hyperbolized character. Incest was equated to rape in its nature, purpose, extent, and consequences. The "incest survivor movement" served as a prominent atrocity story, as real victims and pseudovictims alike were encouraged to emerge—and did so—throughout the nation. Therapists catering to this concern integrated the gender feminist view of incest. Soon, incest and then all CSA became equated with violence. All victims became "survivors," borrowing vocabulary from the Nazi Holocaust to maximize dramatic effect. As a result, survivorship became an identity (Jenkins, 1998).

Sexual victimology prospered in a general climate of emerging victimologies in the wake of various 1960s and 1970s protest movements (Best, 1997), but it far surpassed its "siblings" because of the staying power of sexual sensationalism. As it transformed, with the help of therapists and their theories, into a matter of identity, it turned from victimology into victimism, a new secular religion. Sexual victimization became all-explaining in terms of personal problems. Acknowledging one's victim status relieved one of personal responsibility for life's errors and faults. Victimhood created a sense of purpose in many who previously had been without purpose—it identified the perpetrator as a demon, who needed to be pursued and extirpated. This externalizing provided a mission for both the victim and her confidant—that is, the therapist, who took the role of the cleric in this imagined healing ritual. The therapist in turn derived inspiration from sacred "truths" revealed by Janet, Charcot, and Freud; the lack of any sort of generally accepted modern empirical verification of the founders' notions acted as no more of a problem for the believing therapist than a corresponding lack of empirical verification in religious assertions had bothered the cleric. Finally, victim status created group identity, in which members shared a common, organizing trait and sense of solidarity. The religious-like aura of victimism helps to account for the zeal with which advocates promoted the 1980s' fictions of day-care abuse and recovered memories, as well as the general hyperbole concerning CSA, which gained much of its steam during this period and was a direct result of these two fictions. That aura also helps to elucidate the compatibility of the extreme left and right on this issue, both of which came to it with a degree of religious fervor.

CONCLUSION

Certainly adult–child sex is not the moral equivalent of other forms of sex. It is unambiguously immoral in our society. We did not question this view in our review. Morality, however, is a separate issue from harm. Since the rise of

Christianity, morality in the West, especially in regard to sexual behavior, has often not centered on minimizing harm or pain and maximizing benefit or pleasure of a bodily or psychological nature (Bentham, 1978; Russell, 1977). Until a few hundred years ago, clerics were the designated experts on sexual behavior; sin against the Christian god was their criterion for judgment. When medicine grew in prestige and influence, clinicians took over the role of designated experts on sex, and sickness replaced sin as the criterion. However, sickness was inferred from sinfulness, as in labeling female sexual desire as pathological, defining masturbation as dangerously harmful self-abuse, or calling homosexuality a perversion and disease (Szasz, 1990). Today, mainstream science and sexology reject these pathologizations as pseudoscientific. All this is to say that it is a fallacy to assume that a behavior is harmful just because it is regarded as immoral.

Our review was concerned with psychological harm, not moral harm. As such, we felt no obligation to adhere to the language of morality. Our recommendation for professionals to use the term *abuse* less indiscriminately reflected the concern that this term in scientific discourse implies measurable psychological or physical harm, which is inappropriate when the empirical results suggest otherwise. A possible effect of freely using the term *abuse* when no harm occurs is biasing recipients of the communication to perceive harm nonetheless. Priming and framing, as psychological research has demonstrated, can have such effects (Rind et al., 1998, 2001).

Our recommendation for terminology was even more appropriate for adolescent–adult sex, where it *is* debatable to categorically define all sexual relations between adults and adolescents up to age 18 as abuse, as is the practice (a) in many jurisdictions in the United States and (b) by many abuse researchers. Even Ondersma et al. (2001), one of our sharpest critics, noted that there is room for discussion about the term *abuse* when adolescents rather than children are involved. Recently, a group of prominent U.S. medical groups concerned with adolescent health offered this opinion in a position paper published in the *Journal of Adolescent Health* ("Protecting Adolescents," 2004). Among the medical groups were the American Academy of Family Physicians, the American Academy of Pediatrics, and the Society for Adolescent Medicine. These groups complained that laws requiring reporting consensual adolescent sex (with peers or adults) hurt physicians' ability to properly treat adolescent patients, and hurt the adolescents themselves. Such laws interfere with confidentiality in treatment, so much so that teens may forgo needed treatment, or may be subject to undue stress if they obtain treatment and honestly report their sexual behavior. The groups argued that, among adolescents, sexual activity and sexual abuse are *not* synonymous.

Physicians, they asserted, should not be required to report sexual activity merely because it is illegal, although they should be required to report sexual abuse. The opinion of these physician groups represents a pragmatically based break with sociolegally based definitions of abuse.

The criminalization and pathologization of sex between adults and adolescents in their midteens is a modern, particularly American, social construction. Throughout history and across culture, girls have married on average between the ages of 12 and 15, often to much older males. In many cultures, boys of similar ages have been initiated into sex through relations with an experienced adult woman. In many other cultures, adolescent boys have been involved in homosexual relations with older males as part of a mentoring relationship (Rind, Bauserman, & Tromovitch, 2000). In all these examples, such relations have been considered to be socially functional rather than abusive or enslaving, as victimologists argue they by nature are. In Canada, the current age of sexual consent is 14; in Europe, the median age of consent is also 14 (Rind et al., 2001). Clearly, the U.S. standard is no basis for universally defining abuse in a scientific sense when adolescents are involved.

In examining the assumption of psychological harm, we adhered to basic scientific principles, much more so than did our critics and their colleagues in their reviews. We brought in precision to our review through use of meta-analysis, and we focused explicitly on important issues such as external and internal validity. In our rebuttal to critics in *Psychological Bulletin* (Rind et al., 2001), we provided a point-by-point comparison of our review against that of Kendall-Tackett, Williams, and Finkelhor (1993), the last review on CSA before ours to be published in *Psychological Bulletin*, and the one most frequently cited by child advocates and victimologists to claim universal and extreme harm from CSA. We showed that whereas we sought out more representative samples and then explicitly compared results to those of national samples, Kendall-Tackett et al. used highly unrepresentative samples and assumed their generalizability, never discussing their severe limitations. Although we devoted much journal space to examining internal validity, Kendall-Tackett et al. assumed causality from CSA-adjustment correlations as a matter of course. In the end, our review brought some measure of balance into a field run amok with extremism. Our review did what science is supposed to do—self-correct, not rubber stamp.

The fact that the U.S. government condemned our review indicates nothing negative about the review's merits, although our critics have often advanced this specious argument. The history of science and philosophy is filled with important and even great works that have conflicted with prevailing opinion and have then been condemned, banned, or burned following campaigns by moral crusaders and power holders. If anything, such treatment speaks to a work's genuine merit, rather than to its invalidity.

REFERENCES

Bagash, B. K. (1995, February 24). Judge dismisses blasphemy charges in Pakistan. *Philadelphia Inquirer.*

Baird, B. N. (2002). Politics, operant conditioning, Galileo, and the American Psychological Association's response to Rind et al. (1998). *American Psychologist, 57,* 189–192.

Bartholow, B. N., Doll, L. S., Joy, D., Bolan, G., Harrison, J. S., Moss, P. M., & McKirnan, D. (1994). Emotional, behavioral, and HIV risks associated with sexual abuse among adult homosexual and bisexual men. *Child Abuse & Neglect, 18,* 747–761.

Becker, G. (1986). Correcting the point-biserial correlation for attenuation owing to unequal sample size. *Journal of Experimental Education, 55,* 5–8.

Bentham, J. (1978). Offenses against one's self. *Journal of Homosexuality, 3,* 383–387.

Best, J. (1997, May/June). Victimization and the victim industry. *Society,* pp. 9–17.

Brandon, S., Boakes, J., Glaser, D., & Green, R. (1998). Recovered memories of childhood sexual abuse. *British Journal of Psychiatry, 172,* 296–307.

Bullough, V., & Bullough, B. (1977). *Sin, sickness, and sanity: A history of sexual attitudes.* New York: Meridian.

Ceci, S. J., & Bruck, M. (1993). Suggestibility of the child witness: A historical review and synthesis. *Psychological Bulletin, 113,* 403–439.

Crews, F. (1998). *Unauthorized Freud: Doubters confront a legend.* New York: Penguin.

Dallam, S., Gleaves, D., Cepeda-Benito, A., Silberg, J., Kraemer, H., & Spiegel, D. (2001). The effects of child sexual abuse: An examination of Rind, Tromovitch, and Bauserman (1998). *Psychological Bulletin, 127,* 715–733.

Dallam, S., Gleaves, D., Spiegel, D., & Kraemer, H. (1999). *An analysis of Rind et al.'s meta-analysis of the long-term effects of child sexual abuse* [unpublished manuscript]. Preliminary analysis in preparation for full review article rebutting the Rind et al. (1998) study.

Divided memories. (1995). O. Bikel (Producer), *Frontline.* New York: Public Broadcasting Service.

Duin, J. (1999, May 13). Hill joins pedophilia-study critics: Lawmakers urge professional journal to disavow report. *Washington Times.*

Finkelhor, D. (1984). *Child sexual abuse: New theory and research.* New York: Free Press.

Finkelhor, D., Hotaling, G. T., Lewis, I. A., & Smith, C. (1989). Sexual abuse and its relationship to later sexual satisfaction, marital status, religion, and attitudes. *Journal of Interpersonal Violence, 4,* 379–399.

Fishman, J. (1991). Prevalence, impact, and meaning attribution of childhood sexual experiences of undergraduate males. *Dissertation Abstracts International, 52,* 114.

Fowler, R. (1999). Retrieved from http://www.apa.org/releases/delay.html

Fromuth, M., & Burkhart, B. (1989). Long-term psychological correlates of childhood sexual abuse in two samples of college men. *Child Abuse & Neglect, 13,* 533–542.

Hergenhahn, B. R. (1986). *An introduction to the history of psychology.* Belmont, CA: Wadsworth.

Hooker, E. (1957). The adjustment of the male overt homosexual. *Journal of Projective Techniques, 21,* 18–31.

Innocence lost. (1991). In O. Bikel (Producer), *Frontline.* New York: Public Broadcasting Service.

Innocence lost: The verdict. (1993). In O. Bikel (Producer), *Frontline.* New York: Public Broadcasting Service.

Jenkins, P. (1998). *Moral panic: Changing concepts of the child-molester in modern America.* New Haven, CT: Yale University Press.

Kendall-Tackett, K. A., Williams, L. M., & Finkelhor, D. (1993). Impact of sexual abuse on children: A review and synthesis of recent empirical studies. *Psychological Bulletin, 113,* 164–180.

Landass, T. (n.d.). *The Evelyn Hooker study and the normalization of homosexuality.* Retrieved June, 1999, from http://www.frc.org

Latané, B. (1981). The psychology of social impact. *American Psychologist, 36,* 343–356.

Leadership Council. (2001). Retrieved from http://www.leadershipcouncil.org/Research/Rind/rind.html

Lilienfeld, S. O. (2002). When worlds collide: Social science, politics, and the Rind et al. (1998) child sexual abuse meta-analysis [special issue]. *American Psychologist, 57*(3), 176–188.

Marmor, J. (1971, July 12). "Normal" and "deviant" sexual behavior. *Journal of the American Medical Association.*

McCarty, R. (1999). A brief comment by APA executive director for science. *Psychological Science Agenda, 12*(6), 2–3.

Mendel, M. P. (1995). *The male survivor.* Thousand Oaks, CA: Sage.

Nathan, D., & Snedeker, M. (1995). *Satan's silence: Ritual abuse and the making of a modern American witchhunt.* New York: Basic Books.

Olafson, E., Corwin, D., & Summit, R. (1993). Modern history of child sexual abuse awareness: Cycles of discovery and suppression. *Child Abuse & Neglect, 17,* 7–24.

Ondersma, S. J., Chaffin, M., & Berliner, L. (1999). Comments on Rind et al. meta-analysis controversy. *The APSAC Advisor, 12,* 2–5.

Ondersma, S. J., Chaffin, M., Berliner, L., Cordon, I., Goodman, G., & Barnett, D. (2001). Sex with children is abuse: The Rind et al. meta-analysis controversy. *Psychological Bulletin, 127,* 707–714.

Pedhazur, E. (1997). *Multiple regression in behavioral research: Explanation and prediction.* New York: Harcourt Brace College.

Pedophilia report controversy. (1999, May 14). On *Watch It!* [Television broadcast]. New York: MSNBC.

Protecting adolescents: Ensuring access to care and reporting sexual activity and abuse. (2004). *Journal of Adolescent Health, 35,* 420–423.

Rind, B., Bauserman, R., & Tromovitch, P. (2000). Science versus orthodoxy: Analysis of the congressional condemnation of a scientific article and reflections on remedies for future ideological attacks. *Applied & Preventive Psychology, 9,* 211–225.

Rind, B., Bauserman, R., & Tromovitch, P. (2001). Moralistic psychiatry, Procrustes' bed, and the science of child sexual abuse: A reply to Spiegel. *Sexuality and Culture, 5,* 75–85.

Rind, B., & Tromovitch, P. (1997). A meta-analytic review of findings from national samples on psychological correlates of child sexual abuse. *Journal of Sex Research, 34,* 237–255.

Rind, B., Tromovitch, P., & Bauserman, R. (1998). A meta-analytic examination of assumed properties of child sexual abuse using college samples. *Psychological Bulletin, 124,* 22–53.

Rind, B., Tromovitch, P., & Bauserman, R. (2000). Condemnation of a scientific article: A chronology and refutation of the attacks and a discussion of threats to the integrity of science. *Sexuality and Culture, 4,* 1–62.

Rind, B. (2001). *Spreadsheet.* Unpublished manuscript.

Rind, B., Tromovitch, P., & Bauserman, R. (2001). The validity and appropriateness of methods, analyses, and conclusions in Rind et al. (1998): A rebuttal of victimological critique from Ondersma et al. (2001) and Dallam et al. (2001). *Psychological Bulletin, 127,* 734–758.

Rosenthal, R. (1984). *Meta-analytic procedures for social sciences.* Beverly Hills, CA: Sage.

Russell, B. (1977). *Why I am not a Christian, and other essays on religion and related subjects.* New York: Simon & Schuster.

Schlessinger, L. (1999a, April 18). Article on pedophilia is just "junk science." *The Times-Picayune,* p. E6.

Schlessinger, L. (1999b, March 23). *The Dr. Laura show* [Radio broadcast]. Los Angeles: Premiere Radio Networks.

Silliman, M. (1993). Self-esteem and locus of control of women who report sexual abuse during childhood. *Psychological Reports, 72,* 1294.

Socarides, C. (1995). Retrieved from www.narth.com/docs/1995papers/socarides.html

Sommers, C. H. (1995). *Who stole feminism? How women have betrayed women.* New York: Touchtone.

Szasz, T. (1990). *Sex by prescription: The startling truth about today's sex therapy.* New York: Syracuse University Press.

10

Is Smiling Related to Interpersonal Power? Theory and Meta-Analysis[1]

Judith A. Hall
Northeastern University

Erik J. Coats
Bala Cynwyd, Pennsylvania

Lavonia Smith LeBeau
Pennsylvania State University

It happens that a *theme*, a *method*, and *two quotations*—all from the writings of Ralph Rosnow—perfectly set the stage for the research that we describe in this chapter. The theme is rumor, the method is meta-analysis, and the two quotations are "surely, God loves the .06 nearly as much as the .05" (Rosnow & Rosenthal, 1989, p. 1277) and "some things you learn aren't so" (Rosnow & Rosenthal, 1995, p. 3). Each of these reflects a different and important way in which Ralph Rosnow has influenced both content and methodology in social psychology. The relevance of the theme, the method, and the quotations become clearer as we discuss our research on the relation between how much a person smiles and that person's position on the vertical dimension of social relations (the term *vertical*, as used here, represents dominance, status, power, and other related concepts). The first author of this chapter has been studying the relation of nonverbal behavior,

[1]Some of the research described in this chapter was supported by a grant from the National Science Foundation to the first author.

including smiling, to these and other manifestations of the vertical dimension for a number of years, and the second and third authors joined with her in performing a meta-analysis of the literature pertaining to smiling and other nonverbal behaviors (Hall, Coats, & Smith LeBeau, in press).

THE THEME: RUMOR

In outlining why rumors are transmitted and suggesting ways in which they can be controlled, Rosnow stated, "Steeped in wishful thinking, rumors about how the world works are theory-driven by stereotypes and illusions as much as they are data-driven by empirical facts" (1991, p. 488). Our research is not about rumor per se, but it does concern something *about which* there has been much rumor, if rumor is taken to mean the transmission of a claim from one person to the next without independent verification. By that definition, beliefs about verticality and smiling constitute a rumor that has been circulated in social psychology for decades. In a seminal statement, Henley (1977) argued that gender differences in nonverbal behavior (including women's tendencies to smile more than men) stem from women's lower social power and status. Although there are many different conceptual and operational definitions relevant to the vertical dimension, Henley (1977) did not make such distinctions, and thus we consider all available definitions of this broad constellation of characteristics. Verticality can be defined in terms of process or outcome; can be state or trait; can be achieved, ascribed, or assigned; and can have many different bases, including coercion, expertise, reward capacity, and outcome dependency. When appropriate, we identify specific operational definitions of the verticality construct.

Henley argued first that there exists a parallelism between women's nonverbal communication and the nonverbal communication of people who are generally low in verticality, and second that this parallelism is no coincidence: Verticality brings about, and reinforces, differences in the nonverbal communication of men and women. Henley discussed several kinds of communication under this rubric, including gazing, nonverbal sensitivity, and smiling. For each behavior, it was assumed to be socially advantageous (in an adaptive or compensatory way) for women to manifest a high level of behavior or performance. Henley described smiling as women's "badge of appeasement" (1977, p. 175), arguing that smiling is a hallmark of subordinate people who feel a need to placate or please others (both more powerful others as well as others in general).

Henley's idea has been repeated often in published works, including textbooks of social psychology and psychology of women (e.g., Crawford & Unger, 2000; Feldman, 1995; Lippa, 1994; Lips, 2001, 2003; Matlin, 2000; Yoder, 2003). Vrugt (1987) noted that "Henley's idea that nonverbal sex differences result from differences in the social position of men and women quickly became widely accepted" (p. 371). As with a rumor, the frequent repetitions of Henley's position have generally been phrased as assertions of fact, not as opinions or as a hypothesis to be tested. As Rosnow (1991) pointed out, much of the time rumors, not unlike stereotypes, are based on a kernel of truth, or at least something that is easily believable.

In terms of the Henley "rumor," we believe that it was the kernel of truth concerning the frequency with which females displayed certain nonverbal behaviors that added credibility to the gender-verticality link, along with people's ability to envision stereotypic scenarios in which a woman's smile suggests weakness or dependency. Of course, a bit of open-minded reflection might bring to mind counterexamples or counterarguments. Nevertheless, these were hardly ever raised, and it was evident that the logic tying gender, verticality, and nonverbal behavior seemed unassailable to many. Indeed, it was too obvious to question: People low in social power are more likely to smile (gaze, etc.), women are lower in social power than men, and that is why women smile (gaze, etc.) more than men do. This three-part chain of argument seemed to provide a sweeping explanation for many nonverbal gender differences, and it appealed both to feminist scholars who felt that the impact of patriarchal society surely must penetrate into the microprocesses of social interaction, and to researchers of nonverbal communication who had suffered the criticism that their field was not adequately theoretical. Henley's was a grand theory that could account for a wide range of nonverbal gender differences (Hall, 1998). Henley's theory was called the "oppression hypothesis" by Hall (1984).

Is the oppression hypothesis correct with regard to smiling? To answer this, we must consider each of the three claims that comprise the hypothesis. The claim that women tend to smile more than men is well justified based on numerous studies that have been summarized in several meta-analyses (Hall, 1984; Hall, Carter, & Horgan, 2000; LaFrance, Hecht, & Levy Paluck, 2003). LaFrance et al.'s (2003) review, more recent and much larger than Hall's (1984) review, found a point-biserial correlation of about .20 between smiling and gender (equivalent to a Cohen's d of about .40). Thus, the difference is modest in magnitude but very well established. The claim that women are lower in verticality than men will not be challenged here, although of course it is an assumption that deserves qualification in terms of time, place, operational definition, and many other factors (Wood & Eagly, 2002). The remainder of this chapter addresses the final claim—that people lower in verticality are more likely to smile than are those who are higher. On what evidence is this claim based?

At the time of Henley's (1977) original statement, there was little empirical research on the topic of verticality and smiling. Henley (1977) did not refer to any, and Hall (1984), in reviewing nonverbal gender differences and discussing their possible causes, did not report any. This lack, as well as limited and/or unconvincing evidence for the oppression hypothesis's ability to explain other nonverbal behaviors and skills, led Hall (1984) to conclude that Henley's hypothesis was as yet unsupported. Vrugt and Kerkstra (1984) reached much the same conclusion in a review of this topic, noting:

> [T]here is a profound lack of sound theoretical background. The observed differences between men and women are often loosely interpreted and thus unjustly viewed as expressions of the supposedly different characteristics of men and women, as for example male dominance. Such interpretations, which start to live a life of their own and gain common acceptance, are not beneficial to the building of a sound theoretical framework for this area of research. (p. 29)

When a claim has a "life of its own," the process of verifying its truth can become difficult, insofar as the evidence must pass not only the scientific bar but also the psychological bar of entrenched belief. And when such verification leads one to suggest that an entrenched belief is not true, the task is harder still, as we show later in this chapter.

Before reviewing empirical findings relevant to the smiling-verticality link, it is instructive to apply our common sense to the question. Even in the absence of empirical data, there are many reasons for questioning the broad claim that a person lower in verticality will smile more than will a person higher on the dimension. Such a person might have a motive to appease others (a motive that Henley emphasized in the case of women), but on the other hand such a person might have quite different motives as well as a range of different emotions. Furthermore, smiling is known to follow from a wide range of motives and emotions (Abel, 2002; Ekman & Friesen, 1982). One can imagine a subordinate in an organization, or someone with a nondominant personality, or someone at the bottom of the pecking order among peers feeling hostile, sulky, anxious, or depressed and therefore not smiling much at all. Alternatively, a low-power person might wish to impress others with his or her competence and seriousness regarding task performance, a motivation that is not likely to foster smiling. At the same time, a person with high power (status, rank, etc.) might wish to reassure or encourage those with less power, and therefore might be motivated to engage in higher levels of smiling. Furthermore, considering that higher-power or higher-status people are generally socially advantaged, the lion's share of happiness might certainly fall to them, which could also lead to greater amounts of smiling (Keltner, Gruenfeld, & Anderson, 2003). Thus, the proximal state (emotion, goal, social motive) of an individual is likely to be a potent—and highly variable—influence on smiling.

Given the many different motives and emotions that both low and high verticality may engender, should one still argue that people low in verticality smile more? Consideration of this question led Hall and colleagues (Hall et al., in press; Hall & Halberstadt, 1997; Hall, Horgan, & Carter, 2002) to propose that verticality (status, dominance, authority, etc.) may be more of a structural variable than a psychological one, and that it may therefore be pointless to make overall predictions. In other words, simply knowing a person's vertical position does not tell you how he or she feels or what he or she is trying to accomplish interpersonally. Just as a person who is high or low on a ladder might feel either fear, determination, thrill, joy, boredom, or any number of other emotions, so it is not possible to predict a psychological state from what rung of the social power ladder one is standing on. What determines behavior (including smiling) is one's emotions and social motives. Therefore, Hall and colleagues have argued that the prediction of a particular relation between verticality and smiling must depend on knowing people's proximal states and motives. Armed with such knowledge, one would then be in a position to develop an understanding of when low or high verticality might, or might not, be associated with an asymmetry in smiling and in other kinds nonverbal communication.

It follows that when one compares the amounts of smiling displayed by dyadic interactants who differ in verticality, any prediction of which individual will smile more must take into account the strength and nature of the individual's respective proximal states. If they are in the same state, differences in smiling may disappear. Alternatively, there may be no smiling difference even if the individuals are in different states, if those states promote equivalent amounts of smiling. Yet another possibility is that smiling differences between the individuals occur because they are in states that promote different amounts of smiling. The latter case fits the prototypical picture of a stern boss and a fawning underling. However, it may be a misleading picture insofar as many situations and roles may promote quite different goals and emotions in people who differ in verticality. This situation represents the *confounding* of verticality and proximal states, opening up the possibility that verticality per se may not actually be the source of the difference. We discuss this important possibility in depth later.

Researchers skilled in studying rumor transmission might make a case study of the spread of Henley's (1977) provocative ideas. However, this chapter has another goal—to examine the empirical evidence bearing on the relation between verticality and smiling. After we offer this review, we return to the role of proximal states in understanding the relation between verticality and smiling.

Five Recent Studies

Over the past few years, the first author has conducted a series of studies to examine the relationship between verticality and smiling. This work has included naturalistic observations as well as controlled experiments. In none can much support for the oppression hypothesis be found.

Status in the Workplace

Most studies in the published literature in this area are laboratory studies. For some purposes this is a good thing, because in the laboratory one can control extraneous and confounding variables better than in field settings. However, interest in the question of how verticality affects social behavior is rooted in a desire to understand what happens in everyday life, not just in the psychology laboratory. Therefore, it was important to do research in more naturalistic settings.

The first study we describe was conducted by Hall, Smith LeBeau, Gordon Reinoso, and Thayer (2001) with employees of a university who were recruited to participate in a study of social interaction. The participants were not told of the investigators' interest in their organizational rank until after the observations were made, in order not to introduce bias into the participants' behavior.

Forty-eight employees, representing a random selection from those listed in the university's phone directory, were asked to recruit an acquaintance from their same department or unit and to have a short conversation about work while being photographed. Several candid photographs (taken at unannounced moments while they were conversing) and one posed photo (taken afterwards under the instruction to look at the camera) were taken and coded for a number of nonverbal behaviors. Smiling data consisted of ratings on a 9-point scale made by five raters for each photo; raters and photos were later averaged for candid and posed photographs separately. After their conversation, the participants rated themselves and their partners on their relative status within the university.

The results of this study did not support the oppression hypothesis. Although status predicted some nonverbal behaviors (e.g., head tilt up or down), it did not predict smiling ($r = .06$). There was mixed evidence on the gender difference in smiling. For candid photographs, there was no gender difference (point-biserial r between gender and smiling $= -.05$ and $-.13$ for the lower- and higher-status dyad members, respectively), but for posed photographs women smiled more than men, especially when they were the lower-status person in the dyad (point-biserial $r = .48, p < .01$, for lower status and .26, not significant, for higher status). The emergence of a bigger gender difference for posed than for candid photographs is consistent with Hall's (1984) and LaFrance et al.'s (2003) meta-analytic observations that the smiling difference is larger when participants are made more aware of being observed. Interestingly, the present study found that none of the behaviors that showed a status difference also showed a gender difference, and vice versa (this finding of nonparallelism was also noted in a different workplace study by Hall & Friedman, 1999). The oppression hypothesis thus received no support.

Status in News Photographs

As a different way to capture information on verticality and smiling in the real world, Hall, Carter, Jimenez, Frost, and Smith LeBeau (2002) gathered 248 news photographs, each featuring two individuals. Because each photograph had a caption and a story accompanying it, it was possible to make judgments about the status of the two people and relate these to how much the two people smiled. To be sure that the data would not be biased by stereotypes held by the coders, the status ratings and the smiling ratings were made by different people who saw only the stimuli appropriate to their respective tasks. Thus, the people who judged smiling saw only the photographs (with the two individuals from each photograph cut apart and mounted in separate scrapbooks), and the people who judged status from the captions and stories did not see the photographs.

Smiling was rated on a 21-point scale, from "obviously negative expression" to "broad obvious smile." Status was judged on five dimensions that were later combined to form a status composite. Of the five dimensions, four were individual traits (fame, respect, power, and wealth) and the fifth was relational (the participants' relative role status in that particular interaction). Other characteristics of the people and the interaction were also coded, such as age and how positive or negative the story was, and of course the gender of the people shown.

Smiling was related to a number of variables. For example, smiling between the two people was very strongly correlated, meaning that if one was smiling, the other was likely to be smiling too. People smiled more when the story was about more positive events. This relation was stronger for women than for men, indicating that women's faces were more reflective of the story content than men's faces were. Women and men did not smile a different amount, a surprising result but not one that invalidated the main analysis of the relation between status and smiling. That relation was essentially zero ($r = .02$ for Member A of the dyad, and $r = -.03$ for Member B, where the A and B designations were assigned at random to the two people in the photograph). It remained zero when several possible confounders were controlled for. Thus, in this naturalistic study, there was no evidence of a relation between status and smiling.

Relative Power in Three Laboratory Studies

The next three studies to be described moved back into the psychology laboratory, where relative power was experimentally manipulated by randomly assigning members of dyads of unacquainted participants to be either the owner of a mock art gallery (high power), or either the owner's assistant hoping for a promotion or someone applying for the job of assistant (low power; Hall, Horgan, & Carter, 2002). There were 60 of these unequal-power dyads in each of the three studies. In their roles, owner and assistant performed several tasks, including discussing and selecting works of art to be displayed in the gallery, with the understanding that the owner was in charge of the discussion and the final selection. During all of the tasks, the owner evaluated the assistant, and postexperimental questionnaires indicated that they experienced relatively high and low feelings of power in the interaction, respectively.

In the first two of these art gallery studies, assistants' and owners' smiling was very similar ($r = -.05$ and $-.15$, both not significant; the negative signs mean assistants smiled slightly more than owners). In the third study, the difference also went in this direction and was marginally significant ($r = -.25$, $p = .06$). Thus, there was some evidence in favor of Henley's hypothesis in this study.

Further analysis allowed for a deeper understanding of this effect. In the third study, there was an additional experimental variable: the manipulation of the owner's attitude. In half of the dyads, the owner was instructed to be authoritarian and controlling; in the other half, the owner was instructed to be supportive and facilitative. For the interview task in that study, the difference in smiling between owners and assistants occurred only in the controlling owner condition. In this condition, smiling increased among assistants and decreased among owners (compared to the supportive owner condition), although neither of these differences was significant. In the supportive owner condition, in fact, owners smiled somewhat more than assistants did, although this was also not significant. This moderating effect of owner's attitude underscores the view put forth earlier that the effect of verticality on smiling (and other nonverbal behaviors) is likely to be determined by proximal factors such as emotions or contextually determined motivations.

We have highlighted five studies by this chapter's first author, but these are not by any means the only studies in the literature. Before summarizing any other studies, we wish to make connection with another important theme in the work of Ralph Rosnow—the nature of statistical evidence.

"SURELY, GOD LOVES
THE .06 NEARLY AS MUCH AS THE .05"

In the process of publishing the results of the three art gallery studies just described, the relevance of Rosnow and Rosenthal's famous (and beloved) quote reproduced earlier became strikingly clear. When Rosnow and Rosenthal wrote this statement, they were making the point that the evidence against the null hypothesis falls on a continuum rather than on a "cliff"—that is to say, it is not correct to conclude that any p-value greater than .05 represents "no difference" or "no effect." Rosnow and Rosenthal, in this and many other writings, helped to educate a generation of students and researchers about the misleading nature of null hypothesis significance testing in the absence of an understanding of effect size and statistical power, and an attendant understanding of the impact of theoretically irrelevant factors, such as sample size, on significance levels. Rosnow and Rosenthal helped to teach students and researchers that there can be information in a so-called "nonsignificant" result.

Of course, their emphasis was on effect size, with one of their points being that a nonsignificant result can actually be of substantial magnitude, indeed larger than the effect size associated with a significant result, if the two results are based on different sample sizes. This teaching helps to counter the once-prevailing attitude that if you don't achieve $p = .05$, you have nothing to say at all.

Unfortunately, the frustrating process of finding a publication outlet for the art gallery studies demonstrated that the assumption that one must "reject the null or bust" has not been laid to rest. It came as no surprise, first, that some of the reviewers wanted any marginally significant (i.e., $p < .10$) result to be removed entirely. This particular manifestation of "cliff" mentality still appears rather often among peer reviewers and journal editors.

But more surprising was evidence of another, more subtle, manifestation of the "cliff" mentality, namely the assumption that an author's *sole goal* is to reject the null hypothesis. This, therefore, is a twist on the point that Rosnow and Rosenthal were making. Their main point was that results of $p > .05$ can have information in them that can help build a case against the null hypothesis; thus, a series of nonzero effects (assuming net directionality one way or the other) can lead one to overturn the null hypothesis even if none of the effects is individually statistically significant. However, as Rosnow and Rosenthal would certainly agree, a series of results of $p > .05$, if the effect sizes are small enough, can also help to build the case *in favor of* the null hypothesis, or—to be more realistic—in favor of concluding that the effect in question is trivially small. This was the case that Hall, Horgan, and Carter (2002) were building in their art gallery studies of verticality and smiling. However, the reviewers repeatedly missed that point because they were blinded by a reject-or-bust mentality. Thus, it was evident that some reviewers considered Hall, Horgan, and Carter's (2002) not rejecting the null hypothesis to be a fully justifiable reason for not publishing the manuscript, *not* because of the inherent difficulty of supporting the claim that the null hypothesis is true, but because the reviewers assumed that the only way to demonstrate something of value is to reject the null hypothesis. In other words, they assumed that any investigator's goal must be to achieve a $p < .05$

result. And this was in spite of Hall, Horgan, and Carter's (2002) clearly stated skepticism about the supposed relation between verticality and smiling and their carefully constructed case for why "failing" to reject the null hypothesis would be important theoretically.

One reviewer's comment well illustrated this blindspot: "In the final analysis, it doesn't seem that the results tell any kind of clear and theoretically interesting story that would justify publication. Studies 1 and 2 found no status effect on smiling, and the results of Study 3 were essentially non-significant also.... Nor was there a clear relationship between self-reported feelings of status and power and smiling." The editor concurred with this opinion, stating, "The primary reason for not accepting this manuscript derives from the limited magnitude of the empirical contribution." It was clear from the context of these comments that the reviewer and editor did not consider the results to be statistically significant enough to justify publication, even though Hall, Horgan, and Carter (2002) made it clear that the finding of interest was the *lack* of statistical significance.

Of course, anyone familiar with the rudiments of statistical power knows that it is difficult to "prove" the null hypothesis (Cohen, 1988), and this is why Hall, Horgan, and Carter (2002) conducted three sizable experiments before trying to publish the evidence. Ironically, however, not a single reviewer at several journals criticized the authors for wanting to "prove" the null hypothesis. We think they were blinded to this potential concern by assuming, as we described previously, that the only good p-value is a small p-value, and, relatedly, that the only good effect size is a big one. To this we would respond by rephrasing Rosnow and Rosenthal's famous statement to say: *Surely, God may sometimes love vanishingly small effects nearly as much as very big ones.*

META-ANALYSIS

The failure to find support for the verticality-smiling hypothesis in our own work led us to wonder what supporting evidence others had found for the crucial link between verticality and smiling. We therefore undertook a meta-analysis of the existing literature on this question. Meta-analysis, so wisely and successfully promoted by Ralph Rosnow among others, is ideally suited for building a strong case either for or against the null hypothesis, because accumulating findings across studies can counter one's unease over the statistical power of individual studies, and also because one can circumvent the issue of the statistical significance of individual studies by accumulating effect sizes rather than p-values. The use of meta-analysis as a powerful research tool has been strongly advocated by many writers, among them (and at the forefront) Ralph Rosnow and Robert Rosenthal.

In our meta-analysis, we asked the question that we have already discussed at length—whether verticality is related to smiling. However, we also asked another question, one that relates to the rumor theme raised earlier: What are people's *beliefs* about this relation? We thought it likely that people do believe that there is such a relation or else Henley's (1977) hypothesis would not have fallen on such fertile ground. In two of the Hall, Horgan, and Carter (2002) studies, owners and assistants in the "art gallery" were asked to rate how much they thought they and their partner smiled, and these ratings could be related to their assigned power along with their actual amount of smiling. In both studies, assistants thought they had smiled more than their respective owners had, effects that were much larger in magnitude than any actual smiling differences that occurred. Thus, it appeared that people do indeed have beliefs on this topic, although interestingly in neither study did the assigned owners have such a belief.

In the description of our meta-analysis that follows, we discuss the method rather briefly; for a complete description, see Hall et al. (in press).

Method

In our meta-analysis search, we cast our net for studies of both *actual* verticality and *perceived* verticality in relation to smiling (the latter we also refer to as *beliefs about* smiling and verticality). These two groups of studies were essentially nonoverlapping because it was rare that a study included both kinds of assessment. We searched PsycINFO through the year 2002 with the terms *dominance, status, rank, power, hierarchy, authority, expertise, subordinate, submissive, personality, socioeconomic, SES, education, income,* and *occupation,* crossed by *nonverbal, emotion, expression, face (facial),* and *smile (smiling)*. In addition, we searched Dissertation Abstracts International, our own reprint files, and the reference lists in retrieved studies and literature reviews.

A study was included if: (a) it fit one of our definitions of the verticality construct, (b) it included a measurement of smiling or beliefs about smiling, (c) it was published in an article or book, (d) it was in English, (e) the age of the primary participants was adolescent age or older, and (f) the primary participants had normal psychological function (not psychiatrically diagnosed or otherwise labeled as a "clinical" sample, and not blind, deaf, learning disabled, alcoholic, incarcerated, autistic, or having developmental disability). Because a given source (e.g., article) might contain several independent studies or samples, and, conversely, a given study or sample might be written up in more than one source, the following distinctions were made: A source was a published article, book, or book chapter with a single bibliographic citation, whereas a study was an independent group of participants (which might be called a *study, experiment, sample, subsample,* or *subgroup* by the original authors). In our meta-analysis, the unit of analysis was the study as defined in this way.

Because we wished to discover the relation of smiling to both *actual* verticality and people's *beliefs* about this association, it was important to have criteria for distinguishing between these two kinds of study. A study measured actual verticality if any of the following were the case: verticality was experimentally manipulated by assignment to different verticality roles, was objectively measured in terms of rank in one's place of employment or social class, or was operationalized as personality dominance or assertiveness as measured with a paper-and-pencil scale. In each such study, the participants' smiling would then be measured by the investigators.

In the great majority of the studies that measured beliefs, perceivers made verticality ratings (typically, ratings of dominance) of photographed or videotaped stimuli that were presented to them; in these stimuli, smiling was either experimentally manipulated or occurred naturalistically and had been measured by the investigator. In two studies, participants imagined their own smiling in different verticality situations; and in another, participants rated verticality in people with whom they had just interacted.

For each result in each study, the following information was extracted: N, direction of effect (disregarding p-value), effect size (Pearson r, transformed to Fisher's z for calculations), and Z (standard normal deviate). Results that were reported as F, t, chi-square, or means and standard deviations were converted using standard procedures to the r-metric (Rosenthal, 1991). All rs and Zs were given signs such that positive values meant that higher verticality was associated with more smiling, and negative signs meant the reverse.

Results for Actual Verticality and Smiling

The literature search yielded 34 studies, 22 of which yielded effect sizes (r) that could be extracted or calculated. Nonindependent effect sizes (i.e., multiple rs from the same study) were averaged before other analyses were undertaken. Table 10.1 shows a summary of study characteristics for these 34 studies.

Table 10.2 shows a stem-and-leaf display of the 34 studies, and Table 10.3 shows the summary statistics. Overall, there was no relation between verticality and smiling. This was the case whether the analysis is based on only the known effects, or on all studies counting the unknown effects as zero. However, the results were highly heterogeneous, with three studies being notably extreme (rs of .52, .52, and −.54). Excluding these studies made essentially no change in the central tendency statistics, although it reduced the heterogeneity to nonsignificance.

TABLE 10.1
Characteristics of Studies on Actual Verticality and Smiling

Characteristic	Description
Publication year	Median = 1990; range = 1969–2002
Publication type	Dissertation = 7, published = 27
Nationality	U.S./Canada = 31, Asia = 3
N males	1,154
N females	1,148
N total	2,422
Age	Adolescents = 2, college = 23, adult = 9
Setting	Laboratory = 31, field = 3
Group size	Individual = 1, dyad = 25, 3–5 people = 5, 6+ people = 2
Group gender composition	Same-gender = 10, opposite-gender = 4, both = 19
Groupmembers' identity	Acquaintance = 9, stranger = 17, experimenter = 1, confederate = 6
Type of task	Free conversation = 8, assigned topic to discuss = 11, structured activity or discussion = 8, interview = 7
Definition of verticality	Personality = 8, socioeconomic status = 3, role or rank = 18

Note. Unknown and "other" categories are not shown.

TABLE 10.2
Stem and Leaf Plot of Actual Verticality Effect Sizes (r)

5	2***	2+														
4																
3																
2	2*															
1	3															
0	0	0	0	0	0	0	0	0	0	0	0	0	3	3	4	6
–0	1	2	3	4	4	5	6									
–1	1	2	5	8												
–2	6+															
–3	6*															
–4																
–5	4***															

Note. Unknown rs are entered as italicized zeros. Decimals are omitted.
$+p < .10$, $*p < .05$, $***p < .001$ (all two-tail).

TABLE 10.3
Summary of Actual Verticality Effects

	Known rs	All studies (unknown rs = 0)
N of studies	22	34
Directional tally	8+/14−	8+/14−/12?
Unweighted mean r	−.02	−.01
Weighted mean r	−.03	−.02
Median r	−.04	.00
Combined Z	−.95	−.76
Homogeneity test	48.15***	

Note. Combined Z was calculated using the Stouffer method (Rosenthal, 1991). Weighting is by sample size. Homogeneity test was calculated only for known rs.
***p < .001.

Results for Beliefs About Verticality and Smiling

The literature search located 35 studies, which yielded 24 known rs. As with "actual" studies reviewed previously, nonindependent effects were averaged before other analyses were undertaken so that each study would contribute only one result. Table 10.4 shows the study characteristics of the 35 studies.

Tables 10.5 and 10.6 reveal an overall relationship for beliefs about smiling and verticality. Including only the 24 known effect sizes, the average weighted effect size (r) was −.25 and the average unweighted effect size was −.20. If the 11 studies that failed to report any relationship between smiling and verticality were included (with rs estimated to be zero), the average weighted effect size became −.19 and the unweighted effect size became −.14. The combined Z associated with this effect size was highly significant.

Despite this overall support for the idea that people believe that people low in verticality smile more often, there is also evidence that this belief may depend on contextual information. The results in Tables 10.5 and 10.6 are highly heterogeneous. Of the 18 statistically significant effects, 12 were negative and 6 were positive. Because 11 of the studies used the same set of photographs, another analysis was done in which the effects were averaged across those 11 studies and then treated as though they were one study. The unweighted average r for the reduced set of 14 studies with known rs was now −.07 and the combined Z was not significant (Z = −.44). Results were still highly heterogeneous, and results still went dramatically in different directions. Careful inspection of methodologies across the whole set of studies suggested no clues about moderator variables that might explain the hetero-

TABLE 10.4
Characteristics of Studies on Beliefs About Verticality and Smiling

Characteristic	Description
Publication year	Median = 1988; range = 1975–2002
Publication type	Dissertation = 1, published = 35
Nationality	U.S./Canada = 17, Europe = 4, Asia = 3, Central/South America = 5
N expressors	1,295
N perceivers	4,365
Age	Adolescents = 2, college = 21, adult = 12
Setting	Laboratory = 21, field = 8
Group size	Individual = 9, dyad = 23, 3–5 people = 3
Stimuli judged	Imagined = 2, drawings = 3, photographs = 18, video = 2, audio and video = 3, live = 6
Nonverbal behavior design	Manipulated = 24, measured = 9, self-reported = 2

Note. Unknown and "other" categories are not shown.

TABLE 10.5
Stem-and-Leaf Plot of Beliefs About Verticality Effect Sizes (r)

Stem	Leaves
6	
5	
4	0^*
3	
2	3^*
1	0 5^* 5^* 5^*
0	0^{***} 0 0 0 0 0 0 0 0 0 2 5
−0	0^* 2
−1	**5+**
−2	0 2^* 6^{**} 6^* 8^{***}
−3	**5+** **6^{***}** **8^{***}** **9^{***}**
−4	**3+**
−5	**3^{***}** **6^{***}** **7^{***}**
−6	**9^{***}**

Note. The 11 effect sizes in bold all used the same photographic stimuli (see text). Unknown rs are entered as zero in italics (with p-value if $p < .10$).

$+p < .10$, $^*p < .05$, $^{**}p < .01$, $^{***}p < .001$ (all two-tail).

TABLE 10.6
Summary of Beliefs About Verticality Effects

	Known rs	All Studies (unknown rs = 0)
N of studies	24	35
Directional tally	8+/16−	12+/17−/6?
Unweighted mean r	−.20	−.14
Weighted mean r	−.25	−.19
Median r	−.24	.00
Combined Z	−9.04***	−8.08***
Homogeneity test	253.95***	

Note.   Combined Z was calculated using the Stouffer method (Rosenthal, 1991). Weighting is by sample size. Homogeneity test was calculated only for known rs.
***p < .001.

geneity. Whatever the important moderating variables in this relationship may be, they are likely to be subtle. It is possible that small details in the experimenters' presentation of stimuli, or other verbal or nonverbal cues displayed by the people being judged, established for participants a context that created highly divergent impressions. Along the same lines, the proximal states imagined or suggested in different studies might have varied in ways that produced very inconsistent results (Hall et al., in press).

One of the included studies sheds light on possible mechanisms for this divergence. Nagashima and Schellenberg (1997) asked college students in the United States and Japan to imagine being in several interactions of equal status (with another student) or unequal status (with a professor), and then to imagine how much smiling they themselves would engage in. Although there were some cultural differences, the main finding was that participants expected to smile more when equal rather than lower in status, unless an ingratiation motive were stimulated. This finding fits with theoretical observations offered earlier concerning the impact of proximal motives on nonverbal behavior.

A final study we would like to highlight came too late for inclusion in the meta-analysis (Carney, Hall, & Smith LeBeau, 2005). This study is one of the very few that asked directly for people's beliefs rather than inferring their beliefs based on how their verticality ratings correlated with measured smiling. Carney et al. (2005) asked participants to imagine how much the individuals would smile in two different kinds of interactions: one involving two people who differed in personality dominance, and one involving two people of differing rank in an organization. For neither scenario did the participants report an imagined difference in smiling between the higher- and lower-vertical person.

HOW COULD PROXIMAL STATES
EXPLAIN THE LITERATURE?

Ideally, we would know what proximal states were present in studies of actual verticality, and we would know what proximal states were imagined or
inferred in studies of perceived verticality and beliefs. However, even in
the absence of such information, we can speculate. When different studies
show significant but contradictory results, it suggests that the studies were
characterized by different states. In some cases, these states may be confounded with verticality, as we suggested earlier. The strongest negative
correlation was from Deutsch (1990), who asked the low-verticality participants to try to make a favorable impression on their high-verticality
partners, who were not given such an instruction. If trying to make a favorable impression promotes smiling, then the finding that more smiling
occurred in the low-verticality person could be due either to verticality or
to proximal state.

Alternatively, if a study shows essentially no relation between verticality
and smiling, as many did, proximal states could also be implicated. This is
because within the study, different participants may have been in different
states or imagined different states (in actual and belief studies, respectively),
thus canceling out overall verticality effects.

"SOME THINGS YOU LEARN AREN'T SO"

This quote from the title of Rosnow and Rosenthal's (1995) article on statistical inference is in some ways a variation on Huxley's famous lament that
"the great tragedy of science [is] the slaying of a beautiful hypothesis by an
ugly fact" (Huxley, 1870/1968, p. 244). The parsimony of the oppression hypothesis is beautiful and appealing, because it unifies a diverse collection of
nonverbal gender differences under one theoretical argument. However,
for smiling, the lack of the required negative association with verticality in-
validates this general explanation. On the other hand, we believe there are
certainly situations in which people who are low in verticality do smile more
than people who are higher in verticality. We have seen from this review
that, for both actual verticality and perceptions/beliefs about verticality,
there are instances in which the association is as Henley (1977) proposed,
and we can certainly imagine other situations in daily life that confirm it as
well. However, the available evidence offers no support for a general tendency of greater smiling by low-verticality people and only qualified support
for a general belief in such a relationship. We can thus consider verticality to
be a highly unreliable predictor in the absence of knowledge about potentially moderating and confounding variables. Whether Henley's (1977)
speculation that verticality underlies women's tendency to smile more than

men can be supported will now depend on further research, for example research showing that women's experience of low verticality is systematically associated with certain smile-promoting states. One might argue that such a state is the need to please. If that were the case, we would expect to see a smaller ratio of "felt" (Duchenne) to "unfelt" smiles among women than men (the difference resting on whether the muscles around the eyes are activated in addition to the mouth muscles; Ekman, Davidson, & Friesen, 1990). However, such research as exists on the question does not support this prediction (Hecht & LaFrance, 1998).

Another possibility is that a specific (and complex) confluence of factors determines smiling in men in women. The laboratory study of Schmid Mast and Hall (2004) illustrates this case. Smiling was elevated only in one group: women who were assigned to the low-verticality role *and* who wanted to have that role. Other combinations of gender, role, and role preference did not show elevated smiling. As an interesting return to the rumor theme, perhaps the situation that showed elevated smiling is so prototypical in people's minds that it can influence their general beliefs about verticality, gender, and smiling.

Rosnow's words—that some things one believes are not so—remind us that sometimes knowledge progresses by regressing, that to take two steps forward we must first take one step back. Even our favorite theories must be discarded if they do not continue to demonstrate usefulness. For the past 25 years, the oppression hypothesis was taught and learned on the basis of compelling theory, but with scant evidence for one of its main tenets. Now it is clear that the theory as currently conceived is not useful in organizing findings with respect to smiling. New theories and more research are needed before we will understand the reasons why women and men smile different amounts.

The work described in this chapter is informed in many important ways by the contributions of Ralph Rosnow to social psychology, whether these be substantive (theory of rumor transmission) or methodological (use of multiple methods, combining studies using meta-analysis, understanding statistical inference). His impact is felt far beyond the subject matter of his own research.

REFERENCES

Abel, M. H. (Ed.). (2002). *An empirical reflection on the smile.* Lewiston, NY: Edwin Mellen.

Carney, D. R., Hall, J. A., & Smith LeBeau, L. (2005). Beliefs about the nonverbal expression of social power. *Journal of Nonverbal Behavior, 29,* 105–123.

Cohen, J. (1988). *Statistical power analysis for the behavioral sciences* (2nd ed.). Mahwah, NJ: Lawrence Erlbaum Associates.

Crawford, M., & Unger, R. (2000). *Women and gender: A feminist psychology* (3rd ed.). Boston: McGraw-Hill.

Deutsch, F. M. (1990). Status, sex, and smiling: The effect of role on smiling in men and women. *Personality and Social Psychology Bulletin, 16*, 531–540.

Ekman, P., Davidson, R. J., & Friesen, W. V. (1990). The Duchenne smile: Emotional expression and brain physiology: II. *Journal of Personality and Social Psychology, 58*, 342–353.

Ekman, P., & Friesen, W. V. (1982). Felt, false, and miserable smiles. *Journal of Nonverbal Behavior, 6*, 238–252.

Feldman, R. S. (1995). *Social psychology*. Englewood Cliffs, NJ: Prentice Hall.

Hall, J. A. (1984). *Nonverbal sex differences: Communication accuracy and expressive style*. Baltimore, MD: Johns Hopkins University Press.

Hall, J. A. (1998). How big are nonverbal sex differences? The case of smiling and sensitivity to nonverbal cues. In D. J. Canary & K. Dindia (Eds.), *Sex differences and similarities in communication: Critical essays and empirical investigations of sex and gender in interaction* (pp. 155–177). Mahwah, NJ: Lawrence Erlbaum Associates.

Hall, J. A., Carter, J. D., & Horgan, T. G. (2000). Gender differences in the nonverbal communication of emotion. In A. H. Fischer (Ed.), *Gender and emotion: Social psychological perspectives* (pp. 97–117). Paris: Cambridge University Press.

Hall, J. A., Carter, J. D., Jimenez, M. C., Frost, N. A., & Smith LeBeau, L. (2002). Smiling and relative status in news photographs. *Journal of Social Psychology, 142*, 500–510.

Hall, J. A., Coats, E. J., & Smith LeBeau, L. (in press). Nonverbal behavior and the vertical dimension of social relations: A meta-analysis. *Psychological Bulletin*.

Hall, J. A., & Friedman, G. B. (1999). Status, gender, and nonverbal behavior: A study of structured interactions between employees of a company. *Personality and Social Psychology Bulletin, 25*, 1082–1091.

Hall, J. A., & Halberstadt, A. G. (1997). Subordination and nonverbal sensitivity: A hypothesis in search of support. In M. R. Walsh (Ed.), *Women, men, and gender: Ongoing debates* (pp. 120–133). New Haven: Yale University Press.

Hall, J. A., Horgan, T. G., & Carter, J. D. (2002). Assigned and felt status in relation to observer-coded and participant-reported smiling. *Journal of Nonverbal Behavior, 26*, 63–81.

Hall, J. A., Smith LeBeau, L., Gordon Reinoso, J., & Thayer, F. (2001). Status, gender, and nonverbal behavior in candid and posed photographs: A study of conversations between university employees. *Sex Roles, 44*, 677–692.

Hecht, M. A., & LaFrance, M. (1998). License or obligation to smile: The effect of power and sex on amount and type of smiling. *Personality and Social Psychology Bulletin, 24*, 1332–1342.

Henley, N. M. (1977). *Body politics: Power, sex, and nonverbal communication*. Englewood Cliffs, NJ: Prentice-Hall.

Huxley, T. H. (1870/1968). Presidential address at the British Association for the Advancement of Science, *Biogenesis and Abiogenesis*. In *Collected essays* (Vol. 8). New York: Greenwood.

Keltner, D., Gruenfeld, D. H., & Anderson, C. (2003). Power, approach, and inhibition. *Psychological Review, 110*, 265–284.

LaFrance, M., Hecht, M. A., & Levy Paluck, E. (2003). The contingent smile: A meta-analysis of sex differences in smiling. *Psychological Bulletin, 129*, 305–334.

Lippa, R. A. (1994). *Introduction to social psychology* (2nd ed.). Pacific Grove, CA: Brooks/Cole.

Lips, H. M. (2001). *Sex & gender: An introduction* (4th ed.). Mountain View, CA: Mayfield.

Lips, H. M. (2003). *A new psychology of women: Gender, culture, and ethnicity* (2nd ed.). Boston: McGraw-Hill.

Matlin, M. W. (2000). *The psychology of women* (4th ed.). Fort Worth: Harcourt.

Nagashima, K., & Schellenberg, J. A. (1997). Situational differences in intentional smiling: A cross-cultural exploration. *Journal of Social Psychology, 13,* 297–301.

Rosenthal, R. (1991). *Meta-analytic procedures for social research* (Rev. ed.). Newbury Park, CA: Sage.

Rosnow, R. L. (1991). Inside rumor: A personal journal. *American Psychologist, 46,* 484–496.

Rosnow, R. L., & Rosenthal, R. (1989). Statistical procedures and the justification of knowledge in psychological science. *American Psychologist, 44,* 1276–1284.

Rosnow, R. L., & Rosenthal, R. (1995). "Some things you learn aren't so": Cohen's paradox, Asch's paradigm, and the interpretation of interaction. *Psychological Science, 6,* 3–9.

Schmid Mast, M., & Hall, J. A. (2004). When is dominance related to smiling? Assigned dominance, dominance preference, trait dominance, and gender as moderators. *Sex Roles, 50,* 387–399.

Vrugt, A. (1987). The meaning of nonverbal sex differences. *Semiotica, 64,* 371–380.

Vrugt, A., & Kerkstra, A. (1984). Sex differences in nonverbal communication. *Semiotica, 50,* 1–41.

Wood, W., & Eagly, A. H. (2002). A cross-cultural analysis of the behavior of women and men: Implications for the origins of sex differences. *Psychological Bulletin, 128,* 699–727.

Yoder, J. D. (2003). *Women and gender: Transforming psychology* (2nd ed.). Upper Saddle River, NJ: Prentice-Hall.

11

Some Observations on the Social Psychological Study of Human Values

Charles B. Thomas, Jr.
University of Michigan–Flint

This chapter explores two questions relevant to social psychology: What are values? How is a social psychological understanding of values relevant to efforts to create a better world? It is obvious that these questions can involve issues of vast scope. Thus, the intent of this brief chapter is to provide some valuable reflections on these matters, but not to offer "definitive answers" to the questions. The goal of this agenda is to provide a useful review and perspective on important facets of the literature on the social psychological study of values.

In the context of further exploration of the second question, the chapter identifies a link between values and ethics, and explores some of the ways the work of the social psychologist Ralph Rosnow has importantly influenced understandings of research ethics in the conduct of behavioral research. This chapter is written in tribute to Ralph Rosnow, Professor Emeritus in the Psychology Department at Temple University. A recent search of the PsycINFO online database identified 80 items authored since the 1960s by this immensely productive and respected scholar. Included among his principal interests are the study of rumor and gossip, attitude and impression formation, ethical dilemmas in research, and control of artifacts in research. Ralph Rosnow mentored my first publication in a refereed jour-

nal in psychology (Thomas et al., 1979), and has continued to be an earnest
friend and valued colleague.

WHAT ARE VALUES?

A recent PsycINFO search identified over 6,000 items linked to the keyword *values*. The abstract for item #100 in the search (Rohan, 2000) noted,
in part, "Definitional inconsistency has been epidemic in values theory and
research.... In the past, personal value systems, social value systems, world
views, and ideologies each may have been given the generic label values" (p.
255). At the beginning of the 1970s, Milton Rokeach (1968, 1973, 1979)
made breakthrough contributions in social psychology toward resolving
older problems with defining values. For example, prior to the originative
work of Rokeach, many definitions of values tended to be circular, such that
values were defined as "conceptions of the desirable"; in turn, these conceptions were spoken of in terms of "values."

This problem of circular definitions of values suggests these fundamental
questions: Given the difficult challenges involved in studying values scientifically, why do so? What benefits might come from the scientific study of
values? Rokeach (1973) addressed these basic questions with valuable insights: Despite the complications involved in studying values scientifically,
values are nevertheless an ubiquitous area of study in the social sciences
(e.g., in economics, political science, sociology, psychology, anthropology,
education, history, etc.). Also, given this widespread interest in values as an
intervening variable, the concept has a unique potential for establishing vital links or bridges among subject matters in the various social science disciplines, promoting fruitful interdisciplinary collaboration.

Rokeach (1973) avoided the problem of circularity with the following definitions. A value is an "enduring belief that a mode of conduct or endstate of
existence is personally or socially preferable to an opposite or converse mode
of conduct or endstate of existence" (p. 5). A value system is an "enduring organization of beliefs concerning preferable modes of conduct or endstates of
existence along a continuum of relative importance" (p. 5).

In an earlier article (Thomas, 1997), the present author described the
Rokeach theoretical framework that so substantially advanced social psychological understanding of human values at the time it was proffered. As
noted in that discussion, in his book *The Nature of Human Values* (1973),
Rokeach distinguished between terminal values and instrumental values.
Terminal values concern desirable endstates of existence. Examples of terminal values include a sense of accomplishment, a world at peace, equality,
and mature love. Instrumental values have to do with modes of conduct that
are means to achieve desired ends. Examples of instrumental values include
being broadminded, capable, honest, and loving.

Rokeach identified types of terminal and instrumental values. Terminal (endstate) values may be personal (e.g., salvation, happiness) or social (e.g., a world at peace, equality). A distinction is being made between a self-centered versus a society-centered focus—between an intrapersonal versus an interpersonal focus (Rokeach, 1973).

Instrumental values may be moral values (e.g., honest, responsible) or competence values (e.g., logical, intellectual, imaginative). A violation of moral values, which have an interpersonal focus, leads one to feel pangs of conscience or to have feelings of guilt for wrongdoing (Rokeach, 1973). In contrast, competence values have a personal rather than an interpersonal focus, and when one violates a competence value, one feels shame because of personal inadequacy.

Rokeach furthered the social psychological measurement of values with the Rokeach Value Survey, which was based on his theoretical framework for understanding values (as briefly described earlier). The Rokeach Value Survey has enjoyed wide currency inside and outside of social psychology (Mayton, Ball-Rokeach, & Loges, 1994). For example, a recent PsycINFO search identified over 350 items related to the use of the Rokeach Value Survey. The present author has found the Value Survey useful in understanding characteristics correlated with sympathetic perceptions of problems of sexism confronting women (Thomas, 2001), values correlates with success in organizations (Thomas, 1997), and values correlates with social activist behavior (Thomas, 1986). In furthering social scientific understanding of the question that is the focus of this section—"What are values?"—Rokeach enormously extended previous major contributions of Kluckhohn (1951), Allport , Vernon, and Lindzey (1960), Kluckhohn and Strodtbeck (1961), Scott (1965), Williams (1968), and Smith (1969) (Mayton et al., 1994). Another figure who has advanced the study of values, working in the Rokeach tradition, with important contributions for over 2 decades, is Norman T. Feather (e.g., 1975, 1994).

Since the late 1980s, the work of another social psychologist, Shalom Schwartz, has continued the Rokeach tradition by being extremely heuristic in promoting the study of human values. For example, the results of a recent PsycINFO search pointed to over 40 items of research and theory authored and coauthored by Schwartz since the late 1980s that have deepened our understanding of the answer to the question "What are values?"

Schwartz (1994; see also Schwartz, 1992; Schwartz & Bilsky, 1987, 1990) commented on what scholars studying values have come to hold in widespread agreement concerning five features of the conceptual definition of values. First, a value is a belief. Second, a value pertains to desirable endstates or modes of conduct. Third, a value transcends specific situations. Fourth, a value guides the evaluation or selection of behavior, people, and events. Fifth, a value forms a system of value priorities when it is ordered by importance relative to other values.

By these formal features, values are distinguished from such related concepts as needs and attitudes. For example, using these criteria, we may conclude that security and independence are values, whereas thirst and a preference for blue ties are not.

Schwartz (1994) built on the work of Rokeach and offered the following definition of values, which fit a new theoretical framework he proposed for identifying a manageable number of types of values:

> Somewhat modifying earlier definitions of values, I define *values* as desirable transsituational goals, varying in importance, that serve as guiding principles in the life of a person or other social entity. Implicit in this definition of values as goals is that (1) they serve the interests of some social entity, (2) they can motivate action—giving it direction and emotional intensity, (3) they function as standards for judging and justifying action, and (4) they are acquired both through socialization to dominant group values and through the unique learning experiences of individuals. Other goal-related constructs such as "personal projects" (Little, 1983) and "life tasks" (Cantor & Kihlstrom, 1987) may be seen as expressions of values in specific life domains. (p. 21)

Schwartz (1994) identified 10 types of values: power, achievement, hedonism, stimulation, self-direction, universalism, benevolence, tradition, conformity, and security. He described an ambitious research project that tested his theory of values. The scope of the project involved findings from 97 samples in 44 countries from every inhabited continent. The findings were obtained between 1988 and 1993, and included data from 25,863 respondents. With a sample as diverse as this, it is possible to undertake a strong test of potential universal aspects of value contents and structure.

The ability to compare values in one country with those in a different country is an important feature of the Schwartz approach to the theory and measurement of values, and fulfills an aim desired by Rokeach (Schwartz, 1994). In this research, Schwartz (1994) found that, in the vast majority of samples, the theorized structure reasonably approximated the structure of relations among the 10 types of values. The findings of Schwartz's research also discerned little empirical support for the earlier distinction by Rokeach between terminal (endstate of existence) and instrumental (means to desired ends) values.

A review of several of the 40+ PsycINFO abstracts of work authored or coauthored by Schwartz since the 1980s reveals that his theory of values has received support in many cross-cultural investigations (e.g., Schwartz & Bardi, 2001; Smith, Peterson, Schwartz, et al., 2002), evidence for convergent and discriminant validity and for construct validity has been presented (Schwartz et al., 2001), and this approach to studying values has been used to compare values of different countries (Schwartz, 1999). The Schwartz theoretical and empirical approaches to values have investigated many interesting and important topics, including gender differences in values, values and voting behavior, and values and religiosity.

Summary

This discussion of the question "What are values?" has noted that "values" is a popular topic, as indicated by representation in over 6,000 items identified in a PsycINFO search. However, due to definitional inconsistency, many somewhat different phenomena (e.g., ideologies, personal value systems, social value systems, needs) have been housed under the "values" rubric. Two social psychologists have made breakthrough theoretical and methodological contributions in promoting the rigorous study of values: Milton Rokeach (particularly in the late 1960s, the 1970s, and the 1980s), and, building on the Rokeach work, Shalom Schwartz (in the late 1980s, the 1990s, and the 2000s).

VALUES AND A BETTER WORLD [I]

The second question raised at the beginning of this chapter was: How is a social psychological understanding of values relevant to efforts to create a better world? What, then, is "a better world"? Upon reflection, one can observe that there is a nearly infinite number of ways to create a world that most would acknowledge is in some sense "better." For example, planting a home flower garden increases the available beauty in the world, and can thus be said to help create a better world. Other such examples might include being a better parent to one's children, crafting an attractive sculpture or a fine painting, doing a kind deed for a friend or family member, and so on. Although all such examples possess legitimate value, in the context of the question about how social psychology, through furthering an understanding of values, can contribute to creating a better world, the intended meaning of "a better world" is a broader one than is reflected in the preceding examples.

In exploring a meaning of this question pertinent to the concerns of social psychology, it is useful to consider this statement by Mayton et al. (1994):

> How are human values helpful in our efforts to understand social issues? Are human values useful in explaining the positions people advocate and their behaviors concerning social issues such as racial and ethnic discrimination, political ideology, political reasoning, and political activism? ... [T]hese questions ... were central to the writing and research of Rokeach.... [N]umerous studies have been conducted through the world to assess the value orientations that predispose in-

dividuals to form particular political attitudes and behaviors (e.g., Ball-Rokeach et al., 1984; Rokeach, 1973).... (p. 5)

Thus, from a social psychological standpoint, one way of interpreting what it means to "create a better world" is to view efforts at social and political activism as steps toward (or at least intended toward) creating a better world. Thomas (1986) made distinctions that are valuable to this discussion, pointing out the usefulness of distinguishing "social action" from related concepts such as "social service." Hessell (1972; see also Hammer, 1983) differentiated these concepts and offered this definition: "Social action [or social activism] is a process of deliberate group effort to alter community or social structures for the common good" (p. 29).

Furthermore, political activism and social activism are not the same. In political activism, one participates in the "body politic"; this is only one among many tactics used in social activism, which aims at changing not only political structures or institutions, but others as well (e.g., business institutions, educational institutions, religious institutions). Thomas (1986) also emphasized that there are varieties of social activism, from the activism stressing what have commonly been regarded as "liberal" issues (e.g., antiwar and civil rights movements of the 1960s, disarmament, the environment, women's rights, etc.) to the social activism focusing on "conservative" concerns (in the past, pornography, drinking; more recently, busing, abortion, school prayers, etc.).

As indicated, how one defines what makes for "a better world" will vary depending on one's ideological commitments. For example, those who call themselves "pro-life" will view the enacting of laws that limit or prohibit abortion as an instance of "creating a better world." In contrast, those who see themselves as "pro-choice" see the enacting and strengthening of laws that protect a woman's right to choose abortion as an instance of "creating a better world." However, regardless of such disagreements about what might constitute the "common good," can social psychology assist in explaining the processes that lead people to engage in "deliberate group effort to alter community or social structures for the common good" (i.e., social activism, as noted earlier; see Hessell, 1972, p. 29)?

The answer to this question is clearly "yes" (see Mayton et al., 1994)—examples abound. One eminent illustration is the work of Milton Rokeach on the two-value model of political ideology. Rokeach (1973) put forth the hypothesis that, when examined at the level of their barest essence, the major variations in political ideology are fundamentally reducible to opposing value orientations concerning the political desirability or undesirability of freedom and equality in all their ramifications.

Applying this theoretical framework to the realm of political activism, Rokeach declared that those with high levels of political involvement would exhibit great regard (either positive or negative) for one, or both, of the values "freedom" and "equality." Rokeach (1973) cited a variety of empirical evidence for these assertions. The research of Thomas (1986) showed that the Rokeach two-value model of political activism can be extended to the broader realm of social activism. (See Hessell, 1972, as cited earlier, for a distinction between political and social activism.) In a context of declining interest in Rokeach's two-value model of political ideology, Braithwaite (1994) modified this two-value model and successfully applied the product to an understanding of voting behavior and political activism.

Mayton et al. (1994) pointed out that understandings of values have been useful in the study of support for affirmative action policies (Peterson, 1994), and peace activist behavior (Mayton & Furnham, 1994).[1] Further instances of research on values and their relation to understanding involvement with social issues or social activism can be found in PsycINFO. A search on "values" and "Shalom Schwartz" yielded 72 items, including: work investigating values and emigration behavior and the well-being of immigrants; values and voting behavior; values and issues related to gender, or the role of women in society; values and adaptation to communist rule in Eastern Europe; values and fear of nuclear war; values and the role of religion in society; and values and issues related to race and ethnic relations. In their relation to social activism, values can be independent variables (impelling a person toward involvement with social activism) or dependent variables (social activist involvement may lead to a change in values; Thomas, 1986).

Summary

In this section, it was observed that there is a nearly infinite number of ways to create, in one sense or another, "a better world." However, from the standpoint of the concerns of social psychology, the relevance of the question "How is a social psychological understanding of values relevant to efforts to create a better world?" is usefully interpreted to relate to efforts to understand the relationship between values and social activism or social issues. This was a principal concern of Milton Rokeach. The work of Shalom Schwartz has also reflected this interest in values and social issues. Political activism is one type of social activism; and what can loosely be called "liberal social activism" can be distinguished from "conservative social activism." What makes for a better world and the common good can vary depending on whether one's perspective stems from liberal or conservative social activism.

---

[1]Methodologically, Mayton and Furnham (1994) demonstrated how the Rokeach Value Survey can be used to provide measures for the value types proposed by Shalom Schwartz.

There are many examples of social psychological (or other) research that contributes to explaining the processes that lead people to engage in "deliberate group effort to alter community or social structures for the common good" (i.e., social activism; Hessell, 1972, p. 29). Illustrations would include the work of Rokeach and his posited two-value model of political activism (extended by the research of Thomas,1986, to apply more broadly to social activism; and modified by Braithwaite, 1994). Furthermore, there are many examples in Schwartz's work of efforts to understand the relationship between values and social issues or social activism.

VALUES AND A BETTER WORLD (II): ETHICS

As previously noted, in the Rokeach theoretical framework for work on values, instrumental values can be either moral values (with an interpersonal focus—"honest," "responsible") or competence values (with a personal focus—"logical," "imaginative"). Ethics can be conceptualized as a system of moral values ("Ethics," Dictionary.com, 2004; see also Rosnow, 1997). The following discussion reconsiders, from a different vantage point, the question "How is a social psychological understanding of values relevant to efforts to create a better world?"

The contribution of social psychological insights that encourage greater adherence to high ethical standards (or systems of moral values) in the pursuit of scientific investigation makes for a better world. Such a contribution certainly benefits the practitioners of science; for example, by aiding in maintaining the good reputations of various disciplines and helping to avoid deleterious research scandals. The general public and research participants also benefit by a decreased likelihood of being victimized by falsified, invalid findings, by research studies that harm the participants, and so on.

Some vital contributions of this nature, which promote research ethics and deepen our understanding of issues related to research ethics, are found in the work of the social psychologist Ralph Rosnow, who from 1992 to 1993 chaired the Committee on Standards in Research of the American Psychological Association. For example, in "Hedgehogs, Foxes, and the Evolving Social Contract in Psychological Science: Ethical Challenges and Methodological Opportunities" (Rosnow, 1997), he offered insights about balancing the needs of the technical concerns of research with the demands of numerous ethical rules in ways that can benefit both science and society. Among other issues, Rosnow discussed the discouraging problem investigated by Kimmel (1991) concerning how institutional review boards can display predictable biases when evaluating research studies for ethical clearance. (For example, decisions of ethics committees have been shown to be influenced by characteristics of the decision makers, such as gender, degree of active involvement with their own research, etc.; see Kimmel, 1991.)

Rosnow (1997) commented on some of his earlier work with Rosenthal (Rosenthal & Rosnow, 1984), which described a very useful tool in making ethical judgments: a "decision plane" diagram in which the costs of doing a particular research study are weighed against the benefits of doing that study. Rosnow (1997) noted the vital insight that ethical decisions about whether a particular research study is undertaken must also consider the costs (e.g., to society or to the discipline) of not doing the research.

Rosnow (1997; Rosnow, Rotheram-Borus, & Ceci, 1993) advocated educating members serving on institutional review boards in ways that would lead them to have greater regard for the costs of preventing important but socially sensitive research studies (see also Kimmel, 1988). Useful in this process of providing relevant training for institutional review boards could be a role-play strategy that has been found to be effective in sensitizing students to ethical judgment standards (Rosnow, 1990, 1997). Rosnow (1997; Blanck, Bellack, Rosnow, Rotheram-Borus, & Schooler, 1992) valuably reminded researchers that the climate of accountability to numerous ethical rules offers advantages that shouldn't be ignored. For example, debriefing research participants can provide researchers with leads that might be useful in future research, or might help them identify problematic aspects of the methodology they are using in a present study (Blanck et al., 1992). Kimmel (1988), in reviewing ideas on research ethics presented by the social psychologist Herbert Kelman, also pointed to the importance of considering methodological and ethical issues in the context of one another (see also Kimmel & Smith, 2001).

Summary

In this section, the topic of values has been linked to ethics. It has been noted that ethics may be viewed as a system of moral values. This section has considered again, from a different perspective, the earlier question "How is a social psychological understanding of values relevant to efforts to create a better world?" The argument has been advanced that contributions in social psychology that promote and assist in elucidating high ethical standards in scientific investigation make for a better world by, for example, helping to safeguard the good reputation of scientific disciplines, and decreasing the likelihood that research participants will be harmed or that society will suffer instances of falsified, invalid research results.

One social psychologist who has made significant contributions to understanding ethical issues in research is Ralph Rosnow. The work of Rosnow and his associates has maintained that both science and society can benefit from ways of balancing methodological and ethical concerns in research. Not only must the costs of doing a particular study be weighed against the benefits of doing the study, but the costs of not doing the research must also be evaluated in ethical terms. Rosnow's work calls for training ethical decision makers who serve on institutional review boards, using a role-play technique that has proven effective in sensitizing students to the complexities of ethical decision making. There are important advantages to considering methodological issues and ethical issues in the context of one another.

REFERENCES

Allport, G., Vernon, P., & Lindzey, G. (1960). *A study of values* (3rd ed.) Boston: Houghton Mifflin.

Ball-Rokeach, S., Rokeach, M., & Grube, J. (1984). *The great American values test.* New York: Free Press.

Blanck, P. D., Bellack, A. S., Rosnow, R. L., Rotheram-Borus, M. J., & Schooler, N. R. (1992). Scientific rewards and conflicts of ethical choices in human subjects research. *American Psychologist, 47*(7), 959–965.

Braithwaite, V. (1994). Beyond Rokeach's equality-freedom model: Two-dimensional values in a one-dimensional world. *Journal of Social Issues, 50*(4), 67-94.

Cantor, N., & Kihlstrom, J. F. (1987). *Personality and social intelligence.* Englewood Cliffs, NJ: Prentice-Hall.

Dictionary.com. (2004). "Ethics." Retrieved September 1, 2004, from http://dictionary.reference.com

Feather, N. T. (1975). *Values in education and society.* New York: Free Press.

Feather, N. T. (1994). Human values and their relation to justice. *Journal of Social Issues, 50*(4), 129–152.

Hammer, D. (1983). The practice of urban ministry: A postscript. *Review and Expositor, 80*, 537–541.

Hessell, D. T. (1972). *A social action primer.* Philadelphia: Westminster.

Kimmel, A. J. (1988). Herbert Kelman and the ethics of social-psychological research. *Contemporary Social Psychology, 12*(4), 152–158.

Kimmel, A. J. (1991). Predictable biases in the ethical decision making of American psychologists. *American Psychologist, 46*, 786–788.

Kimmel, A. J., & Smith, N. C. (2001). Deception in marketing research: Ethical, methodological, and disciplinary implications. *Psychology & Marketing, 18*(7), 663–689.

Kluckhohn, C. (1951). Values and value-orientations in the theory of action. In T. Parsons & E. A. Shills (Eds.), *Toward a general theory of action* (pp. 388–433). Cambridge, MA: Harvard University Press.

Kluckhohn, F. R., & Strodtbeck, F. L. (1961). *Variations in value orientations.* Westport, CT: Greenwood.

Little, B. (1983). Personal projects: A rationale and methods for investigation. *Environment and Behavior, 15*, 273–309.

Mayton D. M., II, Ball-Rokeach, S. J., & Loges, W. E. (1994). Human values and social issues: An introduction. *Journal of Social Issues, 50*(4), 1–8.

Mayton, D. M., II, & Furnham, A. (1994). Value underpinnings of antinuclear political activism: A cross-national study. *Journal of social Issues, 50*(4), 117–128.

Peterson, R. S. (1994). The role of values in predicting fairness judgments and support of affirmative action. *Journal of Social Issues, 50*(4), 95–116.

Rohan, M. J. (2000). A rose by any name? The values construct [Abstract]. *Personality and Social Psychology Review, 4*(3), 255–277.

Rokeach, M. (1968). *Beliefs, attitudes, and values.* San Francisco: Jossey-Bass.

Rokeach, M. (1973). *The nature of human values.* New York: Free Press.

Rokeach, M. (Ed.). (1979). *Understanding human values: Individual and societal.* New York: Free Press.

Rosenthal, R., & Rosnow, R. L. (1984). Applying Hamlet's question to the ethical conduct of research: A conceptual addendum. *American Psychologist, 39*, 561–563.

Rosnow, R. L. (1990). Teaching research ethics through role-play and discussion. *Teaching of Psychology, 17*(3), 179–181.

Rosnow, R. L. (1997). Hedgehogs, foxes, and the evolving social contract in psychological science: Ethical challenges and methodological opportunities. *Psychological Methods, 2*(4), 345–356.

Rosnow, R. L., Rotheram-Borus, M. J., & Ceci, S. J. (1993). The Institutional Review Board as a mirror of scientific and ethical standards. *American Psychologist, 48*(7), 821–826.

Schwartz, S. H. (1992). Universals in the content and structure of values: Theoretical advances and empirical tests in 20 countries. In M. Zanna (Ed.), *Advances in experimental social psychology* (Vol. 25, pp. 1–65). Orlando, Fl: Academic Press.

Schwartz, S. H. (1994). Are there universal aspects in the structure and contents of human values? *Journal of Social Issues, 50*(4), 19–45.

Schwartz, S. H. (1999). A theory of cultural values and some implications for work [Abstract]. *Applied Psychology: An International Review, 48*(1), 23–47.

Schwartz, S. H., & Bardi, A. (2001). Value hierarchies across cultures: Taking a similarities perspective [Abstract]. *Journal of Cross-Cultural Psychology, 32*(3), 268–290.

Schwartz, S. H., & Bilsky, W. (1987). Toward a psychological structure of human values. *Journal of Personality and Social Psychology, 53*, 550–562.

Schwartz, S. H., & Bilsky, W. (1990). Toward a theory of the universal content and structure of values: Extensions and cross-cultural replications. *Journal of Personality and Social Psychology, 58*, 878–891.

Schwartz, S. H., Melech, G., Lehmann, A., Burgess, S., Harris, M., & Owens, V. (2001). Extending the cross-cultural validity of the theory of basic human values with a different method of measurement [Abstract]. *Journal of Cross-Cultural Psychology, 32*(5), 519–542.

Scott, W. A. (1965). *Values and organizations.* Chicago: Rand McNally.

Smith, M. B. (1969). *Social psychology and human values: Selected essays.* Chicago: Aldine.

Smith, P. B., Peterson, M. F., Schwartz, S., et al. (2002). Cultural values, sources of guidance, and their relevance to managerial behavior: A 47 nation study [Abstract]. *Journal of Cross-Cultural Psychology, 33*(2), 188–208.

Thomas, C. B., Jr. (1986). Values as predictors of social activist behavior. *Human Relations, 39*(3), 179–193.

Thomas, C. B., Jr. (1997). The relationship between values and success for managers in large corporations. *Journal of Social Behavior and Personality, 12*(3), 671–688.

Thomas, C. B., Jr. (2001). Characteristics correlated with perceptions of gender inequality. *Michigan Sociological Review, 15*, 20–28.

Thomas, C. B., Jr., Hall, J. A., Miller, F. D., Dewhirst, J. R., Fine, G. A., Taylor, M. & Rosnow, R. L. (1979). Evaluation apprehension, social desirability, and the interpretation of test correlations. *Social Behavior and Personality, 7*, 193–197.

Williams, R. M. (1968). The concept of values. In D. L. Shils (Ed.), *International encyclopedia of the social sciences* (Vol. 16, pp. 283–287). New York: Free Press.

12

Rumor in Brand Community

Albert M. Muñiz, Jr.
DePaul University

Thomas C. O'Guinn
University of Illinois, Urbana-Champaign

Gary Alan Fine
Northwestern University

Talk is cheap, so the popular expression goes; yet hearsay can be a precious commodity in the marketplace of social exchange.

— Rosnow and Fine (1976, p. 1)

Over the course of the 20th century, the marketplace came to occupy a more central position in the daily lives of much of the world's population (Bauman, 2001; Cohen, 2000; Cross, 2000; Iyer, 2000; Marchand, 1985; Schudson, 1984). Most of the world now is exposed to consumer culture. Branded goods are the defining icon, the prime mover, in this social transition. A little more than a century ago, relatively few things were branded. Soaps, beers, and most "soft goods" were purchased by number, volume, or weight. They were unbranded commodities. Today, even water and dirt are branded. The desire for branded consumer products and the social agenda that derives from their unequal distribution are reputed to be significant factors in events such as the fall of the former Soviet Union and geopolitical struggles the world over. Brands are major markers of social identity (Cova, 1997; Frank, 1997; Gladwell, 2000; Kotlowitz, 1999). Clearly, consumption is important in its own right, not just in terms of inequities of labor, production, or income (Lasch, 1991).

As consumption of branded goods and services increases, so does discussion of them. Consumers discuss their consumption, their purchases, and their favored brands. One form of these discussions involves spreading rumor. As in other contexts, consumption rumors often are analyzed in a pejorative fashion. The reasons for this are many, but one is gender (i.e., most marketing is directed at women, and marketplace rumor has been appended to gendered stereotypes about gossip). In addition, marketplace rumors are more likely viewed as false than as true, further stigmatizing them. And perhaps most important, rumors are outside the "marketing communication channel"; that is, outside of the marketer's control. This alone makes them undesirable for marketing practitioners. The industrial response to marketplace rumors has largely been to formulate strategies of control. Public relation firms may be hired to limit the impact of rumor. In fact, many public relations firms owe their very existence to detecting, stopping, or occasionally starting rumors. The role of public relations in several "whispering campaigns" is legendary.

Yet, in academic marketing, the study of rumor has a much smaller presence. In the 1950s and 1960s, the nascent discipline became obsessed with the larger category of consumer word of mouth (including rumor) and its impact on the firm's marketing activity. World War II optimism about modern and scientific propaganda efforts, a 1950s fascination with neo-Freudian thought (particularly the unconscious), and the advent of television led marketers to believe that they could directly and effectively motivate consumer behavior (O'Guinn & Faber, 1991). However, by the mid-1950s the idea of socially unmediated mass communication had vanished. At that point, marketing researchers began to focus on opinion leadership. This idea was a significant development in that it acknowledged that certain individuals were key players in the communications channel, and served to edit, translate, amplify, and dismiss mass-mediated messages via interpersonal communication. This two-step flow (Katz, 1957) rejected the theory of powerful direct media effects; that is, marketing information, without social mediation, directly (and powerfully) getting consumers to respond as marketers wished. The folly of the powerful direct effects position was underscored by practical experience. More and more advertising was required to move goods and services. People talked to each other about the things they were thinking of buying and what they thought about the things they had already bought and the ads they had seen. Prominent marketing failures such as the Ford Edsel underscored the role of the stubborn social public. For about a decade, academic attention focused on interpersonal communication (including rumor) and its interaction with marketing communication.

Research on most forms of word of mouth, including marketplace rumors, subsided as a topic area in academic marketing by the mid-1970s. Although universally recognized as important, marketing academics avoided the topic due to what seemed to be profound methodological limitations and an unproductive search for "generalized marketing opinion leaders." Rumors moved too fast for easy analysis. Not coincidentally, the marketing field simultaneously ended its flirtation with sociology and embraced the social psychology of "information processing." Rumor had little place in this new paradigm.

Now, 30-some years later, the Internet has created an acute need for more rumor studies, as well as providing an empirical venue for collecting rumor data in computer-mediated environments. The Internet has allowed consumers to form important social aggregations that act as rumor agents. One key form of these groups is the *brand community*.

BRAND COMMUNITY

The fields of marketing and consumer behavior have lately focused on consumption communities. A growing number of consumer researchers (Celsi, Rose, & Leigh, 1993; Kozinets, 2001; Muñiz & O'Guinn, 2001; Schouten & McAlexander, 1995) demonstrated that these communities exist, are of significant numbers and varieties, and have an important impact on consumers and consumption, including the use of rumor.

Muñiz and O'Guinn (2001) defined a brand community as "a specialized, non-geographically bound community, based on a structured set of social relationships among admirers of a brand. It is specialized because at its center is a branded good or service. Like other communities, it is marked by a shared consciousness, rituals and traditions, and a sense of moral responsibility" (p. 412). Because brand communities are centered on a branded good/service, the focal ideology is unabashedly commercial. An individual can be a member of the community even if he or she has never purchased the branded product or service but instead merely admired it. Brand communities share defining characteristics with other communities: consciousness of kind, the presence of rituals and traditions, and a sense of commitment.

Each of these traditional communal markers is closely tied to consumer narratives and rumor. For the purposes of this chapter, we are defining rumor as "a recurrent form of communication through which [members of a group], caught together in an ambiguous situation, attempt to construct a meaningful interpretation of it by pooling their intellectual resources" (Shibutani, 1966, p. 16). This definition has several important components. First, it focuses on how a group interacts with a rumor, as opposed to how an individual makes sense of a rumor or distorts it (as in serial transmission studies). Second, this definition focuses on the processes by which a group constructs and responds to a rumor when faced with an uncertain environment. Third, the truth or falsity of the rumor is not the focus of the Shibutani definition; rather, the focus is on the ways that members of the community collectively attempt to make sense of it. Thus, the veracity of the rumor is incidental relative to the effects it produces on individuals and groups.

Brand communities are, to a large degree, defined by the stories that members share (Muñiz & Hamer, 2001; Muñiz & O'Guinn, 1995, 2001; Muñiz & Schau, 2005; O'Guinn & Muñiz, 2000; Schau & Muñiz, 2002). Not every brand will have a strong community of admirers—major consumer products (e.g., cars, computers, electronics) and those aimed at specialized markets seem particularly likely to generate enthusiastic groups and groups that are autonomous or semi-autonomous from the manufacturer. In this account, we focus on six examples: brand communities of Saab, Miata, and Volkswagen drivers, and of Linux, Mac, and Newton PDA users.

Consciousness of Kind

Like all communities, brand communities possess what Gusfield (1978) referred to as "consciousness of kind"—the intrinsic connection that members of a community feel toward one another, as well as a collective sense of difference from those outside the community. It is a shared consciousness and bond that is more than shared attitudes or perceived similarity—it is a shared sense of belonging (Fine & Harrington, 2001; Weber, 1922/1978). In brand communities, members share a sense of "we-ness" (Bender, 1978). Members feel an important connection to the brand, as well as a connection to one another. Members feel that they know each other, even if they have never met. They have established parasocial relations through assumptions about identity (Caughey, 1984). Frequently, this understanding includes a boundary between users of their brand and users of competing brands. Such a demarcation often includes a reference to brand users being "different" or "special" in contrast to users of other brands.

Terms of collectiveness are common in this consciousness. Members refer to "the cult of Macintosh," "Saab spirit," "the spirit of Miata," or note feeling they had "wandered into the wrong part of town" when describing visiting a store that sold only a competing brand. Consider the following Usenet newsgroup posting. The member began by sharing what he believed to be a prototypical brand consumption experience, and then rejoiced in finding a forum in which members of the Miata brand community could congregate in virtual space:

> Here in Las Vegas it's always a great Miata day! Even the few days that it rains I find that my little baby can float with the best speed boats, these roads always flood when it rains hard the 3 days out of the year that we get it. The best fun to be

had is zipping in and out around the tourists that drive down the road and don't really watch what they're doing. :-) Truth be told I just "found" this group and I'm a happy little person now that I've found there are other people out there like me that love their Miatas! By the by I've got a 93 white conv. (message posted to Usenet, February 1998)

This quote illustrates several points. First, brand communities are centered on narratives, just as is true for leisure domains (Fine, 1998; Mitchell, 1983). Tales concerning the history and performance of the brand are exchanged like currency. Second, such sentiments illustrate consciousness of kind in their recognition of a distinct social category: "other people out there like me" or community members. Third, this example also indicates the importance of computer-mediated communication. Although brand communities can and do exist in face-to-face settings as well (Muñiz, 1998; Muñiz & O'Guinn, 2001), computer-mediated environments (CMEs) allow much larger and geographically dispersed brand communities.

Brand communities, like the brands on which they are centered, transcend geographic boundaries. Members feel part of a larger, unmet, but easily imagined community. They know that others are out there, just like them (e.g., Mac users, Saab owners), even though they might only have met a small percentage. Some researchers suggest that most contemporary communities must be, to some extent, sustained by notions of unknown, understood others (Anderson, 1983; Gellner 1983). Like other forms of community, a brand community is "a network of social relations marked by mutuality and emotional bonds" (Bender, 1978, p. 145). This conceptualization of community is consistent with a social network perspective (Granovetter, 1973; Oliver, 1988; Wellman, 1979), stressing the functioning of individual ties over notions of local solidarity.

Two critical processes operate to perpetuate consciousness of kind in brand communities: legitimacy and oppositional brand loyalty. Both are affected or even sustained by rumor. Legitimacy is the boundary-maintenance process by which members of a brand community differentiate between those who are true members of the community and those who are not. Whether one belongs largely stems from that person's appreciation and understanding of the brand. Legitimacy discriminates between true devotes of the brand and all that it stands for as an expressive object (e.g., culture, history, rituals, symbols, traditions) and "shallow", fair-weather users. For example, many long-time Saab drivers view with skepticism the new drivers being attracted to the Saab brand in recent years. As one such driver remarked: "A lot of people actually purchased the cars who I feel shouldn't have purchased them. There's a certain type of owner who is proper for the car and people who buy one just because it's something that they really don't have intentions of keeping for a long time" (interview with first author).

This member noted that during the 1980s, Saab was embraced by "the Yuppies," a reality that he did not relish because he asserted that this group was attracted to the car for the wrong reasons: It was trendy.

In a similar way, members of the Volkswagen (VW) community differentiate between the original Beetle, produced between 1945 and 1981, and the New Beetle, introduced in 1997. The original Beetle was central to the meaning of the VW brand community. Its unusual appearance and underdog origins were a source of pride among VW enthusiasts (reflected in many jokes about the original Beetle). To most long-term VW afficionados, the New Beetle is nothing but a pale, marketing-inspired imitation of the original Bug, designed to move VW upstream and further away from its economy-minded roots. Hence, long-term members of the Volkswagen brand community view those attracted to the brand by the new Beetle as being less legitimate members of the community. In both the Saab and VW cases, rumors about new models, the use of the original plans, and the rehiring of retired designers are an important part of the mythology surrounding the brand.

Consider the following exchange, taken from a Volkswagen Internet forum 2 years before the New Beetle was reintroduced:

> I remember hearing (reading perhaps) that VW wants to target the new Bug at around $8 000. I'm sure that all the luxuries (leather seats etc.) are just for the show car, the Concept 1. Wasn't VW working on some new car design that would reduce the time needed to actually build the car by 2/3? (Or was this the Ford executive VW stole, err, hired in Germany?) That would keep costs way down, and still allow them to offer things such as a CD player and dual air-bags. (message posted to Usenet, February 1994)

Another member responded by expressing indignation that the New Beetle would include so many things that he viewed as antithetical to the values of the original Beetle (simplicity, efficiency, pragmatism): "I find this hard to believe. I don't think VW is so far out of touch that they would offer the [Beetle] in such a configuration. There has got to be some misinformation here" (message posted to Usenet, February 1994). Such rumors feed the desire for legitimacy. Members want assurance that the brand will remain true to what they feel it stands for, and will seek this information out wherever they can.

Cultural capital and issues of credibility loom large in brand communities. These communities are hierarchically structured (Muñiz & O'Guinn, 2001; Schau & Muñiz, 2002). The longer one has been using the brand, the more knowledge of the history surrounding the brand that a member knows, and the higher that member's status is in the community. There are rewards to be gained from bringing solid information to the community (Rosnow &

Fine, 1976). Prior work has suggested that when operating in an uncertain environment, status is afforded to members who contribute insight (Scheibel, 1989; Shibutani, 1966). The same is true in brand communities.

Simultaneously, there are risks to being naive or gullible, and also risks to expressing opinions or beliefs that are perceived to be harmful to the group. Some cynicism might be expected with regard to "truth claims" in order for a member to be considered a sophisticated, well-versed member of the community. A member may feel the need to be skeptical, arguing against accepting claims, in order to maintain his or her status (Bordia & Rosnow, 1998; Kapferer, 1990; Shepherd, 1987). Members must balance maintaining credibility with not damaging communal morale. If the community is interconnected, it might be harder for members to distance themselves from having believed or announced rejected information.

Consider a recurring rumor in the Apple Newton community. The Apple Newton was one of the earliest entrants into the personal digital assistant (PDA) category. Rushed to market in 1993, the Newton was riddled with errors (Tesler, 2000). The problems with the Newton were widely reported (and lampooned) in the media, and discouraged many potential adopters. Consequently, the Newton never achieved critical mass. In February 1998, Apple officially discontinued the Newton and all related products. However, a community of 20,000 Newton users still exists (Kahney, 2002). Few suppliers carry replacement parts or software or perform repairs on the machine. As a result, these users have been largely left to their own ingenuity. Members strive to keep the devices viable, creating software and hardware that they exchange in online forums. These forums are characterized by informed discussion, as well as a fair amount of speculation.

A recurring rumor in these forums is that Apple is planning to reintroduce the Newton. Such rumors have made their way through the community at least eight times since the device was discontinued in 1998. Each time, the details surrounding the device are slightly different, and each time it generates considerable discussion. Analysis of these repeated rumors suggests that members of these communities use these rumors to provide a basis for their social investment, even though most long-term members believe such rumors are false (Muñiz & Schau, 2005). Hence, in the Newton community, those who don't believe the rumors and think that a new Newton would be impossible tend not to say so, because it could hurt group morale. By repeatedly partaking in the reintroduction rumor, the community enables members to believe that the reintroduction might not be imminent, but is still very possible. To believe anything else would be a blow to the community. A recent rumor outbreak ended with an addition to the community FAQ concerning such rumors. The entries are far from definitive. Under the portion of the FAQ devoted to hardware, one can find the following question and answer:

> I heard a rumor that Apple is making a new Newton. Is this true?

That's very probably just a rumor based on the interest of Apple for Palm devices. BTW, Palm Desktop which is to be found on iBooks is compatible with NCU (the format is like Claris Organizer). (FAQ for the Newton Community, www.chuma.org)

Even here, the desire to allow for the possibility that another Newton will get introduced is present. This possibility generates an important source of optimism. By leaving open the possibility that the Newton can be reintroduced, members find reassurance.

Oppositional brand loyalty is the other process that operates to perpetuate consciousness of kind in brand communities. Oppositional brand loyalty is a process by which members of the brand community denigrate users of competing brands (Muñiz & Hamer, 2001; Muñiz & O'Guinn, 2001). This opposition is an important part of community affiliation and is a significant component of brand identity and group idioculture (Fine, 1979). Oppositional brand loyalty delineates what the brand is not, and who the community members are not. This process is consistent with findings in urban sociology suggesting that neighborhoods define themselves in opposition to one another (Hunter & Suttles, 1972; Keller, 1968); boundary work is crucial for the structuring of identity (Snow & Anderson, 1987). For example, many members of the Linux brand community derive an important aspect of their collective identity and group culture from their opposition to PCs, PC users, and PC giants Microsoft and Intel (derisively referred to as "WinTel"). The following exchange is from an online conversation in which users of the two platforms debated which system was best:

>> Life is too short to use Windows.

> Preach it brother!

Can I get an "Amen", my children? Another story: in 1997, it was discovered that because of a time-keeping error, Win95 would always crash after 42 days of continuous (2 billion milliseconds or something). Why did it take TWO YEARS to discover this problem? Because no one could keep a Win95 box running for 42 days reliably enough to notice the problem! (message posted to Usenet, August 2000)

The Linux community, like the Apple Macintosh community, opposes the WinTel establishment for its market dominance. Moreover, they define themselves in opposition to it. Many communities pull together and experience their tightest bonds during periods of social threat (Bensman & Vidich, 1995; Erikson, 1966). Oppositional brand loyalty probably explains some of the tensile strength of these communities. As in the case of legitimacy, rumors about "the other" in opposition to the communal brand are common. They help keep the threat (and the image of the other) alive. They also provide "insider knowledge" of one's revered brand's strengths and the "evil" other's weaknesses. For example, rumors about Apple technology "stolen" by WinTel serve multiple cohesive functions.

One topic of repeated interest in the Apple Newton brand community concerns Apple's decision to discontinue the Newton. Rumors abound as to why the Newton was discontinued and why Apple has failed to reenter the PDA market. One recurring theme blames the failure of the original Newton on Microsoft. The following exchange is typical:

> Anyway, I heard a rumour that it wasn't a lone gunman (SJ) that killed
> the Newt, apparently, Big Billy Gates had his dirty paws all over it
> too!!! Rumor has it that he injected a *whole*
> lotta cash into Apple (which we know as fact) and one of his bargaining
> chips was to kill the Newton, so that Win CE could take over that market
> space (which is conjecture). Does
> anyone else have any extra info on this? Or am I plainly wrong?

I'm pretty much sure you are wrong. I would be surprised if Bill Gates even spent a thought on the Newton when he bought that 150 million $$ worth of Apple shares. Frankly, the Newton's market share at that time wasn't worth bothering with. (message posted to Newtontalk listserv, February 2002)

The appearance of Microsoft as conspirator could reflect the fact that it is Apple fans' favorite villain, easily envisioned as a suppressor of superior technology, as well as because it is a dominant company and its inclusion reflects the "Goliath effect" that is common in consumer myths (Fine, 1992; Kapferer, 1990). In this way, the Newton reintroduction rumor may provide a cathartic outlet through which group participants actively project blame on outgroups. The group agrees on these targets, either explicitly or through inference.

Rituals and Traditions

The second marker of brand communities is shared rituals and traditions. Rituals and traditions perpetuate a community's shared history, culture, and consciousness. Rituals create "visible public definitions" (Douglas & Isherwood, 1979, p. 65) and social solidarity (Durkheim, 1915/1965), whereas traditions are "social practices which seek to celebrate and inculcate certain behavioral norms and values" (Marshall, 1994, p. 537). In brand communities, rituals and traditions reflect how the meaning of the community is reproduced and transmitted within and beyond the community. Most typically, they center on shared consumption experiences with the brand. For example, two members of the Saab brand community discussed a common Saab greeting ritual:

> George: If you drove a Saab, whenever you passed someone else driving a Saab on the road, you beeped or flashed your lights.

> Mark: Or you'd wave at each other. I did it today, I was driving around downtown Kenosha, and it was a four-door, nothing special, but that's OK, Hey, how you doing? Yeah I still flash my headlights at people. (interview with first author)

These greeting rituals involve public recognition of brand users and include a knowing nod, honking, waving, and asking about their brand model. Such rituals may at first appear insignificant, but they perpetuate the consciousness of kind. Every time a greeting ritual is initiated or returned, members are validated in their understanding of the community. Their belief that the other users of the brand are just like them is affirmed. These traditions are often passed along as rumor, particularly with respect to their origins and acceptance by the brand's maker.

The history of the brand is important to community members, and may be transmitted as rumor. The celebration of the brand keeps the community vital and perpetuates the culture of the community and the brand. Appreciation of such history differentiates true believers from the more opportunistic, and is a form of cultural capital within brand communities. Thus, user-created Web pages devoted to these brands are replete with historical narratives. The textual nature of the Internet provides an excellent forum in which members share their knowledge of the brand's origins, often replete with illustrations and photographs. Consider the following, from an ambitious user-created Volkswagen Web site:

> The idea for the Beetle came from a German engineer, Ferdinand Porsche, in the early 1930's. The final design for the Beetle was completed in 1938 and the first bug prototype saw the light of day in 1939. Unfortunately, WW2 ceased production shortly thereafter. Fortunately, in the summer of 1945, production restarted and Beetles couldn't be produced fast enough. In 1958, Volkswagen of America was established and Beetles soon made their way onto American soil. By the mid 1960's the VW Beetle was out selling all American made vehicles in the US. The Beetle was mass produced for a record 30 years, undergoing over 50,000 design modifications along the way. Loved for its unique road handling and its adorable

style, the Beetle stands proudly today as the top selling imported car in US automotive history. (from a now-defunct user-created VW Web site)

Similar texts and retellings are common within most brand communities,
and frequently include rumors and other unverified data. In the following,
two members of the Macintosh community debated some of the finer points
of Macintosh history:

> The order of these events were:
> 1) Apple gives Xerox an option on Apple stock ($1M) in return for a look
> at what PARC had done (a one day visit)
> 2) Apple invents a number of technologies (overlapping windows etc.)
> based on what they thought the PARC machine could do.
> It was no where near as advanced as Apple thought it was.
> 3) Lisa & Macintosh introduced
> 4) Bill Gates blackmails Apple into licensing some code to produce
> Windows 1.0 (Bill wrote the OS for the Apple II)

Not quite. MicroSoft wrote AppleSoft BASIC for the Apple II, not the
original Apple DOS or ProDOS. In fact, I think a good chunk of the original Apple II DOS was written by Steve Wozniak. (message posted to
Usenet, August 1995)

The history of the brand is an important source of pride for members of
the community. Macintosh users, like Volkswagen drivers, enjoy their product's history as outsider, underdog and innovator. However, Macintosh users
share a slight paranoia in this regard, particularly in relation to arch-rival
Microsoft. Historical details, accurate or not, are more likely to be accepted
by the community if they confirm this relationship.

Beliefs such as these, transmitted and accepted as true by loyal community members, can be dangerous for the company, because it holds them to
standards—real or imagined—that they cannot or may not wish to meet.
Many in the Saab brand community feel that Saab has moved away from
what it once stood for since being taken over by General Motors. As a result,
members spend considerable time discussing the future of Saab, including
rumors about future Saab plans. Recently, such speculation has been fueled
by statements from GM that they plan on making dramatic changes to the
Saab brand line. Members of the community consider this significant, because it could dilute the brand or move from what it once stood for. Such

changes could affect the meaning of the brand and, by extension, its community. Consider the following from a Saab newsgroup:

> Okay next is a piece of text I found some days ago ... I don't know what is true and what is just made up by the author, but I find it quit disturbing. Read and be afraid, be very afraid. Sorry for my comments in between.

> Saab is on the verge of a product explosion. Today GM's Swedish subsidiary has four models: the 9-3 fastback and convertible, and the 9-5 fastback and station wagon. GM says Saab will have five to eight models based on the Epsilon platform. According to the following roundup of what's coming, it looks like at least five Epsilon 9-3s: fastback, sedan, wagon, roadster and coupe, plus however many styles of new Epsilon 9-5s arrive at the debut in 2004.

> a car like the country master is good (see the Volvo V70XC which is a nice car, except it is a Volvo of course). I don't know what the writer means with the sedan version of the 9-5, maybe he means hatchback? (message posted to Usenet, July 2000)

This member shared an unverified piece of news seen in another Internet posting. This message generated great discussion among members. Several offered other possibilities based on rumors that they had heard—competing and comparing texts. In a similar vein: "I heard a blurb somewhere that Saab might make a new model to challenge, or at least match in size, the BMW 7 series. Does anyone know if this is true?" (message posted to Usenet, November 1998).

Reactions to such rumors are fueled by the ambiguous information available from more authorized channels. The community is embedded in the brand history. As members discuss the possibilities of such new models, unsubstantiated information enters the discourse. Sources for these rumors posted about Saab included Saab dealers and mechanics, other Saab drivers, and participants on a variety of other automotive discussion forums:

> has anyone seen news about a new model smaller than a 9-3? Jetta-sized?
> It would look great next to my 9-5 wagon!
> Especially with wide rubber ...
> Some time ago I saw sketches in an auto-mag of a proposed 9-2 hatchback.
> So something is brewing.

Try www.saabzone.f2s.com [an unofficial site] and look at the galleries ... you'll see plenty of nice stuff, including the 9-2. (message posted to Usenet, May 2001)

The concern over these plans is a preoccupation of the community. Similar rumor-fueled speculation is common in the Macintosh community. Here, topics have included possible takeovers of Apple by Disney and IBM, and also whether or not Apple would stop producing computers to focus solely on operating systems and software.

Personal stories based on common experiences are also important (Stahl, 1989). As in all aspects of group culture, they invest the brand with meanings understood by other members of the community. The telling of these stories tends to be ritualistic, reflecting a narrative tradition. Consider the following "war story" (Fine, 1998) in which a Miata driver, under the subject heading "Miatas ARE Waterproof," shared an account of miraculous survival:

I'm in the Navy, we work very late sometimes, I knew there was a 'noreaster coming in but figured I had parked my 97M in high enough ground not to worry. WRONG. I came back home at high tide to find water about half way up my doors (it was over the tires of the truck parked next to me). There was nothing I could do about it then so I went to bed then to work today. When I got home from work today my Miata was on high ground again. There was no water at all inside, it cranked right up ... The water was too high to get it out of the parking lot so I left it running for about 20 minutes to evaporate all the water out of the exhaust. Except for needing a bath she's just like I left her! OUTSTANDING!!! (message posted to Usenet, February 1998)

The fact that this poster's Miata survived unscathed is a testament to its worth as a car and validation of his choice of the brand, as well as that of other members of this community. The story makes a claim for the existence of a "Miata culture." As members retell such tales, the details change to fit the circumstances, but the traditions and ideals remain intact.

Similarly, among Saab brand community members, a popular war story is the "Saab saved my life" narrative:

The car I had before this one, I was going down the road and a fella in a garbage truck made a left hand turn in front of me and I hit him broadside and totaled the Saab. The policeman sitting at the corner having lunch saw it happen and thought I was dead. I stepped out of the car and didn't have a scratch on me. Yeah. It looked like an accordion. The whole thing just collapsed right up in front. Actually, it broke the door wheel on the garbage truck. Broke it off. (interview with first author)

Most members of the Saab community have such a story in their reper-
toire, a firsthand experience or the account of a friend (Muñiz, 1998). The
consistency of these stories is remarkable. Consider the following, told by a
different Saab driver, to participants in an Internet Saab forum:

> I love my Saab. It is my second one, the first one got totaled when a stupid young
> girl pulled right out in front of me. I was going about 50mph and slammed on my
> brakes as hard as I could (there was a truck coming in the other lane). Everything
> went into slow motion and I braced myself for the crash. My car held straight, did-
> n't waver or slip on the wet pavement and it also saved my life. I walked away …
> she wasn't so lucky. The cop told me Saabs & Volvos are the safest in crashes that
> he has seen. (message posted to Usenet, August 2000)

These stories are often transmitted in the register of rumor: "I heard that
this story is true …" or "I know this guy who …" The presence of the policeman—or some other unbiased observer—makes a claim that the story is objective and transparent, open for all to see. Similar rumors are common in
brand communities.

Communal Responsibility

The third marker of brand communities is a sense of communal responsibility, including responsibility to the community as a whole, as well as to
individual members. This helps produce collective action during times of
threat to the community. This commitment is evidenced in recruiting, integrating, and retaining members, as well as in assisting other members.
The functional, anonymous nature of market relations has been tran-
scended, because a brand community reflects a strong sense of
embeddedness in consumption practices. Economic choices have become
moral choices. Consider a dialogue in which two members of the Saab
brand community discussed their practice of stopping to help other Saab
drivers with mechanical problems:

Researcher: Have either of you ever stopped to help a Saab driver on the
side of the road?

George: More than once.
Mark: Yeah.

George: Sure. In fact, on the way home from work, Thursday, … Wednes-
day or Thursday last week, I got off the Interstate and I see this car sitting

there. It's got Wisconsin plates. I drove him into the gas station and had [Midwestern Saab] club cards with me and said "Here, you want one of these?"

Mark: Yeah, we see another Saab on the side of the road, we pull over to help no matter what it is. (interview with first author)

Consider the following newsgroup posting in which a VW driver thanked his fellow members for help and reminded them of community protocol: "So if you are driving through Cincinnati and see a white 67 Beetle at the side of the highway, hopefully it will not be me this time. If you do see a bug stranded by the side of the road, remember that it is good VW etiquette to stop and see what is wrong" (message posted to Usenet, February 1998). This responsibility to provide assistance not only manifests itself in helping to solve problems, it is also apparent in the sharing of brand-related resources. Members share important brand-related and community relevant information. On the Internet, members create elaborate pages devoted to the brand, designing them to be useful resources, independent from the manufacturers. Often this information includes rumors. For example, "I heard that Saab is going to reintroduce the Saab 98. There's going to be a waiting list, so you better call the dealer and get on it."

An example from the Macintosh community illustrates the role of rumors and communal responsibility. One member posted a message to an online forum concerning a problem with the e-mail program Eudora. In the responses that followed, several members offered their own solutions, as well as rumors related to problem. For example:

> My main complaint about Steve Dorner's excellent email program Eudora is that it suffers from the 32K text limit so common to Macintosh programs. This isn't inherently Eudora's fault—after all, Steve currently uses TextEdit (a component of the Mac operating system essentially designed to handle minimal text editing in dialog boxes, scrolling lists, and so on) to provide text services, and TextEdit causes the 32K text limit. (Rumor has it that the next version of Eudora, at least the commercial version, will eliminate the 32K limit entirely). (message posted to Usenet, September 1996)

In this example, the member suggested that the problem under discussion would be fixed in the future, according to unverified sources. The responsibility in this community to provide information, any information, is high, so the temptation to rely on informal and unverified sources is substantial. Rumors are such a common part of the Macintosh community that there are actually multiple Web sites that specialize in debating and analyzing Macintosh rumors.

Marketers and Shills

Marketers have long understood the value of word of mouth in promoting products and services. Recently, marketers have recognized the potential to create fake or contrived word of mouth. This practice has been relabeled "buzz marketing." It has been successfully employed in promoting Christina Aguilera and the movie *The Blair Witch Project* (Khermouch, 2001). Marketers have also recognized the existence and value of brand communities, particularly with regard to the value these communities have for generating word of mouth. To capitalize on this, marketers have increasingly begun attempting to manipulate these communities, either by supporting them with information, or by planting confederate members, or shills, and thus undercutting the authority of the community. As a result, the manufacturer may have a hand in the construction and spread of rumors, as Coke attempted to prior to the introduction of Vanilla Coke ("Coca-Cola," 2002). Indeed, the rumor may shape or manipulate the community. Through a shill, a marketer might plant a rumor in a brand community to test an idea. Thus, Saab might "leak" pictures of a new prototype and then track reaction. Alternatively, someone from Palm, posing as a member of the Palm Pilot brand community, might start a rumor about performance tests favorably comparing a Palm Pilot to a competing PDA. The idea of brand sabotage via a brand community exists, too. A manufacturer, upon learning of the strength of the community for the competitor's brand, could be motivated to corrupt that community in order to encourage migration to the manufacturer's own brand. It is not known whether this has ever happened, but given the power of brand communities, it is conceivable.

The Presence of Agency

One virtue of a brand community is that it provides consumers with measure of agency (real and/or supposed). They come to exercise some measure of perceived power and control over life events that are otherwise outside of their control, creating a sense of self-efficacy. This has traditionally been an explanation for how rumors spread, particularly in relatively powerless groups (Bordia & Rosnow, 1998; DiFonzo & Bordia, 1998; Parsons, Simmons, Shinhoster, & Kilburn, 1999; Scheibel, 1989; Scott, 1985). By allowing members to vent frustrations, these rumors serve as an extrajudicial complaint processing system (Nader, 1980). Given that they may lack other means of righting brand-related and product-related wrongs, members of a brand community use these rumor discussions to seek symbolic redress from those parties that have treated them unjustly. In very real terms, the ability of consumers to aggregate rapidly and cheaply, and communicate among themselves, involves greater agency in and of itself.

There are other ways that rumor commingles with agency. The significant recurrence of rumors in brand communities could be a response to the need to negotiate a new definition of the situation (Shepherd, 1987), one that provides more control, or at least the perception of greater control. The Apple Newton reintroduction rumor is one such example. At present, Newton owners face the reality of an aging technological product with no replacements being made. Without new equipment, the community will atrophy over time. But what if Apple came out with a new Newton? The community could migrate en masse to the new device, or it could dissipate. Both eventualities are potentially threatening to the extant Newton community. In this context, rumors can be very powerful. Rumor construction can act to assuage communal fears by constructing more palatable alternative outcomes, such as Apple deciding to reembrace the Newton. In a similar way, the recurrence of rumors concerning General Motors in the Saab brand community reflects the communal concern for its future as a group.

These brand community rumors exist in the context of what Fine (1979, 1987) called "idioculture," which refers specifically to the culture of small groups, capable of being referred to by members with the expectations that the meanings will be shared by other participants. These idiocultures play a vital part in maintaining social consensus (Deighton & Grayson, 1995), cohesion (Fine & Holyfield, 1996) and expectations regarding the future of the community. Participation in such rumors contributes to solidarity among members. By simplifying these explanations, they provide a common history on which members of the community can agree, or at least be familiar with. These conceptual reductions produce simple patterns of dialogue that are similar to scripted discourse, in which the community has an agreed-on set of beliefs regarding the technology and its history and circumstances. The discourse is traditional with slight personalized variations on common themes and amounts. The script fortifies the community and expresses group-based meanings and social processes. Rumor is always responsive to the cultures of the groups in which it is embedded.

Michel Maffesoli (1996) noted, "We have so dwelled on the dehumanization and the disenchantment with the modern world and the solitude it induces that we are no longer capable of seeing the networks of solidarity that exist within" (p. 72). Brand communities offer an example of just such a thing: networks of social solidarity typically overlooked or even seen as evidence of the destruction of "real community." Supposedly, there was once a time and place where community was completely outside mercantile exchange; in this imagined pastoral vale, material objects yet unmarked by the heavy hand of mass commerce had a benign function. Then came the branded good, and paradise was lost. It is a story told and retold, reproducing a central mythology of modernist social thought. Commerce is to blame for hordes of wandering spirits, experiencing only simulacra, lacking community. Such a historical record is suspect, because contemporary communities centered on brands do exist. They possess the traditional defining characteristics of community. As a result, we must abandon the idea that just because something is commercial, social phenomena like community cannot occur around it. A brand community is a contemporary and particular form of community, but a form of community nonetheless.

This returns us to rumor. As embedded communities, participants in groups focused on brands search for information as best they can, sharing and critiquing the communications of each other, reminding us that knowledge is always social. In groups that lack formal authority—such as brand communities—given their distance from manufacturers, what is transmitted is often unauthenticated, and sometimes incorrect as well. It is the distance of brand communities from those products that they celebrate that make these communities storehouses of rumor. Yet, it is the presence of rumor—a function of their independence—that makes brand communities consequential in their ability to question the claims of the powerful. The trust that members place in each other permits them to evaluate claims in light of the politics of plausibility, placing affiliation ahead of authority, and communal cohesion ahead of corporate strategy. Rumor is, as Ralph Rosnow well recognized, a means by which an insistent and continuing questioning of the ambiguities of social life can be the basis for creating a community of equals.

REFERENCES

Anderson, B. (1983). *Imagined community*. London: Verso.

Bauman, Z. (2001). *Community: Seeking security in an insecure world*. Cambridge, UK: Polity.

Bender, T. (1978). *Community and social change in America*. New Brunswick, NJ: Rutgers University Press.

Bensman, J., & Vidich, A. J. (1995). Race, ethnicity and new forms of urban community. In Philip Kasinitz (Ed.), *Metropolis: Center and symbol of our times* (pp. 196–203). New York: New York University Press.

Bordia, P., & Rosnow, R. L. (1998). Rest stops on the information superhighway—transmission patterns in a computer-meditated rumor chain. *Human Communication Research*, 25(2), 163–179.

Caughey, J. (1984). *Imaginary social worlds: A cultural approach*. Lincoln: University of Nebraska Press.

Celsi, R. L., Rose, R. L., & Leigh, T. W. (1993). An exploration of high-risk leisure consumption through skydiving. *Journal of Consumer Research*, 20, 1–23.

Coca-Cola creates "myth" online to help sell vanilla flavor. (2002, July 12). *Sun-Sentinel*, p. D1.

Cohen, L. (2000). From town center to shopping center: The reconfiguration of community marketplaces in postwar America. In Jennifer Scanlon (Ed.), *The gender and consumer culture reader* (pp. 243–266). New York: New York University Press.

Cova, B. (1997). Community and consumption: Towards a definition of the linking value of product or services. *European Journal of Marketing, 31,* 297–316.

Cross, G. (2000). *An all consuming century: Why commercialism won in modern America.* New York: Columbia University Press.

Deighton, J., & Grayson, K. (1995). Marketing and seduction: Building exchange relationships by managing social consensus. *Journal of Consumer Research, 21,* 660–676.

DiFonzo, N., & Bordia, P. (1998). A tale of two corporations: Managing uncertainty during organizational change. *Human Resource Management, 37,* 295–303.

Douglas, M., & Isherwood, B. (1979). *The world of goods.* New York: Basic Books.

Durkheim, E. (1915/1965). *The elementary forms of the religious life.* New York: Free Press.

Erikson, K. (1966). *Wayward Puritans.* New York: Wiley.

Fine, G. A. (1979). Small groups and culture creation: The idioculture of little league baseball teams. *American Sociological Review, 44,* 733–745.

Fine, G. A. (1987). *With the boys: Little league baseball and preadolescent culture.* Chicago: University of Chicago Press.

Fine, G. A. (1992). *Manufacturing tales: Sex and money in contemporary legends.* Knoxville: University of Tennessee Press.

Fine, G. A. (1998). *Morel tales: The culture of mushrooming.* Cambridge, MA: Harvard University Press.

Fine, G. A., & Harrington, B. (2001, August). *Tiny publics: Small groups and civic society.* Paper presented to the American Sociological Association, Anaheim, CA.

Fine, G. A., & Holyfield, L. (1996). Secrecy, trust, and dangerous leisure: Generating group cohesion in voluntary organizations. *Social Psychology Quarterly, 59,* 22–38.

Frank, T. (1997). *The conquest of cool: Business culture, counterculture, and the rise of hip consumerism.* Chicago: University of Chicago Press.

Gellner, E. (1983). *Nations and nationalism.* Ithaca, NY: Cornell University Press.

Gladwell, M. (2000). *The tipping point: How little things can make a big difference.* New York: Little, Brown.

Granovetter, M. S. (1973). The strength of weak ties. *American Journal of Sociology, 78,* 1360–1380.

Gusfield, J. (1978). *Community: A critical response.* New York: Harper & Row.

Hunter, A. J., & Suttles, G. D. (1972). The expanding community of limited liability. In G. D. Suttles (Ed.), *The social construction of communities* (pp. 44–80). Chicago: University of Chicago Press.

Iyer, P. (2000). *The global soul: Jet lag, shopping malls, and the search for home.* New York: Vintage.

Kahney, L. (2002, August 29). Apple's Newton just won't drop. *Wired News.* Retrieved December, from http://www.wired.com/news/mac/0,2125,54580,00.html

Kapferer, J. (1990). *Rumors: Uses, interpretations, and images.* New Brunswick, NJ: Transaction.

Katz, E. (1957). The two-step flow of communication: An up-to-date report on an hypothesis. *Public Opinion Quarterly 21,* 61–62.

Keller, S. (1968). *The urban neighborhood.* New York: Random House.

Khermouch, G. (2001, July 30). Buzz marketing. *Business Week,* pp. 50–60.

Kotlowitz, A. (1999). False connections. In J. B. Schor & D. B. Holt (Eds.), *The consumer society reader* (pp. 253–258). New York: New Press.

Kozinets, R. V. (2001). Utopian enterprise: Articulating the meanings of *Star Trek's* culture of consumption. *Journal of Consumer Research, 28*(1), 67–88.

Lasch, C. (1991). *The true and only heaven: Progress and its critics.* New York: Norton.

Maffesoli, M. (1996). *The time of the tribes: The decline of individualism in mass society.* Newbury Park, CA: Sage.

Marchand, R. (1985). *Advertising: The American dream.* Berkeley: University of California Press.

Marshall, G. (1994). *The concise Oxford dictionary of sociology.* Oxford, UK: Oxford University Press.

Mitchell, R. (1983). *Mountain experience.* Chicago: University of Chicago Press.

Muñiz, A. M., Jr. (1998). *Brand community.* Unpublished doctoral dissertation, University of Illinois, Urbana-Champaign.

Muñiz, A. M., Jr., & Hamer, L. O. (2001). Us versus them: Oppositional brand loyalty and the cola wars. In M. C. Gily & J. Meyers-Levy (Eds.), *Advances in consumer research* (Vol. 28, pp. 355–261). Provo, UT: Association for Consumer Research.

Muñiz, A. M., Jr., & O'Guinn, T. C. (1995). *Brand community and the sociology of brands.* Paper presented at Association for Consumer Research Annual Conference, Minneapolis, MN.

Muñiz, A. M., Jr., & O'Guinn, T. C. (2001). Brand community. *Journal of Consumer Research, 27, March,* 412–431.

Muñiz, A. M., Jr., & Schau, H. J. (2005). Religiosity in the abandoned Apple Newton brand community. *Journal of Consumer Research, 31, March,* 66–676.

Nader, L. (1980). *No access to law: Alternatives to the American judicial system.* New York: Academic Press.

O'Guinn , T. C., & Faber, R. J. (1991). Mass communication and consumer behavior. In T. S. Robertson & H. H. Kassajarian (Eds.), *Handbook of consumer behavior* (pp. 349–400). Englewood Cliffs, NJ: Prentice-Hall.

O'Guinn, T. C., & Muñiz, A. M., Jr. (2000). *Correlates of brand communal affiliation strength in high technology products.* Paper presented to Association for Consumer Research Annual Conference, Salt Lake City, UT.

Oliver, M. L. (1988). The urban Black community as network: Toward a social network perspective. *The Sociological Quarterly, 29*(4), 623–645.

Parsons, S., Simmons, W., Shinhoster, F., & Kilburn, J. (1999). A test of the grapevine: An empirical examination of conspiracy theories among African Americans. *Sociological Spectrum, 19,* 201–222.

Rosnow, R. L., & Fine, G. F. (1976). *Rumor and gossip: The social psychology of hearsay.* New York: Elsevier.

Schau, H. J., & Muñiz, A. M., Jr. (2002). Brand communities and personal identities: Negotiations in cyberspace. In S. Broniarczyk & K. Nakamoto (Eds.), *Advances in consumer research* (Vol. 29, pp. 344–349). Provo, UT: Association for Consumer Research.

Scheibel, D. (1989). If your roommate dies, you get a 4.0: Reclaiming rumor with Burke and organizational culture. *Western Journal of Communication, 63,* 168–192.

Schouten, J. W., & McAlexander, J. (1995). Subcultures of consumption: An ethnography of the new bikers. *Journal of Consumer Research, 22,* 43–61.

Schudson, M. (1984). *Advertising, the uneasy persuasion: Its dubious impact on American society.* New York: Basic Books.

Scott, J. C. (1985). *Weapons of the weak: Everyday forms of peasant resistance.* New Haven, CT: Yale University Press.

Shepherd, G. (1987). The social construction of a religious prophecy. *Sociological Inquiry, 57,* 394–414.

Shibutani, T. (1966). *Improvised news: A sociological study of rumor.* Indianapolis: Bobbs-Merrill.

Snow, D., & Anderson, L. (1987). Identity work among the homeless: The verbal construction and avowal of personal identity. *American Journal of Sociology, 92,* 1336–1371.

Stahl, S. D. (1989). *Literary folkloristics and the personal narrative.* Bloomington: Indiana University Press.

Tesler, L. (2000). Why the Apple Newton failed. *TechTV.* Retrieved January, 2001, from www.techtv.com/print/story/0,23102,3013675,00.html

Weber, M. (1922/1978). *Economy and society.* Berkeley: University of California Press.

Wellman, B. (1979). The community question: The intimate networks of East Yorkers. *American Journal of Sociology, 84*(5), 1201–1231.

13

Rumor
in Organizational Contexts

Nicholas DiFonzo
Rochester Institute of Technology

Prashant Bordia
University of South Australia

Rumors—a regular feature of social and organizational life—fascinate, foment, and infuriate. Some examples: Many customers were alarmed—falsely—that Kentucky Fried Chicken had changed its name to "KFC" because it had replaced real chicken meat with "genetically engineered organisms cultured from chicken cells and grown in vats" (Mosemak, 2000, p. 3D). Erie, Pennsylvania, moviegoers draped newspaper, coats, and cloth hand towels over their seats after hearing unsubstantiated rumors of head lice at the new 17-screen Tinseltown theatre (Wesman, 1997). Rumors of school violence kept many secondary students home across the United States in the aftermath of the Columbine School shootings in Colorado (Breen, 1999). Rumors in Baghdad of Israeli conspiracies are common; one rumor claims that Israel is training the Kurdish army so Kurdistan can protect itself in preparation for a Kurdistan secession ("What's the Word," 2004). False rumors originating from late-night talk radio that a "metallic object full of aliens" trailed the Hale-Bopp comet may have inspired the "Higher Source" cult belief that it was time to "shed their containers" (i.e., commit suicide) in order to rendezvous with the UFO; 39 members of the group were found dead, their faces and chests draped with triangular shrouds of purple cloth ("Distorted View," 1997; "Tragedy in California,"

1997). Rumors alter social perceptions, affect attitudes and behaviors, exacerbate hostilities, help groups to cope with the unknown, and reflect the predispositions of the collective. They are an important social psychological phenomenon encountered everywhere.

It is therefore not surprising that the study of rumor has a long and distinguished history in the field of social psychology. The list of scholars interested in this phenomenon is illustrious: Floyd Allport, Gordon Allport, Leon Festinger, Kurt Back, Stanley Schachter, Dorwin Cartwright, and John Thibaut (Bordia & DiFonzo, 2002). However, interest since World War II—with one notable exception—has tended to diminish. That exception is the work of Ralph L. Rosnow and his colleagues; over the last 3 decades, these researchers have contributed a great deal to our understanding of rumor phenomena (e.g., see Rosnow, 1991, 2001). This chapter overviews theory and updates findings in the psychology of rumor (see also DiFonzo & Bordia, in press-a). Many of these findings originated from studies performed in organizational contexts; therefore, we focus on organizational rumor. In addition, special emphasis is placed on Ralph L. Rosnow's important contributions to this area.

RUMOR DEFINED

Rosnow and his associates have done much to clarify the concept of rumor and to delineate it from other forms of informal communication, especially gossip.

Toward a More Contextual Definition

Gordon W. Allport and Leo Postman's seminal work, *The Psychology of Rumor* (1947), defined rumor as "a specific (or topical) proposition for belief, passed along from person to person, usually by word of mouth, without secure standards of evidence being present" (p. IX). Rosnow (1980, 2001) showed how parts of this definition were outdated. Today, print, electronic media, and the Internet may be added to word-of-mouth channels of communication through which rumors flow. Rosnow also noted that, although the content of the rumor may be of topical (i.e., current) interest, it often expresses themes of long-standing interest, such as student-teacher liaisons and flying saucers (Jung, 1910/1916, 1959). Third, the classification of a statement as a "rumor" is dependent on a person's frame of reference. A statement is considered "fact" to someone who can authenticate it, but "rumor" to someone for whom it is in doubt (Rosnow, 1980).

In addition, we note that embedded in Allport and Postman's definition is the notion of *person-to-person* transmission—implying a serial chain of communication through individuals—whereas rumors are often communicated to a cluster of people (Davis, 1972; Hellweg, 1987). Finally, the idea of rumor inherent in this definition is mainly about message *transmission* (i.e., the proposition is passed along). Although a rumor may sometimes be best described as a statement transmitted through a group, it can also be conceived of as a hypothesis temporarily set forth during group discussion in which people are attempting to make sense of an ambiguous situation (Rosnow, 1988; Shibutani, 1966; Turner, 1994). For example, many Americans find it difficult to make sense of the events of September 11, 2001; why would Arab terrorists destroy so many innocent people? False rumors of widespread Arab celebration of the events of September 11 help to explain these actions by casting Arabs as "predators" (Fine & Khawaja, 2005).

Rosnow and Kimmel's recent entry for rumor in the *Encyclopedia of Psychology* avoids these problematic features. They defined rumor as "an unverified proposition of belief that bears topical relevance for persons actively involved in its dissemination" (2000, pp. 122–123). The central notion of rumor as a statement without authentication is retained. The method of dissemination is not specified, however, nor is the type of active involvement in its dissemination. This revision allows for rumor as a message that is transmitted from person to person *and* as the means by which groups make sense of a situation. More important, the definition focuses on the *relevance* of the proposition for persons. Such a modification shifts the emphasis away from the specific *content* of the rumor to the *context* of the situation that makes the given content relevant to the people involved in rumor activity (Rosnow, 1988). Rosnow and Kimmel's reformulation thus highlights the more contextual and constructivist aspects of rumor.

Rumor Versus Gossip

In common parlance, *rumor* and *gossip* are often used synonymously (Rosnow, 1974; Rosnow & Fine, 1976). Indeed, the APA PsycINFO *Thesaurus* currently lists *rumor* under the term *gossip*. Rosnow and his associates have distinguished rumor from other important genres of communication—especially gossip—in terms of both the characteristics of the communication and its function. Rosnow and Kimmel (2000) posited three distinguishing characteristics of a message: whether or not it is based on *evidence*, is *significant*, and is primarily *about individuals*. Rumor is *not* based on solid evidence, *is* significant (i.e., is about a topic of some urgency or importance as perceived by participants), and *may or may not* be about individuals. News shares these characteristics, except that news is based on firm evidence (Shibutani, 1966). Gossip may or may not be firmly substantiated, is not typically perceived as significant/urgent by participants, and is about individuals (Rosnow, 1974; Rosnow & Georgoudi, 1986). Rumor and gossip have also been distinguished by primary function. Rumor is often intended as a hypothesis to help make sense of an unclear situation (Shibutani,

1966), whereas gossip has more to do with important group identity and solidarity functions—it provides social information, entertains, defines who is part of the group (and who is not), fosters friendship bonding, defines social hierarchy, and conveys group norms (Foster, 2004; Gluckman, 1963; Rosnow & Georgoudi, 1986; Wert & Salovey, 2004).

Taking our cue from the preceding discussion, we delineate *organizational* rumors as those unverified propositions of belief that bear topical relevance to members of an organization or to the organization as a whole. Organizational rumor is not firmly substantiated, is perceived as significant by members of the organization, and may or may not be about individuals.

PREVALENCE AND TYPES OF ORGANIZATIONAL RUMORS

Prevalence

Rumors are a ubiquitous part of organizational life (Koenig, 1985). A survey of top corporate public relations (PR) personnel found that harmful or potentially harmful rumors appear to be widespread and frequent, reaching participants' ears almost once per week on average (DiFonzo & Bordia, 2000). Rumors seem especially prevalent during times of change, such as restructuring, downsizing, or mergers (DiFonzo & Bordia, 1998). A recent quip—"We are *swimming* in rumors"—from a software firm manager undergoing downsizing accurately characterizes our repeated observations.

Types

With Rosnow, we categorized organizational rumors as stemming from common and collective organizational concerns (DiFonzo, Bordia, & Rosnow, 1994). These rumors may be primarily transmitted within an organization—we have dubbed these *internal* rumors—or mostly transmitted outside formal organizational boundaries—*external* rumors. In our survey of experienced corporate PR personnel, participants estimated that half of all rumors were primarily internal; a significant minority were primarily external, and about 1 in 10 were both (DiFonzo & Bordia, 2000). Rumors pertaining to job security, job satisfaction, and personnel change constituted most internal rumors. Rumors affecting an organization's reputation, the reputation of its products or services, and stock value characterized most external rumors. Similarly, a more recent survey of personnel undergoing change in a large hospital setting collected internal rumors that reflected four collective concerns *about change*: changes to job and working conditions, the nature of the organizational change, poor change management, and consequences of the change for organizational performance (Bordia, Jones, Gallois, Callan, & DiFonzo, in press).

EFFECTS OF HARMFUL ORGANIZATIONAL RUMORS

Not all rumors are harmful or potentially harmful. Office grapevine rumors are often quite accurate and serve the helpful function of preparing organizational members for significant events (DiFonzo & Bordia, in press-a). Other rumors—for example, those concerning personnel changes—are often not detrimental. Those rumors that are injurious, however, can severely damage both tangible and intangible assets (DiFonzo & Bordia, 2000).

Tangible Effects

First consider tangible effects. Rumors hindering sales are particularly troublesome. In March 1991, false rumors that Tropical Fantasy Soda Pop was manufactured by the KKK and caused African American men to become sterile caused sales to plummet 70% (Freedman, 1991). Delivery trucks were attacked and vendors dropped the product. False allegations that Pop Rocks candy, when eaten with soda, would explode in the stomach caused a substantial sales loss (Unger, 1979). Bubble Yum bubble gum sales plummeted when false rumors alleged its contamination with poisonous spider eggs (Unger, 1979). Rumors also affect stock values (Lazar, 1973; Pound & Zeckhauser, 1990; Rose, 1951).

It is important to note that these effects can occur even in the absence of strong belief in rumors. Put another way, I need not possess strong confidence in a rumor before it substantially affects my behavior (e.g., my consumer purchase behavior). Merely hearing the false rumor that MacDonald's used worm meat in its hamburgers appeared to have a negative effect on people's intentions to visit the fast-food chain, even though the rumor was disbelieved (Tybout, Calder, & Sternthal, 1981). Although subjects denigrated a rumor source as eminently untrustworthy, merely hearing the rumor affected their stock market trading behavior in precisely the same manner as those subjects who heard the same message presented as *Wall Street Journal* news (DiFonzo & Bordia, 1997, 2002a). Subjects put rumors down but traded on them as if they were news. Sense-making explanations, once formed, are difficult to eradicate, despite thorough discrediting of the evidence on which the connection was formed (Anderson, 1983, 1985; Anderson, Lepper, & Ross, 1980; Ross, Lepper, & Hubbard, 1975) and even despite forewarning that forthcoming evidence is bad (Wegner, Coulton, & Wenzlaff, 1985). If thoroughly discredited data provoke changes in behavior, then it is reasonable to infer that rumors from even noncredible sources would do likewise. Similar findings have obtained in studies of rumor's frequent companion, innuendo (Wegner, Wenzlaff, Kerker, & Beattie, 1981).

Intangible Effects

More commonly, harmful rumors impinge on intangible assets—especially trust. In interviews we conducted with a variety of corporate managers and PR personnel, harmful consequences were found to be rooted in the depletion of trust (DiFonzo et al., 1994; DiFonzo & Bordia, 1998). Rumors inflicted harm by eating away at faith in coworkers, management, or the corporation. One manager, facing innuendo that his consulting firm was incompetent, feared the consequences brought on by a loss of credibility: "When credibility is undermined, that undermines just about everything else. Your client can't trust you; they can't trust your word, your future activity, nor any dealings with you whatsoever" (DiFonzo et al., 1994, p. 50). Another manager in the same study, at a manufacturing corporation, feared "strained relationships" when a rumor arose that the manufacturer was "going directly to product vendors and circumventing marketing representatives" (DiFonzo et al., 1994, p. 50). Consistent with these concerns are empirical results indicating employees' reliance on rumors over formal announcements (Harcourt, Richerson, & Wattier, 1991).

Evidence for both types of losses was further corroborated in our survey of 74 top-level corporate PR professionals (DiFonzo & Bordia, 2000). Participants were questioned about the effects of rumor based on their extensive overall experience. They were presented with a list of 17 different effects and then were asked to indicate the average severity of each (i.e., "small," "medium," or "large"). Results (presented in Figure 13.1) showed that negative effects of rumors were commonplace. The most widespread and deleterious rumor effects included negative effects on worker morale, bad press, loss of management–employee trust, and increased worker stress. Using principle components analysis, we categorized the locus of effects as either external (e.g., loss of consumer trust, sales, stock value) or internal. Internal effects were further categorized as negatively affecting either attitudes (e.g., employee morale, trust) or behaviors (e.g., turnover, withdrawal, productivity). Of these three loci, harmful effects on internal attitudes were the worst overall and were rated as "moderately severe" on average.

RUMOR TRANSMISSION

Research investigating the antecedents of rumor transmission, much of it done by Rosnow and his colleagues, points toward four important predictors: generalized uncertainty, personal anxiety, outcome-relevant involvement, and belief in the rumor (Rosnow, 1991). The associations between

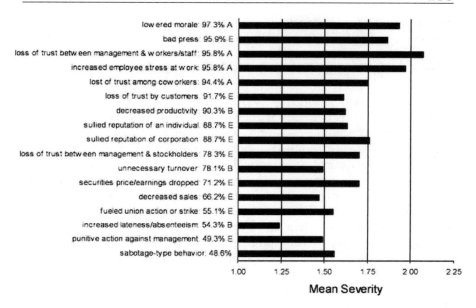

FIG. 13.1. Rumor effects and mean severity ratings.

Note. Effects are in decreasing order by the percentage of respondents (*n* ranged from 66 to 73) who had ever observed the effect in their overall experience. Mean severity ratings are on scale, where 1, 2, and 3 indicate small, medium, and large average effects, respectively. E indicates an external ramification, A indicates an effect related to internal attitudes, and B indicates effects associated with internal behaviors (see text). From "How Top PR Professionals Handle Hearsay: Corporate Rumors, Their Effects, and Strategies to Manage Them," by Nicholas DiFonzo and Prashant Bordia, 2000, *Public Relations Review, 26,* p. 180. Copyright 2000 by Elsevier Science Inc. Reprinted with permission of the author.

these variables and rumor spread has been observed in field settings for a long time (e.g., Prasad, 1935; Shibutani, 1966; Turner, 1994), but their systematic measurement and subjection to focused hypothesis testing is in large part due to the work of Rosnow and his associates (for recent reviews, see Bordia & DiFonzo, 2002; Rosnow, 1991).

Anxiety

Rosnow defined anxiety in the context of rumor as "an affective state—acute or chronic—that is produced by, or associated with, apprehension about an impending, potentially disappointing outcome" (1991, p. 487). Anxiety, as both a trait characteristic (Anthony, 1973) and a situational variable (Esposito, 1986/1987), has been linked to the likelihood of transmitting a rumor (Anthony, 1992; Bordia, DiFonzo, & Chang, 1999; Bordia

& Rosnow, 1998; DiFonzo et al., 1994; Jaeger, Anthony & Rosnow, 1980; Rosnow, Esposito & Gibney, 1988). For example, students made to feel anxious over an impending unpleasant interview with a professor spread rumors more quickly than did controls (Walker & Beckerle, 1987).

Rosnow's (1991) meta-analysis of seven empirical studies found a large average linear association ($r = .48$) for anxiety and rumor transmission. Rosnow (1980) speculated that the relation between rumor and anxiety may indeed be curvilinear—an inverted "U" shape—in which moderate anxiety yields greater rumor transmission than do low and high anxiety. Too little anxiety may not be enough to motivate transmission, but too much may result in an aversion to communicate at all. Although Rosnow et al.'s (1988) investigation of rumors surrounding a campus murder did not support this relation, a recent investigation by Mark Pezzo and Jason Beckstead (in press) did. In a high-anxiety set of rumors concerning an unexpected student death from spinal meningitis, a curvilinear relationship obtained between anxiety and the number of people to whom participants passed the rumor (this occurred only at low levels of belief in the rumor). The purported curvilinear anxiety-transmission relationship awaits further empirical testing.

At least two explanations underlie the general correspondence between anxiety and rumor transmission. First, rumors are a way to justify the presence of anxiety (Turner, 1994). Prasad (1935) explained the presence of unreasonable post-earthquake rumors by proposing that people transmitted rumors in order to justify their feelings of anxiety: "I feel anxious, it must be because there is something to feel anxious about." In other words, rumors reduced cognitive dissonance arising from unexplained feelings of apprehension (Festinger, 1957). Second, rumors are a vehicle by which people seek to reduce anxiety by regaining a sense of control. Rumors may afford a sense of control in that they help people to prepare for and/or to understand events (Bordia, Hobman, Jones, Gallois, & Callan, 2004; Bordia, Hunt, Paulsen, Tourish, & DiFonzo, 2004; Walker & Blaine, 1989). In two field studies, most of the variance in anxiety (or psychological strain) accounted for by uncertainty was mediated by a reduced sense of control among staff from a public sector organization undergoing restructuring (Bordia, Hobman, et al., 2004) and a sample of rumor episodes recalled by experienced corporate PR officers (DiFonzo & Bordia, 2002b).

Uncertainty

Uncertainty may be defined as a psychological state of doubt about what current events mean or what future events are likely to occur. Uncertainty is sometimes referred to as "cognitive unclarity" (Schachter & Burdick, 1955) and is the psychological side of "ambiguous" and "undefined" situations (Rosnow, 1991). Uncertainty has been linked to rumor transmission (Allport & Postman, 1947; Prasad, 1935, Rosnow, 1991). Indeed, "[r]umour depends upon uncertainty" (Belgion, 1939, p. 12). According to Tamotsu Shibutani (1966), rumors are "improvised news" necessitated by uncertain situations: When formal information is not available or not trusted, people compensate with informal speculation. Shibutani and other sociologists advocated thinking of rumor as collective problem solving to define (i.e., make sense of) undefined situations (Turner & Killian, 1972); "undefined" situations are by definition filled with uncertainty. Similarly, rumors have been conceived as an adaptive response in organizations in which clearly specified organizational contingencies are absent (Houmanfar & Johnson, 2003). A recent study of rumor discussions on the Internet supported and extended these ideas; a substantial portion of these discussions was devoted to sense making (Bordia & DiFonzo, 2004). Rosnow's meta-analysis of five studies found a small—although practically significant—average linear effect ($r = .19$) between uncertainty and rumor transmission. Rosnow (1980) speculated that a curvilinear relation may also exist between uncertainty and transmission: too little uncertainty and one is not motivated to transmit a rumor; too much uncertainty and one lacks enough information to participate meaningfully in rumor transmission.

Importance

Importance refers to the significance of the topic on which a rumor bears. Allport and Postman's (1947) basic law of rumor (rumor transmission = importance of the rumor × by the ambiguity of the situation) points to the necessity of importance in rumor transmission. According to this law, ambiguity alone would not result in rumors. The authors noted, "an American citizen is not likely to spread rumors concerning the market price for camels in Afghanistan because the subject has no importance for him, ambiguous though it certainly is" (p. 34). Importance has been linked to rumor transmission (Kimmel & Keefer, 1991; Schachter & Burdick, 1955), but the result has not been uniform (Back et al., 1950; Jaeger et al., 1980). Rosnow (1991) speculated that these discrepant findings might have resulted from differences in how study participants operationalized importance. Rumors that evoke caring or involvement are said to be *outcome relevant* to participants—this is really what Allport and Postman had in mind. Participants in studies failing to find importance effects may have rated a rumor (e.g., that a student was caught smoking during a final exam) as "important" but it may not have been important *to them* (i.e., outcome relevant). Rosnow therefore renamed importance to "outcome relevant involvement" to more clearly reflect this meaning.

We note that, for rumors portending negative events (e.g., layoffs), the caring/involvement about rumor-relevant outcomes is closely related to the sense of dread that defines anxiety. We found evidence for this in a sample of rumors recalled by corporate PR personnel (DiFonzo & Bordia, 2002b): Anxiety mediated the effect of importance on rumor activity. Given caring/involvement, a rumor that evokes negative consequences makes one anxious. Conversely, when a rumor fails to evoke caring/involvement/anxiety, it is less likely to be transmitted.

Belief

Belief—designated as "credulity" by Rosnow (1991)—refers to how much trust one puts in the truth of a rumor. Belief in a rumor has been linked with its transmission (Rosnow et al., 1988). For example, during a strike by university faculty, rumors that were firmly believed were transmitted more than were those in which there was less confidence (Rosnow, Yost, & Esposito, 1986). Presumably, if people don't trust a rumor, they won't pass it along for fear of losing credibility (Caplow, 1947). Rosnow found a moderate average linear effect ($r = .30$) across six studies that correlated belief in rumor with transmission.

Prasad (1935) and others (Shibutani, 1966; Turner & Killian, 1972) proposed a moderating role for anxiety in the relation between belief and transmission. Extreme anxiety results in decreased critical ability, or "heighten[ed] social suggestibility" (Prasad, 1935, p. 12). For example, Prasad observed that some highly improbable rumors ("there will be a change of sex on February 27th," p. 4) that were apparently not believed were nevertheless widely spread. This agrees with Rosnow's more recent empirical research. Rosnow et al. (1988) found that the relationship between credulity and rumor transmission was weakest for people experiencing high anxiety ($r = .20$, with correlations of .24 & .56 for low and medium anxiety), and concluded that anxiety might moderate critical ability. Put another way, the association between belief and transmission is strongest in situations of moderate anxiety.

Similarly, Rosnow proposed a moderating role for outcome-relevant involvement in the relation between belief in the rumor and transmission (Rosnow, 1980, 1991; Rosnow et al., 1988). The relation between belief and transmission is strong for high-outcome-relevant rumors because they evoke greater scrutiny; that is, people devote cognitive resources to evaluating rumors and pass on only those that seem credible to them. Low-outcome-relevant rumors, however, receive little or no evaluation, and belief has little bearing on whether the rumor is passed on.

The Gun Analogy

As a rough analogy for how these four variables act in concert, Rosnow (1991) proposed that rumor transmission is similar to the loading and firing of a gun. In an atmosphere of anxiety and uncertainty, people load a gun and shoot at a perceived target. This process is analogous to passing a rumor in situations of anxiety and uncertainty. Furthermore, the gun is usually fired when one is confident that it will hit a target; this is analogous to passing a rumor in which one has confidence. Normally, misfires are costly; that is, if the stakes surrounding the rumor are important, people tend not to spread it if they believe it is false. If a rumor is unimportant, however, misfires are not costly and people may take a "shot in the dark"—belief and transmission are then unrelated.

Motivational Approaches

These causes of rumor transmission may be viewed motivationally; elsewhere we have proposed that people transmit rumors in order to find facts and act effectively, to enhance or maintain relationships, and to self-enhance (Bordia & DiFonzo, 2005). These motives may overlap or oppose one another, depending on the circumstances. The fact-finding motive highlights the roles of uncertainty, anxiety, and outcome-relevant involvement: In situations of uncertainty about important topics, people feel anxious and are motivated to "ferret out the facts" and make sense of the situation (reduce uncertainty and anxiety), and thereby to act effectively in their environment. For example, employees kept in the dark about the details of a departmental downsizing will experience uncertainty, anxiety, and a reduced sense of control (Bordia, Hunt, et al., 2004)—they will be motivated to find out the facts of the downsizing so as to prepare effectively for the future. The motivation to find facts is powerful; under conditions of uncertainty, people will seek out and pay for even useless information (Bragger, Bragger, Hantula, & Kirnan, 1998; Bragger, Hantula, Brager, Kirnan, & Kutcher, 2003).

Second, people are motivated to build and maintain relationships; transmitting, withholding, or distorting a rumor may enhance their ability to do so. For example, people generally avoid transmitting bad news of any sort—this is the well-known minimize unpleasant messages (MUM) effect (Tesser & Rosen, 1975)—because it generally makes people feel bad. Likewise, MBA students were less likely to transmit a rumor to student peers that their own school rankings—as compared to a rival school's rankings—had fallen (Kamins, Folkes, & Perner, 1997). This motivation doubtless explains the common experience that occurs in relation to ingroup (the group with which I closely identify) and outgroup (the group with which I do not closely identify): When speaking with ingroup members about rumors of violence, people tend to share rumors that reflect positively on the ingroup and negatively on the outgroup. This is presumably because a rumor that an ingroup member committed a violent act is unlikely to enhance one's relationship with others in the group! The finding that people tend to spread rumors they believe to be true rather than those they believe to be false can also be explained in part by this motivation: When people are concerned about their reputational standing among others, they will attempt to transmit only true rumors.

Third, rumors may also be spread because they are self-enhancing, either psychologically or materially. Rumors may enhance one's sense of self by denigrating others. Racist rumors are perhaps the best example of this; by putting down the outgroup one can boost the image of one's ingroup by comparison—and, by extension, oneself. Rumors can self-enhance in that they protect us from feeling guilty about prejudice; for example, a rumor among some Pakistanis alleges that no Jew reported to work at the World Trade Center on September 11, 2001 (Hari, 2002); such rumors offer "evidence" that the terrorist attacks were in reality a Jewish scheme to foster aggression against Muslims. Needless to say, this type of rumor worsens ethnic hostility (Knopf, 1975). For example, the *Report of the National Advisory Commission on Civil Disorders* (Kerner et al., 1968) cited rumor as being responsible for exacerbating racial tensions in "more than 65% of the disorders studied by the Commission" (p. 173). On a more commercial level, people often identify their ingroup according to what brand of product they purchase (e.g., "I am a SAABer," "I am a Mac-person"; Muniz & O'Guinn, 2001). We speculate that rumors enhancing one's own brand—and/or denigrating competing brands—would readily flourish among persons who closely identified with such "brand communities."

Rumors in the service of self-enhancement may be more practical in their goals, such as when they are purposely spread to achieve financial or political gain by denigrating or dividing an opponent. For example, rumors about a business competitor's products or ingredients to these products may be spread to attract consumers away from the competitor. Of course, for these "planted" rumors to achieve their intended aim, they must resonate with the target's existing beliefs and concerns (Kapferer, 1993). Rumors of this nature sometimes allege that rival products contain harmful (e.g., carcinogenic) ingredients, and feed on consumer fears of contamination (Fine, 1992; Kapferer, 1987). Indeed, one such false rumor that a common ingredient in shampoo causes cancer is disseminated principally by "websites maintained by 'independent distributors' for various multi-level marketing companies hawking 'natural personal care products,' etc." (Emory, 1998). In interviews we conducted with managers, we encountered an instance in which one faction spread rumors for political gain in order to eliminate a competing group within the company (DiFonzo et al., 1994). One person—materially threatened by a computer consultant's presence—purposely and repeatedly spread rumors of the consultant's incompetence. This underhanded use of rumor as a form of propaganda and manipulation is not new (DiFonzo & Bordia, in press-b). Germans used rumors in World War II to demoralize the French (Knapp, 1944).

RUMOR ACCURACY

Organizational members often depend on rumors for information (Burlew, Pederson, & Bradley, 1994; Davis, 1972; Newstrom, Monczka, & Reif, 1974; Smeltzer & Zener, 1992; Walton, 1961; Zaremba, 1988). Many middle managers in a national sample "rated the grapevine as superior to formal communication" and as the best source of information for certain topics such as promotion opportunities, company future plans, departmental future plans, and salaries and raises (Harcourt et al., 1991, p. 357; see also Modic, 1989). How justified are people in this reliance on rumors? That is, how well do groups fare in ferreting out the facts? We address questions of rumor accuracy in this section (cf., DiFonzo & Bordia, in press-a).

Conceptualization and Measurement

Rumor accuracy has two meanings. One refers to a rumor's correspondence with facts, reality, and truth. We term this sense of accuracy as "rumor verity." The other meaning of accuracy refers to a rumor's correspondence with some prior version of the rumor. We call this sense of accuracy "rumor precision." Thus, a rumor may be (a) true or false, and (b) precisely transmitted or distorted during transmission.

Rumor verity accuracy has tended to be measured in studies that assume that rumors are mostly about collaborative sense making in an undefined situation. In such studies, rumors are collected in a field setting and the percentage of these rumors (or bits of one rumor) that are true is assessed (e.g., Davis, 1972; Marting, 1969; Rudolph, 1971; Walton, 1961; Weinberg & Eich, 1978). Rumor verity accuracy is the percentage of such rumors that are true. Rumor precision accuracy has tended to be measured in serial transmission (ST) studies. Lab ST studies involve a "whisper-down-the-lane" methodology: Subjects observe an original stimulus (e.g., a drawing) and pass a description of that stimulus through a chain of participants without discussion (e.g., Allport & Postman, 1947; Higham, 1951; Werner, 1976) or with discussion (e.g., Leavitt & Mueller, 1951; McAdam, 1962). In field settings, the original stimulus is a planted rumor in an actual organization; transmission here, of course, involves discussion (e.g., Schachter & Burdick, 1955). Rumor precision accuracy is the percentage of the final report that corresponds to the original stimulus.

Researchers have measured rumor precision, but they were truly interested in rumor verity. They assumed that rumor precision was the same as rumor verity in real-life settings. Like our rumor researcher forebears, we are likewise interested in rumor verity. Unless otherwise specified, we therefore mean rumor verity when using the term *accuracy*.

How Accurate Are Rumors Overall?

Several studies have assessed rumor accuracy in field settings; rumors (or rumor components) were collected and the percentage of rumors that were true was ascertained. Overall, rumor accuracy varied widely. Two crisis events—a landslide (Sinha, 1952) and an earthquake (Prasad, 1935)—produced accuracy rates near zero. Rumors among graduate students calling a hotline during a university faculty strike were accurate 16.2 % of time (Weinberg & Eich, 1978). Financial takeover rumors published in *The Wall Street Journal*'s "Heard on the Street" column came true 43% of the time (Pound & Zeckhauser, 1990). However, rumors in established organizational settings, especially those characterized as "grapevine" rumors, produced accuracy rates above 80% (Caplow, 1947; Davis, 1972; Marting, 1969; Rudolph, 1971; Walton, 1961). This agrees with the Hellweg's (1987) review of organizational grapevine research: Grapevine information (including rumor) tends to be accurate, although incomplete.

Our own, more recent, empirical studies have been consistent with the conclusion that rumors within organizations tend to be accurate (DiFonzo & Bordia, in press-a). First, we conducted a set of six in-depth field interviews about harmful or potentially harmful rumors with organizational communications personnel from large corporations in a U.S. metropolitan area. Rumors in these organizational settings, especially if given time, tended to be very accurate (above 80%). False rumors existed only for a brief time period and were "corrected" during group interaction and/or contact with authoritative sources. Next, from employed students we collected 42 workplace rumors that had proven to be either true or false. These recalled workplace rumors tended to be 100% or nearly 100% true. In addition, participants indicated that workplace rumors tended to become more accurate over the life of the rumor. Indeed, most of the rumors in this sample were "converts"—they were true and had become more accurate during the rumor episode.

Finally, from employed students we collected 244 workplace rumors (DiFonzo & Bordia, in press-a). To counteract a possible memory bias toward true rumors, we asked each student for a true rumor and a false rumor.

Results mimicked and expanded earlier results. Rumors tended to be all/mostly true or all/mostly false; there were very few partly true/false rumors. Of the true rumors recalled, most by far were converts. Most false rumors had either remained false during their lifetime or become less accurate. In summary, rumors tended to change toward or away from verity. True rumors especially tended to mutate toward accuracy; false rumors tended to become either more false or to remain false.

Thus, there is substantial empirical evidence that organizational rumors tend to be accurate. Apparently, the reputation of workplace rumor as "inaccurate" is itself inaccurate! In addition, of those rumors that prove true or false, the true tend to get "truer" and the false either stay the same or become more false. Rumor verity trends tend to bifurcate.

RUMORS AND ORGANIZATIONAL CHANGE

Rumors and organizational change go together like a horse and carriage. Organizational changes—such as restructuring, downsizing, layoffs, reorganization, mergers, new technology, and culture change—are often experienced as stressful and may dramatically affect organizational commitment and productivity (Damanpour, 1987; Hunsaker & Coombs, 1988). Good communication surrounding such transformations has the potential to ameliorate these difficulties (Covin & Kilmann, 1990; Richardson & Denton, 1996); poor communication has the potential to worsen them (Burlew et al., 1994; Kimmel, 2004).

Poor Communication→Uncertainty→Rumors

Poor communication efforts produce widespread uncertainty. Uncertainty, in turn, leads to an abundance of rumors. Excessive rumor activity is therefore indicative of poorly managed uncertainty during organizational change (DiFonzo & Bordia, 1998; DiFonzo, Bordia, & Winterkorn, 2003). Excessive rumor activity has been associated with unsuccessful change communication efforts (Schweiger & Denisi, 1991; Smeltzer, 1991). An active rumor mill during the preacquisition phase of a merger eroded trust, lowered moral, and reduced organizational commitment (Burlew et al., 1994). Smeltzer and Zener concluded, "[R]umors have such a large impact on culture, climate, and timing that organizations need to recognize the importance of grapevine information and [to] monitor it. During layoff situations an informal rumor control system is essential" (1992, p. 468). As discussed earlier, rumors arise out of situations of uncertainty. Organizational grapevine researcher Keith Davis stated, "[A] major cause of rumor is lack of information about things important to employees" (1975, p. 3). Esposito (1986/1987) found a direct association between how frequently patrons of a striking transit system passed strike-related rumors and their level of uncertainty. The effective management of uncertainty—evident by an absence of rampant rumor activity—is therefore critical to successful communication during change.

These ideas accord with uncertainty reduction theory (Berger, 1987). Change in organization signals future events that cannot be predicted with certainty, and employees thus experience uncertainty and a reduced sense of control (Blake & Mouton, 1983; Bordia, Hunt, et al., 2004; Hunsaker & Coombs, 1988; Mirvis, 1985). Rumors are aimed at reducing uncertainty and regaining a sense of control by increasing one's preparedness or understanding (Shibutani, 1966; Walker & Blaine, 1989). For example, faced with a company merger about which little official information is disseminated, employees will attempt to prepare for such a transformation and/or understand it more fully by participating in the rumor mill. Employees in a banking conglomerate, for example, experienced a flood of anxious rumors during a major reorganization in which managers were sworn to secrecy (DiFonzo & Bordia, 1998). Out of a desire to help employees, management invoked a "don't talk 'til you get the facts" approach, but this policy backfired; employees experienced much more anxiety than was necessary.

In in-depth field interviews with management and PR personnel from primarily multinational corporations, we investigated the links between ineffective communication, uncertainty, and rumor activity (DiFonzo & Bordia, 1998). Effective change communication efforts tend to reveal rather than conceal, use collective planning, and proactively establish and maintain trust.

Reveal Versus Conceal

During change, managers often don't have access to complete information, are wary of its credibility, or are required to keep silent. Not wanting to mislead their employees, they therefore end up passing out *no* information (Richardson & Denton, 1996). However, organizations typically have a well-developed grapevine and it is very difficult to hold information in secret; leaks almost inevitably occur (Bastien, 1987; Covin, 1993; DiFonzo et al., 1994). Given this fact of organizational life, management's withholding of information is likely to fail. Worse, as in the previous example, this policy is likely to backfire. In general, change communication researchers advocate erring on the side of revealing rather than concealing information as a way to promote successful change efforts (DiFonzo & Bordia, 1998; Richardson & Denton, 1996; Smeltzer, 1991). Even the partial disclosure of information—along with an explanation of why complete information is not available—is advocated rather than waiting. Management can do this, for example, by clarifying values, timelines, and procedures by which change decisions will be made. Often, however, this does not occur. Why? Hirschhorn (1983) maintained that managers' concerns about partial information disbursement are rooted in fears about the collective process.

Collective Planning

Two (or more) heads are usually better than one. Facing problems collectively avoids several liabilities common to noncollective planning, and garners several benefits (Hirschhorn, 1983). Facing problems individually forces employees to rely on rumors, causes them to focus on their own concerns over the company's, and reinforces feelings of "I" versus "them" (Bastien, 1987). In contrast, collaborative planning is likely to lead to more effective solutions. Open communication enhances a sense of procedural justice and leads to a greater acceptance of change. Collaborative planning cannot occur, however, without the reduction of uncertainty. To this end, Hirschhorn (1983) suggested that management form committees with employees to openly explore alternative solutions to the problems necessitating change and arising from change. Hirschhorn argued that such exploration will occur informally through the rumor mill anyway; collaboration harnesses this energy. Experienced PR personnel rated this strategy as being moderately effective overall (DiFonzo & Bordia, 2000).

Trust

Attitudes of mistrust provide fertile ground for negative rumors during organizational change. In our research, we have frequently observed this association (DiFonzo et al., 1994). Distrust may occur during organizational change when employees learn of change first through news media (Richardson & Denton, 1996), or when change communiqués are written with a stockholder, rather than an employee, audience in mind (Smeltzer & Zener, 1992). Conversely, management practices that foster trust procure greater cooperation during change (Hirschhorn, 1983). For example, the director of communications of a large consumer products manufacturer was inundated with inquiries after the new CEO revealed that several subsidiaries were being carefully scrutinized (DiFonzo & Bordia, 1998). Executives at the time were developing a downsizing plan; however, it should be noted that this had been announced early in the change process. In addition, management outlined the general extent of layoffs, committed to a timeline when further information would be forthcoming, and explained why it could give no further details. As a result, rumors quickly abated. Notably, employees trusted management's announcements because of previous trust-generating experiences. This corporation emphasized frequent supervisor-to-employee communication and quarterly companywide meetings; in other words, they fostered communication and trust.

Our investigation of a corporation undergoing radical downsizing accorded with the notion that distrust of formal information sources leads to negative rumor activity (DiFonzo & Bordia, in press-a). Monthly questionnaires were administered to employees in four waves. During this time period, negative rumors (rumors of dreaded future outcomes) abounded. Results indicated that distrust of the company predicted rumor transmission. In addition, trust moderated the important role played by anxiety; employees who trusted the company spread rumors only when they were anxious, but distrustful employees spread negative rumors regardless of their level of anxiety. Taken together, these findings suggest that distrust of formal communication sources is a major ingredient in negative rumor transmission.

PREVENTING AND MANAGING HARMFUL ORGANIZATIONAL RUMORS

There is currently little empirical research on effective methods of preventing and managing harmful organizational rumors, be they internal or external; managers must often rely on their own savvy experience and intuition (DiFonzo, 2000). Issues needing empirical investigation include the ramifications of a "no comment" policy and effective methods for rumor refutation (DiFonzo et al., 1994; cf., Esposito & Rosnow, 1983).

With Rosnow, we identified and categorized rumor prevention and management strategies currently in use by managers, according to variables involved in rumor generation, evaluation, and dissemination (DiFonzo et al., 1994). Practitioners' timely explanations of ambiguous events, for example, can prevent rumors by reducing uncertainty during rumor generation. Establishing trust reduces credulity when negative rumors are evaluated. Detecting—and responding to—rumors early in their lifetimes reduces the likelihood that people will hear a rumor repeatedly, a factor occurring during dissemination that affects belief. Some rumors are so impotent as to not require neutralization. For those that do, confirming a true rumor and commenting on it reduce uncertainty and anxiety. Effective refutation (e.g., based on truth, internally consistent, from an appropriate spokesperson, and understandable) reduces belief in a rumor (Bordia, DiFonzo, Haines, & Chaseling, in press; Bordia, DiFonzo, & Schultz, 2000; Bordia, DiFonzo, & Travers, 1998; DiFonzo et al., 1994).

These strategies, and others, were presented to our sample of 74 experienced corporate PR personnel (DiFonzo & Bordia, 2000). The PR specialists identified whether or not they had ever used the strategy and indicated its overall effectiveness. The strategies, percentages of respondents who had ever used them, and mean effectiveness ratings of those who had are presented in Fig. 13.2. These strategies are widespread; nearly all of them had been employed by a majority of respondents. Strategy prevalence was generally related to rated effectiveness. Using principle components analysis, we categorized strategies into two components: *structuring uncertainty* and *enhancing formal communications*. Strategies that structure uncertainty are aimed at placing bounds on what is not known. For example, stating the values (e.g., division profitability) that will be used to guide upcoming changes (e.g., downsizing) limits the uncertainty (e.g., it is less likely that profitable divisions will be downsized). Strategies that enhance formal communications are designed to reduce uncertainty or to increase the effectiveness of a rumor refutation. Average ratings for each component were rated, on average, as being moderately effective.

Experienced PR professionals, overall, strongly advocated a "*do* comment" approach rather than "no comment" (DiFonzo & Bordia, 2000). Similarly, they championed strategies that strongly refuted negative rumors. In sum, managers can best inhibit rumor activity and its associated effects by reducing and/or placing bounds upon uncertainty and by reducing belief in the rumor through effective formal communications, including strong refutations. It seems probable to us, however, that the success of such efforts presupposes perceptions of honesty, a climate of trust, and communiqué content that is helpful in structuring uncertainty.

CONCLUSION

This chapter has reviewed several facets of rumor in organizational contexts; much of this body of knowledge is due—directly and indirectly—to the work of Ralph L. Rosnow. We reviewed Rosnow's updated and more contextual conceptualization of rumor and his helpful differentiation of rumor from gossip. Organizational rumors occur frequently and can be distinguished according to collective and common concerns of the organization. Effects of harmful rumors are tangible and intangible, and may be categorized as affecting both attitudes and behaviors inside and outside of an organization; these effects are often severe. We reviewed Rosnow's extensive investigations of the antecedents of rumor transmission: anxiety, uncertainty, outcome-relevant involvement, and credulity. At a motivational level, we have posited fact-finding, relationship-enhancement, and self-enhancement goals in rumor transmission. The concept of rumor accuracy and evidence that organizational rumors tend to be accurate were presented. A plethora of rumors during organizational change indicates that uncertainty is not well managed; our research points toward the efficacy of revealing rather than concealing, collective planning, and developing trust.

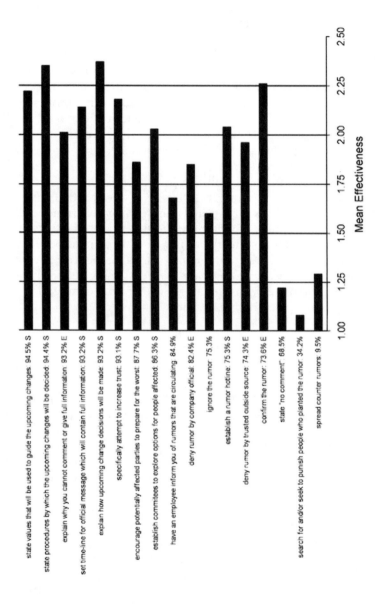

FIG. 13.2. Rumor strategies and mean effectiveness ratings.

Note. Strategies are in decreasing order by the percentage of respondents (*n* ranged from 72 to 74) who had ever used them to prevent and/or neutralize rumors. Mean effectiveness rating are on scale, where 1, 2, and 3 indicate low, medium, and high average effectiveness, respectively. S indicates a structuring-uncertainty strategy, and E indicates a strategy that enhances official communication (see text). From "How Top PR Professionals Handle Hearsay: Corporate Rumors, Their Effects, and Strategies to Manage Them," by Nicholas DiFonzo and Prashant Bordia, 2000, *Public Relations Review, 26*, p. 182. Copyright 2000 by Elsevier Science Inc. Reprinted with permission of the author.

Finally, strategies that limit uncertainty and enhance formal communication are likely to be effective in rumor management.

REFERENCES

Allport, G. W., & Postman, L. J. (1947). *The psychology of rumor.* New York: Holt, Rinehart & Winston.

Anderson, C. A. (1983). Abstract and concrete data in the perseverance of social theories: When weak data lead to unshakable beliefs. *Journal of Experimental Social Psychology, 19,* 93–108.

Anderson, C. A. (1985). Argument availability as a mediator of social theory perseverance. *Social Cognition, 3,* 235–249.

Anderson, C. A., Lepper, M. R., & Ross, L. (1980). Perseverance of social theories: The role of explanation in the persistence of discredited information. *Journal of Personality and Social Psychology, 39,* 1037–1049.

Anthony, S. (1973). Anxiety and rumour. *Journal of Social Psychology, 89,* 91–98.

Anthony, S. (1992). The influence of personal characteristics on rumor knowledge and transmission among the deaf. *American Annals of the Deaf, 137,* 44–47.

Back, K., Festinger, L., Hymovitch, B., Kelley, H., Schachter, S., & Thibaut, J. (1950). The methodology of studying rumor transmission. *Human Relations, 3,* 307–312.

Bastien, D. T. (1987). Common patterns of behavior and communication in corporate mergers and acquisitions. *Human Resource Management, 26,* 17–33.

Belgion, M. (1939). The vogue of rumour. *Quarterly Review, 273,* 1–18.

Berger, C. R. (1987). Communicating under uncertainty. In M. E. Roloff & G. R. Miller (Eds.), *Interpersonal processes: New directions in communication research* (pp. 39–62). Newbury Park, CA: Sage.

Blake, R. R., & Mouton, J. S. (1983). The urge to merge: Tying the knot successfully. *Training and Development Journal, 37,* 41–46.

Bordia, P., & DiFonzo, N. (2002). When social psychology became less social: Prasad and the history of rumor research. *Asian Journal of Social Psychology, 5,* 49–61.

Bordia, P., & DiFonzo, N. (2004). Problem solving in social interactions on the Internet: Rumor as social cognition. *Social Psychology Quarterly, 67*(1), 33–49.

Bordia, P., & DiFonzo, N. (2005). Psychological motivations in rumor spread. In G. A. Fine, C. Heath, & Campion-Vincent, V. (Eds.), *Rumor mills: The social impact of rumor and legend* (pp. 87–101). New Brunswick, NJ: Transaction.

Bordia, P., DiFonzo, N., & Chang, A. (1999). Rumor as group problem-solving: Development patterns in informal computer-mediated groups. *Small Group Research, 30,* 8–28.

Bordia, P., DiFonzo, N., Haines, R., & Chaseling, L. (in press). Rumor denials as persuasive messages: Effects of personal relevance, source, and message characteristics. *Journal of Applied Social Psychology.*

Bordia, P., DiFonzo, N., & Schultz, C. A. (2000). Source characteristics in denying rumors of organizational closure: Honesty is the best policy. *Journal of Applied Social Psychology, 11,* 2301–2309.

Bordia, P., DiFonzo, N., & Travers, V. (1998). Denying rumors of organizational change: A higher source is not always better. *Communications Research Reports, 15,* 189–198.

Bordia, P., Hobman, E., Jones, E., Gallois, C., & Callan, V. (2004). Uncertainty during organizational change: Types, consequences, and management strategies. *Journal of Business & Psychology, 18*(4), 507–532.

Bordia, P., Hunt, L., Paulsen, N., Tourish, D., & DiFonzo, N. (2004). Communication and uncertainty during organizational change: Is it all about control? *European Journal of Work & Organizational Psychology, 13*(3), 345–365.

Bordia, P., Jones, E., Gallois, C., Callan, V., & DiFonzo, N. (in press). Management are aliens! Rumors and stress during organizational change. *Group & Organization Management: An International Journal.*

Bordia, P., & Rosnow, R. L. (1998). Rumor rest stops on the information highway: Transmission patterns in a computer-mediated rumor chain. *Human Communication Research, 25,* 163–179.

Bragger, J. D., Bragger, D., Hantula, D. A., & Kirnan, J. (1998). Hysteresis and uncertainty: The effect of uncertainty on delays to exit decisions. *Organizational Behavior and Human Decision Processes, 74*(3), 229–253.

Bragger, J. D., Hantula, D. A., Bragger, D., Kirnan, J., & Kutcher, E. (2003). When success breeds failure: History, hysteresis, and delayed exit decisions. *Journal of Applied Psychology, 88*(1), 6–14.

Breen, K. (1999, May 18). Rumors keep students home. *Rochester Democrat and Chronicle,* pp. 1B, 5B.

Burlew, L. D., Pederson, J. E., & Bradley, B. (1994). The reaction of managers to the preacquisition stage of a corporate merger: A qualitative study. *Journal of Career Development, 21,* 11–22.

Caplow, T. (1947). Rumors in war. *Social Forces, 25,* 298–302.

Covin, T. J. (1993). Managing workforce reduction: A survey of employee reactions and implications for management consultants. *Organization Development Journal, 11,* 67–76.

Covin, T. J., & Kilmann, R. H. (1990). Participant perceptions of positive and negative influences on large-scale change. *Group and Organization Studies, 15,* 233–248.

Damanpour, F. (1987). The adoption of technological, administrative, and ancillary innovations: Impact of organizational factors. *Journal of Management, 13,* 675–688.

Davis, K. (1972). *Human behavior at work: Human relations and organizational behavior* (4th ed.). New York: McGraw-Hill.

Davis, K. (1975, June). Cut those rumors down to size. *Supervisory Management,* pp. 2–6.

DiFonzo, N. (2000). Why we measure. In J. Felton (Ed.), *Proceedings of International Symposium IV: Putting the yardstick to PR: How do we measure effectiveness globally?* (pp. 1–7). Gainesville, FL: Institute for Public Relations.

DiFonzo, N., & Bordia, P. (1997). Rumor and prediction: Making sense (but losing dollars) in the stock market. *Organizational Behavior and Human Decision Processes, 71,* 329–353.

DiFonzo, N., & Bordia, P. (1998). A tale of two corporations: Managing uncertainty during organizational change. *Human Resource Management, 37,* 295–303.

DiFonzo, N., & Bordia, P. (2000). How top PR professionals handle hearsay: Corporate rumors, their effects, and strategies to manage them. *Public Relations Review, 26,* 173–190.

DiFonzo, N., & Bordia, P. (2002a). Rumor and stable-cause attribution in prediction and behavior. *Organizational Behavior and Human Decision Processes, 88,* 785–800.

DiFonzo, N., & Bordia, P. (2002b). Corporate rumor activity, belief, and accuracy. *Public Relations Review, 150,* 1–19.

DiFonzo, N., & Bordia, P. (in press-a). *The social and organizational psychology of rumor.* Washington, DC: American Psychological Association.

DiFonzo, N., & Bordia, P. (in press-b). Rumors influence: Toward a dynamic social influence theory of rumor. In A. R. Pratkenis (Ed.), *The science of social influence.* Philadelphia: Psychology Press.

DiFonzo, N., Bordia, P., & Rosnow, R. L. (1994). Reining in rumors. *Organizational Dynamics, 23*, 47–62.

DiFonzo, N., Bordia, P., & Winterkorn, R. (2003, February). *Distrust is a key ingredient in negative rumor transmission.* Paper presented at the 4th Annual Meeting of the Society for Personality and Social Psychologists, Los Angeles, CA.

Distorted view of star spurred UFO rumors. (1997, March 28). *Rochester Democrat and Chronicle*, p. 8A.

Emory, D. (1998, September 9). *What is sodium laureth sulfate … and why are people saying those awful things about it?* Retrieved January 2, 2003, from http://urbanlegends.miningco.com/library/weekly/aa090998.htm

Esposito, J. L. (1986/1987). Subjective factors and rumor transmission: A field investigation of the influence of anxiety, importance, and belief on rumormongering (Doctoral dissertation, Temple University, 1986). *Dissertation Abstracts International, 48*, 596B.

Esposito, J. L., & Rosnow, R. L. (1983, April). Corporate rumors: How they start and how to stop them. *Management Review*, pp. 44–49.

Festinger, L. (1957). *A theory of cognitive dissonance.* Evanston, IL: Row, Peterson.

Fine, G. A. (1992). *Manufacturing tales: Sex and money in contemporary legends.* Knoxville: University of Tennessee Press.

Fine, G. A., & Khawaja, I. (2005). Celebrating Arabs and grateful terrorists: Rumor and the politics of plausibility. In G. A. Fine, C. Heath, & V. Campion-Vincent (Eds.), *Rumor mills: The social impact of rumor and legend* (pp. 189–205). New Brunswick, NJ: Transaction.

Foster, E. K. (2004). Research on gossip: Taxonomy, methods, and future directions. *Review of General Psychology, 8*(2), 78–99.

Freedman, A. M. (1991, May 10). Rumor turns fantasy into bad dream. *The Wall Street Journal*, pp. B1, B5.

Gluckman, M. (1963). Gossip and scandal. *Current Anthropology, 4*, 307–316.

Harcourt, J., Richerson, V., & Wattier, M. J. (1991). A national study of middle managers' assessment of organization communication quality. *Journal of Business Communication, 28*, 348–365.

Hari, J. (2002, December 31). "Well, they would say that, wouldn't they?" *Australian Financial Review*, p. 42.

Hellweg, S. A. (1987). Organizational grapevines. In B. Dervin & M. J. Voigt, *Progress in communication sciences* (Vol. 8, pp. 213–230). Norwood, NJ: Ablex.

Higham, T. M. (1951). The experimental study of the transmission of rumour. *British Journal of Psychology, 42*, 42–55.

Hirschhorn, L. (1983). *Cutting back: Retrenchment and redevelopment of human and community services.* San Francisco: Jossey-Bass.

Houmanfar, R., & Johnson, R. (2003). Organizational implications of gossip and rumor. *Journal of Organizational Behavior Management, 23*(2/3), 117–138.

Hunsaker, P. L., & Coombs, M. W. (1988). Mergers and acquisitions: Managing the emotional issues. *Personnel Journal, 67*, 56–78.

Jaeger, M. E., Anthony, S., & Rosnow, R. L. (1980). Who hears what from whom and with what effect: A study of rumor. *Personality and Social Psychology Bulletin, 6*, 473–478.

Jung, C. G. (1910/1916). Ein Beitrag zur Psychologie des Gerüchtes. *Zentralblatt für Psychoanalyse 1*: 81–90. Reprinted in *Collected papers on analytical psychology* (pp. 176–190) (C. E. Long, Trans.). New York: Moffat Yard.

Jung, C. G. (1959). A visionary rumour. *Journal of Analytical Psychology*, 4, 5–19.

Kamins, M. A., Folkes, V. S., & Perner, L. (1997). Consumer responses to rumors: Good news, bad news. *Journal of Consumer Psychology* 6(2), 165–187.

Kapferer, J. N. (1987). A mass poisoning rumor in Europe. *Public Opinion Quarterly*, 53, 467–481.

Kapferer, J. N. (1993). *Rumors: Uses, interpretations, and images.* New Brunswick, NJ: Transaction.

Kerner, O., Lindsay, J. V., Harris, F. R., Abel, I. W., Brooke, E. W., Thornton, C. B., Corman, J. C., Wilkins, R., McCulloch, W. M., Peden K. G., & Jenkins, H. (1968). *Report of the National Advisory Commission cn Civil Disorders* (Report No. 1968 O-291-729). Washington, DC: U.S. Government Printing Office.

Kimmel, A. J. (2004). *Rumors and rumor control: A manager's guide to understanding and combating rumors.* Mahwah, NJ: Lawrence Erlbaum Associates.

Kimmel, A. J., & Keefer, R. (1991). Psychological correlates of the transmission and acceptance of rumors about AIDS. *Journal of Applied Social Psychology, 21,* 1608–1628.

Knapp, R. H. (1944). A psychology of rumor. *Public Opinion Quarterly,* 8, 22–27.

Knopf, T. A. (1975). *Rumor, race and riots.* New Brunswick, NJ: Transaction.

Koenig, F. W. (1985). *Rumor in the marketplace: The social psychology of commercial hearsay.* Dover, MA: Auburn House.

Lazar, R. J. (1973). Stock market price movements as collective behavior. *International Journal of Contemporary Sociology, 10,* 133–147.

Leavitt, H. J., & Mueller, R. A. (1951). Some effects of feedback on communication. *Human Relations,* 4, 401–410.

Marting, B. (1969). *A study of grapevine communication patterns in a manufacturing organization.* Unpublished doctoral dissertation, Arizona State University, Tempe.

McAdam, J. R. (1962). *The effect of verbal interaction on the serial reproduction of rumor.* Unpublished doctoral dissertation, Indiana University, Bloomington.

Mirvis, P. H. (1985). Negotiations after the sale: The roots and ramifications of conflict in an acquisition. *Journal of Occupational Behaviour,* 6, 65–84.

Modic, S. J. (1989, May 15). Grapevine rated most believable. *Industry Week,* pp. 11, 14.

Mosemak, J. (2000, January 18). Caught in the grips of a hoax. *USA Today,* p. 3D.

Muniz, A. M., & O'Guinn, T. C. (2001). Brand community. *Journal of Consumer Research, 27*(4), 412–432.

Newstrom, J. W., Monczka, R. E., & Reif, W. E. (1974). Perceptions of the grapevine: Its value and influence. *Journal of Business Communication, 11*(3), 12–20.

Pezzo, M. V., & Beckstead, J. W. (in press). A multi-level analysis of rumor transmission: Effect of anxiety and belief in two field experiments. *Basic and Applied Social Psychology.*

Pound J., & Zeckhauser, R. (1990). Clearly heard on the street: The effect of takeover rumors on stock prices. *Journal of Business, 63,* 291–308.

Prasad, J. (1935). The psychology of rumour: A study relating to the great Indian earthquake of 1934. *British Journal of Psychology, 26,* 1–15.

Richardson, P., & Denton, D. K. (1996). Communicating change. *Human Resource Management, 35,* 203–216.

Rose, A. M. (1951). Rumor in the stock market. *Public Opinion Quarterly, 15,* 461–486.

Rosnow, R. L. (1974). On rumor. *Journal of Communication, 24*(3), 26–38.

Rosnow, R. L. (1980). Psychology of rumor reconsidered. *Psychological Bulletin, 87*, 578–591.

Rosnow, R. L. (1988). Rumor as communication: A contextualist approach. *Journal of Communication, 38*, 12–28.

Rosnow, R. L. (1991). Inside rumor: A personal journey. *American Psychologist, 46*, 484–496.

Rosnow, R. L. (2001). Rumor and gossip in interpersonal interaction and beyond: A social exchange perspective. In R. M. Kowalski (Ed.), *Behaving badly: Aversive behaviors in interpersonal relationships* (pp. 203–232). Washington, DC: American Psychological Association.

Rosnow, R. L., Esposito, J. L., & Gibney, L. (1988). Factors influencing rumor spreading: Replication and extension. *Language and Communication, 8*, 29–42.

Rosnow, R. L., & Fine, G. A. (1976). *Rumor and gossip: The social psychology of hearsay*. New York: Elsevier.

Rosnow, R. L., & Georgoudi, M. (Eds.). (1986). *Contextualism and understanding in behavioral science: Implications for research and theory*. New York: Praeger.

Rosnow, R. L., & Kimmel, A. J. (2000). Rumor. In A. E. Kazdin (Ed.), *Encyclopedia of psychology* (Vol. 7, pp. 122–123). New York: Oxford University Press & American Psychological Association.

Rosnow, R. L., Yost, J. H., Esposito, J. L. (1986). Belief in rumor and likelihood of rumor transmission. *Language and Communication, 6*, 189–194.

Ross, L., Lepper, M. R., & Hubbard, M. (1975). Perseverance in self-perception and social perception: Biased attributional processes in the debriefing paradigm. *Journal of Personality and Social Psychology, 32*, 880–892.

Rudolph, E. (1971). *A study of informal communication patterns within a multi-shift public utility organizational unit*. Unpublished doctoral dissertation, University of Denver.

Schachter, S., & Burdick, H. (1955). A field experiment on rumor transmission and distortion. *Journal of Abnormal and Social Psychology, 50*, 363–371.

Schweiger, D. M., & Denisi, A. S. (1991). Communication with employees following a merger: A longitudinal field experiment. *Academy of Management Journal, 34*, 110–135.

Shibutani, T. (1966). *Improvised news: A sociological study of rumor*. Indianapolis: Bobbs-Merrill.

Sinha, D. (1952). Behaviour in a catastrophic situation: A psychological study of reports and rumours. *British Journal of Psychology, 43*, 200–209.

Smeltzer, L. R. (1991). An analysis of strategies for announcing organization-wide change. *Group and Organization Studies, 16*, 5–24.

Smeltzer, L. R., & Zener, M. F. (1992). Development of a model for announcing major layoffs. *Group and Organization Studies, 17*, 446–472.

Tesser, A., & Rosen, S. (1975). The reluctance to transmit bad news. In L. Berkowitz (Ed.), *Advances in experimental social psychology* (Vol. 18, pp. 193–232). New York: Academic Press.

Tragedy in California: Cult mixed monasticism, computers, fixation on UFO. (1997, March 28). *Rochester Democrat and Chronicle*, p. 8A.

Turner, R. H. (1994). Rumor as intensified information seeking: Earthquake rumors in China and the United States. In R. R. Dynes & K. J. Tierney (Eds.), *Disasters, collective behavior, and social organization* (pp. 244–256). Newark: University of Delaware Press.

Turner, R. H., & Killian, L. M. (1972). *Collective behavior* (2nd ed.). Englewood Cliffs, NJ: Prentice-Hall.

Tybout, A. M., Calder, B. J., & Sternthal, B. (1981). Using information processing theory to design marketing strategies. *Journal of Marketing Research, 18*, 73–79.

Unger, H. (1979, June). Psst—heard about Pop Rocks? Business rumors and how to counteract them. *Canadian Business*, p. 39.

Walker, C. J., & Beckerle, C. A. (1987). The effect of anxiety on rumor transmission. *Journal of Social Behavior and Personality, 2*, 353–360.

Walker, C. J., & Blaine, B. E. (1989, April). *The virulence of dread rumors: A field experiment.* Poster presented at the meeting of the Eastern Psychological Association, Boston.

Walton, E. (1961). How efficient is the grapevine? *Personnel, 38*, 45–49.

Wegner, D. M., Coulton, G. F., & Wenzlaff, R. (1985). The transparency of denial: Briefing in the debriefing paradigm. *Journal of Personality and Social Psychology, 49*, 338–346.

Wegner, D. M., Wenzlaff, R., Kerker, R. M., & Beattie, A. E. (1981). Incrimination through innuendo: Can media questions become public answers? *Journal of Personality and Social Psychology, 40*, 822–832.

Weinberg, S. B., & Eich, R. K. (1978). Fighting fire with fire: Establishment of a rumor control center. *Communication Quarterly, 26*(3), 26–31.

Werner, W. P. (1976). *The distortion of rumor as related to prejudice and stereotypes.* Unpublished master's thesis, Montclair State College, Montclair, NJ.

Wert, S. R., & Salovey, P. (2004). A social comparison account of gossip. *Review of General Psychology, 8*(2), 122–137.

Wesman, G. (1997, April 17). Myths, lice and theater seats. *Erie Morning News*, p. 1B.

What's the word on the streets of Baghdad? (2004, June 25). *Baghdad Mosquito*, p. 7.

Zaremba, A. (1988). Working with the organizational grapevine. *Personnel Journal, 67*, 38–42.

14

Making Sense of Escalating Commitment to a Failing Course of Action

Donald A. Hantula and David Landman
Temple University

Throughout his career, Ralph Rosnow puzzled about how people make sense of their social worlds. He often went beyond the safe world of the laboratory for ideas and problems to solve, and did not shy away from gleaning bits of wisdom from the popular culture, as recounted in his "personal journey" inside rumor (Rosnow, 1991). This chapter takes the 1991 paper as an inspiration to tackle another vexing problem in the organizational world: escalation and persistence of commitment to a failing course of action. At first glance, it would appear that continuing in a failing course of action would be a reflection of irrationality, or an intellectual deficit. However, another perspective views decision makers in escalation situations as individuals striving to divine the right direction amid a quagmire of conflicting and confusing information. Popular attention sees that these individuals' decisions are losing dollars, but a more nuanced analysis reveals that the individuals are trying to make sense.

CONTEXT

In his antiwar folk song, "Waist Deep in the Big Muddy," Pete Seeger described the quandary of the Vietnam War, marked by escalating setbacks leading to increasing U.S. commitment. The decision-making processes that led to involvement and escalation in Vietnam have been cited by psychologists as a prototype of escalation of commitment (Staw, 1976). In retrospect, it appears that decisions made early in the process set the stage. On May 6th, 1950, the United States began what was to become a 25-year commitment to stifling the spread of communism in Indochina. For the next 15 years, the United States provided an increasing amount of support to South Vietnam, support that proved to be inadequate in defending the country. At this point, President Lyndon B. Johnson was faced with a crucial decision: escalate support to full military involvement or allow South Vietnam to lose to the North. This decision was a critical point in the United States' involvement, because escalation to war would mark a great increase in the United States' commitment to achieving the objectives of containing communism. In a memo to the president, Undersecretary of State George Ball (1965) warned that "Once we suffer large casualties, we will have started a well-nigh irreversible process. Our involvement will be so great that we cannot—without national humiliation—stop short of achieving our complete objectives. Of the two possibilities I think humiliation would be more likely than the achievement of our objectives—even after we have paid terrible costs."

Despite the negative prospects for the war, the United States landed the first American ground troops in Vietnam on March 6th, 1965. The troops were met with fierce opposition and suffered setback after setback. Following each setback, more troops were sent to battle in what was becoming an impossible war to win. Just as Undersecretary Ball had suggested, once the United States suffered significant casualties, political leaders were unable to withdraw without achieving their objectives. However, in 1969, a deescalation process began, and in 1972, America pulled the last U.S. ground troops from South Vietnam. On April 30th, 1975, Saigon fell to the North Vietnamese and the United States evacuated the American embassy in Vietnam, ending over a decade of escalating conflict that resulted in the loss of 58,721 American lives, $165 billion of direct war expenses, and defeat by the North Vietnamese communists (Mohr, 1985).

The purpose of this example is not to comment on whether or not the United States should have become involved in the situation in Vietnam, nor should it be taken as a veiled reference to current U.S. foreign policy and military action. Instead, it serves as a riveting example of a decision-making process that is marked by a situation in which "we become more deeply a prisoner of the process" (Janis, 1972, p. 103) with each increase in our commitment to a decision (acknowledged by Staw, 1976, who used the title of Seeger's song in the title of his journal article).

ESCALATION AND PERSISTENCE OF COMMITMENT

Escalation and persistence of commitment have been defined as situations in which "decision makers recommit resources to a failed or failing course of action" (Bowen, 1987, p. 52). In escalation situations, a decision maker will choose to continue a failing course of action rather than cut losses and end the project, sometimes referred to as "throwing good money after bad." Escalation and persistence of commitment have been used to explain decision making on individual, organizational, and governmental levels. Individual escalation is evident in decisions of whether to continue repairing an aging automobile or whether to continue investing in a declining stock (Goltz, 1992, 1993; Hantula & Crowell, 1994a). Organizational-level escalation is apparent in decisions of whether to continue to fund a failing product venture or to continue investing in a failing information technology (IT) project (Drummond, 1998). Government-level escalation has been applied to explain the United States' involvement in the Vietnam conflict (Staw, 1997) and to London's construction of the Millennium Dome (Drummond, 1998). Escalation of commitment in the face of failure appears to be a direct violation of rational choice theory, which dictates that decision making should be a maximization process whereby the decision maker maximizes reward or returns (Herrnstein, 1990). This apparent violation has sparked research for over 2 decades into the causes of escalation, and it continues to intrigue researchers today, perhaps because escalation costs individuals, organizations, and governments a great deal of resources.

For example, the massive monetary loss incurred as a result of the Long Island Lighting Company's (LILCO) continued investment in the failing Shoreham Nuclear Power Plant has been identified as an example of escalation and persistence of commitment on an organizational level (Ross & Staw, 1993). Over a period of 23 years, LILCO escalated their initial investment in the construction of a new power plant from $75 million in 1966 to $5 billion when the project was finally abandoned in 1989. Initially, planners estimated that the project would cost $75 million and be completed in 1973. However, over the following 2 decades, nuclear power declined in popularity, resulting in a great deal of public opposition that hindered the completion of the plant. In the face of this negative feedback, LILCO invested greater and greater amounts of money into the completion of the plant, accumulating a total cost of $5 billion for a plant that never went into full operation. In another hallmark example of escalation, decision makers in British Columbia increased their investment in plans to host a World's Fair in 1986 (Ross & Staw, 1993). Over the course of 7 years (1978–1985), the provincial government escalated its investment from $78 million to $1.5 billion, despite increasingly negative prospects for success. In this case, the gradual growth of escalation decisions led to a situation that has been described by Ross and Staw (1993) as a prototype of escalation of commitment.

In an analysis of National Basketball Association (NBA) teams from 1980 through 1986, Staw and Hoang (1995) examined sunk costs (operationalized as draft order pick) incurred to acquire players and those players' subsequent amount of court time and tenure with the team. According to rational decision making, after the draft teams should play and retain players with the best performance, without regard to sunk costs. However, Staw and Hoang found a significant sunk cost effect influencing coaches' decision making. After controlling for performance, injuries, trade status, and position, Staw and Hoang noted that players selected earlier in the draft received more court time, enjoyed longer team tenure, and were less likely to be traded to other teams than those players who were selected later in the draft. Camerer and Weber (1999) replicated Staw and Hoang's study using a new set of NBA data, finding evidence of escalation but only half as strong in magnitude and statistical strength as that reported in Staw and Hoang's study.

Several explanations have been offered to account for escalation and persistence of commitment. The majority of these explanations can be categorized as psychological determinants, social determinants, organizational determinants, or project determinants. Psychological determinants of escalation include the desire to recover sunk costs (Arkes & Blumer, 1985; Garland, 1990), the self-justification of prior decisions (Staw, 1976; Staw & Fox, 1977; Whyte, 1991), reinforcement issues (Hantula & Crowell, 1994b; Platt, 1973), framing effects (Kahneman & Tversky, 1984; Whyte, 1993), individual differences and anonymity (Rao & Monk, 1999), and the involvement of the confirmation bias when evaluating decisions. Social determinants of escalation include modeling (Brockner, Rubin, & Lang, 1981), cultural norms, and the desire not to appear wasteful (Staw & Fox, 1977). Organizational determinants include the organization's tolerance for failure and the level of political support for the project. Project determinants include level of project completion (Garland & Conlon, 1998), closing costs, salvage value, causes of the setbacks hindering the project's success, and the economic results of pursuing or abandoning the project. Although all of these factors may have an influence on escalation, the majority of escalation studies have focused on self-justification, sunk costs, and reinforcement issues and their influence on decision making.

Self-Justification

According to self-justification theory (Staw, 1976), decision makers have a strong drive to rationalize their behavior. This theory, which was based on cognitive dissonance theory (Festinger, 1962), suggests that decision makers feel responsible to justify the rationality of their decisions. In escalation scenarios, decision makers escalate in the prospect of turning a failing project around, hoping that the potential success of the project will rationalize past decision making. The failure of their initial decision causes them to feel dissonance that they believe can be resolved by turning the project around, leading to an escalation of commitment to the failing course of action.

Staw (1976) asserted that individuals were more likely to escalate commitment in an ongoing project when they were induced to feel responsible for a prior project-related decision that incurred an initial sunk cost. Following Staw's findings, the self-justification explanation of escalation emerged as a dominant theory of the phenomenon. However, the self-justification effect has been difficult to replicate in single-choice decision scenarios, wherein a task involves a single reallocation decision over one decision round (Armstrong, Coviello, & Safranek, 1993), and has never been found in multiple-allocation scenarios, wherein a task involves several reallocation decisions over repeated decision rounds (Bragger, Bragger, Hantula, & Kirnan, 1998; Goltz, 1993; Hantula & Bragger, 1999; McCain, 1986; Staw & Fox, 1977).

Sunk Costs

Sunk costs are defined as any prior investments of money, effort, or time that are unrecoverable regardless of final investment outcome. Because sunk costs are unrecoverable, rational decision making would dictate that they should not influence future decision making. However, decision makers are sometimes misguided by the belief that they can recover sunk costs through continued investment, and feel that they have too much invested to quit (Teger, 1980) without turning around their investment.

A classic scenario of the sunk cost effect was demonstrated by Arkes and Blumer (1985), who provided participants with a scenario involving a decision to continue investing in a failed stealth aircraft project in which 90% of the budget has been spent. Participants were told that although their plane was 90% complete, another company had just completed a more cost-effective model, thereby rendering the model obsolete. Although rational choice theory would dictate the investors' immediate withdrawal from the failed investment, over 85% of the participants chose to commit the final 10% of the research funds to complete the project. However, when participants were presented with a similar situation without the initial sunk cost, fewer than 17% of the participants decided to invest. The sunk cost effect has been replicated several times for single-choice decision scenarios (Garland, 1990; Garland & Newport, 1991).

However, the sunk cost effect does not always occur in experimental research. Garland, Sandefur, and Rogers (1990) noted a negative sunk cost effect on escalation in experienced petroleum geologists; the greater the sunk cost was, the less likely the participants were to escalate following negative feedback. Bornstein, Emler, and Chapman (1999) found no sunk cost effect in a sample of medical residents making a one-shot decision of whether to continue a failing medical treatment plan. Furthermore, no sunk cost effect has been demonstrated in multiple-allocation studies (Goltz, 1992, 1993; Hantula & Crowell, 1994b). It is important to note that the research that has found sunk cost effects deals with decision making in single-choice scenarios; in fact, these studies showed an opposite effect, namely that those individuals who initially invested the most money early on invested the least when failing. However, given that most real-world decisions involve several investments over a period of time in a dynamic environment, the relevance of the experimental sunk cost research is questionable.

Equivocality and Reinforcement Schedules

Initially discussed by Bowen (1987), *equivocality* refers to uncertainty of information; feedback high in equivocality provides ambiguous information, and feedback low in equivocality (unequivocal) provides clear information. Bowen suggested that decision makers escalate under conditions of uncertainty in order to reduce equivocality. Equivocality is operationalized as information that is temporally ordered so that a decision maker is unable to discern a predictable pattern and make accurate predictions of future performance. In addition, Bowen proposed that the presence of a standard by which to measure feedback might serve to decrease equivocality and attenuate its effect on escalation and persistence. A similar theory of escalation as decision dilemmas comes from the economic literature. Dixit's (1992) theory of hysteresis posited that decision makers persist in their investment merely as a way to gather more information (reduce uncertainty) with which to make their withdrawal decision. According to both theories, an escalation scenario is a decision dilemma in which the decision maker attempts to make sense of highly uncertain conditions by persisting or escalating, thereby generating more information (at a cost) by which to make a final decision.

Goltz (1992) examined the relationship between reinforcement and escalation using a dynamic multi-allocation, computer-based Microworld (DiFonzo, Hantula, & Bordia, 1998) investment simulation. The innovative use of a dynamic computer simulation allowed Goltz to investigate escalation beyond the traditional single-choice decision scenarios. Investment feedback varied and was presented under either a partial reinforcement (PRF) or continuous reinforcement (CRF) schedule during an acquisition phase. Despite the fact that during an extinction (failure) phase all participants received losses of 10% of their investment, participants in the PRF group invested more dollars than did those in the CRF group. This finding—that reinforcement history influences escalation tendencies—began a new line of escalation research that examined escalation as a dynamic, multiple-decision process (Goltz, 1993; Hantula & Crowell, 1994b).

In the first empirical study directly testing equivocality's effect on escalation, Bragger et al. (1998) manipulated uncertainty by manipulating feedback variability and information availability regarding a failing investment. Escalation was greater in both the highly variable feedback condition (compared to less variable feedback) and in the information unavailable condition (compared to information available), providing support for both Dixit's (1992) hysteresis theory and Bowen's (1987) equivocality theory. In both cases, escalation was directly related to the level of uncertainty experienced by the participants. Further support for these theories came from Hantula and Bragger's (1999) study[1] that manipulated both feedback variability and the presence of a standard (in the form of a sales quota) by which to measure feedback. Hantula and Bragger reported that participants receiving feedback high in equivocality were more likely to escalate commitment compared to those in a low-equivocality situation, and, more importantly, that the standard served to attenuate escalation by reducing feedback ambiguity and therefore reducing equivocality.

Both equivocality theory (Bowen, 1987) and hysteresis theory (Dixit, 1992) resemble reinforcement processes and suggest that escalation of commitment is not irrational. Instead, escalation and persistence in the face of uncertainty are a function of the decision maker seeking more information about the status of their situation. This idea—that escalation is more reasonable than once thought—contrasts with earlier descriptions of escalation as a decision-making error. Instead, equivocality theory and hysteresis theory view escalation as a decision dilemma in which escalation is a method of seeking to clarify equivocal information. Once a substantial sunk cost has been incurred, unless the perceived probability of failure is high, continuance (although sometimes costly) leads to more information by which to make a final decision.

Deescalation of Commitment

Although escalation of commitment attracted attention and inspired initial work in this area, deescalation was explored in later years. Garland et al. (1990) found that, when presented with high sunk costs and clearly

---

[1]Bragger et al. (1998) was actually a follow-up study to Hantula and Bragger (1999), but, due to differing publication schedules, Bragger et al. (1998) was published first.

negative feedback, experienced decision makers were more likely to deescalate than escalate, in line with Bowen's (1987) equivocality hypothesis that unequivocal failure leads to rapid deescalation. Similarly, Drummond (1995) found that when people are presented with obviously negative feedback, they will quickly withdraw instead of escalate. Furthermore, multiple-decision round approaches to escalation have demonstrated that the escalation effect fades fairly quickly after repeated negative feedback is provided (Goltz, 1992). Logically, because escalation is often a destructive force in organizations, several strategies for attenuating escalation have been explored. The following moderators have been identified as reducing the likelihood that decision makers will escalate their commitment in the face of failure.

Threat Reduction.   One method that has been proposed to reduce escalation is to reduce the perceived threat of failure to the decision maker. Campbell's (1969) trapped administrators committed themselves (and resources) to social programs and were not able to admit error (withdraw) because of the severe consequences for failure. Organizations that have a higher tolerance for failure and that do not impose severe punishment for failure reduce the threat of repercussions that facilitate escalation (Keil & Robey, 1999). Through interviews with experienced information systems auditors, Keil and Robey discovered significant deescalation in software companies that had a high tolerance for failure. Simonson and Staw (1992) noted a reduction in escalation when they told participants before an experiment that the task would be very difficult and that prior research had indicated that the participants' performance on the experiment did not reflect on their intelligence or real-world decision-making skills. Heng, Tan, and Wei (2003) discerned that deescalation was facilitated when managers and peers provided the decision maker with assurance that failure would not effect his or her reputation (or job), but this effect was only seen in low sunk cost scenarios and not when high sunk costs were incurred.

Decision-Making Responsibility.   Keil and Robey (1999) suggested that separating the decision-making process and decision maker may attenuate the self-justification effect by reducing the perceived responsibility for a prior sunk cost. They found a significant deescalation effect in information systems (IS) audit managers when the initial decision maker did not make project evaluation decisions following his or her initial decision. This responsibility effect has been supported in several prior studies that found escalation in situations in which the decision maker was responsible for past sunk costs versus when the decision maker was not (Staw, 1976). Furthermore, Staw, Barsade, and Koput (1997) noted significant deescalation in problem loan scenarios when senior managers responsible for the initial loan decisions left the firm, passing the responsibility to a new decision maker. However, it is important to note that when a project is passed along to a new champion, the consequences for failure may remain with the original decision maker. Therefore, lack of consequences, and not level of responsibility, may be responsible for the deescalation effect.

Thorough Decision Making.   One method to reduce escalation is directed toward encouraging people to think about the problem from multiple perspectives rather than use a single-minded approach. One aspect of this method is a strategy labeled *counterexplanation,* in which a decision maker is required to list any potential unexpected outcomes to his or her decision. Beeler (1998) discovered that when participants engaged in counterexplanation following an initial allocation decision, they escalated less than did those who did not engage in counterexplanation. A similar method came from Brody and Frank (1999), who posited that when considering bank loans, the loan officers should play "devil's advocate" and write down all the reasons that the loan could go bad. Brody and Frank indicated that doing this allows loan officers to be more alert for signs that the loan should be discontinued. In a meta-analysis on the devil's advocate method, Schwenk (1990) discerned that the controversy introduced by the devil's advocate improves managerial decision making. However, Simonson and Staw (1992) did not see significant differences between decision makers who used this method or those who did not, potentially because increasing the amount of alternatives may also increase equivocality.

Goal Setting.   Goal setting was proposed by Drummond (2003) as a method to limit the effects of escalation. Simonson and Staw (1992) had found that when decision makers set goals beforehand (as minimum targets) and determined that if these goals were not met would then immediate withdrawal from the situation would result, escalation was attenuated in the face of failure. Keil and Robey (1999) discovered that when these goals were made public, significant deescalation followed failure. Goal setting is another way to reduce equivocality; if returns fall below a certain point, then the decision maker has unequivocal feedback to withdraw. Hantula and Bragger (1999) demonstrated this by providing some participants with a sales goal and some with no goal in a multiple-decision marketing simulation. The participants with the goal deescalated more quickly than did those without a goal.

Outcome Accountability.   Simonson and Staw (1992) noted attenuation in escalation when they told participants in their study that their overall evaluation would not be based on the decision outcome but rather on the logic of their decision-making process. Furthermore, Kite, Katz, and Zarzfski

(1996) found that frequent performance evaluations led to increased escalation in project managers working on long-term capital-budgeting projects. Kite et al. hypothesized that such frequent evaluations force decision makers to escalate commitment in an attempt to maximize their short-term performance appraisals rather than concentrate on long-term results. Furthermore, Kite et al. asserted that long-term performance appraisals are more effective, because they allow decision makers to accept short-term losses and concentrate on long-term results. Keil and Robey (1999) also found that, when organizations evaluate their decision makers on decision process rather than decision outcome, deescalation was facilitated.

Decision-Making Experience. Garland et al.'s (1990) assertion that experience and training can lead to more "rational" decision making is interesting and leads us to question of whether escalation decreases as decision-making expertise increases. This idea, although logical, has not been supported by research—in fact, quite the opposite trend has emerged in the escalation literature. Although limited, most escalation studies have found significant escalation in experienced decision makers. These decision makers included experienced accounting and finance managers (Beeler, 1998), IS audit and control professionals (Keil, Mann, & Rai, 2000), and bank executives (Staw et al., 1997). Furthermore, all of the case studies discussed in this chapter involved decision makers with extensive experience, including the LILCO debacle (Ross & Staw, 1993), British Columbia's World Fair escalation (Ross & Staw, 1986), escalation in the NBA (Staw & Hoang, 1995), and escalation in the Vietnam War. Experience does not attenuate escalation in the face of failure; in fact, it can make such escalation worse (Bragger, Hantula, Bragger, Krinan, & Kutcher, 2003).

Escalation Outside of the Laboratory

Although real-world examples of escalation inspired this line of research and continue to rivet people's attention, most if not all empirical studies of escalation and persistence have been conducted in a laboratory setting, with participants ranging from introductory psychology students to graduate business students. The one laboratory study that examined escalation within the realm of the participants' decision-making experience (petroleum geology) found no escalation in the face of unequivocal failure (Garland et al., 1990). There have been several case-study qualitative analyses of organizational and public decision-making escalation (Drummond, 1994, 1998; Ross & Staw, 1986, 1993), but real-world quantitative analysis has been limited because of legal and ethical barriers (Arkes & Blumer, 1985; Staw & Hoang, 1995). However, the limited number of real-world analyses have been important in illuminating the nature of escalation outside of the laboratory.

Staw et al. (1997) examined escalation of commitment in bank executives, hypothesizing that the turnover of senior bank managers would be followed by deescalation of problem loans. This hypothesis was based on the assumption that when the initial decision makers depart from the firm, the new decision makers will feel less self-justification pressure than did the initial decision makers. As predicted, Staw et al. found that increased turnover predicted a higher likelihood that banks would not escalate their commitment to problem loans.

Lind, Kutcher, Bragger, and Hantula (1999) searched for evidence of escalation or persistence of commitment in articles describing business failures in two business magazines, *Fortune* and *Business Week,* covering a period of 2½ years (January 1996–June 1998). Through their analysis of 128 articles that were identified as escalation/persistence situations, Lind et al. identified the major determinants involved in the escalation or persistence situation. The escalation determinants used were proposed by Staw and Ross (1987) and included project variables, psychological variables, social variables, and organizational variables. Lind et al. (1999) discovered that 49.1% of the scenarios included characteristics from all four determinants, 36.8% from three, and less than 13% included two or fewer determinants. In addition, they also found that escalation/persistence developed over time in many cases, with 63% of the cases involving multiple decisions over a period of time. This analysis was unique in that it strengthened the laboratory concept of escalation and persistence as a real-world business event that is based on several factors, including project, social, psychological and organizational variables.

In another qualitative analysis of escalation, Keil, Mann, and Rai (2000) surveyed over 2,000 IS audit and control professionals, hoping to identify the frequency and drivers of escalation in software projects. Software projects are particularly susceptible to escalation, with reports of overspending and difficulty meeting time constraints common in the managing information systems (MIS) literature. In fact, Johnson (1995) reported that only 16% of software projects were completed on time and within budget in a survey of over 8,000 projects. On average, these projects went more than 200% over initial budgeting. Escalation in software projects has been highly publicized, including Drummond's (1996) lengthy discussion of London's Taurus project and California's Statewide Automated Child Support System (Newcombe, 1998). Keil et al. (2000) noted that escalation of commitment occurred on average in 38% of all software projects. In fact, 81% of the respondents indicated that one or more of their past five projects involved escalation. Consistent with studies showing that deescalation eventually occurs, 75% of respondents said that escalation lasted a period of 2 years or less (Bragger et al., 1998; Garland, 1990; Goltz, 1992, 1993; McCain, 1986). However, cases of escalation up to 255 months were reported. In addition, as Lind et al. (1999) found, escalation of commitment was influenced by several variables, including project variables, psychological variables, social variables, and organizational variables. It is important to note, however, that Keil et al. (2000) operationalized escalation as an individual's continued investment in a project despite the *existence* of negative feedback rather than the individual's *knowledge* of negative information.

Although real-world escalation studies are limited, the past 2 decades of escalation research has provided us with a model by which to understand escalation and its causes. However, stark differences between laboratory and real-world research findings now lead to serious questions regarding the future of escalation research. First, the majority of laboratory studies of escalation have measured one decision at one point in time, yet have then been generalized to repeated and extended decision scenarios. Real-world escalation situations always involve repeated decisions. Second, most laboratory research has tested only one or two moderators of escalation. However, recent qualitative investigations suggest that project, psychological, social, and organizational variables are all operating in these situations. Third, decisions of any sort of importance are most often made in groups or teams in the world of modern organizations, yet nearly all laboratory escalation research has focused on individual decisions.

Whyte (1991) and Bazerman, Giuliano, and Appelman (1984) studied escalation in individuals and groups and did not find greater escalation in groups when using a single decision methodology. Schmidt, Montoya-Weiss, and Massey (2001) found the same. Kameda and Sugimori (1993) came to the same conclusion using a repeated decision methodology. In contrast, Seibert and Goltz (2001) found greater escalation in three-person decision-making groups than in individuals using a repeated decision methodology. Because these appear to be the extant studies comparing group and individual escalation, there is little to conclude from this research except to say that much more needs to be done.

AN AGENDA FOR FUTURE RESEARCH

Some 30 years after the initial studies appeared, escalation remains a riveting and often terrifying phenomenon. However, much has changed in the interim. In their 1993 paper that highlighted the LILCO debacle, Ross and Staw pointed out the discrepancy between the single-choice laboratory research on escalation and the temporal reality of escalation, commenting on the dearth of dynamic, multi-investment research on escalation and our lack of laboratory knowledge on escalation over time. Methodologically, early studies were by necessity of the paper-and-pencil, single-decision variety, but in the ensuing years access to inexpensive and easily programmable microcomputers has rendered such a static methodology largely irrelevant in the face of the sort of realism and interaction that can be created in a Microworld (DiFonzo et al, 1998). Indeed, given the ubiquity of computers in the workplace, computerized interactive studies should be high on both mundane as well as experimental realism. Furthermore, research with Mircroworlds has shown that the types of psychological variables that may be present at the beginning of an escalation situation (e.g., self-justification) may fade quickly (Goltz, 1993), or not be important at all (Bragger et al., 1998, 2003; Hantula & Bragger, 1999; McCain, 1986) when considering repeated decisions and that other variables they may engender escalation such as partial reinforcement (Hantula & Crowell, 1994b) or momentum (Goltz, 1999) change in time. Considering the definition of escalation, these prior one-shot studies may not be relevant to escalation of commitment at all. Instead, the phenomenon must be examined as a process over time rather than as a single decision. As such, paper-and-pencil, single-decision studies are now minimally informative and should not be continued.

The original emphasis on individual decision making in escalation should also be reconsidered. Although most psychological theory is developed clearly at the level of the individual—and, for theoretical ease, studies of individual decision makers initially makes sense—such a practice may also be myopic. In the case of escalation, where real-world studies show a preponderance of escalation decisions made in a group, this focus on individual decision makers may well have led research away from some important findings. Although it is acknowledged that individuals, not groups, make decisions, a group may be an important context that could conceivably limit or facilitate escalation, as shown by Seibert and Goltz (2001). Furthermore, the types of decisions made by groups versus individuals and the kind of information sought out (or ignored) by groups and individuals in escalation situations may be important clues, especially in light of Bowen's (1987) and Dixt's (1992) work on equivocality and hysteresis. Hence, further studies of escalation should include conditions with explicit group membership (if group decisions are to be compared to individual decisions), or study group processes during the course of escalation. Studies of individual decision makers may be minimally generalizable to escalation in the world outside the laboratory.

Theoretically, the initial emphasis on isolating a single controlling psychological variable should also be reconsidered. Analyses of real-world escalation dilemmas show clearly that no one single variable, state, trait, or mechanism accounts for escalation. In contrast, it appears that multiple variables at different levels and at different time scales may be operating in escalation situations. Furthermore, escalation is of interest to scholars from diverse disciplines, and each field may bring insights to individuals working in other fields. No one discipline or field holds a monopoly on truth, and—as current syntheses of psychological and economic theory in studies of escalation have shown (Bragger et al., 1998, 2003; Hantula & Bragger, 1999)—a deft combination of the best of both literatures leads to innovative questions and explanations that neither field would have developed on its own. Future escalation research should be deliberately interdisciplinary.

CONCLUSION

Ralph Rosnow studied, advanced, and catalogued many ways that we try to make sense of our social worlds, both as individuals in our daily lives and as scholars. As individuals, we are enlightened by his insights about our capacities and foibles; as scholars, we are guided by his careful articulation of methodological and theoretical issues. When trying to understand something as counterintuitive and frightening as escalation and persistence of commitment, it is crucial to have such a beacon to lead the way, reminding us that we are studying failing situations rather than failing people, and that the people caught in these situations are doing the best they can with the information they have available to them. Much like in scholarship, what is needed is not recrimination or criticism, but rather further research and more information.

REFERENCES

Arkes, H., & Blumer, C. (1985). The psychology of sunk cost. *Organizational Behavior & Human Decision Processes, 35*(1), 124–140.

Armstrong, J., Coviello, N., & Safranek, B. (1993). Escalation bias: Does it extend to marketing? *Journal of the Academy of Marketing Science, 21*(3), 247–253.

Bazerman, M., Giuliano, T., & Appelman, A. (1984). Escalation of commitment in individual and group decision making. *Organizational Behavior & Human Decision Processes, 33*(2), 141–152.

Beeler, J. (1998). Effects of counter-explanation on escalation of commitment: An experimental assessment of individual and collective decisions. *Advances in Accounting Behavioral Research, 1*, 85–89.

Bornstein, B., Emler, C., & Chapman, G. (1999). Rationality in medical treatment decisions: Is there a sunk-cost effect? *Social Science and Medicine, 49*(2), 215–222.

Bowen, M. G. (1987). The escalation phenomenon reconsidered: Decision dilemmas or decision errors? *Academy of Management Review, 12*(1), 52–66.

Bragger, J. D., Bragger, D., Hantula, D. A., & Kirnan, J. (1998). Hysteresis and uncertainty: The effect of uncertainty on delays to exit decisions. *Organizational Behavior & Human Decision Processes, 74*(3), 229–253.

Bragger, J. D., Hantula, D. A., Bragger, D., Kirnan, J., & Kutcher, E. (2003). When success breeds failure: History, hysteresis, and delayed exit decisions. *Journal of Applied Psychology, 88*(1), 6–14.

Brockner, J., Rubin, J., & Lang, E. (1981). Face-saving and entrapment. *Journal of Experimental Social Psychology, 17*(1), 68–79.

Brody, R. G., & Frank, K. (1999). Don't throw good money after bad. *Commercial Lending Review, 14*(3), 72–75.

Camerer, C. F., & Weber, R. A. (1999). The econometrics and behavioral economics of escalation of commitment: A re-examination of Staw and Hoang's NBA data. *Journal of Economic Behavior and Organization, 39*(1), 59–82.

Campbell, D. (1969). Reforms as experiments. *American Psychologist, 24*(4), 409–429.

DiFonzo, N., Hantula, D. A., & Bordia, P. (1998). Microworlds for experimental research: Having your (control and collections) cake, and realism too. *Behavior Research Methods, Instruments & Computers, 30*(2), 278–286.

Dixit, A. (1992). Investment and hysteresis. *Journal of Economic Perspectives, 6*(1), 107–132.

Drummond, H. (1994). Too little too late: A case study of escalation in decision making. *Organization Studies, 15*(4), 591–607.

Drummond, H. (1995). De-escalation in decision making: A case of a disastrous partnership. *Journal of Management Studies, 32*(3), 265–281.

Drummond, H. (1996). *Escalation in decision-making: The tragedy of Taurus.* Oxford, UK: Oxford University Press.

Drummond, H. (1998). Is escalation always irrational? *Organization Studies, 19*(6), 911–929.

Drummond, H. (2003). Take off optional, landing compulsory: Risk and escalation in decision making. *Business Strategy Review, 14*(1), 39–44.

Festinger, L. (1962). Cognitive dissonance. *Scientific American, 207*(4), 93–107.

Garland, H. (1990). Throwing good money after bad: The effect of sunk costs on the decision to escalate commitment to an ongoing project. *Journal of Applied Psychology, 75*(6), 728–731.

Garland, H., & Conlon, D. (1998). Too close to quit: The role of project completion in maintaining commitment. *Journal of Applied Social Psychology, 28*(22), 2025–2048.

Garland, H., & Newport, S. (1991). Effects of absolute and relative sunk costs on the decision to persist with a course of action. *Organizational Behavior & Human Decision Processes, 48*(1), 55–69.

Garland, H., Sandefur, C. A., & Rogers, A. C. (1990). De-escalation of commitment in oil exploration: When sunk costs and negative feedback coincide. *Journal of Applied Psychology, 75*(6), 721–727.

Goltz, S. M. (1992). A sequential learning analysis of decisions in organizations to escalate investments despite continuing costs or losses. *Journal of Applied Behavior Analysis, 25*(3), 561–574.

Goltz, S. M. (1993). Examining the joint roles of responsibility and reinforcement history in recommitment. *Decision Sciences, 24*(5), 977–994.

Goltz, S. M. (1999). Can't stop on a dime: The roles of matching and momentum in persistence of commitment. *Journal of Organizational Behavior Management, 19*(1), 37–63.

Hantula, D. A., & Bragger, J. D. (1999). The effects of feedback equivocality on escalation of commitment: An empirical investigation of decision dilemma theory. *Journal of Applied Social Psychology, 29*(2), 424–444.

Hantula, D. A., & Crowell, C. R. (1994a). Behavioral contrast in a two-option analogue task of financial decision making. *Journal of Applied Behavior Analysis, 27*(4), 607–617.

Hantula, D. A., & Crowell, C. R. (1994b). Intermittent reinforcement and escalation processes in sequential decision making: A replication and theoretical analysis. *Journal of Organizational Behavior Management, 14*(2), 7–36.

Heng, C.-S., Tan, B., & Wei, K.-K. (2003). De-escalation of commitment in software projects: Who matters? What matters? *Information and Management, 41*(1), 99–110.

Herrnstein, R. J. (1990). Rational choice theory: Necessary but not sufficient. *American Psychologist, 45*(3), 356–367.

Janis, I. L. (1972). *Victims of groupthink: A psychological study of foreign-policy decisions and fiascoes.* Oxford, UK: Houghton Mifflin.

Johnson, J. (1995) Chaos: The dollar drain of IT project failures. *Application Development Trends, 2*(1), 41–57

Kahneman, D., & Tversky, A. (1984). Choices, values, and frames. *American Psychologist, 39*(4), 341–350.

Kameda, T., & Sugimori, S. (1993). Psychological entrapment in group decision making: An assigned decision rule and groupthink phenomenon. *Journal of Personality and Social Psychology, 65*(2), 282–292.

Keil, M., Mann, J., & Rai, A. (2000). Why software projects escalate: An empirical analysis and test of four theoretical models. *MIS Quarterly, 24*(4), 631–675.

Keil, M., & Robey, D. (1999). Turning around troubled software projects: An exploratory study of the deescalation of commitment to failing courses of action. *Journal of Management Information Systems, 15*(4), 63–87.

Kite, D. M., Katz, J. P., & Zarrzeski, M. T. (1996). Can managers appraise performance too often? *Journal of Applied Business Research, 13*(1), 41–51.

Lind, R. S., Kutcher, E., Bragger, J. D., & Hantula, D. A. (1999, May). *Why do managers try, try, and fail? A real-world analysis of factors affecting escalation and persistence of commitment.* Paper presented at the Eastern Academy of Management, Philadelphia.

McCain, B. E. (1986). Continuing investment under conditions of failure: A laboratory study of the limits to escalation. *Journal of Applied Psychology, 71*(2), 280–284.

Mohr, C. (1985, April 30). History and hindsight: Lessons from Vietnam. *The New York Times*, pp. 1, 6.

Newcombe, T. (1998). Big project woes halt child support system. *Governmental Technology, 28*, 34–35.

Platt, J. (1973). Social traps. *American Psychologist, 28*(8), 641–651.

Rao, V. S., & Monk, A. (1999). The effects of individual differences and anonymity on commitment to decisions: Preliminary evidence. *Journal of Social Psychology, 139*(4), 496–515.

Rosnow, R. L. (1991). Inside rumor: A personal journey. *American Psychologist, 46*, 484–496.

Ross, J., & Staw, B. M. (1986). Expo 86: An escalation prototype. *Administrative Science Quarterly, 31*(2), 274–297.

Ross, J., & Staw, B. M. (1993). Organizational escalation and exit: Lessons from the Shoreham Nuclear Power Plant. *Academy of Management Journal, 36*(4), 701–732.

Schmidt, J. B., Montoya-Weiss, M. M., & Massey, A. P. (2001). New product development decision-making effectiveness: Comparing individuals, face-to-face teams, and virtual teams. *Decision Sciences, 32*(4), 575–594.

Schwenk, C. R. (1990). Effects of devil's advocacy and dialectical inquiry on decision making: A meta-analysis. *Organizational Behavior & Human Decision Processes, 47*(1), 161–176.

Seibert, S., & Goltz, S. M. (2001). Comparison of allocations by individuals and interacting groups in an escalation of commitment situation. *Journal of Applied Social Psychology, 31*(1), 134–156.

Simonson, I., & Staw, B. (1992). Deescalation strategies: A comparison of techniques for reducing commitment to losing courses of action. *Journal of Applied Psychology, 77*(4), 419–426.

Staw, B. (1976). Knee-deep in the Big Muddy: A study of escalating commitment to a chosen course of action. *Organizational Behavior & Human Decision Processes, 16*(1), 27–44.

Staw, B. (1997). The escalation of commitment: An update and appraisal. In Z. Shapira (Ed.), *Organizational decision making* (pp. 191–215). New York: Cambridge University Press.

Staw, B., Barsade, S., & Koput, K. (1997). Escalation at the credit window: A longitudinal study of bank executives' recognition and write-off of problem loans. *Journal of Applied Psychology, 82*(1), 130–142.

Staw, B., & Fox, F. V. (1977). Escalation: The determinants of commitment to a chosen course of action. *Human Relations, 30*(5), 431–450.

Staw, B., & Hoang, H. (1995). Sunk costs in the NBA: Why draft order affects playing time and survival in professional basketball. *Administrative Science Quarterly, 40*, 474–494.

Staw, B., & Ross, J. (1987). Behavior in escalation situations: Antecedents, prototypes, and solutions. *Organizational Behavior & Human Decision Processes, 9*, 39–78.

Teger, A. I. (1980). *Too much invested to quit.* New York: Pergamon.

Whyte, G. (1991). Diffusion of responsibility: Effects on the escalation tendency. *Journal of Applied Psychology, 76*(3), 408–415.

Whyte, G. (1993). Escalating commitment in individual and group decision making: A prospect theory approach. *Organizational Behavior & Human Decision Processes, 54*(3), 430–455.

15

Influence Processes in Leadership-Followership: Inclusion and the Idiosyncrasy Credit Model

Edwin P. Hollander
City University of New York, Baruch College and Graduate Center

Leadership is not just about a leader. Studying leadership properly needs attention to how followers perceive and respond to a leader, in a two-way influence relationship. Within a particular context, this dynamic process can be called *inclusive leadership,* which begins with the leader's perceived legitimacy, as in election and appointment. Legitimacy depends on acknowledgment by followers and their response to the leader. The overarching point here is that the leadership process involves more than the leader's qualities alone; it also involves those of followers and their mutual situation.

Inclusive leadership also emphasizes doing things with people, not to people. The traditional dichotomy of leader or follower overlooks many shared features of these interdependent roles, not least activity level. In all settings, those rising to higher levels are likely to be identified as leaders for such qualities as effective communication and dependability—qualities that they had shown as active followers.

To understand the leader–follower relationship, it is useful to conceive of credits accorded to leaders by followers. This view departs from the long-standing "leader-centric" focus on leader qualities, independent of how they engage and are viewed by followers. By contrast, these "idiosyncrasy credits"

293

(Hollander, 1958, 1964, 2004) accrue from two major sources of follower perception, and lesser inputs from seniority. These sources are competence in the main group task, and loyalty to group norms by living up to expectancies for appropriate behavior. The latter is not slavish conformity so much as providing for an ease of relationships. Once earned, credits may be drawn on to take needed initiatives, or may be lost for failing to do so. Experimental and other research is presented here on these relational features of leadership, which reveal conditions that animate this process, are open to study, and help understanding.

Using the critical incidents technique (Flanagan, 1954), a mode of event analysis, my colleagues and I asked many hundreds of respondents from management settings to describe their experiences with either "good" or "bad" leadership (Hollander, 1993, 1995a, 1995b; Hollander & Kelly, 1992; Hollander, Schwager, Russeva, & Nassauer, 1996). Content analyses of their responses provided a fuller picture of how followers perceive leaders. These respondents also gave semantic differential ratings of the leaders involved. With the content analyses of the qualitative material, plus the quantitative ones, it was then possible to relate these to what respondents reported in follow-up questions on the consequences of the incident. For example, interpersonal qualities of sensitivity to and support of followers were found to engender loyalty and trust. These two qualities were also among the best for differentiating good from bad leadership. In turn, loyalty and trust were significantly associated with both sustaining relationships and respondents remaining in or leaving an organization, across gender. Ultimately, these relational elements were found to keep followers involved in productive and satisfying activities. These paid off in producing the attainment of mutual goals associated with inclusive leadership.

STUDYING LEADERSHIP

The heartland of social psychology is the study of social influence, which is basic to leadership. Ralph Rosnow's work has long enriched many parts of this terrain. It can be found in such seemingly diverse matters as looking at experimenter effects on volunteer research subjects (Rosnow & Rosenthal, 1975) and the effects of rumors and gossip on behavior (Rosnow & Fine, 1976). The latter research has special pertinence to understanding leadership, as was earlier evident in the classic research on personal influence by Katz and Lazarsfeld (1955).

Years ago, George Homans (1961) made the point that we "must not confuse the particular sort of situation in which research is conveniently carried on with the subject of that research" (p. 8). If leadership is what we study, then where we study it may not be as crucial as is made to appear, not least because it often omits followers and their perceptions of what is going on there. A rectification of that omission is seen, for example, in the seminal re-search of Offermann and Schrier (1985) on sex, role, and the impact of power. In practice, the fundamental task in studying leadership is to observe leadership phenomena and seek understanding of as much of the whole as possible. Although they are different in various ways, laboratory and field research both contribute to the study of leadership.

Surely, laboratory and field research should be better integrated (See Locke, 1986). However, they are not quite as divergent as has been made to appear. Methodologically speaking, there are supplemental tech-niques used in leadership research that transcend the setting. These in-clude such methods as observation, ratings or nominations by peers, and attitude scaling, which can all incorporate the inclusion of the followers' perspective. In addition, experimentation may be conducted in the field as well as in the laboratory.

Essentially, the question at issue is one of external validity with respect to application. Field studies need not necessarily have any greater claim on such validity than do laboratory experiments. For example, a study of deci-sion making among the top executives of a particular organization may be less generalizable or applicable than a laboratory experiment on variables af-fecting group decision making. It may also be that laboratory experiments on equity, or fairness, as perceived as an attribute of leaders by followers, may be quite pertinent (see, e.g., Hollander & Julian, 1970, 1978).

Laboratory experimentation does not necessarily precede field research. The sequence may be quite the reverse, as occurs when work in the field calls attention to a relationship that can be probed further by an experiment in the laboratory. Another consideration is the reality element that, accord-ing to Weick (1969), requires financial sponsorship and social support if the linkage between knowledge and practice is to be made.

There is also the issue of intentionality regarding a research approach. In fact, the choice of field or laboratory research may be dictated by circum-stances rather than by personal predilections. My own research on leader-ship began conveniently in the field when I was on active duty as an aviation psychologist officer assigned to the Naval Air Training Command at Pensacola from 1951 through 1953 during the Korean War. Although inter-ested in laboratory experimentation as a graduate student, my experiments on leadership did not occur until after I had completed leadership field re-search in the Navy. Instead, my research began in spring 1954, when I was starting in my first academic position, at the Carnegie Institute of Technology (now Carnegie-Mellon University) in Pittsburgh.

Note that pioneering research on leadership by Lewin, Lippitt, and White (1939) is often cited as an instance of laboratory experimentation opening the way to field research. Actually, it was not a laboratory experi-ment but a field experiment. The boys' clubs were real enough, they met recurrently over a period of several weeks, and the situation was quite involving. The circumstances were, therefore, quite different from those of many laboratory experiments. In addition, the boys studied in this research were 10 and 11 years old, even though the research findings frequently have been generalized well beyond to adult groups.

Although gaining knowledge about leadership can make organizations more "humane," even further it helps to deal with the crisis and challenge presented in such settings. The study of leadership is significant to the health and well-being of organizations and the people who populate them. Leadership and the leader-follower relationship are the most central processes affecting these outcomes, as pointed out elsewhere (Hollander, 1978a, 1978b; 1986, 1995a, 1995b).

Regarding the strengths and weaknesses of laboratory and field research, there may be strong but nonetheless unreal effects in the laboratory. For instance, Hovland (1959) found differential effects of laboratory and survey studies in attitude change, with the laboratory showing the greater impact. This fits the general observation from Rosenthal and Rosnow (1969) that the demand characteristics of experiments may tip the balance toward compliance by subjects.

Perhaps a greater problem with laboratory experiments on leadership is that the groups studied have no past or future, unless the latter is induced. In one experiment precisely on this point (Lewis, Langan, & Hollander, 1972), a group discussion task centered around urban problems was used. Half the participants were told that they would have future interaction (i.e., that the group would have an extended life), and the other half were not. Cross-cutting this treatment, the attractiveness of the decisional alternatives in the problems was varied. When participants believed that there would be future interaction and the alternatives were of relatively equal attractiveness, based on pretests, we found the greatest conformity to the group's majority judgments. By contrast, the lack of any anticipation of future interaction, coupled with unequal attractiveness of the alternatives, gave the highest level of nonconformity by participants.

The significance of this finding rests primarily in what it reveals about the greater pressure that may exist to conform to majority judgments in persisting groups. There are easily understandable reasons why this may be so. A major reason is that disagreement is more costly in continuing interaction, compared with a lesser cost in short-term interaction. A person who takes a different stand may be obliged to defend it later, which represents a cost likely to be considerably higher than that created in a shorter-term situation. This is related to conformity in rumor transmission, as in DiFonzo, Bordia, and Rosnow's (1994) study of this organizational effect. It also is associated with the central matter of uncertainty reduction during organizational change, which was the focus of related research by DiFonzo and

Bordia (1998, 2000). These results clearly implicate important leadership functions, because of the necessity to offset the potentially damaging effects of wayward rumors.

The experiment by Lewis et al. (1972) also is illustrative of the utility of the laboratory in helping to sharpen our understanding of the relationship between variables. Although the laboratory experiment may not be the method of choice, its use can be instructive in this respect. In another instance, an experiment (Hollander, Fallon, & Edwards, 1977) was done on the succession of elected and appointed leaders, a phenomenon deserving more study than it has received. Hollander et al.'s results have some interesting implications for further investigations. For example, it was found that eventual successors were identifiable as having been influential in the early stages of the group's life. They did not emerge suddenly in the election condition, but clearly had built a following before reaching the leader threshold.

In another laboratory experiment (Gleason, Seaman, & Hollander, 1978), it was possible to create groups of male students composed of one high, one low, and two who were medium on the Machiavellianism scale, a measure of the tendency to seek and use power in relationships. The hypothesis of immediate interest was that those high in Machiavellianism would be most likely to show ascendance in the low structure condition (Geis, 1968). Although we did not find that as a significant effect, those who were medium on Machiavellianism were found to be significantly preferred as leaders, as opposed to those who were at the extremes. A point of interest is that this experiment followed the injunction to study the relationship of personality and situational factors that had been urged in a critique of leadership research by Hollander and Julian (1969) a decade before.

This line of work helps to recognize the significance of a leader's cognitive ability, as Fiedler and Garcia (1987) indicated in their instructive research on this topic. It has been bolstered by more recent efforts by Aditya and Rosnow (2002). Indeed, social perceptiveness was one of the qualities thought to be especially important to the leader role, for example, in the development of leadership concepts in the 1940s and 1950s and later evolved by Argyle and Little (1972; see Hollander, 1985).

There is another technique that transcends the particular situation—the use of critical incidents. Developed by Flanagan (1954) to evaluate bomber pilots in World War II, the technique has been applied successfully to describe the major variables distinguishing effective and ineffective flight crew commanders and managers. The technique also has been used to get at those relational qualities of leadership that stand out in distinguishing good from bad leadership (see Hollander, 1995b; Hollander & Neider, 1978). The primary finding of this work was that, for good leadership, the characteristics differentiating appointed and elected leaders were fairness and facility in interpersonal relations. Further investigation has corroborated the basic importance of these and other relational qualities. Whether in the laboratory or the field, in general there is a need to pay more attention to these processes and to the perceptions of each other and the context by the participants in leadership events.

IDIOSYNCRASY CREDIT (IC) MODEL

Traditionally, little attention has been given to followers, who accord or withdraw support to leaders. As alluded to earlier, the idiosyncrasy credit, or IC model, is distinctive for its emphasis on followers' perceptions and evaluations of the leader. Hollander (1958, 1964, 2004) conceived it regarding the apparent paradox that leaders may appear to conform to the group's norms and yet are likely to be influential in bringing about innovations. This is partly reconcilable by recognizing that leaders are distinctly granted latitude to innovate for the benefit of the group's goal attainment. Hence, status in the eyes of followers can be seen as a credit balance that a leader can draw on to take innovative actions in behalf of group goals. This dynamism contrasts with the usual, more static emphasis on the directive effects of the leader on followers (see Hollander, 1992a, 1992b). Furthermore, the IC model makes explicit the vital role of followers in the latitudes of a leader's action (see Kelley, 1992). This is also seen in the negative effects of "toxic" followers, described in a penetrating analysis by Offermann (2004) about the dysfunction they present.

The idea of credit is embedded in everyday language in such general terms as *receiving credit, taking credit,* and *being discredited.* For example, Porter (1985) noted, "Managers are reluctant to spend time and resources on interrelationship projects if they are uncertain to receive credit for them" (p. 389). An early precursor of this evaluative component was Chester Barnard's (1938) "acceptance theory of authority." It stated that the follower has a pivotal role in judging whether an order is authoritative, insofar as he or she understands it, believes it is not inconsistent with organizational or personal goals, has the ability to comply with it, and sees more rewards than costs in complying and remaining within the organization or group (Hollander, 1978a).

Taking off from Barnard's (1938) acceptance theory of authority, a following can come about in various ways. For the moment, the focus here is on how legitimacy and credit serve as two significant interrelated factors in the process. *Legitimacy* is the basis for a person's attainment of the leader status. In short, it is the validation of the leader, acknowledging him or her in the leader role. Most important, legitimacy becomes a pivotal part in the leader–follower relationship because it is the base on which followers perceive and respond to the leader. Research by Hollander and Julian (1970) demonstrated that election and appointment produce differing expectations and evaluations by followers, further found in research by Ben-Yoav, Hollander, and Carnevale (1983), among others. Legitimacy is seen as a fundamental factor, such as in granting trust to a leader. *Credit* is another, more psychological, way of considering the leader–follower bond, in regard to positively disposed perceptions. In both cases, followers can affect the strength of a leader's influence, the style of a leader's behavior, and the performance of the group or larger entity. In short, influence and power flow both from legitimacy and those additional elements affected by followers through their perceptions, attributions, and judgments.

The IC model treats innovative leadership and the latitude that followers give a leader to render change beyond that accorded by legitimacy of authority. The model describes a dynamic process of interpersonal evaluation in which the effects of leader authority are not fixed, but instead are determined significantly by the support of followers. It does not tell how things ought to be; rather, it reflects how they seem to operate in relatively noncoercive situations in which power is not absolute but instead dependent on the context and persons there.

Essentially, the model also postulates credits to be positive perceptions of a person earned from others by showing competence in helping to achieve the group's task goals, and conformity to the group's norms, as a sign of loyalty. Credits may then be drawn on to take innovative actions in line with expectations associated with the leader role. Therefore, it becomes possible that "early signs of competence and conformity will permit later nonconformity to be better tolerated" (Hollander, 1958).

"As the individual is perceived to behave in accordance with commonly applied expectancies, and makes contributions toward the group's activities, his (or her) status moves upward. Where an individual fails to live up to expectancies, i.e. nonconforms, he (or she) loses credits, but may maintain some appropriate level of credits by continuing to be perceived as a contributor to the fulfillment of the goals of the group. When an individual's credit balance reaches zero, he (or she) may be thought of as having been excluded from the group, so far as the group's perception is concerned. On the other hand, credits may accumulate to such a level that the expectancies applicable to the individual are directed toward innovation. The critical feature here is that status will allow greater latitude in the manifestation of behavior which would be seen to be nonconformist for the other members of the group" (Hollander, 1964, p. 158).

This formulation was verified in a set of experiments the first of which was with groups of engineering students involved in a joint decision task (Hollander, 1960, 1961). It has subsequently been supported in various ways and settings (see, e.g., Estrada, Brown, & Lee, 1995), with certain refinements.

Earlier, for example, Alvarez (1968) found that the credit loss, in his term of "esteem," was significantly less for a leader's nonconformity when the organization was successful rather than failing.

Additionally, the model postulates that unused credits can be lost by failing to live up to follower expectations for leader action. The drainage may be compounded by first overpromising and then appearing not to act in the face of stated need. Not least, the leader's self-serving and other negatively viewed behaviors can also drain credits, as can perceptions of weak motivation, incompetence, and the responsibility for failure.

As a refined model, the idiosyncrasy credit concept indicates how credits accumulate and have operational significance in permitting innovations that would be perceived to be deviations if introduced by another person with less credit. Seniority can contribute to the accumulation of credits, but without uniform impact. A person may also benefit from having "derivative credit"—a favorable reputation from another group, or from the society (as in high socioeconomic status).

Most usually, however, a new member of a group is in a poor position to assert influence, especially in the direction of change, unless he or she has a unique qualification. An example would be providing a solution to a major group problem, or having a needed knowledge. In these circumstances, the new member's credit is gained by maximizing on the competence factor. Also, credit may not accrue as readily to those who are perceived to be different, as in the case of a woman in an otherwise male group (see Wahrman & Pugh, 1974).

As the saying goes, "A new member must learn the ropes." An example I heard occurred when a new manager, after his first departmental meeting, was told by his superior, "In our meetings, we don't speak up to disagree." (I heard the new manager tell this story at a professional meeting.) A new leader, whether appointed or elected, must still build credits by establishing a following. This is especially evident when the legitimacy of his or her authority is weak, as in a narrow election victory.

These features of the IC model highlight some essentially relational aspects of leadership and followership affecting team and organizational performance. Such an emphasis represents an alternative to the traditional "solar system model" of the leader placed at the center of attention and power. Although perhaps less dominant, leader-centrism continues to hold venerable allure. Granted that qualities of leaders are important, Reich (1987) nonetheless made the point that "We need to honor our teams more, our aggressive leaders and maverick geniuses less" (p. 78). This underscores the need for leaders to have the knowledge, skills, and abilities to engage followers in productive and satisfying mutual pursuits. Moreover, this presents a distinct departure from the traditional way of seeing leader qualities as possessions, rather than as interpersonal links to others involved in shared activities.

Because leaders are often disinclined to be participative, overcoming their resistance to having active followers has special significance. An important source of resistance is the problem of shared responsibility, with the inevitable question, often unstated, being "Who will be accountable?"

A body of research shows how inattention to these matters can lead to dysfunctional outcomes. For instance, Hogan, Raskin, and Fazzini (1990) discerned that organizational climate studies from the mid-1950s onward showed 60% to 75% of organizational respondents reporting their immediate supervisor as the worst or most stressful aspect of their job. Such findings highlight the importance of followers as perceivers with expectations of and attributions about leader performance. From a 10-year perspective, DeVries (1992) estimated the base rate for executive incompetence to be at least 50%. Lord and Maher (1988) maintained that these perceptions are checked against prototypes held by followers and their related expectations of how leaders should perform; that is, "implicit leadership theories" (ILTs).

Regarding prototypes, the leader role traditionally has been seen to be masculine. Although women have made inroads in leadership roles, in mixed-gender situations there are still outmoded ideas about activity and dominance by gender. With respect to being dominant, assertive, or competitive, women in mixed-gender company are often constrained to be less obviously so than men. Among the situational influences affecting this pattern of behavior are the gender composition of the group, subordinates' attitudes, task demands, success or failure of the group, and the leader's source of status (Hollander & Yoder, 1980).

Denmark (1977, 1993) considered that the behavior of women managers is not basically different from men, but women do show a greater concern for interpersonal relations, which should be seen as a plus. Based on her comprehensive research with police partner teams, Gerber (2001) found that men are assigned more often to higher-status positions than are women officers. Furthermore, she noted that gender preconceptions presented a fallacy about gender differences in personality. Her extensive analyses revealed that police supervisors had used gender norms as the basis for evaluating performance, thus disadvantaging the women but not the men. Also, women officers used indirect power so as not to challenge the leadership position of male partners.

LEGITIMACY AND POWER

A major figure in studying political power, Neustadt (1990) also has considered follower perceptions of legitimacy as one of two main sources of presidential power. (The other source he cited involves the sentiments of loyalty, which can be partly accounted for in the favorable impressions—i.e., credits accorded by followers.) However, whether elected or appointed, effective leadership is more likely to be achieved by a process involving persuasion and the sharing of power. By contrast, the unfettered use of power can be dysfunctional and severely limiting to leader–follower relations.

The emphasis on power over others tends to give it greater salience, at the expense of empowerment and resistance to unwanted power assertions, which we have called "power to" and "power from" (Hollander & Offermann, 1990). In that paper, we reviewed and assessed research on organizational leadership and power. Among other things, we considered the benefits of and sources of resistance to delegation and empowerment of followers. On balance, we found that by sharing power and allowing followers to influence them, leaders can foster leadership skills in others, as well as achieve other gains through their greater participation and involvement. However, a major question posed is how to reconcile a return to leader-centered approaches with this trend toward greater follower empowerment and influence.

Rather than be separate, leadership and followership exist in a reciprocal, interdependent system as a unity (Hollander, 1992a, 1992 b, 1993). Fundamental to this system is a relationship "in which the leader both gives something and gets something" (Homans, 1961, p. 286).

Optimally, the leader provides added value as a resource in terms of "adequate role behavior directed toward the group's goal attainment with status, recognition, and esteem [contributing to] 'legitimacy' in making influence assertions and in having them accepted" (Hollander & Julian, 1969, p. 388). In varying degrees, a leader's legitimacy can be altered by his or her contributions that affect his or her standing with followers.

The usual expectation of the follower role as low power and passive is therefore misleading. More likely, followership is best viewed as an active accompaniment to leadership (see Kelley, 1992). Although leaders are usually more active, especially in their directive function, followers can affect a leader as an attentive and responsive strategic audience. Two-way support and influence are therefore essential to the leader–follower bond, which can be construed in credit terms, with followers according them to or withholding them from their leaders, indicating the degree of the followers' loyalty and trust.

THE INTERACTION
OF LEADER LEGITIMACY AND CREDIT

As indicated, legitimacy depends on followers perceiving the leader's source of authority, and then responding accordingly to that leader. The evidence suggests that a major difference exists in the realm of appointment or election as sources of a leader's authority (Hollander & Julian, 1970, 1978).

In both cases, the possibility of being perceived to be a leader, and acting as one, depends on some validation by those who are to be followers.

The election case is of course an obvious instance of emergence, which more closely approximates the IC model. Election can be seen to enhance the psychological identification between followers and the leader, with followers having a greater sense of responsibility for and investment in the leader (see, e.g., Hollander & Julian, 1978). One explanation is to view this as a social exchange in which the group gives the leader a reward in advance, by electing him or her, and then group members feel a claim on the leader to pay them back by producing favorable outcomes (Jacobs, 1970). Correspondingly, it is also true that the support of followers exacts a higher demand on the leader. Elected leaders who fail to perform well have been found to be more vulnerable to criticism than are appointed leaders, particularly if they are seen to be competent in the first place (Hollander & Julian, 1970, 1978).

Although election and appointment may create different psychological climates between leaders and followers, there is the prospect for even appointed organizational leaders to attain a following by doing more than exercising authority. Katz and Kahn (1966) observed this in defining organizational leadership as "the influential increment over and above mechanical compliance with the routine directives of the organizations. Such an influential increment derives from the fact that human beings rather than computers are in positions of authority and power" (p. 302).

CHARISMATIC LEADERSHIP

Recent decades have seen a revitalization of interest in the concept of the "charismatic leader," although charisma is of doubtful value in determining a leader's performance (Howell & Avolio, 1992). Max Weber (1921/1946), the eminent sociologist of bureaucracy fame, coined the term from the Greek word *charisma* for divine gift. Such a leader, he said, has considerable emotional appeal to followers and a greater hold over them, especially in a time of crisis when there are strong needs for direction. Weber contrasted this mode of leadership with the traditional kind, which is handed down, and the legalistic kind, which is based on a constitutional process. Weber asserted that charisma provides a personal authority that evokes awe in followers, which is less likely to be seen in the other forms of leadership. Alternatively, it can be seen as a vast amount of idiosyncrasy credit at the leader's disposal. Indeed, charisma is a quality that can be considered to be invested by followers and accorded or withdrawn by them. In that regard, Weber (1921/1946) stated that if the leader was "long unsuccessful, above all if his leadership fails to benefit followers, it is likely that his charisma will disappear" (p. 360).

Burns (1978) made the point that charisma "is so overburdened as to collapse under close analysis" (p. 243). In this vein, Corry (1993) reported on the acknowledged appeal of John Lindsay, a Republican mayor of New York in the 1960s, who was often said to be charismatic. If anything, Lindsay raised excessively high expectations that could not be met. Corry added, "Charisma is the most attractive but least substantive of political qualities and is useless as a guide to predicting what a candidate will do after he is elected. By the end of Lindsay's first term as Mayor, New York was having second thoughts" (p.111).

Nonetheless, Lindsay managed to win reelection by expressing contrition for the things he said "had gone wrong," and by running as an independent after losing the Republican party endorsement. He tried to regain his following, but given the multiple constituencies to be served, he never again had quite as much allure and support as he had had during his first election. This decline was accelerated by the surfacing of corruption scandals that raised doubts about Lindsay's performance of mayoral duties. When publicized, these helped to squash his effort to run as the 1972 Democratic presidential candidate.

In a parallel fashion, we see here that credits are inevitably transitory, inconstant (as in "What have you done for us lately?"), and therefore in need of replenishing. This is less so regarding legitimacy that has more stability, usually signalized by a public rite. Yet, legitimacy itself still needs to be reaffirmed, as is obvious in the electoral process.

RELATIONSHIP TO TRANSFORMATIONAL AND TRANSACTIONAL LEADERSHIP

Interest in charisma is now mostly associated with *Transformational leadership* (TF) (Bass, 1985; Burns, 1978), and reveals the importance of the followers' perspective in understanding such phenomena. Weber originally conceived of charismatic leaders as attracting others because of their strong appeal and extraordinary determination, especially in time of crisis; however, he also noted charisma's dependence on follower affirmation, as indicated in the previous section.

There is a need, too, to take account of the ethical distinction Burns (1978) made between the self-serving and socially responsible kinds of transformational leaders. In the world of organizations, as well as in politics, charismatic leaders are still sought as saviors. However, they also may present difficulties, such as tendencies toward narcissism (e.g., Post, 1986) and unethical behavior. As examples of the latter, Howell and Avolio (1992) cited the dubious ethical standards associated with such business leaders as Robert Campeau, John DeLorean, and Michael Milken, all of whom were acknowledged to have charisma for many of their followers.

Unethical leaders are more likely to use their charisma for power over followers, directed toward self-serving ends, usually in a calculated manipulative way. Ethical leaders are considered to use their charisma in a socially constructive way to serve others.

Charisma and transformational leadership are frequently linked in the literature. *Transactional leadership* (TA) refers to a fair exchange in which the leader gives something to followers and receives esteem and latitude for action in return, as exemplified by Homans (1961) and Jacobs (1970). Although charisma need not be part of TF leadership, it is routinely imputed to the TF leader; for example, as in Bass' first aspect of TF, and in House and Shamir's (1993) work. However, the research by Ehrlich, Meindl, and Viellieu (1990) suggested that "more transactionally oriented activities by a leader may also contribute to a leader's charismatic appeal" (p. 242). Ehrlich et al. asserted that "Conceptually, the basis for either form of leadership is relational and perceptual exchange developed between a leader and his or her subordinates" (p. 36). At its heart, charisma is attributed to a leader by followers, as indicated in the Weber quote earlier.

TF leaders do provide rewards to followers, as Bass (1985) noted in listing personal attention and intellectual stimulation. However, the followers' reciprocation to the leader is usually unacknowledged, because that would support the view that a transaction has occurred. This would breach the artificial separation of measures maintained by Bass (1985), by defining TA leadership quite differently from how it was originally described. Curphy (1993), for one, found that TF and TA leadership were not independent, but were highly related in ratings given by cadets to their officers at the U.S. Air Force Academy.

The actuality of this transaction between leader and followers is usually denied in accounting for the TF phenomenon. Instead, a rigid dichotomy between TA and TF leadership is maintained by considering only tangible rewards and failing to acknowledge the intangible ones that followers receive from TF leaders as well as TA leaders. Chemers (1993) contended that intrinsic rewards of "self-esteem, a sense of purpose, or salvation ... become highly attractive and supremely motivating" when followers needs are intense enough. "Under such circumstances charismatic or transformational leadership may be seen as a special, elevated case of the more mundane transactional exchange processes that are the basis for all, person-to-person, team leadership" (p. 312).

Accordingly, as defined by Bass (1985), TF leaders do provide intangible rewards to followers, such as personal attention and intellectual stimulation, which he listed among TF qualities. However, he did not acknowledge them as such, nor followers' reciprocation to the leader found in giving credit, support, and trust. To do so would make plain that a transaction had occurred, which would breach the artificial view of TA leadership maintained by presenting it in a caricatured form. This is far from the actual, richer TA conception that incorporated an earlier dynamic element of the TF form,—that is, the idiosyncrasy credit model, dealing with acceptance of change by followers (see Hollander, 1958, 1964, 2004).

Curphy's (1993) findings, noted previously from ratings given by cadets to their officers at the U.S. Air Force Academy, showed that TA and TF leadership are not independent but instead are highly related. Furthermore, leaders wishing to bring about change need TA qualities to establish a relationship with followers based on trust. Similarly, Bensimon (1993) discovered from her research that new college presidents who were successful had the ability to adapt by displaying both kinds of qualities as needed. For instance, they were initially able to be more transactional, and only then transformational in their attempts to make changes. Wallace (1996) noted a similar "middle way" pattern of flexibility in her research among corporate executives considered to be effective.

Whether called TA or TF leaders, the common element evident in good leadership and not in bad are such significant relational factors as intangible rewards. Burns (1978) argued, "[O]nly the followers themselves can ultimately define their own true needs. And they can do so only when they … can make an informed choice among competing 'prescriptions'" (p. 36). Both intangible as well as tangible rewards are found to be essential, however, to the motivation to follow. Our findings reported later in this chapter on their consequences of rewards are consonant with this view of the basis for motivation to follow, particularly when people are engaged in compelling mutual pursuits. Usually satisfaction is involved. Indeed, Burns (1978) related a study of nurses in a hospital setting for whom sources of their satisfaction were found to be motivators. Clearly, this speaks to a TA process, although possibly contributing to a TF one later.

In sum, TF leadership can be seen as an extension of TA leadership, in which there is likely to be greater leader intensity and follower arousal. This amounts to having a large fund of credits accorded to the leader by followers, thereby granting esteem and more sway in being influential. Finally, to achieve a responsive following it is essential at the outset to establish and build on TA leadership before expecting an adequate response to TF leadership.

RECENT RESEARCH ON RELATIONAL QUALITIES OF LEADERSHIP

As is obvious, followers are the ones who experience the actuality of a leader's approach to leadership, and are uniquely able to evaluate it and its effects. A prominent example of the usefulness of this source was shown in a study on "derailment" (McCall, Lombardo, & Morrison, 1988), with 400 promising managers seen to be on a fast track. Those who failed to reach their expected potential were more often found to lack interpersonal skills, especially in relating to subordinates, but not a deficit in their technical skills. Also, research by Kouzes and Posner (1987), with a sample of 3,400 organizational respondents, dealt with qualities that the respondents admired in their leaders, and found the relational realm to be significant. The four qualities that more than half of these respondents said they admired most were being honest, competent, forward looking, and inspiring.

Our own research program (Hollander et al., 1996; Hollander & Kelly, 1990, 1992; Kelly, Julien, & Hollander, 1992; Schwager, Julien, Kelly, & Hollander, 1993) involved critical incidents to study these relationships further. They were supplemented by open-ended questions and rating scales, to get at followers' perceptions of actual leader behavior in good or bad leadership situations, and followers' perceptions of ideal leader behavior. Based on our previous work, we found that relational qualities were emphasized in these reports and evaluations distinguishing good leadership from bad leadership. We also found that characteristics reported for good leadership closely corresponded to those independently described by other respondents as being characteristic of ideal leadership (Hollander & Kelly, 1992).

The latest results came from a total sample of 293 respondents, approximately half male and half female, drawn primarily from organizationally based master's degree students enrolled in evening courses on organizational behavior or leadership. Two thirds held professional and/or administrative positions, and the great majority (four fifths) were employed full time.

Respondents were first asked to describe an incident that had occurred between them and a superior in which either good leadership (for one half of the respondents) or bad leadership (for the other half) was displayed. No identifying information was requested, to protect anonymity. Other follow-up questions asked respondents what they found rewarding or not from what that superior did or said as leader, what their own response was, and what effect this event had on the relationship with this superior. Respondents also rated the leader on 6-point Likert rating scales of seven leader characteristics (e.g., involvement and directiveness, as representative of major qualities of leadership reported in the literature). In addition, respondents evaluated the leader in the incident on 10 6-point semantic differential scales (e.g., capable–incapable and helpful–unhelpful, summed as a "favorability index").

Content analyses of the first open-ended question indicated that, in good leadership, leaders were seen to: be supportive, have good communication skills in providing clarity and/or being good listeners, be action/results oriented, delegate to and/or empower subordinates, and be fair. In bad leadership, leaders were reported to be: unsupportive; to show a lack of communication skills; to be uninvolving, unfair, angry or harsh, autocratic; and at times to be poor managers of resources.

Perhaps most important, we studied the consequences of the good or bad leadership incident with regard to the effect on the relationship and subsequent actions. This approach parallels the work of Komaki (1998) on followers knowing consequences of their behavior. We found that the experience of good leadership was associated most with such intangible rewards as communicating (e.g., "provided a clear message which helped me interact more effectively") and support (e.g., "backed up his staff"). Conversely, bad leadership elicited accounts of poor communication and such unrewarding behaviors as unfairness (e.g., "rules do not go for everyone") and harshness (e.g., "constantly sought to demean me"). Respondents in the good condition reported that the incident developed/strengthened their relationship with the leader and increased their respect for him or her. In the bad condition, respondents most often mentioned a loss of respect, passivity/withholding, discouragement, and a weakening of that relationship, sometimes ending in departure.

CONCLUSION

In general, the follower perspective offers a route to understanding the basis for effective or ineffective leadership. Although by no means the complete account, research such as this identifies some fundamental features of leader–follower relations (see Kouzes & Posner, 1987; Hollander, 1995b). Obviously, a leader's self-presentation skills may still obscure the truth about his or her intentions and dealings. There remains the essential need to have a basis on which followers are able to evaluate the leader's performance, to balance a more common leader-centric view.

As to how these research findings speak to the relationship between legitimacy and credits, clearly they can and do bolster one another. Those leaders granted legitimacy may then exercise their authority to say and do things that gain credits for subsequent actions. Such actions, if evaluated positively by enough followers, create the basis for retaining legitimacy, as in the political world. The reverse is equally true. This cycle is one way of considering the process of ascent and decline of a leader in the eyes of followers, and the consequences to associated relationships. Not least, this implicates how influence flows, as Ralph Rosnow has so trenchantly revealed in his work on what is believed or not about rumors and gossip.

ACKNOWLEDGMENT

Many of the points made here were part of talks given when receiving the New York Academy of Sciences Helmut E. Adler Award from the Psychology Section on December 6, 2004, and the 2004 Walter F. Ulmer, Jr. Applied Leadership Research Award for career contributions, from the Center for

Creative Leadership in Greensboro, North Carolina, on March 8, 2005. I am grateful to both institutions for these awards. Thanks are also extended to Kira Barden, my research assistant, for her help in preparing this chapter.

REFERENCES

Aditya, R., & Rosnow, R. L. (2002). Executive intelligence and interpersonal acumen: A conceptual framework. In B. Pattanayak &V. Gupta (Eds.), *Creating performing organizations: International perspectives for Indian management* (pp. 225–246). New Delhi: Sage/Response.

Alvarez, R. (1968). Informal reactions to deviance in simulated work organizations: A laboratory experiment. *American Sociological Review, 33,* 895–912.

Argyle, M., & Little, B. R. (1972). Do personality traits apply to social behavior? *Journal of the Theory of Social Behavior, 2*(1), 1–35.

Barnard, C. I. (1938). *The functions of the executive.* Cambridge, MA: Harvard University Press.

Bass, B. M. (l985). *Leadership and performance beyond expectations.* New York: Free Press.

Bensimon, E. M. (1993). New presidents' initial actions: Transactional and transformational leadership. *Journal for Higher Education Management, 8*(2), 5–17.

Ben-Yoav, O., Hollander, E. P., & Carnevale, P. J. D. (1983). Leader legitimacy, leader–follower interaction, and followers' ratings of the leader. *Journal of Social Psychology, 121,* 111–115.

Burns, J. M. (1978). *Leadership.* New York: Harper & Row.

Chemers, M. M. (1993). An integrative theory of leadership. In M. M. Chemers & R. Ayman (Eds.), *Leadership theory and research: Perspectives and directions* (pp. 293–319). San Diego: Academic Press.

Corry, J. (1993). *My Times.* New York: Putnam.

Curphy, G. J. (1993). An empirical investigation of the effects of transformational and transactional leadership on organizational climate, attrition, and performance. In K. E. Clark, M. B. Clark, & D. P. Campbell (Eds.), *Impact of leadership* (pp. 177–188). Greensboro, NC: Center for Creative Leadership.

Denmark, F. L. (1977). Styles of leadership. *Psychology of Women Quarterly, 2,* 99–113.

Denmark, F. L. (1993). Women, leadership, and empowerment. *Psychology of Women Quarterly, 17,* 343–356.

DeVries, D. L. (1992). Executive selection: advances but no progress. *Center for Creative Leadership: Issues and Observations, 12,* 1–5.

DiFonzo, N., & Bordia, P. (1998). A tale of two corporations: Managing uncertainty during organizational change. *Human Resource Management, 37*(3 & 4), 295–303.

DiFonzo, N., & Bordia, P. (2000). How top PR professionals handle hearsay: Corporate rumors, their effects, ad strategies to manage them. *Public Relations Review, 26*(2), 173–190.

DiFonzo, N., Bordia, P., & Rosnow, R. L. (1994). Reining in rumors. *Organizational Dynamics, 19,* 47–62.

Ehrlich, S. B., Meindl, J. R., & Viellieu, B. (1990). The charismatic appeal of a transformational leader: An empirical case study of a small, high technology contractor. *Leadership Quarterly, 1*(4), 229–247.

Estrada, M., Brown, J., & Lee, F. (1995) Who gets the credit? Perceptions of idiosyncrasy credit in work groups. *Small Group Research, 26*(1), 56–76.

Fiedler, F. E., & Garcia, J. E. (1987). *New approaches to effective leadership: Cognitive resources and organizational performance.* New York: Wiley.

Flanagan, J. C. (1954). The critical incident technique. *Psychological Bulletin, 51,* 327–358.

Geis, L. (1968). Machiavellianism in a semi-real world. Paper presented at the 76th Annual APA Convention.

Gerber, G. L. (2001). *Women and men police officers: Status, gender, and personality.* Westport, CT: Praeger.

Gleason, J. M., Seaman, F. J., & Hollander, E. P. (1978). Emergent leadership processes as a function of task structure and Machiavellianism. *Social Behavior and Personality, 6,* 33–36.

Hogan, R., Raskin, R., & Fazzini, D. (1990). The dark side of charisma. In K. E. Clark & M. B. Clark (Eds.), *Measures of Leadership* (pp. 343–354). West Orange, NJ: Leadership Library of America.

Hollander, E. P. (1958). Conformity, status, and idiosyncrasy credit. *Psychological Review, 65,* 117–127.

Hollander, E. P. (1960). Competence and conformity in the acceptance of influence. *Journal of Abnormal and Social Psychology, 61,* 365–369.

Hollander, E. P. (1961). Some effects of perceived status on responses to innovative behavior. *Journal of Abnormal and Social Psychology, 63,* 247–250.

Hollander, E. P. (1964). *Leaders, groups, and influence.* New York: Oxford University Press.

Hollander, E. P. (1978a). *Leadership dynamics: A practical guide to effective relationships.* New York: Free Press/Macmillan.

Hollander, E. P. (1978b). What is the crisis of leadership? *Humanitas, 14,* 285–296.

Hollander, E. P. (1985). Leadership and power. In G. Lindzey & E. Aronson (Eds.), *The handbook of social psychology* (3rd ed., pp. 485–537). New York: Random House.

Hollander, E. P. (1986). On the central role of leadership processes. *International Review of Applied Psychology, 35,* 39–52.

Hollander, E. P. (1992a). The essential interdependence of leadership and followership. *Current Directions in Psychological Science, 1*(2), 71–75.

Hollander, E. P. (1992b). Leadership, followership, self, and others. *Leadership Quarterly, 3*(1), 43–54.

Hollander, E. P. (1993). Legitimacy, power, and influence: A perspective on relational features of leadership. In M. Chemers and R. Ayman (Eds.), *Leadership theory and research: Perspectives and directions* (pp. 29–47). San Diego: Academic Press.

Hollander, E. P. (1995a). Ethical challenges in the leader-follower relationship. *Business Ethics Quarterly, 5*(1), 55–65.

Hollander, E. P. (2004). Idiosyncrasy credit: Upward influence. In *Encyclopedia of Leadership* (pp. 695–700; 1605–1609). Great Barrington, MA: Berkshire/SAGE.

Hollander, E. P. (1995b). Organizational leadership and followership: The role of interpersonal relations. In P. Collett & A. Furnham (Eds.), *Social psychology at work: Essays in honour of Michael Argyle* (pp. 69–87). London: Routledge.

Hollander, E. P., Fallon, B. J., & Edwards, M. T. (1977). Some aspects of influence and acceptability for appointed and elected group leaders. *Journal of Psychology, 95,* 289–296.

Hollander, E. P., & Julian, J. W. (1969). Contemporary trends in the analysis of leadership processes. *Psychological Bulletin, 71,* 387–397.

Hollander, E. P., & Julian, J. W. (1970). Studies in leader legitimacy, influence, and innovation. In L. L. Berkowitz (Ed.), *Advances in experimental social psychology* (Vol. 5, pp. 33–69). New York: Academic Press.

Hollander, E. P., & Julian, J. W. (1978). A further look at leader legitimacy, influence, and innovation. In L. Berkowitz (Ed.), *Group processes* (pp. 153–165). New York: Academic Press.

Hollander, E. P., & Kelly, D. R. (1990, March). *Rewards from leaders as perceived by followers*. Paper presented at the Eastern Psychological Association, Philadelphia.

Hollander, E. P., & Kelly, D. R. (1992). *Appraising relational qualities of leadership and followership*. Paper presented at the 25th International Congress of Psychology, Brussels.

Hollander, E. P., & Neider, L. (1978, August). *Critical incidents and rating scales in comparing "good" and "bad" leadership*. Paper presented at the APA Convention, Toronto.

Hollander, E. P., & Offermann, L. (1990). Power and leadership in organizations: Relationships in transition. *American Psychologist, 45,* 179–189.

Hollander, E. P., Schwager, E., Russeva, K., & Nassauer, F. (1996). *Intangible rewards contributing to leader–follower relations*. Paper presented at the 26th International Congress of Psychology, Montreal.

Hollander, E. P., & Yoder, J. (1980). Some issues in comparing women and men as leaders. *Basic and Applied Social Psychology, 1,* 267–280.

Homans, G. C. (1961). *Social behavior: Its elementary forms.* New York: Harcourt, Brace and World.

House, R., & Shamir, B. (1993). Toward the integration of transformational, charismatic and visionary theories. In M. M. Chemers & R. Ayman (Eds.), *Leadership theory and research: Perspectives and directions* (pp. 81–107).San Diego: Academic Press.

Hovland, C. I. (1959). Reconciling conflicting results derived from experimental and survey studies of attitude change. *American Psychologist, 14,* 8–17.

Howell, J. M., & Avolio, B. J. (1992). The ethics of charismatic leadership: Submission or liberation? *Academy of Management Executive, 6,* 43–54.

Jacobs, T. O. (1970). *Leadership and exchange in formal organizations.* Alexandria, VA: Human Resources Research Organization.

Katz, D., & Kahn, R. L. (1966). *The social psychology of organizations.* New York: Wiley.

Katz, E., & Lazarsfeld, P. (1955). *Personal influence.* Glencoe, IL: Free Press.

Kelley, R. L. (1992). *The power of followership.* Garden City, NY: Doubleday.

Kelly, D., Julien, T., & Hollander, E. P. (1992, April). *Further effects of good and bad leadership revealed by critical incidents and rating scales*. Paper presented at the Annual Meeting of the Eastern Psychological Association, Boston.

Komaki, J. L. (1998). *Leadership from an operant perspective.* London: Routledge.

Kouzes, J. M., & Posner, B. Z. (1987). *The leadership challenge: How to get extraordinary things done in organizations.* San Francisco: Jossey-Bass.

Lewin, K., Lippitt, R., & White, R. K. (1939). Patterns of aggressive behavior in experimentally created "social climates." *Journal of Social Psychology, 10,* 271–299.

Lewis, S., Langan, C., & Hollander, E. P. (1972). Expectations of future interaction and the choice of less desirable alternatives in conformity. *Sociometry, 15,* 440–447.

Locke, E. A. (Ed.). (1986). *Generalizing from laboratory to field settings: Research findings from industrial-organizational psychology, organizational behavior, and human resources.* New York: Simon & Schuster.

Lord, R. G., & Maher, K. J. (1988). Leadership perceptions and leadership performance: Two distinct but interdependent processes. In J. Carroll (Ed.), *Advances in applied social psychology: Business settings* (Vol. 4, pp. 129–154). Hillsdale, NJ: Lawrence Erlbaum Associates.

McCall, M. W., Lombardo, M. M. & Morrison, A. M. (1988). *The lessons of experience.* Ashland, MA: Lexington.

Neustadt, R. (1990). *Presidential power.* New York: Wiley.

Offermann, L. R. (2004). When followers become toxic. *Harvard Business Review, 87*(1), 55–60.

Offermann, L. R., & Schrier, P. E. (1985). Social influence strategies: The impact of sex, role and attitudes toward power. *Personality and Social Psychology Bulletin, 11*(3), 286–300.

Porter, M. E. (1985). *Competitive advantage.* New York: Free Press.

Post, J. M. (1986). Narcissism and the charismatic leader–follower relationship. *Political Psychology, 7,* 675–688.

Reich, R. B. (1987). Entrepreneurship reconsidered: The team as hero. *Harvard Business Review, 65*(3), 77–83.

Rosenthal, R., & Rosnow, R. L. (1969). *Artifact in behavioral research.* New York: Academic Press.

Rosnow, R. L., & Fine, G. (1976). *Rumor and gossip.* New York: Elsevier.

Rosnow, R. L., & Rosenthal, R. (1975). *The volunteer subject.* New York: Wiley.

Schwager, E., Julien, T., Kelly, D., & Hollander, E. P. (1993, April). *What women and men perceive about good and bad leadership: Further findings.* Paper presented at the Annual Meeting of the Eastern Psychological Association, Arlington, VA.

Wahrman, R., & Pugh, M. D. (1974). Sex, nonconformity and influence. *Sociometry, 37,* 137–147.

Wallace, J. L. (1996). *An examination of comparable behavioral and motivational features of transactional and transformational leadership as regards effectiveness and follower satisfaction.* Unpublished doctoral dissertation, Baruch College and Graduate Center, City University of New York.

Weber, M. (1946). The sociology of charismatic authority (H. H. Gerth & C. W. Mills, Trans.). In H. H. Gerth & C. W. Mills (Eds.), *Essays in sociology* (pp. 245–252). New York: Oxford University Press. (Original essay published 1921)

Weick, K. E. (1969). Social psychology in an era of social change. *American Psychologist, 24,* 990–998.

IV

Theory and Epistemology

16

An Rx for Advancing and Enriching Psychology[1]

Robert Perloff
Joseph M. Katz Graduate School of Business, University of Pittsburgh

ROSNOW'S WAY

The material that follows constitutes but a small sample of the ways in which Ralph L. Rosnow has, throughout his illustrious career, advanced and enriched our field by creatively bridging psychology with literature and the everyday experiences that occupying individuals. Although the examples discussed in this chapter are from Rosnow's impressive oeuvre of publications, his dazzling capacity to connect literature and objects from people's daily lives extends as well to the scores of talks and colloquia that he has given, to his considerable gifts as teacher and mentor, to the benefits he has bestowed on his clients in his capacity as consultant, and also, I expect, to departmental politics! He has, moreover, erected these linkages between psychology and the universe of metaphors with great wit, and has deftly avoided a slippage into trivia and meaninglessness. Finally, because most of his work in recent years has been in the domains of methodology, statistics, and quantitative psychology, his ability to lighten and make more digestible inherently complex material is all the more noteworthy and is, therefore, deserving of widespread emulation.

---

[1]This chapter is an extension of an earlier article: Perloff, R. (2003). Beyond psychology: Literature and the arts as supplements for understanding, predicting, and controlling behavior—thinking outside the box. In S. Natale and A. F. Libertella (Eds.), *Immortal Longings* (Vol. VIII, pp. 128–136). Lanham, MD: University Press of America.

Trailblazing psychologists dare to stray from their comfortable pastures circumscribed by conventional thinking and pathways indigenous to mainstream psychology. To use a common cliche, they sally forth into alien terrains by "thinking outside the box," by defying weary run-of-the-mill, risk-free procedures, and by reaching out to other fields and disciplines for ideas, metaphors, and approaches for broadening and deepening psychology's theoretical and empirical excursions into unknown behaviors and experiences. This is their prescription for breaking new ground in psychology and this is precisely Ralph L. Rosnow's Rx for advancing and enriching psychology—a Rx I designate as "Ralph L. Rosnow's Way."

Not content to play it safe by traveling the tried and true highways and byways of psychological research throughout his distinguished and productive career, Rosnow reached out creatively for metaphors beyond psychology, where, for example, in his very first publication (1962) he wrote about pigeons—*pigeons*—in "Pigeons, Predictions, and Political Scientists"; about poultry—*poultry*—in "Poultry and Prejudice" (1972); about horses—yes, *horses*—in "Van Osten's Horse, Hamlet's Question, and the Mechanistic View of Causality: Implications for a Post-Crisis Social Psychology" (1983); and, with Robert Rosenthal, again involving Hamlet, in "Applying Hamlet's Question to the Ethical Conduct of Research: A Conceptual Addendum (1984).

In somewhat greater detail and moving beyond the titles of articles referenced in the preceding paragraph, here are three additional articles, one by Rosnow himself and the other two by Rosnow and Rosenthal—a psychological partnership redolent of Gilbert and Sullivan, Currier and Ives, Ben and Jerry, Abercrombie and Fitch, Lewis and Clark, Dun and Bradstreet, Richard Rodgers and Oscar Hammerstein II, Lord and Taylor, and Laurel and Hardy! First, Rosnow (1991), addressed a rumor involving Paul McCartney of The Beatles, the nature of which led Rosnow to gain insights into the psychology of rumors, insights that were at variance with the then-current thinking about the psychology of rumors. Later in this paper, he found it "convenient to conceptualize rumormongering as a process like loading and firing a gun. The gun is the rumor public, and the bullet is the rumor, which is loaded in an atmosphere of anxiety and uncertainty. The trigger is pulled when it is believed the bullet will hit the mark, much as an evolving rumor is likely to be passed on if it is perceived as credible" (p. 485). Also, he referred to insights "as fresh as bread from the oven" (p. 494). Next, Rosnow and Rosenthal (1995) pointed out throughout their paper that some of the things graduate students learn about data analysis are simply not so. For example, Rosnow and Rosenthal noted that "if one claims an interaction, then in almost all cases one is obliged to interpret the residuals and not adopt the traditional mind-set of inspecting only the condition means (i.e., overall effects) generated by a computer" (p. 9). Finally, Rosnow and Rosenthal (1996), in "Contrasts and Interactions Redux: Five Easy Pieces," called their first principle "Tarzan's Leap," and the title of the article was borrowed from the diner scene in the movie, *Five Easy Pieces,* starring Jack Nicholson.

In a nutshell (itself a metaphor!), then, what I am saying is that it is Ralph Rosnow's way to metaphorically extend his psychological research and theorizing into pigeons, poultry, horses, Shakespeare, and bread in the oven; into abandoning traditional mind-sets and embracing Tarzan and movies. As developed in a theme presented later in this chapter, Rosnow's way asserts that behavior is too complex and vast to be handled by psychology alone; therefore, one must grope for help and guidelines in animal lore, the theater, literature, the movies, and the kitchen sink!

An earlier version of this chapter, developed independently of the idea of "Rosnow's Way," was palpably congruent with the Rosnow doctrine, and simply validated again—indeed, probably for the nth time—how many ideas are more or less independently derived by more than one person. For example—and here it is not my intent to compare Rosnow and Perloff with the following luminaries, but rather to make the point that, if you will, lightning can strike twice in the same place—Charles Darwin and Alfred Russel Wallace independently struck on the idea of evolution through natural selection, whereas Sir Isaac Newton and Gottfried Wilhelm Leibniz insightfully struck gold with their formulations of the calculus, and Gregor Johann Mendel and Hugo Marie deVries hit the jackpot with their insights into the laws of heredity. This heretofore earlier version, my own foray into the world of metaphors so fetchingly fashioned by Rosnow, follows.

BEYOND PSYCHOLOGY: LITERATURE AND THE ARTS AS SUPPLEMENTS FOR UNDERSTANDING, PREDICTING, AND CONTROLLING BEHAVIOR

Generally speaking, research methodology and strategies conventionally used in mainstream psychology—for example, child psychology, clinical psychology, consumer psychology, counseling psychology, educational psychology, industrial/organizational psychology, and social psychology—are confined to protocols indigenous to psychology itself, never straying from psychology's familiar pastures and not daring to venture forth into the happy hunting grounds of the arts and other learned disciplines. To illustrate, in industrial psychology job descriptions are prepared by observing workers at their jobs, by interviewing workers and their supervisors, and by consulting such references as *The Dictionary of Occupational Titles;* not, more's the pity, by attending to what nonpsychologists have to say about jobs and about work, its (mostly) agonies and (seldom) ecstasies!

In support of extending our boundaries, Zimbardo (personal communication, 2002) said, "Yes, it is time for psychology to open the box of human nature and let old ideas and conceptions in." By "old ideas" I infer that Zimbardo was referring to the musings of poets, novelists, and other creative artists. His use of the phrase "open the box" must surely direct attention to the popular phrase today of "thinking outside the box," which I used as a subhead for the earlier version of this chapter. Psychology's "box" is the vast literature, theorizing, studies, experiments, and conceptualizing found in our comfortable journals, monographs, and books. Thinking outside the box, on the other hand, is to reach out to the legions of observers of behavior, poets, and the handful of Shakespeares in our midst, and to others who see snippets of behavior that, although less rigorous and less capable of empirical verification and replication, reveal the richness and texture (examples of which are provided later in this paper) of life's joys, tears, tragedies, exultations, sentiments, and emotions, which are barred from insinuating themselves on to the landscapes of traditional scientific psychology.

Elizabeth F. Loftus (personal communication, 2002) was moved to write the following after she saw an early abstract of this chapter:

> This made me think that in fact that they [psychologists] ought to get on board with helping our writing too ... we write in such a stodgy style (not you, Bob, but generally), and God forbid you try to deviate from it ... your hand gets slapped and you're accused of being "too chatty" or "too informal" or too something. Think of how much fun it would be if psychological concepts were embedded in an artistic endeavor.... Here's an analogy: If you asked me whether I wanted to read a book on the politics, history and geography of Chile, I'd say "forget it." But reading the book, Missing, a fabulous nonfiction tale about a man [played by Jack Lemmon in the film version] who searches for his missing son in Chile, causes you to absorb all this information without effort.

> And this is from a psychologist, Beth Loftus, recently elected to the National Academy of Sciences, who has been shown to be one of "The 100 Most Eminent Psychologists of the 20th Century" (Haggbloom et al., 2002).

It is my strong conviction that the scope, richness, and texture of job descriptions—and please be reminded that job descriptions are used only as an example, and my conviction covers the entire landscape of psychology's specialties—are capable of dramatic enhancement and probing at greater lengths and wider latitude (thus increasing the accuracy and usefulness of job descriptions as well as decreasing error variance) by resorting to, for example, the perceptions and finely chiseled observations that poets, lyricists, librettists, and novelists render automatically, intuitively, without batting an eyelash. As an illustration, ruminate over the lovely and authentic life experiences inherent in the lyrics of songs such as "As Time Goes By," "Always," "Showboat," "You're the Top," "Someone to Watch Over Me," "Accentuate the Positive and Eliminate the Negative," "My Way," "Over the Rainbow, "

"The Lady Is a Tramp," "Embraceable You," and "My Man." To illustrate how the pulsating and foot-stomping lyrics like these—and there are thousands of others just waiting, to be plucked—can energize our research designs, hypotheses, and treatment protocols, selected lyrics from three of the foregoing popular songs follow:

- "As Time Goes By": "Moonlight and love songs never out of date, hearts full of passion, jealousy and hate, that no one can deny. It's still the same old story, a fight for love and glory, a case of do or die!"
- "Always": "When the things you've planned need a helping hand, I will understand always, always. That's when I'll be there, always. Not for just an hour, not for just a day, not just for a year. But always."
- "My Man": "He's not much for looks and no hero out of books, is my man. But I love him! I don't know why I should. He isn't any good. He isn't true, but I'll stick to him like glue. What else can I do? Oh my man, I love him so! He'll never know.

    "All my life is just despair, but I don't care! When he takes me in his arms the world is bright, all right. I just like to dream of a cottage by a stream, with my man, where a few flowers grew and perhaps a kid or two, like my man ..."

Look at the love affair this worker has with his machine in "Factory Love" (Daniels, 1990):

Machine, I come to you 800 times a day

like a crazy monkey lover:

in and out, in and out, in and out. [A thrusting redolent

of sexual intercourse!]

And you, you hardly ever break down,

such clean welds, such sturdy parts [*private* parts?]

Oh how I love to oil your tips. [This is shamelessly erotic!]

Machine, please come home with me tonight.

I'll scrub off all the stains on your name,

grease and graffiti. [Let's take a shower together.]

I'm tired of being your part-time lover

Let me carry you off

into the night on a hi-lo. [Or as Frank Sinatra croons, "Come fly with me."]

that guy on midnights,

I know. he drinks,

and beats you. [or as Fanny Brice famously reveled in "My Man,"

"above, still, he's my man and I'll stick to him like glue.] (p. 45)

Along this same line of thought, heed Wanda Coleman's "Drone" (1995):

i am a clerk [note the lower case "i," indicating an insignificant person],

i am a medical billing clerk, a nonperson, a drone,

i sit here all day and type the same type of things all day long

insurance claim forms

---

for people who suffer chronic renal failure

most of them are poor, black, or latin

---

they are problem cases

some of them are very young

which means they died within a year of beginning treatment

---

sometimes they get drunk and call up

the nurses or attendants and curse them out

---

the cash flows and flows and flows

so that the doctors can feed their racehorses

and play tennis and pay the captains of their yachts

---

i sit here and type is what I do and that's very important day after

day/adrift in the river of forms

---

i sit here all day and type

i am a medical billing clerk

i am a clerk

i clerk (pp. 103–104).

This concept of reaching out into the arts and humanities for behaviors that will enrich and extend almost limitlessly the range and depth of our hypotheses opens up an entirely new and improved realm for preparing job descriptions, inter alia, and for conceptualizing, inquiring, and probing in other areas of psychology—and, if I am permitted to be so bold, as in other social and behavioral sciences as well, not only in psychology.

THE CENTRAL IDEA

I am thus proposing that psychologists partner with the aforementioned specialists in the arts and humanities to craft their variegated research and practice endeavors. In a word, behavior is too complex and far-reaching to be left to psychologists alone. Poets, for example, see, hear, smell, and feel things, sensations, and throbbings that psychologists are immune from seeing, hearing, smelling, and feeling. Mind you, it was a poet, William Blake, and not a psychologist with a PhD, who transported us to lofty aesthetic realms with "To see the world in a grain of sand, and a heaven in a wild flower, hold infinity in the palm of your hand, and eternity in an hour." It was Henry David Thoreau who urged us to step to a different drummer, and lamented that men lead lives of quiet desperation. Job descriptions, not to mention paradigms in social psychology and in other psychological domains, must embrace grains of sand, different drummers, and lives of quiet desperation.

EXAMPLES OF EFFORTS
AT THINKING OUTSIDE THE BOX

- Kipnis (2001) showed how influence tactics and strategies for achieving and increasing power are capable of being gleaned from an examination of four plays: *King Lear*, *Hamlet*, *A Doll's House*, and *The Caretaker*. After all, Shakespeare, Ibsen, and Pinter all went around the block once or twice in their quest for examining human behaviors and dissecting the rhythm and riddles of life.
- David Attenborough (2002), in a PBS documentary, showed that "music made by animals usually serves to mark out and protect territory and to attract mates." He suggested further that "we humans developed music for much the same purposes—for territorial war dances and for ancient tribal ceremonies where women selected their mates based on musical performances by men." The lesson in this for the basic argument in this chapter is that undoubtedly a study of various musical themes or compositions, alongside of conventional ways of studying love and attrac-

tion, will open up a broader and clearer window on the phenomenon of love and mate attraction.

- Overbye (2002), in an insightful essay about Princeton physicist John Archibald Wheeler, maintained that Wheeler had a "poet's flair for metaphor" (p. 1) and that Wheeler "indulged his taste for fireworks and mischief and became the hippiest poet-physicist of his generation, using metaphor as effectively as calculus to capture the imaginations of his students and colleagues and to send them, minds blazing, to the barricades to confront nature" (p. 1).

- Green and Brock (2000) opined that "public narrative predominates over public advocacy: novels, films, soap opera, music lyrics, stories in newspapers, magazines, TV and radio, and command far more working attention than do advertisements, sermons, editorials, billboards, and so forth. The power of narratives to change beliefs has never been doubted and has always been feared" (p. 701). This thesis has been broadened and deepened by Green, Strange, and Brock (2002).

- Madey et al. (1996) pointed out that the song "All the Girls Get Prettier at Closing Time" suggested that "as closing time approaches members of the opposite sex become more attractive" (p. 387). This is, of course, redolent of the classic observation in psychology, the goal gradient hypothesis that "an organism makes greater effort the closer it gets to its goal" (Corsini, 1999, p. 417).

- Csikszentmihalyi (2001) suggested in a book review of Karl E. Scheibe's (2000) *The Drama of Everyday Life* that "the best way to understand human behavior is through the lenses of a dramaturgical perspective" (p. 336); that is, through drama, through stories, and through narratives.

- Hood (1862–1863) cut to the chase, as it were, in the domain of work, expressing the drudgery, the tedium, the mindlessness of work for both some people and some forms of work, via the following memorable verses from "Song of the Shirt." These verses, I realize, are unmistakably tinted with a heavy dose of anticapitalism. Still, ideology aside, they convey an important message—that is, the nagging presence of behavioral pain, agony, and wretchedness. My intent in citing these lyrics is rooted in their psychological implication, and not in their political rhetoric. Don't Hood's words stir in you a vision of the brutality that can be associated with work?

  "With eyelids heavy and red, a woman sat in

  unwomanly rags [work strips a woman of her femininity],

  Plying her needle and thread—

> Stitch, stitch, stitch! [as if with machine-gun rapidity]
> In poverty, hunger, and dirt [Third world depravities].
> and still with a voice of dolorous pitch
> She sang, the "Song of the Shirt."
> Work-work-work [as a whip lashes her weary back]
> Till the brain begins to swim;
> Work-Work-Work
> Till the eyes are heavy and dim!
> Seam, and gusset, and band,
> Band, and gusset, and seam,
> Till over the buttons I fall asleep,
> And sew them on in a dream.
> Oh, men, with sisters dear!
> Oh, men, with mothers and wives
> It is not linen you're wearing out.
> But human creatures' lives! [The dehumanization of some work—if not ac-
> tually stitch-stitch-stitch dehumanizing, then some workers may perceive
> their work to be dehumanizing.]
> In poverty, hunger, and dirt,
> Sewing at once, with a double thread,
> A shroud as well as a shirt. [Work, for some, can be deadly.] (pp. 353–355)

- The poem " My Father Is" (Petrosky, 1990) punctuates piercingly the
  punishing effect work may sometimes wreak on a fragile human being:

  > My father is a small man
  > who wears flannel shirts,
  > silver-blue workpants,
  > a matching blue billed hat,
  > and works on an assembly line
  > in a shed that stretches for acres [which could well describe a Wal-Mart em-
  > ployee]
  > every day he stands on concrete,
  > The noise from the machines
  > vibrating through him. [How can such an automaton, a robot, bond with
  > his son?] (p. 200)

- Fred Bryant (personal communication, 2002) reported the following
  illustrations of psychologists who associate themselves with humanistic endeavors:

  1. Stanley Schacter's idea for his theory of emotion originated from
     Thomas Mann's *The Magic Mountain*.

2. There are literally dozens of instances of theorists or researchers naming a social or intrapersonal phenomenon after Greek or Roman mythology. Examples include the Oedipus and Electra complexes, narcissism, and the Sisyphus parable.
3. Cattell named some of his statistical techniques after classic characters (e. g., King Procrustes).
4. Richard Christie took statements directly from Nicolò Machiavelli's books to postulate a personality construct that he called "Machiavellianism."
5. Rosenthal's "Pygmalion effect" (the theory that teacher expectancies shape students' actual levels of performance) is based on a 1912 play, *Pygmalion,* by George Bernard Shaw.

- Hultberg (1997), in discussing C. P. Snow's celebrated lecture on two cultures concluded that "science and literature should be regarded not as two different cultures but rather as different forms of expression within one culture" (p. 194). My paradigm seeks to bridge Snow's two cultures—the culture of the natural sciences and the literary culture—where, in particular, I plead for the science of psychology to be bejeweled by literary culture.
- Krumhans (2002) asserted that "the expression of emotion in music shares properties with the expression of emotion in speech and dance" (p. 45), which I interpret as saying that at rock bottom, the basic phenomenon of the foundation itself, the noun, is emotion—a holistic entity whose compartments consist of physiological, glandular, musical, dance, and speech elements—and it is incomplete to characterize emotion as being any one of these things. It consists of all of them, and to overlook one element is to shortchange the totality of what emotion is. This reasoning in effect is at the heart of the argument in this chapter: Behavior is a complex multifaceted entity, consisting of classical psychological elements as well as elements that are explicated in fields other than and beyond psychology. A metaphor from the world of business, of the corporate world, of manufacturing, might be in order here. A firm consists of marketing, finance, human resources, manufacturing, social and ethical responsibility, and strategic planning elements. To satisfy oneself with the myopic view that a company is, by and large, what it makes, what it manufactures, and what services it provides, is to overlook the larger picture and offer an incomplete and even deceiving view of the phenomenon we are seeking to elucidate.
- Kugelman (2001) revealed that psychologist and architect Henry Rutgers Marshall (the 16th president of the American Psychological Association) generated his classic thinking on pleasure and pain through concepts and ideas from architecture. This suggests that,

congruent with my thesis in this chapter, a metaphorical orientation shrieks out at us as a fruitful way of understanding, predicting, and controlling behavior. Let us borrow from other fields and learned disciplines the concepts and processes underlying the idea of knowing, thinking, and indeed of actually being

- Franklin (2001), in an article revealing a heretofore (at least for me) aspect of Sigmund Koch's brilliance and creativity, noted that "Koch saw aesthetic endeavors as standing at the center of human life [which indeed is the thesis of my chapter here and now] and thus warranting psychologists' closest attention" (p. 445).
- Lowman (2000), under the rubric of advocating paradigm shifts, urged that we "let a thousand flowers bloom so that, in time, we can create a brilliant bouquet with orderly predictability. In the meantime, in encouraging diverse growth, we must learn about which flowers flourish in which soil, and how to prune, fertilize and water those that later make for stellar displays" (p. 240).
- Dumont (personal communication, 2002) lent support to my position by calling forth "two parallel universes at the same time." On the one hand we embrace the mechanistic-organistic conception of the human animal, and on the other we are drawn to the universe whose fundamental principles are free will and responsibility, intuitive insight and mystical experience, transcendence and disembodied spirituality. Dumont asserted:

  > The first universe is a deterministic one; the latter a free one.... The former has advanced science; the latter has nourished a rich, "soulful" experience of what it means to be human. The former has launched "thousand-ton vehicles into the air," the latter built mansions whose walls put their arms around us and comfort us as we face awful existential issues: death, isolation, meaninglessness, our doomed and eventually imploding solar system.

- Consilience. The central idea in "beyond psychology" is that everything is related to everything else, which is precisely the point made by Damsio et al. (2001), wherein they wrote about the unity of knowledge. This notion was particularly and thoroughly depicted by Wilson (1998), in which he addressed consilience, the unity of knowledge.

CONCLUSION: RALPH L. ROSNOW'S WAY REDUX

This chapter is a first effort, a beginning, a coarse blueprint of the truism—and I insist that it is, *indeed,* a truism—that behavior is not understood and used to better the human condition and to inform public policy exclusively via the protocols of psychology conventionally writ. An intensive, enduring, *extensive,* and replicable science of behavior is one in which psychology joins hands with the arts, narratives, literature, and the humanities. After all, men, women, and children are entertained, experience emotional and intellectual excitement, and receive stimulation not from the bland strictures embedded in psychology. but rather from plays, ballet, opera, music, poetry, novels, and narratives. It thus goes without saying that a sophisticated and efficient psychological science needs to embrace these venues of what it means to be human and what it takes to stir people emotionally, and, in a way, to elicit behavior and inform decision making. Behold the adage that "man does not live by bread alone." So, too, it is true that behavior does not thrive and pulsate with reality and vigor through psychology alone. I am also considering, it should be noted, the possibility of religion and spirituality as handmaidens of the study of behavior, along with the arts, the humanities, literature, and narratives.

This chapter is viewed as a conceptual segue into what I hope will turn out to be a series of papers exploring this issue, including proposals for empirical studies seeking to show—as I am confident will be shown—that a behavior informed by stepping stones to understanding that transcend psychology will be a behavior that is more robust and more useful than is the current limiting approach, wherein behavior is exclusively probed via the psychology highway rather than via a network of highways, byways, and thoroughfares, streets, roads, and lanes that, unfetteredly, traverse all of the universe rather than a rigidly circumscribed portion of it. Such an eventuality would be the crowning endgame of "Ralph L. Rosnow's way."

REFERENCES

Attenborough, D. (2002, April 7). *Nature: song of the earth* [Television broadcast]. New York: Public Broadcasting Service.

Coleman, W. (1995). Drone. In N. Coles & P. Oresick (Eds.), *For a living: The poetry of work* (pp. 103–104). Urbana: University of Illinois Press.

Corsini, R. J (1999). *The dictionary of psychology*. Philadelphia: Brunner/Maze.

Csikszentmihalyi, M. (2001). This strange, eventful history [a review of K. E. Scheibe (2000)]. *Contemporary Psychology: APA Review of Books, 46*(4), 000–000.

Damsio, A. R., Harrington, A., Kagan, J., McEwen, B. S., Moss, H., & Shaikhi, R. (Eds.). (2001). *Unity of knowledge: The convergence of natural and human science*. New York, New York Academy of Sciences.

Daniels, J. (1990). "Factory love." In P. Oresick & N. Coles (Eds.), *Working classics: Poems in industrial life* (p. 45). Urbana: University of Illinois Press.

Franklin, M. B. (2001). The artist speaks: Sigmund Koch on aesthetics and creative work. *American Psychologist, 56*(5), 445–452.

Green, M. C., & Brock, T. C. (2000). The role of transportation in the persuasiveness of public narratives. *Journal of Personality and Social Psychology, 79*, 701–721.

Green, M. C., Strange, J. J., & Brock, T. C. (Eds.). (2002). *Narrative impact: Social and cognitive foundations*. Mahwah, NJ: Lawrence Erlbaum Associates.

Haggbloom, S. J., Warnick, R., Wamick, J. E., Jones, V. K., Yarbrough, G. L., Russell, T. M., Borecky, C. M., McGahhey, R., Powell, J. L., III, Beavers, J., & Monte, E. (2002).

The 100 most eminent psychologists of the 20th century. *Review of General Psychology, 6,* 139–152.

Hood, T. (1999). Song of the shirt. In K. Thomas (Ed.), *The Oxford book of work* (pp. 353–355). New York: Oxford. (Original work published 1862–1863)

Hultberg J. (1997). The two cultures revisited. *Science Communication, 18,* 194–215.

Kipnis, D. (2001). Influence tactics in plays. *Journal of Applied Social Psychology 31,* 542–552.

Krumhans, C. L. (2002). Music: A link between cognition and emotion. *Current Directions in Psychological Science, 11*(2), 45–50.

Kugelman, R. (2001). Introspective psychology, pure and applied: Henry Rutgers Marshall on pain and pleasure. *History of Psychology, 4,* 34–58.

Lowman, R. L. (2000). Paradigm shift! *The Psychologist-Manager Journal, 4,* 239–240.

Madey, S. F., Simo, M., Dillworth, D., Kemper, D., Toczynski, S., & Perella, A. (1996). They do get more attractive at closing, time, but only when you are not in a relationship. *Basic and Applied Social Psychology, 18,* 387–393.

Overbye, D. (2002, March 12). Peering through the gates of time. *New York Times,* pp. 1, 5.

Petrosky, A. (1990). My father is. In P. Oresnick & N. Coles (Eds.), *Working classics: Poems in industrial life* (pp. 353–355). Urbana: University of Illinois Press.

Rosnow, R. L. (1962). Pigeons, predictions, and political scientists. *Darshana, 2,* 62–67.

Rosnow, R. L. (1972). Poultry and prejudice. *Psychology Today, 5*(10), 53–56.

Rosnow, R. L. (1983). Von Osten's horse, Hamlet's question, and the mechanistic view of causality: Implications for a post-crisis social psychology. *Journal of Mind and Behavior, 4,* 319–338.

Rosnow, R. L. (1991). Inside rumor: A personal journey. *American Psychologist, 46,* 319–338.

Rosnow, R. L., & Rosenthal, R. (1984). Applying Hamlet's question to the ethical conduct of research: A conceptual addendum. *American Psychologist, 39,* 561–563.

Rosnow, R. L., & Rosenthal, R. (1995). "Some things you learn aren't so": Cohen's paradox, Asch's paradigm, and the interpretation of interaction. *Psychological Science, 6,* 3–9.

Rosnow, R. L., & Rosenthal, R. (1996). Contrasts and interactions redux: Five easy pieces. *Psychological Science, 7,* 253–257.

Scheibe, K. E. (2000). *The drama of everyday life.* Cambridge, MA: Harvard University Press.

Wilson, E. O. (1998). *Consilience: The unity of knowledge.* New York: Knopf.

17

Twenty Questions
for Perspectivist Epistemologists

William J. McGuire
Yale University

Ralph Rosnow is not adverse to publishing collaboratively. Even casual observers will have noticed that Ralph Rosnow and Robert Rosenthal have not infrequently coauthored their roaring (rrrr!) books and articles, which they typically compose at a distance but publish together. I am more of a loner, so despite Ralph's and my substantial overlappings of interests and our long friendship (almost family), the nearest we have to a joint publication is that both of us contributed chapters to Ralph L. Rosnow's & Marianthi Georgoudi's (1986) book, *Contextualism and Understanding in Behavioral Science*. Mention of Marianthi reminds us that, gone before her time, she is sorely missed. In this chapter I return to some of the epistemological issues raised in that 1986 book, issues that have long interested Ralph and me.

In my chapter in the 1986 book, I proposed that each of the successive half-century intellectual cohort or generation of psychologists has been driven by its characteristic defining mode of wonder. Ralph and I, like many entering psychology around mid-20th century, were epistemologists joining the discipline just when an epistemological generation was achieving hegemony in psychology. In rejoicing at this lucky timing I paraphrase Wordsworth's *Prelude*: "Bliss it was in that dawn to be [a social psychologist] but to be [an epistemologically oriented cognitive social psychologist] was very heaven." Throughout Ralph's and my half-centuries of research efforts so far, a number of our studies have had the basic epistemological issue of what it is "to know" as part of our agenda. Ralph and I have not agreed on all the answers (McGuire, 1986b; Rosnow, 1986) but I think we agree that the important questions have often been epistemological. Hence, in this chapter, for harmony's sake, I focus on epistemology and on questions rather than answers.

OUR EPISTEMOLOGICAL GENERATION

Let me describe my bases for claiming that when Ralph and I entered psychology in the mid-20th century we were in at the creation of an epistemological hegemony that dominated the discipline for the ensuing half century, 1950–2000. The preceding generation who had dominated the field in the 1900–1950 half-century was a cosmogonical cohort, preoccupied with origins and development. The generation that will succeed us and dominate psychology during the coming 2000–2050 half-century will, I predict, focus on issues of power and influence.

Do academic disciplines advance by such waves of episodic enthusiasms constituting successive hegemonies? Insofar as they do, what determines the decline of the old flourishing and what shapes the new? I have conjectured (McGuire, 1986a, 1999) that psychology has evolved by the periodic bringing down of successive Establishment hegemonies by internal forces and replacing each with a new hegemony shaped by external forces. The internal forces that eventually bring down a long-flourishing psychological hegemony tend to be excesses of virtue such as extravagant conceptual elaborations, excessive quantifications, and overapplications. This bringing down of the old does not leave a vacuum because, concomitant with the decline of the old, a new hegemony is being shaped by outside forces such as recent politicoeconomic developments, methodological innovations, and advances in neighboring disciplines.

Consider the situation around 1960 and 1955, when Ralph and I received our respective doctorates. For the preceding half-century psychologists had been preoccupied by originational and developmental issues. The topics and theories that dominated psychology during that first half of the 20th century emphasized growth and acquisition, topics such as evolutionary social Darwinism, conditioning (learning theory, behaviorism), psychoanalytic (and other) theories of personality development, and group formation and dynamics. In the 1900–1950 period psychologists had been wrestling with how we got here from there. By the time Ralph and I stepped up to the plate—as typical communication-and-attitude-change rookies to take our early times at bat—these growth topics were getting tired and were yielding to fascination with the epistemological topics like cognition, language and thought, and inference and reasoning. As Ralph and I matured professionally, cognition replaced behavior as psychology's core topic of inquiry.

Now that we have entered the 21st century, it seems to me that our long-dominant social cognition (epistemological) generation is past its prime, and we of the 1950–2000 cohort are being invited politely to take the topic into retirement with us, weighed down as it is by myriad excesses of virtue. The enthusiasms of the successor 2000–2050 generation are being shaped by outside forces such as political-economic realities in the broad society, development of new methods (and especially imaging technologies), and enthusiasms emanating from neighboring disciplines. My conjecture is that soon the Establishment enthusiasm in the new 2000–2050 half-century will focus on issues of power and influence. When Thomas Mann asserted a bit prematurely, "In our time the destiny of man presents its meaning in political terms," W. B. Yeats disagreed and we hoped he would prevail; however, in the long run Mann, albeit dead, proved prescient. Let the new generation go where it will. I prefer to wrestle stubbornly with the still-to-be-resolved epistemological issues left behind. Even if our epistemological generation is no longer hegemonic, our work still raises significant questions that call for challenging answers. Not all the drama in a given era is performed on the Establishment center stage. I submit here an agenda for our future epistemologizing in terms of 20 question sets left behind, each to be wrestled with like angels in the night by Ralph Rosnow and by me in retirement. As Alfred Lord Tennyson said in *Ulysses* (1842), "… Old age has yet his honor and his toil. / … Some work of noble note may yet be done/ Not unbecoming men that strove with Gods./ We are not now that strength which in the old day/ Moved earth and heaven, that which we are, we are;/ … Made weak by time and fate but strong in will/ to strive, to seek, to find, and not to yield."

HOW WE GOT HERE FROM THERE: EVOLUTION OF EPISTEMOLOGICAL ORTHODOXY FROM DOGMATISM TO PERSPECTIVISM

Because the broad "perspectivist" epistemological approach (McGuire, 1989) that I use to organize this chapter is somewhat unorthodox and has some differences as well as agreements with Ralph Rosnow's (1986) contextualism and other provocative epistemological positions (Lana, 1991, 2002; see also ch. 18 in this volume). I give a précis of perspectivism here, describing the main line of its past evolution and its currently exciting distinctive features.

A fundamental principle in any epistemological system (especially when considered as a knowledge-evaluation process but even when considered as a knowledge-creation process) is what criteria one uses to judge the adequacy of knowledge representations. During the past three millennia of Mediterranean/Atlantic cultural history, or at least since the Common Era miscegenation of the Judeo-Christian with the Hellenic-Roman tradition, the orthodox criterion for discovering and evaluating knowledge can be seen as passing through five accelerating stages, from dogmatism through rationalism, positivism, and logical empiricism, to perspectivism.

Dogmatism

During the dogmatism stage that dominated the first half of the past two millennia the Establishment criterion for the acceptability of a knowledge representation was its agreement (or at least freedom from disagreement) with a canon of revered dogma. The canonical dogmata, often of a religious nature, were typically revered primarily for their origin (e.g., purportedly the revealed word of God) rather than for their intrinsic qualities (although literary artistry is often an added attraction). Dogmatism has shortcomings as a criterion (e.g., disagreements about source credibility, internal contradictions, lack of relevance, authenticity questions, etc.) that gradually wears away its hegemony among the intellectual Establishment who developed more sophisticated criteria. However, dogmatism continues to be a popular, if no longer the overwhelming criterion, not only in the form of current religious fundamentalisms but also in secular movements such as Marxist-Leninism and psychoanalysis of the strict observance.

Rationalism

Gradually, by the 10th century CE, a more sophisticated rationalism replaced dogmatism as the reigning epistemological criterion. In rationalism the truth status of knowledge representations is judged by their deductibility from self-evident principles (self-evident either by their inherent plausibility, e.g., "An effect cannot be greater than its cause," or by their sensory feedback or repeated observation, e.g., "A straight line is the shortest distance between two points"). One marker event in the gradual replacement of dogmatism by rationalism during the 900s CE was St. Anselm's *Monologium,* demonstrating that rationalism suffices to derive all the truths of Christianity so that a canon of sacred revealed dogmata is not necessary. An even stronger marker event was Abelard's *Sic et Non* treatise in the next generation, demonstrating that dogmatism was not only unnecessary but was also insufficient because any dogmatic canon tends to be incomplete, internally contradictory, or otherwise inadequate.

Positivism

Rationalism dominated the medieval schoolmen from the second millennium through the 13th century of the common era. After the 14th century, rationalism's dominance was gradually lost to positivism (empiricism). From the 14th to the 17th century its ascendancy was chipped away by attacks by William of Occam, R. Bacon, British empiricists, and continental enlightenment inductive observationalists. Positivism used induction from objective observation as its preferred criterion for judging the truth of or advancing the scope of knowledge representations, setting the stage for modern empirical science. The transition from Stage 2 rationalism to Stage 3 positivism was a dramatic reversal. The earlier transition from Stage 1 (dogmatism) to Stage 2 (rationalism) had involved a modest substitution of one set of principles for another (from divine revelation to frequent observation), whereas this Stage 2 (rationalism) to Stage 3 (positivism) transition involved a more dramatic switch between opposites, from deduction to induction.

Logical Empiricism

In the first half of the 20th century the Establishment epistemological criterion moved to a fourth stage, logical empiricism (also known as logical positivism), honed by central and peripheral members of the Vienna Circle (e.g., Carnap, Popper) who argued more complexly that the scientific-acceptability criterion for a knowledge representation in the a priori phase was its derivability from a valid theory, and in the a posteriori phase was its survival when put into empirical jeopardy. This evolution of the epistemological criterion from Stage 3 (positivism) to Stage 4 (logical empiricism) was particularly sophisticated in that logical empiricism's criteria combine the opposite criteria of its two predecessors, the Stage 2 (rationalism's) deduction criterion on the a priori side and the Stage 3 (positivism's) inductive criterion on the a posteriori side. Over the two millennia of epistemology's evolution in the Mediterranean/Atlantic world there seems to have been progressively more rapid replacements of old by new criterial hegemonies and progressively more complex relation to the preceding Establishment criteria. These long-term tendencies appear to be continuing in the emerging perspectivist position (although the two tendencies may reflect cognitive distortions rather than historical realities).

Perspectivism: A Contemporary Epistemology

The formulation of my perspectivism epistemology began in the closing decades of the 20th century, with a tragic view of knowledge that morphed into a happy concept of knowing. Its dour origins emerged from the realization that knowledge, whose function is arguably to represent the known, seems rather to triply misrepresent the known by over-, under-, and mal-representation. What we cannot do well, do we must. The only thing more maladaptive than knowing is not knowing. Yet, if all knowledge representations are false, so also must the contradictory (and, a fortiori, the contrary) of each knowledge representation be false, which implies that each knowledge representation is true. In William Blake's terms, "Everything possible to be believed is an image of truth." A resolution of this truth-through-falsity paradox is that any representation of the known may be adequate from some perspectives (and in some contexts) and inadequate from many others.

Perspectivism's Stances on Logical Empiricism's A Priori Innovations. The Stage 5 (perspectivism) advance over Stage 4 (logical empiricism) involves a complex but symmetrical pattern of disagreements and elaborations of desiderata for knowledge representations. Logical empiricism took two pairs of provocative positions, one pair having to do with the a priori deductive aspects of knowing and the other pair with it's a posteriori evaluative aspects. Perspectivism agrees with and advances one member of each pair and disagrees with and transforms the other member. First, on the a priori side, logical empiricism stresses that the knower should have a hypothesis (and a theory from which the hypothesis can be derived) prior to making the empirical observations (collecting which observations should be guided by the a priori theory). Perspectivism agrees and goes a step further in asserting that there should be not only an a priori theory from which the hypothesis can be derived, but also an a priori theory from which the contrary hypothesis can be derived.

A second position that logical empiricism takes regarding the a priori aspects of knowledge is that the truth values of one's alternative a priori hypotheses and theories differ, and that when these a priori propositions conflict at least one must be false. Perspectivism, on the other hand, disagrees regarding this falsity and adopts the working assumption that when there are multiple a priori hypotheses and theories, even contrary ones, they are all true (at least from some perspective, in some context).

Perspectivism's Positions on Logical Empiricism's A Posteriori Innovations. On the a posteriori side also, perspectivism agrees with and develops one of logical empiricism's basic advances and disagrees with and replaces a second logical-empiricism advance. First, it agrees with the logical empiricism postulate that a hypothesis and theory, once formulated, should be subjected to an empirical confrontation. Perspectivism agrees and goes further in maintaining that this empirical confrontation should be programmatically designed, including interactional and mediational variables that (a) influence the predicted size and direction of the relation between the hypothesized variables, and (b) affect the theoretical explanations of these relations.

Finally, whereas logical empiricism maintains that the purpose of the empirical confrontation is to ascertain whether a fixed a priori hypothesis and theory can be shown to be true or false, perspectivism maintains rather that the confrontation's purpose is to identify the pattern of contexts in which the hypothesis is versus is not adequate. That is, logical empiricism asserts that the purpose of the empirical observations is to determine if the hypothesis/theory is true or false, whereas perspectivism asserts that its purpose is to determine what the a priori hypothesis/theory means (i.e., the pattern of perspectives from which the hypothesized relation and its contrary are versus are not the case). Thus, logical empiricism sees the a priori and the a posteriori phases of research as having opposite functions: The a priori phase is attributed a creative hypothesis-generating purpose, and the a posteriori phase is attributed a critical hypothesis-testing purpose. Perspectivism, on the other hand, sees more continuity between the purposes of the two phases, the empirical phase continuing the creative momentum of the a priori phase; and both phases also apply criteria for critical advancement of the knowledge.

What's in a Name?   I may, over the years, have caused some confusion by several relabelings of my Stage 5 approach, calling it first "constructionism," then "contextualism," and since Rosnow and Geogordi's (1986) contextualism book I have labeled it "perspectivism." The renamings were not intended to present a moving target to my enemies, but instead to bring out different aspects of my concept of knowledge: "Constructionism" connotes the subjectivity of knowledge such that a knowledge representation reflects the knower as well as the known. "Contextualism" (McGuire, 1983) conveys a similar point and stresses that the knowledge representation depends on the context in which the knower perceives the known. "Perspectivism" similarly emphasizes that the truth value of the knowledge representation varies with the perspective from which the knower views the known. All these labels were meant to convey a similar basic assumption—that one's knowledge representation of any known is partly adequate and partly inadequate, depending on the knower's perspective and the known's context. All these terms imply that the purpose of research is to use both a priori conceptualization and a posteriori empirical confrontation to determine not just the truth but also the meaning of the proposition; that is, the conditions under which a proposition (or its contrary) is true and those under which it is false.

Why these rechristenings? Each term has been used in other fields, from art to ethics, with the result that each term already carries a heavy baggage of controversy. I am loath to shoulder these exogenous burdens in addition to the more inherent burdens they carry from their relevant epistemological usages. Varying the positions serves also to catch the spirit of this approach in that it stresses the variability of the knowledge representation of a given known.

The relabelings remind us of another innovation of perspectivism. Most other epistemological systems seek to coordinate only two subsystems: the knowledge in relation to the known. Perspectivism goes further, distinguishing and dealing with coordination among three subsystems: the known, the knowledge, and the expression of the knowledge. Indeed, perspectivism asserts that the epistemological responsibility and opportunity is a matter of bringing the knower's expression of the knowledge (how the knower communicates the knowledge to self and others) into accord with the knower's knowledge representation per se more than it is a matter of coordinating the knowledge and the knower. Most conventional epistemological approaches maintain rather that the knower's main responsibility is to coordinate knowledge with the known. Perspectivism's emphasis on the third (communication) component is discussed and exploited more fully below in section B9.

Organization of the Twenty Questions

Many epistemological issues are sufficiently studied, so that we know what questions to ask if not yet what answers to give. As a first step to mapping the epistemology domain, I have drawn up a long list of questions, organized for manageability by ordering and grouping. In all, 20 sets of questions are listed here, the first 10 of which, A1 through B10, raise descriptive issues about knowledge as a product (content); the second 10 sets of questions, C11 through D20, raise prescriptive issues about knowing as a process (an activity). Notice my implied claim that one tends to deal with product (content) issues (the first 10) by description and with process (action) issues by prescription. Table 17.1 provides an overview of the 20 questions.

The first 10 questions, those about knowledge as a product, are further subdivided into 5 subsets of questions (A1–A5) that raise peripheral issues about how context affects knowledge, and 5 subsets of questions (B6–B10) that raise core issues about knowledge per se. The second 10—the questions about knowing as a process (an activity)—similarly subdivide into 5 (C11–C15) that raise issues about creative, knowledge-generating processes, and 5 subsets of questions (D16–D20) that raise issues about critical, knowledge-evaluating processes.

I. DESCRIPTIVE EPISTEMOLOGY:
KNOWLEDGE AS PRODUCT (CONTENT)

The first 10, more abstract, descriptive sets of questions about knowledge as product subdivide into two subsets of five. The first five question sets, A1

TABLE 17.1

Epistemological Inquiry Organized into 20 Sets of Questions

I. Descriptive Epistemology: Knowledge as Product (Content)
  A. Descriptive epistemological issues involving the context in which knowledge arises as product
    A1. Why ask these questions about the nature of knowledge?
    A2. Is there a known independent of the knower's knowledge of it (realism vs. solipsism)?
    A3. What position is to be taken regarding phenomenological awareness, consciousness?
    A4. Nomenclature issues: What to call knowledge and related concepts?
    A5. Who (what species) is it that know?
  B. Descriptive epistemological issues involving the essence of knowledge per se
    B6. Why do (some) species know? Cost/utility and the evolution of knowledge
    B7. What is it, "to know"?
    B8. What is the nature of the known?
    B9. How are the known, the knowledge, and the expression of that knowledge related?
    B10. How do we know?
II. Prescriptive Epistemology: Knowledge as Process (Method, Activity)
  C. Prescriptive epistemological issues involving creative hypothesis generating
    C11. What are creative versus critical aspects of research, of the knowledge process?
    C12. What are some heuristics for creating knowledge?
    C13. How can worksheets be used to train students in knowledge production?
    C14. What different styles of research differentiate knowledge production?
    C15. Theorizing: What is it "to explain"?
  D. Prescriptive epistemological issues involving evaluative hypothesis testing
    D16. What is the tragedy of knowledge?
    D17. What criteria (desiderata), intrinsic and extrinsic, serve for evaluating knowledge?
    D18. What antinomies need rebalancing in generating and evaluating knowledge?
    D19. What reemphases need to be put on research strategy as compared to research tactics?
    D20. Why and how express knowledge in multiple modalities and scaling cases?

through A5, ask questions about knowledge's context, ranging from A1, Why ask these questions about the nature of knowledge?, to A5, Who or what species of beings know? The second set of five product questions, B6 to B10, deal with the nature of knowledge per se (not just the contexts in which knowledge develops) and go from B6, What are costs/benefits of knowledge? through B10, How do we know? The first half of the rest of this chapter, then, raises questions that fall in these first 10 question categories about knowledge and the research process.

A. Descriptive Epistemological Issues Involving the Context in Which Knowledge Arises as Product

The first 10 sets of questions involve descriptive epistemological issues that arise with knowledge as product (content) rather than as process (method). The initial five (A1–A5) deal with prolegomena, in that they deal with the contexts in which knowing occurs and they are preliminary to the second five (B6–B10) that deal with knowledge per se.

A1. Why Ask These Questions About the Nature of Knowledge?
Why should one raise epistemological questions? One might curtly answer, "Why not?" but the enterprise does need justification rather than begging off that the question is too obvious to need discussion or, conversely, too abstruse to be understood. We may not ignore the task of seeking knowledge of knowledge because it risks tautology or redundancy or the hermeneutic dilemma.

Epistemological questions have long seemed fascinating and important to me, but I must acknowledge that others have regarded epistemological questioning as a wimpy copout, a Martha/Mary thing where we should be careful not to choose the less worthy part. G. B. Shaw may be making such a complaint when, in the foreword to Man and Superman (1903), he writes cattily, "He who can, does; he who cannot, teaches" (p. 36). Karl Marx (1845/1946) may be expressing similar hostility when he complained that philosophers have only interpreted the world in various ways; the point is, to change it. This criticism may seem peripheral to Marx's more ponderous expositions (e.g., it has been transmitted only by being quoted by Engels). However, the centrality of this challenge is suggested by its being carved into the London Highgate tomb that Marx shares with his women as the epitaph with which he confronts his neighbor across the cemetery path, Herbert Spencer (joined in a first Marx & Spencer competition).

A particularly worrisome argument against engaging in discussions of epistemological issues is that discussing such topics gets one little respect and considerable disdain at many of psychology's Establishment high tables. Although epistemologists among us wrestle proudly with abstract questions about knowledge and feel that our inquiries are important, difficult, and honorable, such questions glaze the eyes of some observers more than it impresses them. A new Ph.D., giving his or her young job talk, should be aware that raising abstract epistemological issues is likely to antagonize more than a few power figures in the hiring department who come to job talks to hear about empirical work guided by operational specificity and middle-range theories. The job candidate can, of course, stick to his or her guns, even at the risk of frightening the horses, but this may call for having a private source of income at periods when day jobs are scarce. Perhaps one should wait until one has tenure before letting one's epistemological interests show. Epistemology may be a game to be played by old persons, retired on irrevocably vested pensions.

A2. Is There a Known Independent of the Knower's Knowledge of It (Realism vs. Solipsism)?   A second set of epistemological questions, almost as demoralizing as the preceding A1 set, deals with what may be phrased in terms of one pole or the other, either the "realism" or the "solipsism" pole. Can it be proved that anything exists out there independently of being known and to which one's knowledge representation should correspond? One can confront this solipsism issue head on and answer yes or no; or one can answer evasively that the question cannot be answered or that whatever answer one gives makes little difference. One can answer at one extreme that the known obviously exists outside the knowledge of it, and that one is being perverse if one denies the external world's existence or even if one asserts only that realism's contradictory, solipsism, cannot be disproved. At another extreme, one can argue that the nonexistence of a knowledge-independent world is demonstrable. Surprisingly often in the history of philosophy the solipsism issue has been sidestepped by taking the position that the question cannot be answered with confidence, sometimes with the further contention that the answer does not matter because whatever position one takes on solipsism will have little impact on generating or even evaluating knowledge. An alternative way to go would be to analyze which knowledge would and which would not be affected, and how affected, by the position one takes on solipsism.

The realism questions and the proposed answers and nonanswers to them tend to be annoying to the antagonists. Participants in contention regarding solipsism sometimes strike out in exasperation as in the famous August 6, 1763, anecdote in Boswell's *Life of Johnson* (1791/1957), in which Boswell asserted that Bishop Berkeley's argument for the nonexistence of matter was impossible to refute. Thereupon, "Johnson striking his foot with mighty force against a large stone, till he rebounded from it, answered, 'I refute it thus!'" (p. 333). May we thus move the discussion from the cognitive to the behavioral realm?

Perspectivism's triadic division of knowing into the known, the knowledge, and the expression (communication) of that knowledge shifts the solipsism question in a more answerable way (see section B9). Previous psychologies of knowledge, with their dyadic analysis into the known and knowledge, had to focus on correspondences between these two, one of which (the known) is elusively outside the knower. Perspectivism, on the other hand, devotes more effort to reconciling knowledge and its expression, both of which processes are more accessibly inside the knower so that the knower can directly know both components while not having to struggle with the existence, nature, and independence of what is outside the known.

A3. What Is the Relation of Knowledge to Phenomenological Awareness, Consciousness?
This phenomenal (consciousness) issue in knowledge is even more controversial and more complicated than is the A2 solipsism issue. Is knowledge possible without consciousness? Is consciousness necessary but only at the early stages, while becoming unnecessary with habituation? Is phenomenological awareness the essence of knowing, or is it an epiphenomenon of knowing, perhaps a useful diagnostic symptom, a concomitant but not a necessary component of knowing?

For a further, inextricable issue, how is language related to consciousness and to knowledge? Is consciousness essentially subvocal speech? Is knowledge? Is knowledge in some domains dependent on or at least facilitated by consciousness (and what domains especially need be conscious), whereas for knowledge in other domains consciousness is irrelevant? For example, is knowledge of self (self-consciousness) differently demanding of or accessible to consciousness than is knowledge of other persons or of other organic species or of the inanimate world? For epistemological clarification, should we focus on consciousness (or on language) rather than on knowledge?

A few scholars, some perhaps second rate with the Sadim (reverse Midas) touch but others brilliant, have spent lifetimes or at least one unforgettable night of wrestling in the dark like Jacob with the mysterious stranger. How could such struggles be made more enlightening and less laming?

A4. Nomenclature Issues: What Should We Call Knowledge and Related Concepts?
The epistemological domain with which we are wrestling here has a rich vocabulary, especially in terms for its central concepts. It is hard to justify or even describe why I have chosen here to label our core concept by the term *knowledge* and its grammatical variants (*the known, knowing, the knower,* etc.) when many other terms are available and some may be preferable. Instead of *knowledge*, why not label our core topic by a term such as *cognition, thought, perception, awareness, experience, phenomenon, topic, meaning, judgment,* or *representation?* Instead of *the known*, should we use terms such as *reality, the outside world, the environment, noumenon, stimulus, actuality, the data, facts,* or *Ding-an-sich?* (Incidentally, the English use of a generic *to know* obscures a distinction made in many Indo-European languages, al-

though not in English, namely, *connaître/savoir, kennen/wissen, conocer/saber,* etc. That English slights this distinction invites cross-national analysis. Also, the sexual *carnal knowledge* usage deserves attention.)

How to choose among such alternative terms, and why? Is assembling a thick thesaurus of synonyms useful merely in displaying the richness of one's vocabularies, or just in giving literary pleasure? Or would defining and differentiating a long list of near synonyms allow us to get insight into subtle dimensions and structures of knowledge? Or would it at best enhance the literary quality of the discussion only by reducing repetition?

It is worrisomely possible that one's choice of terms has a substantial effect on what answers are given to epistemological questions that we raise. So far we have, with fear and trembling, been using *knowledge* as our core term; our runner-up term has been *thought.* If the choice of terms makes little difference, then we should be able to use these terms interchangeably and ignore distinctions that do not make a difference. However, one's terms often do make a difference. For example, the preceding two sections raised questions about epistemological issues of enduring importance: Section A2 raised the realism-versus-solipsism issue, and Section A3 raised the phenomenological (consciousness) issue. Whether these two sets of questions are worded as being about *knowledge* or about *thought* seems to affect the answers they elicit. When *knowledge* is used, realism (Section A2) seems to be more important and consciousness (A3) less important; when *thought* is used, realism seems unimportant but consciousness seems a central issue.

A5. Who (What Species) Is It That Know?   Strictly, who it is that knows (i.e., how extensive knowing is found across individuals or species) can be ignored in defining *knowing.* Indeed, there is a circularity trade-off between how restrictively one defines knowing and how pervasive one finds knowledge to be: the more leniently one defines knowledge inevitably the more widespread one will find its distribution. So, the answer to "Who knows?" must be given with a qualification like "Compared to what?" or "By which criterion?"

Although not essential for clarifying what knowledge is and although not answerable absolutely, raising the "Who knows?" question is helpful in exploring the limits. Observing others and introspecting on one's own sense of self leaves most of us convinced that most humans know. However, complications suggest themselves almost immediately. Do people know only when awake and perhaps when in REM dreaming sleep? Do catatonic schizophrenics know? Do fetuses or at least neonates know? Do the unconscious, the brain-dead, or the anesthetized know?

Is knowledge found also in some nonhuman species; for example, primates or cetaceans? Do birds know, at least know emotional if not cognitive states? Perhaps mammals in general or at least foxes or hedgehogs or even all species with a dedicated nervous system know? Would anyone argue that plants know?

Are there nonorganic knowers? Can thermostatic monitors or fire alarms be said to know, at least within their narrow range of sensitivity? Are there senses in which computers know, perhaps locally even better than Homo sapiens? Perhaps knowing is ubiquitous, with even stones thinking? It has been argued that being can never be heterogeneous to itself, so any perfection such as knowing that is found in any being is found in all beings. In fairness and efficacy, why should some species evolve with knowledge and others not?

B. Descriptive Epistemological Issues Involving the Essence of Knowledge Per Se

The preceding five question sets, A1 through A5, dealt with issues that arise from the context in which knowledge arises, from the outside (e.g., when discussing why one should study the topic, what nomenclature to use, who knows, etc.). The next five question sets, B6 through B10, confront knowledge per se, coming at knowledge from within, by dealing with intrinsic topics (e.g., what it is to know, what is known, how do we know).

B6. Why Do (Some) Species Know? (Cost/Utility and the Evolution of Knowledge). It is not essential for the survival of members of a species that the members should know—should monitor their environments. Given certain characteristics of selves and environments, it is possible that species should evolve without any capacity for monitoring self or environment. A species whose own needs are stable over time and who lives in an environment extremely homogenous over time and space might well plod on, satisfying its constant needs in its uniform space without monitoring either oneself or one's world. As oneself or one's environment becomes more heterogeneous and varying, it becomes progressively more cost/effective to monitor varied and changing states of self and world.

Although knowledge can be very beneficial, given a varying self and world, it can also be very costly, making it a high-cost, high-benefit process. Consider, for example, the brain, presumably the main organ of knowledge or thought, as regards its histological and metabolic demandingness. The brain has an "astronomical" share of all the cells in the human body and consumes a formidable portion of the oxygen and glucose used by the resting body. Homo sapiens are changing organisms living in an environment heterogeneous and variable as regards the organisms' vital needs, so that knowledge might be cost/beneficial but only very selectively. Consider, for example, the vast range of the electromagnetic spectrum: Homo sapiens are sensitive to (i.e., know directly) only the tiny range that constitutes the visible light range of this vastly wide spectrum. The epistemologist should examine further why knowing evolved in human and certain other species, taking into consideration knowing's inclusive fitness cost/benefits, before attempting to define what knowledge is, being that is what it must be to survive and thrive.

B7. What Is It "To know"?   In this epistemological treatise, intended to be an organized review of what needs to be known about knowledge, it may seem inappropriate, or at least odd, that we arrive at defining what we mean by knowledge only here, one third of the way into the discussion. I plead guilty, with an explanation. Admittedly, it is generally fair to ask that one should define what one is talking about at the outset, but when one's topic is as complicated as knowledge it may be preferable temporarily to defer strict definition of core terms, to allow one's coming at the complex topic in varied contexts from diverse perspectives. As Spinoza (1677/1927) wrote (*Ethics*, V, 42), "Omnia praeclara tam difficilia quam rare sunt" (All things excellent are as difficult as they are rare). Ultimately, it may turn out to be clearer if we concentrate our definitional efforts, not here in the middle, but rather divided between tentative working definitions at the beginning and definitive definitions only at the end.

What terms best get at the essence of *knowledge,* yielding to T. S. Eliot's contention that we have to use words when we talk? I think *monitoring, tracking, representation,* and *correspondence* are especially good at adding more sense than nonsense in clarifying the basic meaning of *knowing.* One knows a given state of self or environment insofar as one can monitor and track it and report (with varying degrees of accuracy) its relation to the world as we find it. That is, the knower knows the known to the extent that it is represented in the knower's knowledge apparatus—primarily in his or her language system, secondarily in his or her neural (especially the left temporal lobes; see fMRI), and tertiary in his or her endocrine states, receptor orientation, and postures. The correspondence should be dynamic rather than just static in that the knower should at a given moment be in some static one-to-one correspondence to relevant aspects of the known, and the correspondence should also be dynamic, that is, that the relevant aspects of the knowledge representation should be covarying with fluctuations of the analogous aspects of the known. (Although I refer conventionally here to correspondence between knowledge and the known, in section B9 I argue that knowing involves three components—the known, the knowledge, and the expression of the knowledge—and that knowing should involve putting the knowledge in close correspondence with the expression (communication) of the knowledge to self and others even more than it involves putting the knowledge in correspondence with the known.)

B8. What Is the Nature of the Known?   If knowledge is some kind of a representation of the known that puts the knower's cognitive apparatus into an analogous one-to-one correspondence or covariation with the known, as I asserted in Section B7, what does knowing tell us about the nature of the known in itself? This question assumes that there is an extra-knowledge reality and that one can know what this "reality" or "the world as we find it" is like, but in considering the solipsism question earlier (see section A2) it seems doubtful that it could be proven that a known exists independent of my knowledge of it, much less that we can judge how closely our knowledge mimics this *Ding-an-sich*. As Kant said in *Critique of Pure Reason* (1787/1958), the world *(Ding-an-sich)* may be forever remote from our knowledge of it.

Might there be ways of studying the nature of the knower's knowing (cognitive) apparatus; for example, analyzing universals in the knowing experience and thus detecting some aspects of the nature of the known, even if only by negating its contradictory or contrary? Four such universal attributes may be that the known is heterogeneous, varying, complicated, and with regularities. Evidence for knowing's requiring heterogeneity is that when a visual field remains undifferentiated or homogenous the visual perception fades and the organism tends toward unconsciousness, unknowing (e.g., Riesen, 1947). Evidence also indicates the necessity of varying in that the organism becomes oblivious in time even to a heterogeneous field if it stays constant (e.g., Riggs, Ratliff, Cornsweet, & Cornsweet, 1953). Evidence for the necessity of complicatedness is that the knower loses interest and becomes oblivious even to a varying heterogeneous stimulus if it does not have at least some intermediate level of complication (predictability), challenging but resolvable (Attneave, 1959). Evidence for the necessity of regularity is that however random the stimulus, the knower perceives regularities, tending to see dots as lines, blots as butterflies, and sets of almost randomly distributed stars as constellations (see the Gestaltists).

However, Kant might argue that such universals tell us more about knowledge and the knowing apparatus than about the known. This is illustrated in section D16, in my example of the multiple knowledge representations of the desktop on which I write; for example, its phenomenal image, the atomic physics wave model, and the particle model. These three contrasting representations are probably all more different from the known than they are from one another. In general, the phenomenological is the ultimate payoff. The elusiveness of the known is fatal but not serious, indicating that we should resign ourselves to the limits of answerability of questions regarding the known, including its very existence, as in the irrefutability of solipsism. In consolation, there is an upside regarding this elusiveness of the known in one of our epistemological revisionisms (see B9)—the epistemological task is more a matter of establishing a correspondence between one's knowledge and one's expression of that knowledge, both of which are directly accessible to the knower, more than establishing a correspondence between the knowledge and the known, the inaccessible thing in itself.

B9. How Are the Known, the Knowledge, and the Expression of That Knowledge Related?   One of the more radical revisionisms in my perspectivist epistemology is my postulate that although the crucial knowledge correspondence has almost always been identified as between the known and the knowledge, I propose that the epistemological domain be regarded as triadic (including the known, the knowledge, and the expression—communication—of the knowledge to the knower and others). Such a triad yields three pairs for correspondence, the most important of which the perspectivist regards as being not the correspondence between the usual pair (known and knowledge), but rather the correspondence between one's knowledge and one's expression (communication) of that knowledge.

Probably one does not fully appreciate most of what one knows until one expresses it in some form that makes it communicable to oneself and others. We know what we know only after we have talked about it or written about it, or discussed it with ourselves or others, or kept a diary that imposes meaning on experience. Although much of one's communication or expression of one's knowledge is via the language medium, some is in nonverbal expression. Some kinds of knowledge are particularly hard to verbalize; for example, I know how to tie my shoes and do so frequently and accurately, but words fail me when I try to express this shoe-tying activity in words, reminding myself or instructing others how the lacing is done. Other knowledge can be expressed better in visual forms (e.g., in diagrams, drawings, graphics, etc.) as described in section D20. Perhaps in these cases manual demonstration and visible images are more communicable because the knowledge is encoded in adjacent motor and sensory areas of the cortex rather than in language's left temporal lobe areas or frontal lobe of the brain, as might be revealed by fMRI imaging studies.

I am proposing here that the possibility of advancing knowledge involves enhancing the correspondence between knowledge and its expression rather than between knowledge and the known. Note that one's knowledge and one's expression of that knowledge are both processes accessible within the knower, and thus study of their correspondence is conveniently amenable to examination. In contrast, the known is less accessible to the knower in most knowledge representations because it is usually outside the knower's self.

B10. How Do We Know?   Describing how people know their world is what we cognitive (social) psychologists are supposed to be doing in our full-time day jobs, until retiring or winning the lottery frees up large blocks of our discretionary time to devote to deep epistemological issues such as those we are asking about in this chapter. Perhaps we epistemologists should leave it to mainstream empirical cognitive scientists to describe how Homo sapiens acquire knowledge, valid or invalid.

Some types of cognitive processing, deep enough to reach an abstract epistemological level, have been described by one or another middle-level theorists in depicting how knowledge is acquired. The processes that they report often yield useful knowledge, but at the risk of also yielding distorting misrepresentations. Such widely needed processes include:

1. Focusing (e.g., concentrating one's attention on specific features of knowledge or the known, thus yielding "observations" if only at the cost of ignoring most of the field).
2. Differentiating (e.g., comparing observations and yielding discriminations, but at the cost of rupturing the seamless web of consciousness).
3. Categorization (e.g., yielding generic topics of thought at the risk of stereotyping).
4. Abstraction (e.g., yielding variables, dimensions of judgments, at the cost of elected ignorance of their other dimensions).
5. Predication (e.g., yielding assertions that project topics of thought on dimensions of judgment at the cost of disregarding other predicates of the topics).
6. Relations between variables (e.g., yielding hypotheses at the cost of the "everything else equal" fallacy).
7. Generalizations (e.g., yielding general principles at the cost of overlooking exceptions).
8. Systematization (e.g., yielding abstract theories at the cost of ignoring specific complexities).
9. Application (e.g., yielding utilizations that guide practice at the cost of misleading extrapolations).

What other general approaches, alternative to such descriptions of processes involved in knowing, might cognitive psychologists utilize to guide their basic empirical research? It might be that we should leave issues resolvable in specific experiments to the cognitive psychologists and their miniature theories. However, are there not intermediate-level theories to which both abstract epistemologically oriented thinkers and research cognitive psychologists can contribute? Admittedly, investigators working on these B10 "How do we know" issues can pay less attention to epistemologizing than do workers on most other of the 20 questions. As Les Terreurists said over their knitting as they sent Lavoisier to the guillotine, "The Revolution has no need for science" (nor, perhaps, science for epistemology?).

II. PRESCRIPTIVE EPISTEMOLOGY: KNOWLEDGE, INCLUDING RESEARCH, AS PROCESS (ACTIVITY)

The preceding 10 epistemological issues, A1 through A5 and B6 through B10, were the half of our epistemological question sets that dealt with descriptions of more abstract, theoretical aspects of knowledge as product (content). The 10 issues discussed in the sections that follow, C11 through C15 and D16 through D20, deal with prescriptions regarding more concrete, practical aspects of knowledge as process (action). Within these latter 10, sections C11 through C15 focus on issues involved in the creative, hypothesis-generating aspects of the knowing process, whereas sections D16 through D20 focus on issues involved in the critical, hypothesis-testing, evaluative aspects of the knowing process.

C. Prescriptive Epistemological Issues Involving Creative Hypothesis Generating

Epistemological analyses of knowledge as a process often divide it, as we do here, into two types of subprocesses: those that generate knowledge representations and those that evaluate them. Here, where we turn to the second (prescriptive, process) set of 10 questions (sections C11–C15 and D16–D20), we adopt this convention on subdivisions. We first describe sections C11 through C15, dealing with knowledge production processes, and then move on to sections D16 through D20, dealing with knowledge evaluation processes.

C11. What Distinguishes Creative from Critical Aspects of Research, of the Knowledge Process?   Gourmets with a particular penchant for freshness of ingredients will be familiar with what Hannah Glasse's (1747) *The Art of Cookery, Made Plain and Simple* might have given as a recipe for Welsh rarebit: "First catch your rabbit." Do scientists need a comparable maître de cuisine to provide a reminder that restores balance between the creative and critical aspects of knowledge-advancing research? Perhaps so. One of the most serious current neglects and most imbalanced antinomies in scientific methodology is our preoccupation with critical hypothesis testing while ignoring the creative hypothesis-generating aspect of research. Just as the cook may in principle be aware that to make a Welsh rarebit one must first catch the rabbit but sometimes needs a cookbook for a reminder, so most research scientists are in principle aware that to test a hypothesis one must first catch the hypothesis.

However, a glance at textbooks and course syllabi on psychological methodology show that they almost always assume that the researcher has the hypotheses and needs only to be trained to acquire proficiency in hypothesis testing. Underlying this costly neglect of the creative in scientific methodology there are probably pulls and pushes. A pull toward hypothesis testing is that it is a distinctive feature of the sciences. All fields of inquiry need novelty in the form of creative hypothesis generation. However, whereas artists, humanities scholars, entrepreneurs, and other professionals all feel that it suffices to generate an interesting and plausible hypothesis and perhaps exhibit it in case studies, the scientist alone goes on routinely to testing the hypothesis, putting it in jeopardy of being empirically disconfirmed (see section D17). It is a well-established principle (McGuire & McGuire, 1988) that distinctive features (here, hypothesis testing) are more salient perceptually. In addition to this pull-to-testing explanation of creativity's neglect, there are some push-from-generating explanations. For example, most scientists would probably agree that creative generating is at least as important as is critical testing, but they may despair of describing, much less teaching, creativity. The psychological epistemologist should divert more effort into developing the other half of methodology, the creative half, and not just the critical half. Developing worksheets (McGuire, 2004) to improve teaching of hypothesis generating (see section C13) is a step in this needed direction.

C12. What Are Some Heuristics to Facilitate Creating Knowledge?

Once the researcher has been sufficiently reminded that the creative aspects of inquiry need teaching as well as the critical aspects, it is important to give the person the confidence that he or she is equipped to achieve creative efficacy in hypothesis generation (and in problem selection, methods, etc.). A useful procedure to this end is to acquaint the researcher with creativity-promoting heuristics and to train him or her in their effective use. By *heuristics* I mean elegant twists of thought that evoke unconventional thinking relevant to the task at hand, such as that of explaining a relation between variables (see section C15). Such heuristics can be described, taught, and utilized by researchers to enhance the originality and effectiveness of their thinking.

McGuire (1997b) described 49 such creativity-promoting heuristics, divided into five broad categories with 14 subtypes. The simplest of the five broad categories includes nine types of heuristics that require no special knowledge but simply enhanced sensitivity to the oddity of perceived natural occurrences (e.g., noticing oddities, assembling propositional inventories, and doing intensive case studies) and recognition of their provocativeness. Slightly more demanding, in that they call for simple conceptual analysis, are 13 types of immediate-inference techniques, such as accounting for the contrary of trite truisms or exploratory nomenclature analysis. A third category includes 10 types that use more complex conceptual analyses, such as mediated inference (e.g., using an idea-stimulating checklist or a thought-provoking metatheory). A more technically demanding fourth category that includes seven types of creativity-facilitating heuristics, demands more knowledge and reinterpretation of past research on the topic (e.g., decomposing complex relations that look like George Washington's profile into several simpler, monotonic relations, or reconciling conflicting or nonreplicating outcomes of past studies). A fifth broad category of 10 creative heuristics requires collection of new or reanalyzing of old data (e.g., allowing open-ended responses or using exploratory analysis such as meta-analyses, multivariate analysis, causal models, etc.).

Work is needed on extending even this long list of 49 heuristics, on more provocative categorizing and dimensionalizing of the heuristics, and on developing pedagogic techniques for teaching their use and evaluating their effectiveness in enhancing creative thinking. Even more needful of further work is improved problem recognition, which, as compared to problem solution, is prior in time, more important, and subjected to greater neglect.

C13. How Can Worksheets Be Used to Train Students in Knowledge Production?   When researchers train our students to adopt effective knowledge-production techniques we tend to use informal, vaguely described, labor-intensive teaching methods of undemonstrated efficacy. This is so even if we are cognitive psychologists whose mission is to acquire knowledge about knowledge acquisition. Our standard pedagogic strategy is to assign the student to a senior researcher to work as an apprentice with vaguely defined duties, perhaps in the hope that the student will absorb the wisdom of the ancient by intellectual osmosis. What do we know about how this apprenticeship relation can be most effectively used as compared with what alternatives? Who makes good mentors, and what procedures on the part of mentors and apprentices work best? Is the use of apprenticeships a copout whose vagueness is excused by the claim that it allows the mentor to teach without being explicitly aware of what or how he or she is teaching?

It will probably be more efficient to lay out explicitly what it is that one wants to teach one's students and how one can do this teaching more effectively (e.g., by teaching effective use of combinations of creativity-promoting heuristics such as those described in section C12). The pedagogically skillful methodologist will be able to formalize knowledge-producing procedures by incorporating a set of heuristics into worksheets that will guide students efficiently in groups rather than letting them thrash around wastefully with little effectual guidance from a mentor who can listen to only one student at a time. Work is needed to develop worksheets (McGuire, 1989, 2004) that will efficiently guide groups of research students in the mastery of strategic programs of knowledge production in addition to acquiring effective tactical specifics.

C14. What Styles of Research Underlie Knowledge Production?

What is a "style" of research and are there different styles of research, some more effective than others, at least for certain researchers or, within researchers, for different kinds of knowledge? Can and should students be taught several styles of research and when to use one or another, or should each student be encouraged to perfect his or her own ego-syntonic style?

To understand what we mean by a style consider that carrying out a research project calls for taking a long series of steps (e.g., selecting the dependent and independent variables, hypothesizing the relation between them, intuiting theoretical explanations for this relation, …, manipulating the independent variable, …, measuring the effect on the dependent variable, …, controlling for extraneous variables, …, choosing the participants, …, measuring where they stand on the variables, …, applying the results, etc.). Each of these numerous steps calls for the researcher's making a choice among multiple alternative options so that there are dozens of potential paths through the whole research process (reduced a bit by the fact that which alternative is chosen at one step tends to reduce the options available at later steps). A given researcher's path—that is, his or her characteristic pattern of optional choices over all the steps—constitutes his or her research style.

At any given era in a discipline or subdiscipline's history just a few of these myriad potential styles (decision paths) actually get popular use: perhaps two contending Establishment styles, a tolerated third deviational style, and a half-dozen rarely used and less respectable styles (McGuire, 1983). During the 1950–2000 epistemological era of psychology, when Ralph Rosnow and I worked, there were two unidirectional styles vying for Establishment popularity: the convergent style favored by the Hovland school, and the divergent style favored by the Festinger school. The eponymous labels may help identify the two styles. The convergentist typically starts with a variable or relation to be explained (e.g., what personality characteristics correlate with persuasibility) and applies multiple theories convergently and eclectically to account for the relation. The divergent theorist starts with a theory (e.g., dissonance theory) and applies it divergently to account for a small amount of the covariance in the relations among a wide range of variables. The two styles are "unidirectional" in that researchers who use them tend to identify variables a priori as antecedent, mediational, or consequent. The two styles differ in many ways, often with strengths and weaknesses that are mutually compensatory. For example, the convergent stylist tends to have weak independent variable manipulations and strong dependent variable measures; the divergent stylist, the reverse. The convergent stylist tends to incorporate extraneous variables by introducing them as orthogonal interaction variables, whereas the divergent stylist tends to keep them out of the design by elaborate manipulations. Both of these two unidirectional styles may be moving offstage as our epistemological era wanes and a "systems" style becomes more suitable to the new era's topics. These style issues were discussed more fully in McGuire (1983, pp. 18–22).

C15. Theorizing: What Is It "To Explain"?
How important and timely is it that we give more attention to what constitutes an explanation? What does it mean to explain, to account for an observation, a hypothesized relation, or a theory? To what extent can an explanation be formally defined? Is there a logic and a psychologic of explanation? Does an explanation have a psychological aspect such that the knower must judge (possibly only on the basis of a feeling?) whether a purported explanation is explaining adequately to him or her? Does what is accepted as an explanation differ among times and persons (e.g., see our earlier introductory discussion of the evolution of epistemological criterial orthodoxy from dogmatism to perspectivism)? What is the logical status of an explanation and a theory (e.g., must an explanation for a hypothesis be a theory and, if so, in what sense)?

On our worksheets, as described in C13 and McGuire (1989, 2004), our students are asked to generate series of hypotheses, each stating a main-effect relation between two variables of interest to them (e.g., a student might respond with "The more television children watch, the more aggressive they are"). Then the student is asked to theorize (to explain) why this relation might hold. The explanations given tend to be mediational theorizing; that is, college students tend to explain a relation between variables by positing a mediational variable that bridges the independent and dependent variables in the hypotheses (e.g., the student might explain the TV $\xrightarrow{+}$ aggression hypothesis by stating a theory that "Seeing all that TV violence makes aggression seem legitimate to the children" or "It makes the children accept that aggression is an effective way to solve problems"). The logical structure of these popular mediational explanations is IV (TV exposure) $\xrightarrow{+}$ MV (perceived legitimacy of aggression) $\xrightarrow{+}$ DV (viewer aggression). Put syllogistically, the logical structure is $[(IV \xrightarrow{+} MV) \& (MV \xrightarrow{+} DV)] \xrightarrow{+} (IV \xrightarrow{+} DV)$. Such mediational explanations merely divide the modest conceptual step from IV to DV in the hypothesis to be explained into two "baby" steps, the IV to MV step and MV to DV step.

Although contemporary scientists and their trained students often use mediational theories to explain observations and relations, nonscientists may be more likely to use set-inclusive explanations (e.g., "All men are mortal; Socrates is a man; thus Socrates is mortal"). Is this "cleric versus laity" gap related to Lewin's Aristotelian versus Galilean distinction? Does this change in logical structure of preferred explanations help resolve the controversy initiated by Karl Popper between verification versus falsification, and does it excuse the seeming falsity of Popper's falsification in his allowing (and even his insisting on) disproving the null hypothesis? Much work is needed, empirically as well as conceptually, to advance descriptively and prescriptively what constitutes a theoretical explanation, what does it mean in both logical and psychological terms to "account for" a hypothesized relation.

D. Prescriptive Epistemological Issues Involving Evaluative Hypothesis Testing

The five question sets just discussed, C11 through C15, deal with creative hypothesis-generating aspects of the scientific research process. The final five question sets to which we now turn, D16 to D20, deal with critical hypothesis-evaluating aspects of the research process.

D16. Why Does the Perspectivist Speak of the Tragedy of Knowledge? If the essence of knowing is representational correspondence (leaving aside temporarily what is representing what), then knowing is tragic because any knowledge representation is necessarily flawed, a triple misrepresentation, faulted by under-, over-, and mal-representation. Underrepresentation is the most serious fault, because the high cost of knowing (section B6) necessarily limits the representation to only the few of the known's most relevant aspects that are most economically monitorable, which results in drastic oversimplification. The case of the electromagnetic spectrum mentioned in section B6 illustrates the vastness of this selectivity: Homo sapiens have evolved to monitor (to know directly) only the tiny visible span of wavelengths of this vast spectrum of electromagnetic energy impinging on the sensorium.

The misrepresentations intrinsic to knowing involve also overrepresentation (extrapolation beyond the observations) as well as underrepresentation. Worse, these two misrepresentations, over- and under-, are not of the mutually correcting type. Rather, knowledge's overrepresentations aggravate our underrepresentations. To provide useful guidance our knowledge representations must make extrapolations in the form of stereotypes, positivity biases, and cognitive heuristics.

The third type of misrepresentations, mal-representations, are qualitative distortions that result from knowledge's reflecting the nature of the knower as well as the nature of the known. Mal-representation of the known can be appreciated by considering the common case in which one has multiple knowledge representations of a given known that are highly different from one another. Consider the workaday example of multiple representations of the desktop on which my computer rests. I have a phenomenal representation of it as a smooth, continuous surface with a brown woodgrain pattern, and so on. In addition, I carry over from my sophomore physics class another "physical science" representation of this desktop in terms of atomic nuclei, electrons, and so on that represent the desktop as almost entirely open space interrupted by scattered particles, often nuclei circled by relatively remote electrons. There is little correspondence, even metaphorical, between these two representations. Indeed, even within the scientific knowledge domain there are alternative wave and particle representations that have little in common and are sometimes even mutually exclusive. These alternative representations, different as they are from one another, are probably more similar to one another than any of them is to the known itself.

D17. What Criteria (Desiderata), Intrinsic and Extrinsic, Serve for Evaluating Knowledge?   When one asks a scientifically sophisticated person what is his or her criteria of the truth (adequacy) for judging a scientific knowledge representation, the person is likely to respond that it is the proposition's truth as indicated by survival when put in empirical jeopardy (or some similar phraseology traceable to the logical empiricist Vienna Circle and its immediate predecessors; see the introductory section of this chapter on logical empiricism). Mention of the Vienna Circle may suggest a secondary criterion of scientific validity, derivability from testable theory. However, knowledge is so flawed (see section D16) and is put to so many uses (see section B6) that we need to utilize multiple criteria for the validity and other desiderata of knowledge representations. Whatever the protestations of the orthodox, other criteria, intrinsic and extrinsic, are and ought to be used, as described by McGuire (1986b, 1997a).

Intrinsic criteria involve characteristics of the knowledge representations themselves. Often pairs of them call for opposite desiderata; for example, freedom from internal inconsistency and having internal inconsistency are both desiderata if one is a dialectical theorist. Similarly, opposite desiderata are banality and novelty (i.e., fitting within vs. lying outside the conventional Establishment paradigm). Another pair of opposite desiderata are parsimony and rich intricacy.

Besides these and other intrinsic criteria of knowledge adequacy, there are also numerous extrinsic desiderata for evaluating knowledge on the basis of characteristics outside the knowledge formulation itself. One widely valued extrinsic desideratum is derivability from an accepted body of postulates (e.g., Euclid's axioms, dogmatic theology, Marxist–Leninist principles, etc.). Status of the advocates of the knowledge is another extrinsic desideratum (e.g., favorable peer review, past track record of the advocates). Wide public acceptance of the representation is yet another criterion, as is also the quite different criterion of the judge's subjective reaction to the knowledge (e.g., Archimedes's "Eureka," Plato's feelings of certainty, and Descartes' clear and distinct ideas). Still other extrinsic criteria are pragmatic utility, heuristic provocativeness, and confirmation (or at least avoidance of falsification) by an empirical test.

Science orthodoxy tends to stress the last-mentioned criterion as if it were the only respectable one, but the issue is more complex. There are many desiderata, even mutually contrary ones. A more catholic position is necessary, such as looking for an optimal mix of evaluative criteria, with different criteria weighted more heavily depending on circumstances.

D18. What Antinomies Now Need Rebalancing in Generating and Evaluating Knowledge? The advancement of any field of knowledge is promoted by periodic skillful and timely rebalancings of its antinomies and thus exploiting these dialectical interpenetrations of contraries. Any approach to knowledge has numerous such benign antinomic polarities that superficially may seem mutually to cancel one another, but actually are complementary. A research field has need for the potentialities at each pole. For a field to advance a quantitative and qualitative balance must be struck between the two poles of each of its challenging antinomies.

Elsewhere (McGuire, 2000, 2003) I have discussed the inevitability and desirability of these antinomies in various aspects of the knowing process. For example, a discipline such as psychology is likely to have problem-selection antinomies and problem-solving antinomies. I pointed out five currently imbalanced antinomies in each of these two processes. On each such antinomy a rebalancing is needed that will allow us to exploit more fully the currently neglected pole without losing the potentialities of the presently overemphasized pole. For example, as regards problem selecting, five antinomies currently needing rebalancing (McGuire, 2000) are: more emphasis on the knowledge-to-expression correspondence relative to the knowledge-to-known correspondence (see section B9), more emphasis on counterintuitive relations relative to obvious propositions, more emphasis on induction of relations between variables relative to deduction, more emphasis on unfashionable topics relative to popular ones, and more emphasis on applied relative to basic research.

Another type of examples are five antinomies having to do with problem solution in science that need rebalancing (at least in psychology): more emphasis on research strategy relative to research tactics (see section D19), more emphasis on creative relative to critical aspects of method (see sections C11 and C12), more use of empirical confrontation as a discovery process relative to a testing process, more exploitation of open-ended as compared to highly structured reactive measures, and more use of neglected desiderata for evaluating knowledge (as mentioned in section D17 earlier) relative to the overused criterion of survival when put into empirical jeopardy.

D19. What Reemphases Need to Be Put on Research Strategy as Compared to Research Tactics? We emeriti whose dates allowed serving in the Good War, better than our students who avoided service in the Bad Wars, have had the opportunity to appreciate the aptness of the military metaphor of tactics versus strategy as applied to research methodology. Tactics have to do with the nitty-gritty of the martial task (e.g., an infantry platoon deployment for reverse-slope defense of a ridge line), whereas strategy has to do with the grand-scale deployments (e.g., whether an army of a half-dozen armored divisions should maintain pressure on its entire front or should it settle for holding the line on most of its front and concentrating its strength for a thrust to achieve a breakthrough to the opponent's rear in a narrow salient).

Tactics and strategy in methodology involve an analogous contrast (Johnston & Pennypacker, 1993). Research tactics involve the concrete minutiae of individual experiments (e.g., how to manipulate the independent variable, what subjects to use, which measures of the dependent variable, and what data analyses to use). Research strategy involves broad issues that must be resolved in working out multiexperiment programs of research (e.g., selecting topics to be studied, deciding where to begin, and choosing which studies are to be published together). In general, tactical issues in research are those that arise in individual experiments; strategic issues are those that arise in multiexperiment programs of research.

Remarkably, textbooks and course syllabi in research methodology focus on research tactics to the almost complete neglect of research strategy, with the result that we and our students stumble through programmatic issues with little thought. Strategic issues probably receive less than 10% of the space in methodology textbooks and courses. This imbalance badly needs readjustment. What is the reason for this almost total neglect of the strategic issues? Failure to recognize and identify the strategic issues is the beginning of the problem. Seldom do we teach how programmatic topics for investigation are or ought to be chosen (e.g., how priorities among experiments are or ought to be assigned, how generalizations and applications of the findings of a programmatic series of studies should and should not be done). On the rare occasions when we think of programmatic, strategic issues we tend to be at a loss for deciding what issues we especially need to deal with and how handling them can be taught. Here, again, we can usefully advance by developing pedagogic worksheets that guide the students through strategic programming (see section C13 and McGuire, 2004).

D20. Why and How Should We Express Knowledge in Multiple Modalities and Scaling Cases?   In several of the earlier sections (especially section B9), I called attention to the importance of expressing our knowledge as distinct from the knowledge per se, and that the importance of advancing the correspondence between knowledge and its expression is even more important than that of advancing correspondence between knowledge and the known. More needs to be said about the modalities in which knowledge can be expressed and how the optimal expression is affected by the scaling of our variables, including the scaling of the measures used to locate our topics of meaning on the dimensions of variability.

Because researchers are verbal people, they usually express their knowledge in the verbal modality, oral or written. When the verbalization is formally scientific (rather than colloquial), it typically takes the form of a hypothesis (proposition, statement) expressing the relation among the two or more variables, usually either a main-effect, interactional, or mediating relation. Still more formally elegant is to express the knowledge in abstract symbolic form. Alternatively, the knowledge may be expressed in pictorial (graphical) form, usually with the independent variable on the abscissa and the dependent variable on the ordinate. To ready the data to be entered into the computer, it may be useful to express the knowledge in tabular form. The knowledge expression may also be in statistical form, most usefully descriptive statistics. Each of these (and other) modalities of expressing knowledge has its uses, and some may be more useful than others, depending on the nature of knowledge, the knower, the audience, or the uses to which the knowledge is to be put. Another pedagogic task that deserves more discussion is how to educate the student regarding the availability of these various modalities of expression and when one or another modality is preferable.

Expressions of knowledge offer choices, not only as regards modalities, but also as regards common scaling cases—how the topic of meaning is measured regarding where it falls on the dimension of judgment. Most basically, scaling affects the expression of the knowledge relation depending on whether the variable measure is on a dichotomous versus a multileveled scale. Often the independent variable is manipulated and scaled dichotomously, whereas the dependent variable is measured on a quasi-continuous multileveled scale, reflecting the manipulational difficulty of the independent variable and the need for statistical sensitivity of the dependent variable measures. The student can be instructed simultaneously on modality and scaling cases by giving him or her a worksheet that guides him or her through expressing a given knowledge proposition in the cells of a matrix whose row headings are a half-dozen common modalities of expression and whose column headings are the common scaling cases, as shown in McGuire (2004).

Looking back over our 20 domains of inquiry one is left with the impression: so many questions, so few answers. Ralph Rosnow and I wouldn't have it any other way.

REFERENCES

Attneave, F. (1959). *Applications of information theory to psychology*. New York: Holt, Rinehart & Winston

Boswell, J. (1791/1957). *Life of Johnson*. London: Oxford University Press.

Glasse, H. (1747). *The art of cookery, made plain and easy*. London: Author.

Johnston, J. M., & Pennypacker, H. S. (1993). *Strategies and tactics of behavioral research* (2nd ed.). Hillsdale, NJ: Lawrence Erlbaum Associates.

Kant, E. (1787/1958). *Critique of pure reason* (N. K. Smith, Trans.). New York: Modern Library.

Lana, R. (1991). *Assumptions of social psychology: A reexamination*. Hillsdale, NJ: Lawrence Erlbaum Associates.

Lana, R. E. (2002). Choice and chance in the formation of society: Behavior and cognition in social theory. *Journal of Mind and Behavior, 23*, 1–30.

Marx, K. (1845/1946). *Thesen über Feuerbach*. Moscow: Progress.

McGuire, W. J. (1983). A contextualist theory of knowledge: Its implications for innovation and reform in psychological research. In L. Berkowitz (Ed.), *Advances in experimental social psychology* (Vol. 16, pp. 1–47). New York: Academic Press.

McGuire, W. J. (1986a). The vicissitudes of attitudes and similar representational constructs in twentieth century psychology. *European Journal of Social Psychology, 16*, 89–130.

McGuire, W. J. (1986b). A perspectivist looks at contextualism and the future of behavioral science. In R. L. Rosnow & M. Georgoudi (Eds.), *Contextualism and understanding in behavioral science: Implications for research and theory* (pp. 271–301). New York: Praeger.

McGuire, W. J. (1989). A perspectivist approach to the strategic planning of programmatic scientific research. In B. Gholson, W. R. Shadish, Jr., R. A. Neimeyer, & A. C. Houts (Eds.), *The psychology of science: Contributions to metascience* (pp. 214–245). New York: Cambridge University Press.

McGuire, W. J. (1997a). Going beyond the banalities of bubbapsychology: A perspectivist social psychology. In A. Haslam & C. McGarty (Eds.), *The message of social psychology* (pp. 221–237). Oxford, UK: Blackwell Publishers.

McGuire, W. J. (1997b). Creative hypothesis generating in psychology: Some useful heuristics. *Annual Review of Psychology, 48*, 1–30.

McGuire, W. J. (1999). *Constructing social psychology: Creative and critical processes*. New York: Cambridge University Press.

McGuire, W. J. (2000). L'evoluzione dialettica psicologia tramite il riequilibrio delle sue antinomie. *Rassegna di Psicologia, XVII*(3), 29–43.

McGuire, W. J. (2003). Doing psychology my way. In R. S. Sternberg (Ed.), *Psychologists defying the crowd: Eminent psychologists describe how they battled the Establishment and won* (pp. 119–137). Washington, DC: American Psychological Association.

McGuire, W. J. (2004). Worksheets for generating a program of research. In J. Jost, M. Banaji, & D. Prentice (Eds.), *Perspectivism in social psychology: The yin and yang of scientific progress* (pp. 319–332). Washington, DC: American Psychological Association.

McGuire, W. J., & McGuire C. V. (1988). Content and process in the experience of self. In L. Berkowitz (Ed.), *Advances in experimental social psychology* (Vol. 21, pp. 97–144). New York: Academic Press.

Riesen, A. H. (1947). The development of visual perception in man and chimpanzee. *Science, 106,* 107–108.

Riggs, L. A., Ratliff, F., Cornsweet, J. C., & Cornsweet, T. N. (1953). The disappearance of steadily fixated visual test objects. *Journal of the Optical Society of America, 43,* 495–501.

Rosnow, R. L. (1986). Summing up. In R. L. Rosnow & M. Georgoudi (Eds.), *Contextualism and understanding in behavioral science: Implications for research and theory* (pp. 303–310). New York: Praeger.

Rosnow, R. L., & Georgoudi, M. (Eds.). (1986). *Contextualism and understanding in behavioral science: Implications for research and theory.* New York: Praeger.

Shaw, G. B. (1903). Foreword to *Man and superman.* Cambridge, MA: The University Press.

Spinoza, B. de (1677/1927). *Ethics* (Vol. 42; W. H. White & A. H. Sterling, Trans.). Oxford, UK: Oxford University Press.

18

Experiment and Interpretation in Social Psychology: A Paradigm Shift?

Robert E. Lana
Temple University

When Thomas Kuhn (1962) wrote *The Structure of Scientific Revolutions,* its principal thesis engaged a number of scientists from a variety of fields who sought to judge the applicability of the concept of the paradigm shift to the development of theory in their own discipline. Ralph L. Rosnow, in his *Paradigms in Transition: The Methodology of Social Inquiry* (1981), discussed the evolution of thinking in American social psychology within the context of Kuhn's sense of the paradigmatic structure of scientific endeavor. Kuhn's thesis has been well absorbed by those interested in scientific metatheory, so only a brief summary of his position is necessary.

Kuhn held that theory within a scientific discipline remained stable with practitioners working out the details of the prevailing view, until a new way of doing research and characterizing the field was introduced. The old way, or paradigm, was then discarded, and theory and research developed that was consistent with the new conceptualization. The process proceeded until the introduction of another new paradigm and the cycle continued. A prime example of this process is the displacement of Galilean-Newtonian mechanics by particle physics.

Rosnow argued that social psychology began, at least in the United States, with theorists actively or tacitly assuming that social phenomena were the results of causal laws that could be discovered through the application of carefully constructed experiments. He called this the *mechanical model*. Rosnow then traced the history of this model, beginning with a review of late 19th-century psychological theory and method as they were inspired and influenced by the success of similar efforts in physics and the other natural sciences. The hypothetico-deductive method, borrowed from physics, thus became the fundamental logical process whereby one fit systematic observation into a coherent whole that allowed for derivation to unobserved phenomena. Social psychology embraced this model of procedure with the assumption that person-to-person interaction could be ordered and made predictable, just as any other psychological or physical phenomenon. Rosnow then traced the history of reliance on the experimental method from the 1930s to the present, noting the pitfalls this approach attracts (which had been cited by a number of leading social psychologists). The principal pitfall is probably that suggested by Gordon Allport in 1954—the controls and definitions required by experimentation often render trivial the subject matter of such a complex field as the study of social activity. Later in this chapter we address other consequences of strict experimentation in social psychology as well.

Rosnow then discussed the self-perceived crisis that resulted when social psychologists recognized some of the implications that came from their experimental methods. The very process of manipulating social variables and the fact that the experimenter operated within a social context was thought to distort the results of an experiment. The expectations of the experimenter, it was shown, were sometimes inadvertently communicated to the subjects, thus affecting the results of the experiment in a manner independent of the experimental manipulation. The subject was also capable of reacting to the experimental situation in a manner outside of the parameters set by the experimenter. Volunteers reacted differently than did nonvolunteers. Subjects not infrequently attempted to guess at the expectation of the experimenter and acted accordingly. These artifacts in behavioral research with human beings were most likely to occur when the subject was placed in a fundamentally social situation, such as being asked his or her opinion about some social issue, or requested to assess the personality characteristics of another person.

The recognition of these artifacts created a situation in which social psychologists were poised for a possible paradigmatic change in the way they constructed knowledge of individuals within the societal context. There were two directions in which the change could take place: They could maintain the classic experimental approach and fine-tune their experimental procedures to eliminate, or at least minimize, artifactual results, or they could abandon or significantly modify the experimental approach and replace it with some other technique or conceptualization (see also Kipnis, 1997). The development of these possibilities is the subject matter of the latter part of this chapter.

Fuel was added to the fire consuming social psychological methods, as Rosnow indicated, when the ethics of social psychological manipulations were also questioned. The experiment that undoubtedly set the ethicists in motion was carried out by Stanley Milgram in the 1960s (Milgram, 1963, 1965, 1974). Milgram, of course, considerably deceived his subjects by communicating the idea that they were successively shocking a person who gave incorrect answers to various questions whereas, in fact, the presumed "subject" was a confederate of the experimenter. Milgram demonstrated that some individuals would follow the directions of the experimenter, who was perceived as an authority figure, even though they were administering pain to someone, an act that they would not have performed under most other circumstances.

Other psychologists, such as Herbert Kelman (1968), vigorously objected to the presumed breakdown in ethical behavior that a deception such as Milgram's implied. As it turned out, most of the significant experiments in social psychology to that time were based on deceiving the subject. Of course, at the completion of the experiments, subjects were informed of the true intent of the study and of the actual conditions that prevailed. Nevertheless, this concern sparked the American Psychological Association to construct a set of stringent ethical guidelines for experimental and applied psychologists. The result, as Rosnow indicated, was to further change the way social psychologists conducted experiments.

Another turn in the process of social psychology (Lana, 2002) was taken when practitioners began to question the relevance of their experimental results, both to theory development and to the settling of actual social problems. The construction of an experiment required such precise definitions of variables and precise ways of measuring them that it proved difficult to maintain a relevance of the experimental results to the solution of an actual social problem. In addition, theory was not frequently served by the results of experiments, because it was difficult to obtain the same results with the same or similar experiments purporting to solidify a proposition derived from a more encompassing theory of social activity. The reasons for these difficulties centered on the nature of social activity in combination with the nature of experimentation. People react to other people in ways that are not always consistent. In short, they change their conclusions about other people and social activity in general depending on environmental and personal circumstances, in much the way someone will vote for a candidate in one election but not necessarily in the next election. Social activity lacks a consistency that is not missing, for example, in the way one's heart functions. An experiment essentially freezes some human phenomenon with the expectation that it will operate in the same way under similar circumstances in every instance of its appearance. This simply does not happen because social activity is so changeable.

Rosnow continued his analysis by examining the ways in which a greatly constrained experimentalism can still be useful in the understanding of social activity. The first is that an experiment, which has been controlled for potential artifacts, can negate the claim of a theoretical generalization supporting the null hypothesis by demonstrating that an effect that was claimed not to be operating was indeed actually operating. The second is that experimentation can support, but not necessarily confirm definitely, a relationship suspected to be operating between designated variables. The third use of experimentation is that it can be used to indicate the subcultural domain of relationships at any given time. With this, Rosnow concluded his analysis. The question now becomes: How has social psychology changed in order to meet these significant assaults on its traditional manner of conducting research? In order to answer this question, we need to review the very nature of the observations that constitute the subject matter of social psychology.

Auguste Comte had a sense of the hierarchy of the sciences, beginning with physics and continuing through chemistry, biology, and eventually what would today be called social psychology. My own sense (Lana, 1976) of such a hierarchy places the various subdisciplines of science in the following order:

Physics   Chemistry   Biology   Psychology   Sociology   History

Understanding that although disciplines such as astronomy, anthropology, and others have legitimate claims to be listed in this hierarchy, those included in the list form key points for delineating the changing nature of the data being studied as one moves from left to right.

In Galilean-Newtonian physics, the size of the unit studied varied from the movement of objects that could be held in one hand to the movement of planets. As theory developed, the model used to explain the movement of any object, regardless of its size, postulated a central core that attracted other objects that orbited it in regular ways. The application of this concept to the planets was obvious. What was not obvious was that the smallest units of matter acted in the same way as did the planets. Physicists then sought to visually examine the substructure of matter to determine whether or not it conformed to this idea of the regular mutual attraction of various objects for one another. Eventually, the electron and the atom were identified and shown to act in a manner similar to those of the planets toward one another. The unit of study of modern physics became very small.

Chemistry, to the extent that it is independent of physics, worked with a unit that was larger than the atom of physics, namely the element. The periodic table of the elements was conceived by Berzelius in 1813 and remains with us today. Elements can be held in the hand if they are solids or liquids, and can be held in containers if they are gaseous. That the elements are composed of atoms and therefore of subatomic particles of various kinds illustrates the difference in the size of the units of study of classical physics and chemistry.

To the extent that modern biology analyzes the chemical structure of organic tissue places it on a par with chemistry in terms of the size of the unit examined. Indeed, the field of biochemistry is designed to examine just such structure. However, much of classical and current biology is concerned with the functions of various internal bodily parts such as the heart, the lungs, and so on, and how these body parts are affected by environmental and bodily conditions. Consequently, we may conclude that the unit of study of biology is often larger than that of chemistry, because biology often focuses on distinct bodily organs.

When we reach psychology's place in the hierarchy, it is necessary to delineate the field into physiological psychology (neuroscience), perception, learning, personality, and social psychology. Adding sociology and history completes the hierarchy. Once we reach biology, any further delineation yields scientific disciplines that become more and more exclusively concerned with various aspects of human existence. Physiological psychology attempts to relate what is biologically true about the organism (both to what is behaviorally observable and to what is true about thoughts) and emotions that do not have direct or easily observable behavioral components. When one ignores the biological underpinnings of behavior and concentrates only on the behavior itself, then he or she is dealing with learning, perception, or emotion as they are immediately observable in the organism. Analysis becomes more complex when one concentrates on those determinants of behavior that are social in origin; that is, people (or symbols for them) that seem to determine behavior in a manner that is not predictable from other classes of stimuli. Finally, when one is interested in the behavior of a group as a group, then one has reached the realms of sociology and history (to the extent that history can be a predictive enterprise).

Assuming the validity of the hierarchy, the question arises as to whether the more complex explanatory levels will eventually be reduced to the simpler levels of the discipline that precedes them. Reduction in science may be roughly defined as the process whereby the major principles of the theory to be reduced become the minor or derivative principles of another theory. For example, when it was discovered that certain biological activity involving enzymes could be explained within the terms and concepts of chemistry better than those afforded by theory referring only to biological entities, a reduction was accomplished and the field of biochemistry came into being. However, all biological theory has not been reduced to theory in chemistry. No such major reductions have as yet occurred in psychology, although not for lack of an attempt.

Fodor (1983), Pinker (1994), and others (e.g., Chomsky, 1966) have interpreted discoveries in neuronal arrangements as the basis of grammatical ability. When considering social arrangements, no such direct reduction has been attempted. However, the context of theory in which to explain social activity has been subsumed under both behavioral and cognitive rhetoric. The behavioral position (Skinner, 1953) considers social behavior to be no different epistemologically than any other behavior observable in human beings. Hence, learning a simple task is a question of reinforcing appropriate responses, and a social communication or interaction is also considered to be an operative acquired in the same manner. There is, therefore, a reduction of most psychological states to the reinforcing properties of the environment of some response at the core of the behavior analytic argument. The cognitive position, focusing as it does on the genetic components producing various responses, assigns a unique status to those activities, such as grammatical language ability, that are not shared with other response systems in the human organism.

The issue then arises as to how one gathers information about those psychological entities that appear to be nonreducible to the simplest forms of human behavior. That is, even though verbal behavior may be acquired in a manner similar to that behavior required to drive an automobile, there may still be significant differences contained in the behaviors that are not attributable to the mode in which they were acquired. The mode in which they are acquired, of course, is the central interest within the behavior analytic position, and that interest yields a methodological reduction if not a reduction in the nature of the actual behavior to some common response or responses.

Clearly, the methodological choice of social psychologists since World War II has been the experiment. However, an experiment requires the manipulation of relevant factors in the present in order to solidify a connection between the independent variable or variables and a predicted change in the dependent variable. This, in turn, requires the assumption that all conditions acquired in the past by the subjects are constant both within and across subjects if more than one subject is used. This is a reasonably safe assumption if a part process, such as the conditioning or perceptual mechanism of the organism, is under examination. That is, it is reasonably safe to assume that all human beings become conditioned by similar processes and the, for example, visual perceptual apparatus works the same in all human beings. However, making these same assumptions regarding the social behavior of an organism has proven to be chancy at best. The social experiences of individuals can be radically different in ways that are not possible when one is studying their perceptual processes or the way that they acquire various responses. The major factor in limiting the use of formal experimentation in social psychological explanation is that social conditions are often the product of the history of a group and, therefore, of the individuals existing within that group context. Rosnow and Georgoudi's *Contextualism and Understanding in Behavioral Science: Implications for Research and Theory* (1986) addressed the issue of the influence of such a history by identifying it as the active context that is crucial in the formation of social action. My position on this issue is contained within a chapter of that volume.

There is a willing suspension of disbelief required in viewing and interpreting the results of an experiment that parallels the suspension of disbelief required in viewing a drama. In a drama occurring on a stage, we may be asked by the playwright to imagine a battlefield, a sword fight, or a drawing room that we know is not actually present. However, we suspend our disbelief in order to enjoy or comprehend the intention of the playwright to inform us, make us laugh, or to ponder the complexities of life. An experiment occurs in a stagelike situation with many of the same elements present. Ideally, all independent variables are controlled except one, and the dependent variable is something to observe in a relatively short period of time outside of the life context of the organism involved. As with a play, the results can be informative and useful. Also, as an actor in a play of sorts, the subject of the experimentation returns to its cage if a laboratory animal, or to its larger life context if a human being, after the experiment is completed. The belief that is suspended in an experimental situation is that the subject is living within the actual totality of his or her life to that time. Instead, an observer concentrates on events occurring in a linear sequence whose successive appearances are contingent on one another. The information gathered may be useful, but of necessity begs the issue of the social reality of the individual's life, not because the experiment is limited in its focus, but rather because it is, of necessity, causal and linear in nature. The idea of context is what is needed to remove the limitations imposed by information gathered via an experiment. The idea of context restores historical meaning and concrete lived reality to the social individual so that we may, as observers, comprehend his or her life.

As with much of psychologists' search for routes for their endeavors, we are still modifying our concept of the proper unit of study for the field. For the Gestaltists, it is the perceptual whole; for the behavioral analysts, it is the observable bit of behavior linked to contingencies in the environment.

The idea of context renders the concept of a proper unit of study no longer useful. Units of study (an attitude, an attribution, a belief, etc.) still have their place within the previously discussed causative, contingent concepts associated with social behavior, but they are not useful if we wish to understand the meaning of a social interaction for the participants. How is one to proceed in examining social context in order to build a solid body of knowledge? One must interpret the meaning of social context. One observer's interpretation may or may not be acceptable, but it can always be appreciated as an instance of subjective reality. By gathering the commonalities present in repeated interpretative assessments of social reality, one may come to learn the fundamentals of perceived social context. This approach remains forever distinct from the approach of natural science appropriated by psychologists from physics and biology. However, the distinction between the two methods—natural science of the one hand and history and interpretation or hermeneutics on the other—provides a genuine dialectical opposition that, although never reaching a thoroughgoing synthesis, allows conceptual progress of a sort.

Hermeneutics has come to mean the theory of the operations of understanding in their relations to the interpretation of texts (Ricoeur, 1981). The texts were originally the classical texts of Greco-Latin antiquity and of the Old and New Testaments. Eventually, hermeneutics addressed itself to any texts of literature, and finally it became a general enterprise that raised exegesis and philology to the level of a technology with presumed general power. When the exegetical and philological sciences are included within historical disquisition, hermeneutics becomes a global enterprise for the revelation of the meaning of the history of humanity. Reality itself in historical time, as the goal of hermeneutics, was opposed to the systematic examination implied by natural scientific laws. Two aspects of hermeneutical analysis are apparent: (a) The grammatical interpretation of a text or of a phase of history is based on discourse that is common to a culture, or (b) interpretation is addressed to the singularity of the individual.

However, a conflict arises. To consider the common historical and linguistic aspects of text or social milieu is to forget the individual (writer, observer), and to understand the individual is to forget his or her language usage and social history. In social psychology, the question was raised by Gordon Allport (1954) as to how it is possible for the individual to both create culture as he or she must and be formed by it as he or she must. This is social psychology as explanation, nomothetic, objective, on the one hand, and understanding, idiographic, subjective on the other. People offer signs of their own existence. To understand these signs is to understand human beings. The signs are linguistic, gestural, and occur within a social historical context. These signs, in turn, yield forms in stable configurations such as feelings, evaluations, and volitions that can be deciphered by others. The deciphering in its formal aspects takes the form of philological and psychological analyses. Regarding how we can understand vanished worlds, we do so because each society generates its own medium of understanding by creating social and cultural worlds in which it understands itself.

In summary:

1. Human beings function among other human beings in a manner in which they are influenced both by the external world of objects and other human beings with whom they interact as both objects and subjects.
2. Examining objective relations yields methodologies that are always positive and quite often (but not always) causative.
3. Examining subjective relationships yields methodologies that are linguistic, social, historical, and therefore contextual.
4. The two epistemologies remain separate in their methodological derivatives.
5. Human beings function holistically in their total environment, and epistemological separations are necessary only when we artifactually, but importantly, wish to grasp specific aspects of their total existence. Being simultaneously conscious of objective and subjective modes of knowing is more encompassing and more satisfying in explaining aspects of total human existence than is either approach applied monistically.

Causative science with its attendant objectivity and contingency analysis has been so successful that the attempt to apply its methods and metaphysics to social existence was both understandable and desirable. However, if the arguments given in this chapter hold, positive science is necessarily, conceptually limited in what it can ever tell us about social existence. Social context is a concept that extends the coverage of understanding begun by positive science by focusing on the creation of social activity by human beings themselves within the frame of their history and the development of their language, itself a totally human creation (Lana, 2002).

Experimental science, besides yielding an epistemology, provides a clear, precise method of procedure that is its glory. Interpretation of context does not per se provide us with a unique method. Rather, it refocuses our perception, our language, and our sense of social history in order to extend beyond mechanistic or causal analyses of them. Presumably, we are left with a clearer picture of which social problems yield themselves to experimental investigation and which do not. Most important, we extend our vision to encompass additional concepts and methods in our attempt to understand social existence.

REFERENCES

Allport, G. (1954). The historical background of modern social psychology. In G. Lindzey (Ed.), *The handbook of social psychology* (Vol. 1, pp. 3–56). Cambridge, MA: Addison-Wesley.

Chomsky, N. (1966). *Cartesian linguistics: A chapter in the history of rationalist thought.* New York: Harper & Row.

Fodor, J. A. (1983). *The modularity of mind.* Cambridge, MA: Bradford.

Kelman, H. C. (1968). *A time to speak: On human values and social research.* San Francisco: Jossey-Bass.

Kipnis, D. (1997). Ghosts, taxonomies, and social psychology. *American Psychologist, 52*(3) 205–211.

Kuhn, T. S. (1962). *The structure of scientific revolutions.* Chicago: University of Chicago Press.

Lana, R. E. (1976). *The foundations of psychological theory.* Hillsdale, NJ: Lawrence Erlbaum Associates.

Lana, R. E. (2002). Choice and chance in the formation of society: Behavior and cognition in social theory. *Journal of Mind and Behavior. 23*(1&2), 1–192.

Milgram, S. (1963). Behavioral study of obedience. *Journal of Abnormal and Social Psychology, 67*(4) 371–378

Milgram, S. (1965). Some conditions of obedience and disobedience to authority. *Human Relations 18*(1) 57–76.

Milgram, S. (1974). *Obedience to authority: An experimental view.* New York: Harper & Row.

Pinker, S. (1994). *The language instinct: How the mind creates language.* New York: Morrow.

Ricoeur, P. (1981). *Hermeneutics and the human sciences.* J. B. Thompson (Ed.). Cambridge, UK: Cambridge University Press.

Rosnow, R. L. (1981). *Paradigms in transition: The methodology of social inquiry.* New York: Oxford University Press.

Rosnow, R. L., & Georgoudi, M. (1986). *Contextualism and understanding in behavioral science: Implications for research and theory.* New York: Praeger.

Skinner, B. F. (1953). *Science and human behavior.* New York: Macmillan.

Author Index

A

Abel, I. W., 260, *272*
Abel, M. H., 198, *212*
Abrahams, D., 122, *140*
Adair, J. G., 95, 116, 118, 122, 123, 125, 129, *135*, *138*
Aditya, R., 93, 120, *138*, 297, *309*
Agard, E., 107, *109*
Aguinis, H., 132, *135*
Aiken, L. S., 94, 96, 104, 108, *111*
Allen, D. F., 121, 122, 123, 126, 127, *135*
Allen, V., 122, *135*
Allport, G. W., 217, *224*, 250, 256, 257, 261, *269*, 360, 366, *368*
Alterman, A. I., 102, *112*
Alvarez, R., 300, *309*
American Psychological Association, *19*, *20*, 80, 82, 84, 86, 89, *91*, 118, *135*
Anderson, B., 231, *244*
Anderson, C., 198, *213*
Anderson, C. A., 253, *269*
Anderson, L., 234, *247*
Anthony, S., 255, 256, *269*
Anyawu, C., 147, *154*
Appelman, A., 286, *288*
Argyle, M., 297, *309*
Arkes, H., 278, 279, 284, *288*
Arms, R., 61, *73*
Arms, R. L., 102, *112*
Armstrong, J., 279, *288*

B

Aronson, E., 103, 107, *109*, *112*, 122, 130, *135*, *310*
Aronson, V., 122, *140*
Attenborough, D., 321, *326*
Attneave, F., 344, *357*
Avolio, B., 303, 304, *311*
Azar, B., 134, *135*

Back, K., 257, *269*
Bagash, B. K., 167, *191*
Baird, B. N., 164, *191*
Baldwin, E., 145, *155*
Ball-Rokeach, S., 217, 220, *224*
Bardi, A., 218, *225*
Bardsley, N., 133, *135*
Barnard, C. I., 298, *309*
Barnes, C., 143, *154*
Barnes, M. L., 99, *109*
Barnett, D., 164, 175, 179, 180, 181, 182, 189, *192*
Barsade, S., 282, 284, 285, *291*
Bartholow, B, N., 168, 169, *191*
Bass, B. M., 304, 305, *309*
Bastien, D. T., 264, 265, *269*
Bauman, Z., 227, *244*
Baumrind, D., 130, 132, *135*
Bauserman, R., 163, 164, 168, 170, *173*, 179, 189, 190, *192*, *193*
Baxter, P. M., 77, *92*

369

Subject Index